DOUGLAS J. BESHAROV
with a chapter by
Susan H. Besharov

the VULNERABLE social worker

LIABILITY FOR SERVING CHILDREN AND FAMILIES

National Association
of Social Workers
Silver Spring, Maryland

Cover by Dan Hildt, Graphics in General, Washington, D.C.

Interior design by Steffie Kaplan

Library of Congress Cataloging-in-Publication Data

Besharov, Douglas J.
  The vulnerable social worker.

  Includes bibliographies and index.
  1. Social workers—Malpractice—United States.
I. Besharov, Susan H.   II. Title.
KF3721.B48   1985   346.7303′3   85-28437
ISBN 0-87101-136-0   347.30633

Printed in U.S.A.

To the children and families who have suffered at the hands of an inadequate child welfare system—and to the social workers who have suffered at the hands of an unfair legal system.

Table of Contents

APPENDICES

Preface

With different professional values, experiences, and needs—and vocabularies—lawyers and social workers often seem to talk past each other, if they talk together at all.[1] This book is purposely cross-disciplinary.

This book is written for social work professionals[2] seeking more information about their potential liability for serving children and families; it describes the expanding liability faced by individual social workers, supervisors, agency administrators, agencies themselves (as corporate or governmental entities), and, in the case of private agencies, their directors or trustees.

The book also seeks to give practical advice on how to respond to this vulnerability. First, it describes an agenda for legal reform that should be pursued by social workers and others concerned with the quality of child welfare services. Second, it gives concrete advice about how social workers can reduce their legal vulnerability and how they should respond to an actual lawsuit. It pays special attention to the personal fears and professional stresses that are almost always triggered by the experience of being sued.

Social workers should be exposed to the practice and ethical issues raised by liability concerns as early as possible. Therefore, this book is designed for use in social work education, either in schools of social work or as part of continuing professional education programs. The materials have been selected and organized to fit into courses on child welfare, social work ethics, and professional methods and practice.

Because this book discusses liability within the context of specific child welfare functions, it should be helpful to others—psychiatrists, psychologists, psychiatric nurses, counselors, caseworkers, foster parents, and volunteers

—who serve children and families in various settings. In addition, because the legal doctrines of *respondeat superior* and vicarious liability generally mean that agency administrators, agency directors, and agencies themselves (as corporate bodies) may be held responsible for the conduct of individual staff members, this book should also help many other professionals whose work is related to mental health and child welfare, and who seek to gauge the degree of vulnerability they face and to reduce that vulnerability.[3]

This book is also written for lawyers desiring a comprehensive summary of the major trends in social worker liability. It identifies the legal theories under which successful cases have been brought, and it identifies those that have so far been unsuccessful in establishing liability. Whether prosecuting or defending cases, lawyers should find the book's framework for analysis useful in understanding the elements of liability established by various case situations. (In fact, the book is designed to be a helpful research tool for both lawyers and social workers.)

Finally, this book is written for policymakers and all those concerned about how growing legal liability affects the quality of service to children and families. As a society, we use the tort law to police the performance of many professions. Whether social work services for children and families should be similarly regulated is the fundamental public policy issue that underlies the cases described in this book. After examining the competing public policy concerns involved, this book makes specific proposals for legal reform designed to reconcile the goal of maintaining individual (and agency) accountability with the often inconsistent goal of guarding professional discretion.

Notes

1. On lawyer–social worker relations, see J. D. Cook and L. Cook, "The Lawyer and the Social Worker: Compatible Conflict," *Buffalo Law Review,* 12 (1963), p. 410; D. T. Dickson, "Law in Social Work: Impact of Due Process," *Social Work,* 21 (July 1976), p. 274; Family Service Association of America, Committee on Lawyer–Family Agency Cooperation, *The Lawyer and the Social Worker: Guides to Cooperation* (New York: Family Service Association of America, 1959); F. Fogelson, "How Social Workers Perceive Lawyers," *Social Casework,* 51 (February 1970), p. 95; H. Foster, "Social Work, the Law and Social Action," *Social Casework,* 45 (February 1967), p. 91; S. Katz, "The Lawyer and the Caseworker: Some Observations," *Social Casework,* 42 (January 1961), p. 10; J. A. Lau, "Lawyers vs. Social Workers: Is Cerebral Hemisphericity the Culprit?" *Child Welfare,* 62 (January–February 1983), p. 21; E. Mueller and P. Murphy, "Communication Problems: Social Workers and Lawyers," *Social Work,* 10 (April 1965), p. 97; National Conference of Lawyers and Social Workers, *Law and Social Work* (Washington, D.C.: National Association of Social Workers, 1973); J. Scherrer, "How Social Workers Help Lawyers," *Social Work,* 21 (July 1976), p. 279; H. W. Sloane, "The Relationship of Law and Social Work," *Social Work,* 12 (January 1967), p. 86; A. Smith and B. Curran, *A Study of the Lawyer–Social Worker Professional Rela-*

tionship (Chicago: American Bar Foundation, 1968). On the subject of joint curricula, see, for example, C. Schottland, "Social Work and the Law—Some Curriculum Approaches," *Buffalo Law Review,* 17 (1968), p. 719; L. Levitt, "Social Work and the Law—Some Curriculum Approaches: A Commentary on Dean Charles Schottland's Article," *Buffalo Law Review,* 17 (1968), p. 741; E. Sparer, "The Place of Law in Social Work Education: A Commentary on Dean Schottland's Article," *Buffalo Law Review,* 17 (1968), p. 733.

2. The general public usually does not distinguish between professionally trained social workers and the untrained and inexperienced "caseworkers" who provide, as best they can, a variety of social work services in public and private agencies. The differences between these two groups are substantial, and the failure to recognize them has been a major obstacle to improving social services generally. However, for convenience, and to avoid unnecessarily clumsy sentences, this book distinguishes between the two only when different legal consequences (or liabilities) result from their differing levels of training and skill.

3. *Respondeat superior,* literally translated, means "Let the master answer." The law holds the master, superior, or employer responsible for the negligent acts of his or her agents committed within the scope of their assignment or employment. See, generally, W. P. Keeton and W. L. Prosser, *Prosser and Keeton on Torts,* 5th ed. (St. Paul, Minn.: West Publishing Co., 1984), Chap. 12.

Acknowledgments

A number of people helped make this book possible, and their assistance should be acknowledged. First, I would like to thank Leila Whiting, associate director, practice advancement department, NASW. She recognized the importance of the project and lent her crucial support to it. Without Leila Whiting's support, this book would not have been written; and without her thoughtful guidance, the book would be far different—and far less useful. Robert Cohen, Lynne Tully, and Myles Johnson, also of the NASW national staff, provided invaluable materials and advice. Jacqueline M. Atkins, director of publications for NASW, helped shape the book and then, more patiently than I like to remember, led me through the long process of writing it.

  This book involved an immense amount of library research, so special thanks should go to my research assistants, Keith Arnold, Avery Muller, and, especially, Dee Mullarkey, for their indispensable help.

  Many of the cases and materials discussed in this book cannot be found in any library. Thus, much of the book's richness comes from the generosity of people who shared with me their experiences, case materials, and other documents. There are too many contributors to list them all, but some deserve individual mention: Chauncey Alexander, former executive director of NASW; Mary Lee Allen, director of Child Welfare and Mental Health, Children's Defense Fund; Alice Kelly, policy associate, American Public Welfare Association; Marcia R. Lowry, director of the Children's Rights Project of the American Civil Liberties Union; John E. Murray, County Attorney, Broome County, New York; and Louise Squeglia, Assistant District Attorney, Kings County, New York. I also received substantial assistance from the staff of Aspen Systems, which operates the Information Clearinghouse for the

National Center on Child Abuse and Neglect, from the Massachusetts Chapter of NASW, particularly Stephen Antler and Sheila Clawson, and from Richard C. Imbert, president of the American Professional Agency, administrator for the NASW Insurance Trust Professional Liability Program.

I also want to thank some of the people whose advice helped clarify my thoughts and correct my misconceptions about liability issues: Austin Campriello, Polstein, Ferrara, & Campriello, New York City; Angela Dowling, reseacher extraordinaire, American Enterprise Institute; Charles H. Fleischer, Ross, Marsh & Foster, Washington, D.C.; Louise Gans, Community Action for Legal Services, New York City; Helen Howerton, director of the U.S. National Center on Child Abuse and Neglect; Robert Mahon, Coordinator, Community Education Office, New Jersey Division of Youth and Family Services; and, especially, Peter Reuter, Rand Corporation senior economist, who graciously served as a friendly but critical sounding board for ideas and arguments. Erwin Krasnow was kind enough to share with me a prepublication copy of his immensely valuable book, *101 Ways to Cut Legal Fees and Manage Your Lawyer: A Practical Guide for Broadcasters and Cable Operators,* from which Chapter 8 benefits greatly.

I also want to acknowledge my special indebtedness to Robert Horowitz and Howard Davidson of the American Bar Association's National Legal Resource Center on Child Advocacy and Protection. This book is an outgrowth of a report I prepared for the Resource Center: *Criminal and Civil Liability in Child Welfare Work: The Growing Trend.* Their early support of my work in this area and their continuing advice and guidance helped extend the scope and quality of this book.

Sally Holland patiently, efficiently, and accurately typed the manuscript for this book. Gregory Besharov spent many evenings helping to proofread the typescript.

Susan H. Besharov, my wife, gets final but greatest thanks. Besides writing the thoughtful and sensitive chapter on personal and agency stress, she lent her wisdom as a social worker and a therapist to the entire book. If this book is able to speak to both social workers and lawyers, it is because of her contribution—to this book and throughout my professional career.

June 1985   *D. J. B.*

1

Introduction to Social Worker Liability

> You are a child protection caseworker, and you closely follow agency policy on all cases. After completing an investigation of a child reported as abused, your assessment is that the child will remain at home and service will be provided to the family. While the case is open, the child dies of injuries allegedly inflicted by a family member. You are called to testify about the case before a grand jury. The next day you are arrested and charged with criminal malfeasance of your public duties.[1]

So opens an article about the newest burden placed on social workers and their agencies—potential criminal and civil liability. In all parts of the country, social workers are being given administrative reprimands and are being fired, downgraded, or reassigned for allegedly mishandling their cases. Hundreds of workers (and their agencies) have been charged with professional malpractice. Clients' claims for monetary damages range anywhere from a few thousand dollars to millions of dollars.

Criminal prosecutions, though still infrequent, are also increasing. Most common are charges of failing to report suspected child abuse, failing to provide information to investigating grand juries, and violating state confidentiality laws. At least a dozen social workers in various communities have been indicted for official malfeasance or negligent homicide. Many others are being brought before investigating grand juries. For example, although it decided not to indict them, one New York Grand Jury issued a report finding a group of child protective workers guilty of "neglect or nonfeasance in public office."[2]

Liability can arise in any social work setting. Lawsuits have been filed against social workers in private practice as well as those employed in mental health clinics, family service agencies, child welfare agencies, medical institutions, schools, juvenile delinquency programs, and a host of other public and private community service agencies. Furthermore, the question of liability can arise for any social work activity. Chart 1-1 lists, by type, the most frequent claims made under the NASW insurance policy.

Categories of Liability

As of now, there is no general civil liability for the failure to "cure" a client, but just about all other aspects of social work practice can lead to liability.[3] The major categories of liability faced by social workers and agencies are briefly summarized below.[4]

Treatment Without Consent

Liability can arise for harm caused by treatment provided without the client's consent. When an individual seeks help from a social worker in private practice, consent to treatment is ordinarily implied. However, the specific circumstances of treatment may enable the client to claim that consent to treatment was "involuntary" or "coerced." For example, one former client claimed that she consented to treatment (in an employee assistance program) because she was threatened with the loss of her job if she did not complete a 30-day residential drug treatment problem. She sued the employer and the social worker for "severe emotional distress and related physical trauma" caused by "involuntary confinement."[5]

Many states require "informed consent" when the hazards of a particular course of treatment might lead a reasonable person to decide against it. Although this is largely an issue for psychiatrists who prescribe electroconvulsive therapy or medications that have possible side effects, social workers wishing to avoid liability should warn their clients about the possible consequences of hazardous treatments. Legal vulnerability is greatest for unusual or radical treatments, such as those that utilize special diets, physical contact, or restraint.

Inappropriate Treatment

Liability can arise whenever a social worker's failure to meet professional standards of competence or conduct injures a client. A common complaint is that the social worker has overstepped the limits of professional training or expertise. Frequently, the social worker is accused of "practicing medicine without a license."

A lawsuit is also possible when the client suffers harm because of a careless or professionally inadequate or inappropriate diagnosis. Although

　　　　　　　　　　　　　　The Vulnerable Social Worker

Chart 1-1
Malpractice Claims Against Social Workers

Type of Claim	Against Individuals	Against Agencies	Total
Sexual impropriety	34	14	48
Incorrect treatment	27	12	39
Improper child placement	18	20	38
Breach of confidentiality	16	8	24
Improper death of patient or others	15	9	24
Child placement removal (including custody disputes)	13	8	21
Violation of civil rights	9	10	19
Bodily injury to client	7	11	18
Defamation (libel/slander)	8	10	18
Failure to supervise client properly, causing injury to client or other	5	11	16
Suicide of patient	9	5	14
Diagnosis—failure to make or improper	13	1	14
Countersuit, due to fee collection	10	3	13
False imprisonment (improper hospitalization)	6	5	11
Breach of contract	7	1	8
Assault and battery	3	2	5
Failure to warn of client's dangerousness	0	3	3
Abandonment of client	2	0	2
Failure to cure, poor results	1	1	2
Failure to refer	2	0	2
Accident on premises	2	0	2
Licensing or peer review	1	0	1
Undue influence	0	1	1
Miscellaneous	17	13	30
TOTALS	225	148	373

Note: This chart is not a complete listing of claims made against social workers and agencies. It covers only those claims made under a policy issued by the American Home Assurance Company for members of NASW (1965–85). Many claims are made against social workers and agencies that are covered by other insurance companies or that carry no insurance.

many social workers avoid categorizing their clients with specific psychological labels, the choice of any course of treatment carries with it an implicit (if not explicit) diagnosis of the client's problem. Failing to identify the true nature of the client's problem makes successful treatment unlikely. One former client, for example, sued on the ground that the "social worker improperly diagnosed and treated plaintiff and tried to convince plaintiff that he had an acute case of alcoholism. Also tried to convince plaintiff to ignore advice of medical doctors who had diagnosed him as severely depressed with acute anxiety."[6] (Half of the claims for erroneous diagnosis made under the NASW insurance policy were based on a charge that the client's problem was actually medical.)[7]

The most extreme forms of inappropriate treatment involve the failure to take adequate steps to prevent a client from committing suicide or from harming others. These issues are discussed separately below because they raise sufficiently different considerations.

Failure to Consult with or Refer the Client to a Specialist

Although it can perhaps be considered a form of inappropriate treatment, this area generates sufficient litigation to be discussed separately. Social workers are frequently not equipped to diagnose or treat all the problems of their clients. Instead, they may need the assistance of psychologists or psychiatrists or of other social workers with more specialized expertise.[8] A common claim alleges the social worker's failure to call upon a psychiatrist for needed diagnostic assistance and possible medical treatment. An example of the failure to refer to a more specialized social worker is the failure to report suspected child abuse, because, besides being government agencies, child protective agencies are specialized social service agencies.

Failure to Prevent a Client's Suicide

Liability can arise for the failure to take adequate steps to prevent a client's suicide if the client's suicidal tendencies were known to the social worker (or if it can be argued that a reasonably diligent social worker would have discovered them). Social workers are obliged to protect their clients from self-destructive impulses that can be identified in accordance with established professional standards. Depending on the circumstances, the social worker may be required to seek hospitalization for the client, to notify the client's family, or to notify the proper authorities.

For hospitalized patients, courts frequently base liability on the unwarranted release of the patient or on the failure to keep the patient in a safe environment, under close observation, or under other constraints to prevent self-harm. For example, the heirs of a patient who was hospitalized for attempting suicide successfully sued for damages because the patient strangled herself after having been placed alone in a locked room.[9]

Causing a Client's Suicide

Most claims involving a client's suicide allege the failure to protect the client from an already existing self-destructive condition, but there have been claims that the therapist's actions were actually the precipitating cause of the suicide. It is usually impossible to establish a clear enough causal connection between the suicide and the therapist's behavior for such suits to succeed. If the connection is established, however, liability is likewise established. For example, a psychiatrist told his female patient, who had been hospitalized for two years, that he would divorce his wife and marry her. The patient divorced her husband, and, when things did not work out, committed suicide. The husband successfully sued both the psychiatrist and the hospital that employed him.[10]

Failure to Protect Third Parties

Liability can arise for the failure to take adequate steps to protect a third party from the client if the client's violent propensities toward that person were known to the social worker (or if a reasonably diligent social worker would have discovered them). As in the case of failing to prevent a client's suicide, the social worker is held accountable for failing to identify such propensities in accordance with established professional standards. Depending on the circumstances, the social worker may be required to seek the client's hospitalization, to retain the client in custody, to notify the potential victim or his or her relatives (especially if the potential victim is a young child), or to notify the police or other appropriate authorities. The most famous case in this area is *Tarasoff v. Regents of University of California,* discussed elsewhere in this book.[11] Courts are in conflict over how far the obligation to protect reaches. Some require that the potential victim have been a particular person whose identity could be determined by the therapist; others impose liability based on the client's general violent propensities.[12] No similar disagreement exists for cases in which the harm to a third party follows the client's inappropriate release from hospitalization, confinement, or supervision.

Inappropriate Release of a Client from Hospitalization, Confinement, or Supervision

Liability can arise if a client is released with suicidal or violent propensities that were known (or should have been known). For liability to attach, the social worker need not have made the actual decision to release the client. It is sufficient that the decision was, at least in part, based on inaccurate or incomplete information negligently provided by the worker.

Unlike liability for failure to warn a third party, the identity of the client's potential victims need not be known; general dangerousness can establish liability. In one case, for example, a lawyer won a $200,000 judgment against both a hospital and a psychiatrist; they had inappropriately released a mental patient who, becoming enraged during a conference with the lawyer, leaped across a desk and bit off the lower half of the lawyer's nose.[13]

Assault and Battery

Social workers using conflict resolution, physical encounter, or fight techniques are particularly vulnerable to lawsuits claiming assault and battery. In one case, for example, malpractice was found when a psychiatrist beat his client, even though the technique he was using enjoyed a reputation for dramatic results in the treatment of schizophrenic patients like the client.[14] In a group setting, the social worker may be liable for injuries caused by other group members. Although the client's consent to such treatment is essential, it is not an absolute defense against a lawsuit.

Physical contact therapies are not the only ways to generate claims of assault and battery. Such claims also arise when a therapist seeks to subdue a violent or self-destructive client. For example, one female social worker was charged with having forcibly knocked a child to the floor and with physically abusing and assaulting the child; the social worker claimed that the child had become hysterical and was out of control, hitting both the mother and the social worker.[15]

Sexual Involvement with Clients

A few therapists claim that sexual intimacy with clients can be a useful treatment technique. However, the NASW Code of Ethics unequivocally prohibits such behavior, stating: "The social worker should under no circumstances engage in sexual activities with clients."[16] Most claims of sexual improprieties involve male social workers, but one case under the NASW insurance policy alleged that a female therapist "so mishandled the transference phenomena that [the male client] fell in love with her and she became his mistress." The plaintiff further alleged that a love triangle was established among the male client, the social worker, and her psychologist colleague.[17]

Breach of Confidentiality

Liability can arise when a social worker divulges information about the client that is made confidential by state statute or by court decisions. (The latter often apply professional standards or theories of implied contract to create a duty to keep client information confidential.) Most social workers are acutely conscious of and deeply committed to the need to maintain confidentiality, so that there appear to be relatively few malicious or intentional violations of a client's right to confidentiality.

More likely to occur are disclosures that are made in good faith but are nevertheless legally wrongful. These can be caused by the social worker's confusion about his or her legal authority—and sometimes obligation—to disclose information to governmental authorities (especially to the police and to prosecutors), to other therapists, to family members, or to persons who appear to be threatened by the potential violence of the client. For this reason, most social workers, before divulging information, are careful to obtain a client release or to consult an attorney. If they do not do so, they should.

A disclosure may also be accidental or careless. For example, during a marital counseling session with both spouses, one social worker inadvertently mentioned the wife's extramarital affair (which she had learned about during a prior, individual session). After this information was used by the husband to achieve a more favorable divorce settlement, the wife sued the social worker.[18]

Defamation

Liability can arise when a social worker says something (either orally or in writing) that is both harmful and untrue about a client. Defamation claims, although often brought together with an alleged breach of confidentiality, need not involve confidential information; in fact, many defamation claims result from statements given by the social worker under legal authority or with the client's actual or implied consent. The key elements are that the information has to be untrue and that the social worker either knew or should have known it to be untrue. For example, social workers are sometimes sued for the contents of reports they prepare for a client's prospective employers or for court purposes. (The usual claim is improper diagnosis or inaccurate information.) The statement's inaccuracy need not be deliberate; liability can be created by negligence. For instance, in one wellknown case, a psychiatrist inadvertently omitted the suffix "Jr." from the client's name on a written diagnosis and request for hospitalization. The court allowed the client's father to sue for libel.[19]

Although most claims of defamation are brought by former clients, they can also be brought by employees and associates. For example, a consulting psychiatrist sued the clinic from which he was fired and his former supervisor when the latter gave an unfavorable evaluation to the consultant's prospective employer. In another case, a social work student sued his field work supervisor when the supervisor's evaluation prevented the student's graduation. The defenses of truth and "reasonable comment," of course, are always available; but in this subjective area they are often hard—and always expensive—to prove.

False Imprisonment

Liability can arise if a client is wrongly detained or committed. The appropriateness of the therapist's actions is judged by prevailing professional standards as well as by relevant statutory and judicial procedures and standards.

Most psychiatric commitments can be made only under the authority of a physician, so that direct liability for such actions is not a major concern for social workers. However, if a physician authorizes a commitment based on a social worker's biased or negligently prepared history, potential liability is established. For example, the social worker may have failed to discover or inform the physician about important information concerning such matters as past psychological tests, past diagnoses, or past treatment of the client. Or the social worker may have inappropriately based the history on information supplied by an unreliable source, such as an estranged relative.[20]

Child protective workers or probation workers often have direct authority to place endangered children in protective custody. As subsequent chapters describe, this authority creates two-edged vulnerability—liability for wrongly removing a child and liability for inappropriately failing to remove a child.[21]

Failure to Provide Adequate Care for Clients in Residential Settings

Liability can arise if the residential facility's failure to provide adequate supervision resulted in the client's being abused by staff or by other patients, or if the facility's failure to provide a minimally acceptable level of care resulted in the client's physical and emotional injury. Although basic liability rests on the institution, social workers can share in this liability if their individual conduct contributed to the client's injury.

Violation of Clients' Civil Rights

The violation of a client's rights, as established by the U.S. Constitution and a particular state's constitution, may establish a cause of action against the social worker. In addition, it has become common for courts to construe the failure to comply with statutory or administrative procedures as a violation of civil rights. For example, the failure to give longtime foster parents notice of the impending removal of a child from their custody and the failure to accord them a hearing or priority in an adoption decision (as required by various statutes or administrative procedures) increasingly form the basis for lawsuits against child welfare workers and their agencies.[22]

Failure to Be Available When Needed

Some clients may need the help of their social worker to deal with various or intermittent crises. If the need to be available was reasonably foreseeable, then liability can arise if the client suffered harm because the social worker was not available and did not take the precaution of having another social worker covering for him or her. (Some commentators have called this area of potential liability "abandonment.") Moreover, the substitute social worker must be adequately skilled and briefed to meet the needs of the client. For example, a social worker could be held liable for a client's suicide if the social worker's failure to tell the person covering of the client's suicidal tendencies contributed to the client's death.

Termination of Treatment

Liability can arise if a social worker terminates treatment abruptly or fails to terminate it at the appropriate time.[23] Social workers in private practice have no duty to treat particular individuals unless they have agreed to do so. However, once begun, treatment can only be terminated in a proper manner. Some clients have claimed that they suffered a setback or even a worsening of their condition because therapy was concluded prematurely. Such claims are unlikely to succeed unless the termination was unreasonably abrupt or occurred during an emergency or a period of crisis in the client's life. On the other hand, some clients have claimed that therapy was continued beyond their need so that their therapists could continue to collect their fees. (Clients rarely initiate a lawsuit on this ground, but it is a likely counterclaim when a social worker seeks to collect unpaid bills.)

Inappropriate Bill Collection Methods

Many states have laws or court decisions that proscribe overzealous methods to collect a client's unpaid bills. Thus, a former client may claim damages for the tort of "harassment" on the basis of any of the following: "threats of criminal prosecution, disclosure or threat of disclosure of *false* information calculated to affect a credit reputation, contacting the debtor's employer *before* obtaining a judgment, disclosure of information about the debt without a legitimate need, abusing or harassing the debtor, or using abusive language."[24] In addition, the confidential nature of the social worker–client relationship coupled with the embarrassment many people feel when others learn of their emotional problems (or even the mere fact that they are under treatment by a psychotherapist) raises an additional dimension of liability when the social worker unnecessarily discloses information about the fact or elements of treatment during bill collection efforts. Some states have passed laws that specify the steps a psychotherapist must take "before referring an account to a collection agency and what information may be revealed when he or she does so."[25] In other states, such special duties have been imposed by court decisions that cite the "fiduciary" relationship between client and therapist.[26]

Extent of Liability

Although many social workers may recognize these broad areas of potential liability, most underestimate the extent of their liability. For example, they tend to assume that they can be held liable only for their own acts. This is not true; they may be liable for the acts of those under their supervision—including social work students, outside consultants, foster parents, and even volunteers.[27] In fact, according to Chauncey Alexander, a former executive director of the National Association of Social Workers, more than one third of all claims made under the NASW insurance policy involve this type of "indirect" liability.[28] He describes some of these cases:

> Twelve cases originated from hospitalization, six from residential treatment, four from foster care, one each from a corrections facility and a school, indicating clients with more severe problems. Nevertheless, social workers were sued because patients were physically or sexually assaulted by other patients, took their own lives, or children were mistreated in residential facilities or foster homes. Several cases point to special sources of jeopardy: two because counselors under the direction of the social worker were not qualified; another regarding improper handling of the estate of a deceased person; and one resulting from a drowning during an outing of a boys' group.[29]

Similarly, many social workers assume that good faith will be an effective defense against most claims. It won't. In most cases, social workers will be held to objective standards of professional skill—as determined by a court *after the fact*. Under certain circumstances—for example, when a statutory mandate is violated—strict liability may be imposed. Although it is not possible to provide a full discussion of the extent of liability, Chart 1-2 seeks to dispel the major misconceptions that exist.

Chart 1-2
Important Points Concerning Social Worker Liability*

- Legal rules and, hence, civil and criminal liability vary from state to state. What is permissible—in fact, what is considered good practice—in one state may create liability in another.

- Social workers are not immune from lawsuits simply because they work for the government or a charitable institution. Few states have retained the doctrines of governmental (or sovereign) immunity and charitable immunity in their original, absolute form.

- State immunity laws, where they exist, provide only limited protection (at best) when a worker is sued in federal court for a violation of federal law or constitutional rights.

---

* Legal rules tend to have many qualifications and exceptions too extensive to discuss in summary form. This chart is meant only to provide a general understanding of the extent of liability faced by social workers. In addition, it does not mention, except indirectly, the many rules that may limit liability or prevent recovery.

The Vulnerable Social Worker

Chart 1-2 (continued)

- Liability can be created by doing nothing (this is called an "act of omission" or "nonfeasance") as well as by doing the wrong thing (called "misfeasance" or "malfeasance").

- The failure to follow a law, rule, or administrative procedure or a professional standard can establish liability, even if its existence was unknown to the social worker or agency.

- Good faith is rarely a defense against the failure to follow a law, rule, or administrative procedure or a well-established professional standard of skill or conduct.

- If particular conduct is mandated by statutory law, court decisions, or legally binding agency rules, adherence to contrary professional standards or ethics is generally not a valid defense.

- Liability can be established by what happened in an individual case or in a particular situation; a long career of outstanding performance is no defense.

- Inadequate training or supervision is rarely a successful defense, although an overwhelming workload, if properly documented, can be.

- Agencies and individual workers may be held responsible for the acts (or omissions) of all those working for them (or under their supervision), including students, outside consultants, foster parents, and volunteers. Liability may be created even if the agency or social worker was unaware of the particular act or omission (because liability is created by inadequate supervision as well as by improper supervision).

- A social worker may be held liable for the erroneous decision of another, if the social worker's wrongful or negligent conduct contributed to the error. For example, although a physician may have the legal authority to decide whether a client should be hospitalized, the physician's reasonable reliance on an inaccurate history carelessly taken by a social worker may shift liability to the worker.

- Directors, trustees, or board members may be held responsible if the agency's liability was caused by their intentional or grossly negligent behavior or if harm could have been prevented by their exercise of minimal care or reasonable diligence.

Chart 1-2 (continued)

- Although most legal judgments establish *joint* liability between the social workers and the agency (and the agency usually pays the entire judgment), sometimes only the workers are found liable. Depending on the circumstances, the agency will probably have no legal obligation to pay a judgment made only against a worker.

- A conflict of interest between an agency and a worker is often discovered only after the agency's attorney elicits damaging evidence from the worker; this evidence can later be used to shift some, or all, liability from the agency to the worker.

- The statute of limitations for actions claiming injuries or other harm to minors does not begin to run out until the child reaches the age of 18. In most jurisdictions, such lawsuits can be brought up to the child's twenty-first birthday.

- Liability is not limited to the plaintiff's actual damages. If bad faith, malicious intent, reckless behavior, or gross negligence is established, punitive damages may be awarded. Furthermore, a sizable judgment is possible even if the plaintiff suffered only small or nominal damages. (Awards for punitive damages have been as high as a million dollars.)

- In federal court actions, successful plaintiffs may have a separate right to obtain reimbursement for their attorneys' fees from the defendant. (These fees can be in the tens of thousands of dollars, even when the actual damages are small or nonexistent. In fact, liability for attorneys' fees may be created even in a nonmonetary settlement in which the defendants agree to change their procedures or practices.)

- Insurance policies (and state indemnification programs) often do not cover punitive damages. They rarely cover the expenses for defending a criminal prosecution (even if there is an acquittal).

- The amount of insurance carried by the worker or agency does not limit the potential size of a judgment; the jury (or judge) is obligated to make an award consistent with the evidence.

- The court's award can exceed the defendant's personal savings. Defendants who have lost may be forced to sell or mortgage most of their property to pay a judgment; sometimes they are forced into bankruptcy.

- Even when social workers successfully defend a lawsuit, it is unlikely that the losing plaintiff will be required to reimburse their legal expenses.

Expanding Legal Vulnerability

Social worker liability is a relatively new phenomenon. As recently as ten years ago, there were almost no lawsuits, let alone successful ones, against social workers. Since then, though, a number of changes, some in the law and some in the social work profession, have combined to increase the likelihood of lawsuits greatly.

On the legal front, courts have all but abolished the doctrines of sovereign, governmental, and public official's immunity, so that it has become progressively easier to bring tort suits against public social service agencies and their employees.[30] Similarly, the abolition of the doctrine of charitable immunity has exposed private agencies and their employees to greater liability.[31] Courts have also expanded the legal concept of "duty" so that agencies and individuals have a broader obligation to take affirmative steps to protect others.[32] For therapists, the "duty to warn" of a client's dangerous propensities is the best known of these new legal duties.[33] Moreover, various federal laws, such as the Civil Rights Act, have been applied to social work services, particularly in the child welfare field.[34]

More lawsuits against social workers are also a manifestation of our increasingly litigious society. There is a touch of truth in Jerold Auerbach's lament: "Few Americans, it seems, can tolerate more than five minutes of frustration without submitting to the temptation to sue."[35] In recent years, a growing list of professions has felt the bite of tort liability. College professors have been successfully sued for giving students a poor grade and for denying tenure to colleagues.[36] Weather forecasters were successfully sued for failing to predict a fierce storm that killed three fishermen.[37] And clergymen have been sued, although so far unsuccessfully, for the harmful effects of their pastoral counseling, which some have called "clergy malpractice."[38]

It may give readers some solace to know that the frequency of malpractice claims against lawyers is also rising sharply. Over the past six years, the number of suits filed has doubled nationwide.[39]

Changes in the nature and structure of the social work profession have also magnified legal exposure. Although the simple increase in the number of private practitioners is probably the most important reason for more lawsuits, there are other factors at work, as Alexander has noted. They include:

1. NASW's emphasis on practice standards in the last dozen years, including the ACSW program and the obtaining of legal regulation in more than one-half of the fifty states.

2. The proliferation and advocacy of therapeutic techniques.

3. The inadequacy of mechanisms for regulating professional behavior and obtaining quality assurance.

4. The limitations in social work education regarding professional discipline and ethical values.

5. The rapid entry into private practice and new areas of social work employment.[40]

The public's declining respect for social workers, sadly, also leads to greater vulnerability. Despite their important responsibilities, social workers are disliked and distrusted by many Americans. Woody Allen is quoted as saying: "I expected something really horrible, with the body of a crab...and the head of a social worker."[41] Of course, such attitudes derive mainly from 1950s clichés about public assistance workers, but they spill over to all social workers, even MSWs, making them inviting targets for a lawsuit.

In recent years, social workers have been alerted to their growing legal vulnerability by newspaper stories, professional journals, conferences, and discussions over lunch.[42] In 1982, the American Humane Association focused the entire agenda of its annual meeting on caseworker liability. George Brager, Dean of the Columbia University School of Social Work, in a letter signed by 22 faculty members, described how one indictment of child protective workers in Queens, New York, "created a riptide of concern among social work professionals."[43]

The extent of legal vulnerability is frequently exaggerated, however. "It is all too easy to spin horror stories about the liabilities that the courts and legislatures have imposed upon social workers and other professionals," wisely counsels social work professor George Sharwell.[44] Certainly, the cases described in this book are still the exception; at most, 1 or 2 percent of all active social workers have ever been sued. Furthermore, many of the cases that are filed can best be described as absurd—like the case of the former mental patient who sued the hospital that had released him on the ground that it should have known that he would kill his girlfriend, or the mother who threatened to sue a child protective agency on the ground that it should have known that she would kill her four children.

It would be equally mistaken, however, to underrate the risk that social workers now face. Even frivolous claims have to be defended—an often stressful and always expensive process. As another writer warns:

> Some therapists...cite the relatively low incidence of suits and the fact that the suits people hear about often involve outrageously unprofessional conduct. It is, of course, easy to point to flagrant misconduct and say, "That's not me," and let the issue drop. The painful reality is that one may be functioning as an ethical and competent therapist on a case and still face a lawsuit....[45]

The small number of reported cases against social workers is misleading. For example, in the writing of this book, substantial efforts were made to identify *all* published court opinions concerning child welfare–related criminal prosecutions and civil damage suits. With over 1.3 million reports of suspected child maltreatment received and investigated each year, and with as many as 400,000 children placed in foster care each year,[46] the relatively few cases found may not seem to constitute evidence of serious vulnerability. However, whenever one digs more deeply, for every published case, ten unpublished cases surface. In discussing a criminal prosecution with one indicted social worker, for example, the author was told of four similar cases—in the same community—that had not reached the media. Likewise, when asked, local agency attorneys invariably shared long lists of unpublicized cases.

Moreover, the profession is entering into a long-term trend toward ever-increasing levels of vulnerability. In the area of child welfare liability, for example, this author found the number of published cases to be almost twice what it had been 30 months before, when he conducted an earlier study on child welfare liability.[47]

It is not just new situations that can generate future liability. In most states, there is a three- or five-year statute of limitations to the bringing of a claim; but if the plaintiff is a minor, most statutes of limitations do not begin to run until the child reaches 18.[48] Thus, a suit could be filed up to 23 years after the events in question. Edward Weaver had been executive director of the American Public Welfare Association for six years when, in 1978, he was sued for events that had occurred in 1971.[49] In another case, the Iowa Department of Social Services and a number of its employees were sued in 1983 for allegedly failing to protect a child. Their last official contact with the family had occurred in 1968.[50]

This higher level of vulnerability might be acceptable if it seemed to be connected to real wrongdoing or obviously inadequate social work services; but it is not. Most criminal prosecutions of social workers seem to be nothing more than attempts to find a scapegoat for a child's death or blatant attempts by prosecutors to gain publicity.[51] Many social workers are successfully sued for making honest mistakes in judgment.[52] Social workers who try to be guided by liability concerns quickly become acquainted with the law's mystifying inconsistencies. A therapist who has reason to think that a client might be dangerous to others, for example, must weigh two competing legal concerns. On the one hand, taking no action might result in a suit for failure to warn. On the other hand, giving a warning might result in a suit for breaching confidentiality.[53] The law should not make social workers feel that they are "damned if they do, and damned if they don't."

Greater—and growing—civil and criminal liability is creating a major challenge for contemporary social workers: how to balance the needs of clients with the need to protect oneself from charges of misconduct and malpractice. Social workers no longer enjoy unfettered freedom to do what they deem is in the best interests of children and parents. As social work professors Stein and Rzepnicki warn: "Workers can expect to have their decisions challenged by review boards or by attorneys representing children or their biological or foster parents, and to have to support their choices with factual evidence, not, as in the past, with impressions and judgments that are not supported by objective data."[54] The profession's response will be a major factor in shaping its future character.

This Book's Purpose

At the practice level, social work will have to be more careful about establishing and maintaining professional standards. Good practice remains the best defense to liability. At the same time, the formal standards established by such groups as the National Association of Social Workers will have to be more realistic; overambitious standards merely create unfulfillable expectations while heightening potential liability.[55]

Insurance has already become a practical necessity for agencies. Family Service America (formerly Family Service Association of America), for example, reports that "as of 1982, 95% of all member agencies possessed some form of malpractice coverage. The comparable figure in 1976 was 69%."[56] Individual social workers, at least those in private practice, will likewise have to carry sufficient insurance.[57]

These responses, however, will be only incomplete ones. Without changes in the basic legal rules governing social work liability, legal vulnerability will continue to grow. At the policy level, there must be a major and sophisticated reassessment of social worker liability to determine its appropriate nature and scope. The competing costs and benefits of greater—and lesser—liability to clients, social workers, and society must be identified and weighed. If the law needs to be changed, thoughtful and effective proposals must be formulated. One hopes that the organized profession will take a leading role in such efforts. The time for action is now, before a crisis like that of medical malpractice develops.

This book seeks to serve as a model for the kind of inquiry that should be made. It addresses only one aspect of social work liability—civil and criminal liability for child welfare–related activities, from reporting suspected child abuse to handling adoptions. To facilitate discussion, the lawsuits to be discussed are divided into four categories:

- reporting suspected child abuse;
- inadequately protecting a child;
- violating parental rights; and
- inadequate foster care services.

This particular focus was chosen for a number of reasons. First, with the exception of claims of sexual exploitation of clients, the most common claims against social workers involve child welfare–related services; and, with the same exception, such claims seem to be the most likely to succeed. Child

The Vulnerable Social Worker

welfare services are, after all, the major involuntary services provided directly by social workers. In addition, this is the only area in which social workers face a tangible chance of being criminally prosecuted for doing their jobs.

Second, this area of social work liability seems to be the fastest-growing. The expansion of child protective programs has involved an increasing number of social workers with child welfare cases. The more frequent appointment of lawyers for both children and parents also raises the chances of a lawsuit, because it establishes the essential first step in litigation—the client's contact with a lawyer. These lawyers can be expected to suggest the possibility of suing because they believe it appropriate or because they themselves fear a subsequent suit for legal malpractice.[58] Ellen Hoffenberg, director of the Florida Guardian Ad Litem Program, describes how such lawyers often learn about possible liability:

> Two years ago, I was appointed to represent a 5 year old who died a few days after appointment, and his 3 year old brother. The agency had had two different units, 6 counselors in the home in 3 years, and had approved an adoption and terminated protective services. One doctor misdiagnosed parental abuse (subdural hematoma) and another a broken arm. The 3 year old was severely abused. We requested appointment of a guardian who did not pursue civil action—surprising, since there were 4 separate liabilities.[59]

Third, this area aptly demonstrates—over and over again—how unfair some lawsuits can be. It is only a small exaggeration to say that the cases in this book illustrate how social workers can be blamed for whatever they do. They can be blamed if they report suspected child abuse, and they can be blamed if they don't. They can be blamed if they remove a child from parental custody, and they can be blamed if they don't. They can be blamed if they return a child to the home, and they can be blamed if they don't. Hence, the title of this book: "The Vulnerable Social Worker."

Fourth, this area was chosen because it raises, in bas-relief, the crucial public policy issues that are often hidden in other areas of social work liability. The dangers of defensive social work, for example, are easily discernible; and the public interest in protecting social work discretion is clear.

Finally, this is still an unsettled area of the law. On the one hand, court decisions are on the brink of a major—and new—expansion of social work liability in child welfare cases. A growing number of courts have held that child protective statutes create a legal "duty" to protect children that can form the basis of liability; but others strongly disagree.[60] Still unresolved, too, is whether a federal civil rights action can be filed seeking damages for inadequately protecting a child.[61] (Federal civil rights liability is clear for violating parental rights and for certain foster care inadequacies.)[62] If federal courts begin holding that such liability exists, then state law protections, such as governmental immunity and special state immunity statutes, will become irrelevant.

Conversely, a number of jurisdictions have adopted various protective devices. Some have adopted insurance or indemnification programs; others have, through court decision or legislation, given social workers good faith immunity from suits.[63] These decisions are, however, hopelessly ambiguous, as courts make unpredictable distinctions between quasi-prosecutorial decisions, which enjoy absolute immunity; discretionary decisions, which enjoy good faith immunity; and ministerial decisions, which are not granted immunity.[64]

This book describes these two seemingly contrary trends and then makes a series of recommendations designed to meet what should be the overriding societal goal—high-quality social work services that respect traditional American values of fairness and redress of grievances.

One *caveat* is in order. Many of the cases described in this book involve the defendant's motion to dismiss a complaint. In deciding whether or not to dismiss a lawsuit, the court assumes that the plaintiff can prove the allegations that have been made. This, of course, is not necessarily so. Thus, unless otherwise indicated, the "facts" described in this book are really only the *untested allegations* contained in court papers.

Notes

1. W. Griffin and J. Kalinowaki, "An Approach to Liability Concerns: Standards for Practice," *Family Life Developments* (Ithaca, N.Y.: College of Human Ecology, Cornell University, April–May 1981), p. 1.

2. Ibid.

3. See Appendix A.

4. Case descriptions, unless otherwise attributed, are based on informal or confidential material collected by the author.

5. C. A. Alexander, "Professional Liability Insurance: Jeopardy and Ethics." (Paper presented at the 1983 Professional Symposium, National Association of Social Workers, Washington, D.C., 21 November 1983), p. 8.

6. Ibid., p. 5.

7. Ibid.

8. Even psychiatrists may sometimes be under a duty to consult with a specialist. See D. Dawidoff, "The Malpractice of Psychiatrists," *Duke Law Journal, 1966* (1966), pp. 696, 713.

9. *Kent v. Whitaker*, 58 Wash. 2d 569, 364 P.2d 556 (1961).

10. Case cited in B. Bernstein, "Malpractice: An Ogre on the Horizon," *Social Work,* 23 (March 1978), pp. 106–107.

11. See pp. 37–38.

12. For a general discussion of this issue, see *Hasenei v. United States,* 541 F. Supp. 999 (D. Md. 1982); and *Thompson v. County of Alameda,* 27 Cal. 3d 741, 614 P.2d 728, 167 Cal. Rptr. 70 (1980).

13. Cited in H. Rothblatt and D. Leroy, "Avoiding Psychiatric Malpractice," *California Western Law Review,* 9 (1973), pp. 260, 271.

14. *Hammer v. Rosen,* 7 N.Y.2d 376, 165 N.E.2d 756, 198 N.Y.S.2d 65 (1960).

15. Alexander, "Professional Liability Insurance," p. 5.

16. National Association of Social Workers, *Code of Ethics* (Silver Spring, Md.: NASW, 1980), II.F, ¶ 5, p. 5.

17. Alexander, "Professional Liability Insurance," p. 6.

18. A similar case is cited in Bernstein, "Malpractice," p. 107. In another case, *Furniss v. Fitchett,* N.Z.L.R. 396 (1958), the "defendant was treating both the plaintiff and her husband. He gave the husband a report on the wife. A year later, the husband's attorney confronted her with this report causing her shock and great mental distress." The wife was able to obtain monetary damages for the harm caused by the disclosure. A description of this case is found in P. Cassidy, "The Liability of Psychiatrists for Malpractice," *University of Pittsburgh Law Review,* 36 (1974), pp. 108, 115–116.

19. *Gasperini v. Manginelli,* 196 Misc. 547, 92 N.Y.S.2d 575 (Sup. Ct., Queens Co., 1949).

20. Two cases in which physicians relied on apparently inappropriate sources are: *Kleber v. Stevens,* 39 Misc.2d 712, 241 N.Y.S.2d 497 (Sup. Ct., Nassau Co., 1963); and *Daniels v. Finney,* 262 S.W.2d 431 (Tex. Civ. App. 1953).

21. See Chapters 3 and 4.

22. See, for example, M. Hardin, ed., *Foster Children in the Courts,* Part 3 (Boston: Butterworth Legal Publishers, 1983).

23. See, for example, Cassidy, "Liability of Psychiatrists for Malpractice," p. 129. Such practices are expressly prohibited by NASW *Code of Ethics,* II.F, ¶¶ 9, 10, 11.

24. J. Klein, J. Macbeth, and J. Onek, *Legal Issues in the Private Practice of Psychiatry* (Washington, D.C.: American Psychiatric Press, 1984), p. 58. Emphasis added.

25. Ibid., p. 58.

26. See, for example, Cassidy, "Liability of Psychiatrists for Malpractice," p. 117.

27. See, generally, W. P. Keeton and W. L. Prosser, *Prosser and Keeton on Torts,* Chap. 12, "Imputed Negligence," 5th ed. (St. Paul, Minn.: West Publishing Co., 1984).

28. Alexander, "Professional Liability Insurance," p. 5.

29. Ibid., p. 6.

30. See, generally, *Prosser and Keeton on Torts,* sections 131 and 132.

31. Ibid., section 133; see also G. Caldeira, "Changing the Common Law: Effects of the Decline of Charitable Immunity," *Law and Society Review,* 16 (1981–82), p. 669.

32. *Prosser and Keeton on Torts,* Chap. 9, "Limited Duty."

33. See, for example, *Semler v. Psychiatric Institute of Washington, D.C.,* 538 F.2d 121 (4th Cir. 1976), holding that the persons under whose supervision a probationer is placed may be held liable for the probationer's reasonably foreseeable acts—in this case murder; *Tarasoff v. Regents of the University of California,* 17 Cal. 3d 399, 131 Cal. Rptr. 14, 551 P.2d 334 (Sup. Ct. 1976), holding that, when therapists determine, or pursuant to the standards of their profession should have determined, that a patient presents a serious danger to another, they incur an obligation to use reasonable care to protect the potential victim.

34. See, for example, *Doe v. New York City Department of Social Services,* 649 F.2d 134 (2nd Cir. 1981) and 709 F.2d 782 (2nd Cir. 1983), *cert. denied,* 104 S. Ct. 195 (1983). See, generally, *Monnell v. Department of Social Services,* 436 U.S. 658 (1978), allowing local governments to be sued under section 1983 of the federal Civil Rights Act.

35. J. Auerbach, "A Plague of Lawyers," *Harper's,* October 1976, p. 42.

36. See, for example, "Prof protection—Liability insurance available," *American Bar Association Journal,* 71 (May 1985), p. 35.

37. "Weather Service Held Liable in Deaths in Unforecast Storm," *Washington Post,* 22 December 1984, p. A4.

38. See, for example, D. Ranii, "Clergy Malpractice—The Prayer for Relief," *The National Law Journal,* 4 March 1985, p. 1; "Malpractice Approaches the Pulpit," *New York Times,* 6 June 1982, p. 8F.

39. M. Galante, "Malpractice Rates Zoom," *National Law Journal,* 3 June 1985, p. 1, 25.

40. Alexander, "Professional Liability Insurance," pp. 1–2.

41. Quoted in W. Holder, "Malpractice in Child Protective Services: An Overview of the Problem," in Holder and K. Hayes, eds., *Malpractice and Liability in Child Protective Services* (Longmont, Colo.: Bookmakers Guild, 1984), pp. 5–6.

42. Appendices A and B contain listings of relevant articles on social work liability.

43. Letter to A. Campriello, 29 January 1985.

44. G. R. Sharwell, "Avoiding Legal Liability in the Practice of School Social Work," *Social Work in Education,* 5 (October 1982), p. 17.

45. B. Schultz, *Legal Liability in Psychotherapy: A Practitioner's Guide to Risk Management* (San Francisco: Jossey-Bass, 1982), p. x.

46. See pp. 24–25 and p. 108, respectively.

47. D. Besharov, *Criminal and Civil Liability in Child Welfare Work: The Growing Trend* (Washington, D.C.: American Bar Association, 1983).

48. See, generally, R. Horowitz, "The Child Litigant," in Horowitz and H. Davison, eds., *The Legal Rights of Children,* section 3.04, "Statutes of Limitation" (Colorado Springs, Colo.: Shepard's, McGraw-Hill, 1984); *American Jurisprudence 2d,* 51 (1970 and Supp. 1981), sections 181–185, "Limitations of Actions."

49. *Chancellor v. Jimi Ann Lawrence and Edward T. Weaver,* No. 78 C 4496 (U.S. Dist. Ct., N.D.E.Ill. Slip Opinion, 9 July 1982).

50. *Rittscher v. Iowa,* 352 N.W.2d 247 (Iowa 1984).

51. See pp. 180–184.

52. See pp. 133–136.

53. See J. Fleming and B. Maximov, "The Patient or His Victim: The Therapist's Dilemma," *California Law Review,* 62 (1974), p. 1025.

54. T. Stein and T. Rzepnicki, *Decision Making at Child Welfare Intake: A Handbook for Practitioners* (New York: Child Welfare League of America, 1983), p. 8.

55. See pp. 139–142.

56. In S. Antler, *Policy Statement on Social Worker Liability. Child Welfare at the Crossroads: Professional Liability* (Boston: National Association of Social Workers, 1985), p. 26.

57. See pp. 175–180.

58. See, generally, L. Miles, "The Guardian Ad Litem and Civil Liability in California Child Maltreatment Cases," *University of California, Davis, Law Review,* 12 (1979), p. 700.

59. Letter to D. J. Besharov, 9 April 1984.

60. Compare *Mammo v. Arizona,* 138 Ariz. 528, 675 P.2d 1347 (Ariz. Ct. App. 1983); *Brasel v. Children's Service Division,* 56 Or. App. 559, 642 P.2d 696 (1982), holding that a duty is created; with *Nelson v. Missouri Division of Family Services,* 706 F.2d 276 (8th Cir. 1983), holding that no duty is created under Missouri law. Cf. *Doe v. Hendricks,* 590 P.2d 647 (Ct. of App. 1097), holding that no "special relationship" (another way to create a legal duty) existed on which to base police liability for the alleged failure to respond immediately to a report of sexual assault by an unrelated adult. See, generally, Annotation, "Liability of Municipality or Other Govern-

mental Unit for Failure to Provide Police Protection," *American Law Reports 3rd,* 46 (1972), p. 184.

61. Compare cases suggesting a cause of action under the Civil Rights Act, such as: *Jensen v. Conrad,* 747 F.2d 185 (4th Cir. 1984), *cert. denied,* ___ U.S. ___, No. 84-1159, *Family Law Reporter,* 11 (19 March 1985), p. 1239; *Estate of Bailey v. County of York,* ___ F.2d ___(3rd Cir. 1985), No. 84-5231, *Law Week,* 54 (23 July 1985), p. 2047; with those denying a cause of action, such as: *Bailey v. County of York,* 580 F. Supp. 794 (M.D. Pa. 1984); *Davis v. Casey,* 493 F. Supp. 117 (D.C. Mass. 1980); cf. *Jackson v. Marsh, Family Law Reporter,* 9 (11 January 1983), p. 2145 (decided 7 December 1982, D.C. Dt.Ct. 1982), denying a cause of action for the death of a child killed by a police officer.

62. See Chapters 4 and 5.

63. See pp. 175–180 and pp. 151–156, respectively.

64. See pp. 152–154.

2

Reporting Suspected
Child Abuse
and Child Neglect

The Basis of Liability

Since 1964, all states have enacted laws that require the reporting of suspected child abuse and neglect. Originally, these laws were directed solely at physicians, who were required to report "serious physical injuries" or "nonaccidental injuries." Over the years, however, reporting laws have been progressively expanded.

To increase the likelihood that maltreated children will be identified, a wide array of professionals are now required to report. *In all states, social workers are required to report.* (So are teachers and most medical professionals.) This reporting mandate applies to all social workers—those in private practice as well as to those who work in schools and other public and private agencies. Almost all states also require reports from the police and child care workers. At least 19 states require all citizens to report, regardless of their professional status. In all states, any person is legally permitted to report.

A corresponding expansion of conditions that must be reported has also taken place. Besides physical abuse, over 45 states now also require the reporting of physical neglect, sexual abuse, and emotional maltreatment. About the same number of states require reports of institutional maltreatment. (Although some states require reports of institutional maltreatment in schools and day care settings, most limit such reports to abuse and neglect in residential or foster care agencies.)[1] (See Chart 2-1.)

Chart 2-1

Reportable Child Maltreatment

Physical battering—physical assaults (such as hitting, kicking, biting, throwing, burning, or poisoning) that caused, or could have caused, serious physical injury.

Physical endangerment—reckless behavior toward a child (such as leaving a young child alone or placing a child in a hazardous environment) that caused, or could have caused, serious physical injury.

Physical neglect—failure to provide food, clothing, hygiene, and other needed care that caused, or over time would cause, serious physical illness or disability.

Medical neglect—failure to provide the medical, dental, or psychiatric care needed to prevent or treat serious physical or emotional injury, illness, or disability.

Sexual abuse—vaginal, anal, or oral intercourse; vaginal or anal penetrations; or other forms of inappropriate sexual contacts that caused, or over time would cause, serious emotional injury.

Sexual exploitation—use of a child in prostitution, pornography, or other sexually exploitative activities that caused, or over time would cause, serious emotional injury.

Emotional abuse—physical or emotional assaults (such as torture and close confinement) that caused, or could have caused, serious emotional injury.

Developmental neglect (sometimes misleadingly called "emotional neglect")—failure to provide needed emotional nurturing and physical and cognitive stimulation that caused, or, over time, would cause, serious developmental deficits.

Improper ethical supervision—parental behavior that contributes to the delinquency of the child.

Educational neglect—failure to send a child to school in accordance with the state's education law.

Abandonment—leaving a child alone or in the care of another under circumstances that demonstrate an intentional abdication of parental responsibility.

Institutional maltreatment—the abuse or neglect of children by public or private residential or foster care agencies.

In general, the maltreatment of any child under the age of 18 must be reported. The laws in Alaska and Wyoming—apparently the sole exceptions—require reports only until children reach 16 years of age. Statutory provisions or administrative policies often lift reporting obligations for young persons who are married or otherwise emancipated, because they are presumed able to protect themselves. In addition, some states establish a higher age limit for reporting (generally 21 years of age) if the child is physically or mentally disabled. Young adults who are disabled are presumed to need this additional period of protection.

State laws do not require that potential reporters be sure that a child is being abused or neglected, or have absolute proof of maltreatment. Instead, the laws require that a report be made if there is "reasonable cause to suspect" or "reasonable cause to believe" that a child is abused or neglected.

Unfortunately, space does not permit a more complete description of reporting mandates—and the variations among states. For a more detailed understanding of state reporting laws, readers can refer to the many publications on the subject.[2] Readers can also contact the appropriate child protective agency in their state for further information and guidance about reporting requirements and procedures.

Mandatory reporting laws and associated public awareness campaigns have been strikingly effective. As mentioned above, in 1963, about 150,000 children came to the attention of public authorities because of suspected abuse or neglect.[3] By 1972, an estimated 610,000 children were reported annually, and in 1981, approximately 1.3 million children were reported.[4]

Nevertheless, there are still major problems in the reporting process. Large numbers of endangered children are not reported to the authorities. According to the National Study of the Incidence and Severity of Child Abuse and Neglect, professionals—physicians, nurses, teachers, child care workers, mental health professionals, police officers, *and social workers*—fail to report *more than half* of the maltreated children whom they see. It is not just minor cases that are not reported. In 1979, according to the same study, over 50,000 children with *observable injuries severe enough to require hospitalization* were not reported.[5] An analysis of child fatalities in one state described how: "In two of the cases, siblings of the victims had died previously. . . . In one family, two siblings had died mysterious deaths that were undiagnosed. In another family a twin had died previously of abuse."[6]

Nonreporting can be fatal to children. A study in Texas revealed that, during a three-year period, over 40 percent of the approximately 270 children who died as a result of maltreatment had not been reported to the authorities—even though they were being seen by a public or private agency at the time of their death or had been seen in the past year.[7]

At the same time that there is serious underreporting, there is extensive overreporting. More than 60 percent of all reports that are now made—involving over 750,000 children each year—are determined to be "unfounded" by the agencies that receive them.[8]

Few of these "unfounded" cases are made maliciously. Most involve situations of poor child care that, though of legitimate concern, are not sufficiently serious to be considered "child maltreatment." In fact, over half of these "unfounded" cases are referred to other agencies that provide various needed services.[9] In addition, child protective workers sometimes wrongly determine that a report is unfounded, and they sometimes use the validation process as a means of controlling their caseload.

Unfortunately, the determination that a report is unfounded is usually made after an unavoidably traumatic investigation, in which the child protective agency questions friends, relatives, and neighbors, as well as schoolteachers, day care personnel, doctors, clergymen, and others who know the family. Besides being unfair to parents, such overreporting places a heavy burden on chronically understaffed child protective agencies. Forced to allocate a substantial portion of their limited investigative resources to these "unfounded" reports, protective agencies are often unable to respond promptly and effectively when children are in serious danger.

High rates of both over- and underreporting are harmful to the children and parents involved, and, by their effect on the system as a whole, they threaten to undo much of the progress that has been made in recent years. In individual cases, either the failure to report or the making of a wrongful report can form the basis of civil and criminal liability.

Criminal Penalties for Failing to Report

The laws of 42 states contain specific penalty clauses for the failure to report. (See Chart 2-2.) In the rest of the states, a general statutory provision may establish criminal liability.[10] (Some states also provide penalties for the failure to perform other mandated protective actions, such as the taking of photographs and X-rays.) The criminal penalty is usually of misdemeanor level, with the potential fine ranging from $100 up to $1,000 and imprisonment ranging from five days up to one year in jail.

There are positive reasons, in terms of treatment, for criminal penalties for failing to report, and for the civil liability discussed in the next section. The existence of penalties makes it easier for mandated reporters to explain to both parents and children why a report must be made. In addition, experience shows that possible penalties are invaluable to individual staff members who often must persuade their superiors of the necessity of making a report. For example, nurses frequently relate how the mention of potential liability for failure to report is the only argument that convinces reluctant hospital administrators to take protective action. Indeed, the main

Chart 2-2
Statutory Liability for Failure to Report
Suspected Child Maltreatment

States and Territories	Criminal	Civil	Test for Civil Liability	States and Territories	Criminal	Civil	Test for Civil Liability
AL	✓			NE	✓		
AK	✓			NV	✓		
AZ	✓			NH	✓		
AR	✓	✓	Willfully fails	NJ	✓		
CA	✓			NM	✓		
CO	✓	✓	Willfully violates	NY	✓	✓	Knowingly and willfully
CT	✓			NC			
DE	✓			ND	✓		
DC	✓			OH	✓		
FL	✓			OK	✓		
GA	✓			OR	✓		
HI	✓			PA	✓		
ID				RI	✓	✓	Knowingly fails
IL				SC	✓		
IN	✓			SD	✓		
IA	✓	✓	Knowingly fails	TN	✓		
KS	✓			TX	✓		
KY	✓			UT	✓		
LA	✓			VT	✓		
ME		✓	Knowingly violates	VA	✓		
MD				WA	✓		
MA	✓			WV	✓		
MI	✓	✓	N/M	WI	✓		
MN	✓			WY			
MS				AS	✓	✓	N/M
MO	✓			GU	✓		
MT		✓	N/M	PR	✓		
				VI	✓		

Note: This chart presents data on specific statutory provisions establishing liability. In any particular state, other general statutes or court decisions may establish liability, as discussed in the text.

N/M = not mentioned

The Vulnerable Social Worker

purpose of penalty clauses is, as the politicians like to say, to "put some teeth" in the statutory mandate to report.

Criminal prosecutions for not reporting have, until recently, been rare. Three reasons why there have not been more prosecutions are: (1) problems of proof; (2) the feeling that criminal sanctions are inappropriate, that there is no criminal culpability, and that an otherwise law-abiding citizen should not be prosecuted; and (3) the fact that the would-be reporter's cooperation is often necessary to prove the case against the parents. A criminal prosecution is also unlikely if the child did not suffer serious injury as a result of the failure to report. For example, in 1979, James Downey, an Assistant County Attorney in Boulder, Colorado, cited "two criminal investigations in Colorado regarding this offense, one involving a doctor and one involving a schoolteacher. In both cases, other persons did report the suspected abuse so that no further injury to the children occurred."[11]

Significantly, the number of criminal prosecutions seems to be increasing. Such cases rarely result in published court opinions, so that they tend to be hidden from wide public and professional view. However, research and interviews by the author have revealed dozens of criminal investigations and a surprising number of successful prosecutions for not reporting. In recent years, there have been prosecutions against doctors, psychiatrists, psychologists, teachers (in one case, a nun), spouses, friends of the family, and, of course, social workers.[12]

The failure to report suspected institutional maltreatment has also resulted in criminal prosecutions. For example, the head of an institution can be criminally liable for the failure to respond to information suggesting that a staff member maltreated a child. In one case, a school principal was fined $200 (the maximum penalty) for failing to report the claims of two sets of parents that a teacher was sexually assaulting their third-grade daughters.[13]

The existence of criminal liability depends on whether the failure to report was an intentional violation of the law. Most state laws impose criminal sanctions only if the failure to report was "knowing" or "willful." Under such laws, which establish a "subjective" standard of intent, a successful prosecution requires proof—beyond a reasonable doubt—that (1) the person was legally required to report, (2) the person had knowledge of this legal mandate, (3) the person had a *conscious* suspicion that the child was abused or neglected, and (4) the person still did nothing.

In states that do not limit liability to "knowing" or "willful" failures to report, an "objective" standard of intent is applied. In these states, the defendant need not intend to violate the law; criminal culpability can be established by proof that the defendant was "*consciously* aware of facts...which would cause a reasonable person to know or suspect that a child was being subjected to abuse or neglect.[14]

Under either test, but depending on the circumstances, the accused may raise the usual defenses to criminal liability. These include ignorance, mistake, necessity, and coercion.[15]

Circumstantial evidence of child maltreatment may be used to prove the accused's knowledge of conditions that should have been reported. Thus, a criminal prosecution may be based on the failure to report the child's "suspicious" or "apparently inflicted" injuries. In Los Angeles, for example, a doctor who apparently knew that a 3-year-old child had been previously removed from her mother's custody was prosecuted for not reporting *repeated* evidence of severe abuse. According to court documents, the doctor did not report evidence of abuse in early 1982 and again in June 1983. When he saw the little girl in June 1983, she was "gravely ill" with pneumonia and showed evidence of "old burns on the chest and left leg, and the absence of the nasal...septum." A report prepared by two UCLA doctors who were child abuse specialists said that the doctor neither reported the child's condition to the authorities nor admitted the child to the hospital because he wanted to "give the mother a chance" to avoid further contact with social service workers. Instead, he attempted to treat the child in his office and at her home. "Thirteen days after [he] began treating her, she died of a massive chest infection resulting from the pneumonia."[16] In December 1984, the doctor entered a no-contest plea to involuntary manslaughter.[17]

A criminal prosecution is more likely, however, when a mandated reporter fails to report direct evidence of child maltreatment; that is, (1) when the person required to report observes the parents' abusive or neglectful behavior, (2) when a child complains to the mandated reporter that he or she is being abused or neglected, (3) when the parents tell such a person about their abusive or neglectful conduct, or (4) when a reputable individual warns such a person that a child is abused and neglected and, instead of disputing the accuracy of the warning, the person says, in effect: "So what? It is none of my business."

A social worker in Arizona did not say, "So what? It is none of my business." Nevertheless, she was prosecuted for failing to report. The social worker's client, an incest victim who was "fearful of authority," told her about "past molestation of her daughter by a family friend. [The social] worker immediately urged the client to report the incident to the police."

> The client asked [the social worker] to interview the girl to determine whether the molestation had caused lasting emotional damage. [She] did so, and found none. Also, because the client had broken off contact with the molester's family, [the social worker] determined that the girl was not in danger of being molested again.
>   [The social worker] continued her effort to get the client to report the incident herself, because [she] believed that urging the client to report it

complied with the law, and that reporting it against the client's wishes "could result in a serious remission to her former state of emotional upheaval" and cause her to "flee therapy." The social worker also feared that no case could be made against the molester without the client's involvement.

[The social worker], however, planned to report the incident if the client would not do so within two months.

After five weeks, the client called in a report to the police, and [the social worker] "followed up on that call as was agreed, but was not contacted by the police for some time."[18]

The social worker was criminally prosecuted because she failed to report "immediately," as required by state law. The reporting law, similar to that in most states, makes no exceptions, not even when a therapist determines that it would be better if the mother were to make the report. The requirement of "immediate" reporting is designed: (1) to prevent the would-be reporter's procrastination (and, perhaps, ultimate failure to report) and (2) to help ensure prompt protection for the child. In justifying the charges in this case, the prosecutor is reported to have said that "any delay in reporting—even if well-intentioned—leaves time for other children to be victimized...."

Almost eight months later, the charges against the social worker were dropped. According to her lawyer, the state's "haphazard" record-keeping system precluded proof that a report was not made in a timely manner. The lawyer is quoted as saying that he and his client "were very pleased with the result," but added that "ideally, we would have liked to have prevailed on the merits. Nevertheless, I am certain that the issue of professional judgment will arise again in the future, and that issue will eventually have its day in court."

Because of the stringent legal requirements involved in criminal prosecutions, they often result in dismissals before trial, acquittals after trial, or reversals on appeal.[19] Nevertheless, the message of these prosecutions is clear: potential criminal liability for failing to report is a realistic possibility and must be kept in mind when working with children or parents.

Chart 2-3 lists the forms of direct and circumstantial evidence that should alert social workers to the possible need to report.

Civil Liability for Failing to Report

The possibility of a *criminal* prosecution for failing to report depends on the existence of a general or specific statute establishing criminal penalties for the violation of the reporting law's mandate. About eight states have specific legislation establishing *civil* liability for the failure to report. No legislation is needed, however, to create civil liability for violating a reporting law. In fact, there are circumstances that can create civil liability even if the report-

Chart 2-3
The Grounds for a Report of Suspected
Child Abuse or Neglect

Direct Evidence

- Eyewitness observations of a parent's abusive or neglectful behavior;

- Children found in physically dangerous situations;

- The child's description of being abused or neglected;

- The parent's own description of abusive or neglectful behavior;

- Demonstrated parental inability to care for a newborn baby; or

- Demonstrated parental disabilities (for example, mental illness or retardation or alcohol or drug abuse) severe enough to make child abuse or child neglect likely.

Circumstantial Evidence

- Suspicious injuries suggesting physical abuse;

- "Accidental" injuries suggesting gross inattention to the child's need for safety;

- Physical injuries or medical findings suggesting sexual abuse;

- Signs of severe physical deprivation suggesting general child neglect;

- Severe dirt and disorder in the home suggesting general child neglect;

- Apparently untreated physical injuries, illnesses, or impairments suggesting medical neglect;

- Unexplained absences from school suggesting educational neglect;

- Apparent parental indifference to a child's severe emotional or developmental problems suggesting emotional maltreatment;

- Apparent parental condonation of or indifference to a child's misbehavior suggesting improper ethical guidance; or

- Apparently abandoned children.

ing law does not require the social worker to report. Although there are only a handful of reported cases on the subject, none denies the cause of action,[20] and the facility with which such claims are settled (even in states without specific legislation) reflects the strong consensus among practicing lawyers—and insurance companies—that such liability exists.[21]

Like a potential criminal prosecution, the prospect of a civil lawsuit for damages arising from the failure to report is a strong incentive to comply with reporting mandates. "In one Michigan district, school administrators responded immediately when faced with a civil action alleging liability for failure to properly report an incident of abuse and distributed pamphlets on child abuse reporting to all faculty members within the district."[22]

Specific Statutory Provision Establishing Civil Liability

The laws that have been enacted in about eight states (as shown in Chart 2-2) apply to all persons required to report. These laws remove whatever question there is about the other bases for civil liability that are described in this section.[23]

All but two of these laws limit civil liability to situations in which there was a "knowing" or "willful" failure to report. A "knowing" failure to report means that the would-be reporter had a *conscious* suspicion (or belief) that the child was abused or neglected, knew that a report was required, and still did nothing. In a civil action, willful misconduct is usually defined to mean "that the actor has intentionally done an act of an unreasonable character in disregard of a risk known to him or so obvious that he must be taken to have been aware of it, and so great as to make it highly probable that harm would follow."[24]

The "knowing" or "willful" standard for liability is narrower than the ordinary tort standard of "negligence." It is usually adopted to avoid penalizing would-be reporters for honest mistakes in interpreting the difficult and ambiguous facts surrounding most cases of child maltreatment.

Sometimes the intentional nature of the failure to report seems relatively clear. For example, in *Beuning v. Waun,* a former high school student in Pontiac, Michigan, sued her former principal, a school social worker, and the school district.[25] The former student claimed that for an entire school year she had consulted with and sought the advice of the principal and the school social worker about sexual abuse at home. According to her complaint, they did not use the information she provided to make a report.

More often, though, such direct evidence of intent is not available. This does not mean that a lawsuit cannot succeed. The defendant's state of mind may be proven "by circumstantial evidence and the inferences which the trier of fact may draw therefrom," as the California Supreme Court explained.[26] Thus, the plaintiff can introduce evidence of the child's condition, its diagnostic significance, and any other surrounding circumstances that would lead the court to infer that the defendant actually suspected (or believed) that the child was maltreated.

Whether a "knowing" or "willful" failure to report falls under one of these civil liability statutes depends on the precise wording of the reporting law. (This is also true for criminal liability.) If the reporting law covers suspected instances of institutional maltreatment (and most do), agency workers, supervisors, and the agency itself may be sued for failing to report the maltreatment of a child in their care. This is what happened in *Borgerson v. Minnesota*;[27] the state and the county, state and county licensing officials, the group home, and staff members of the group home were alleged to have failed to report (and respond to) information that juveniles in a locked residential facility were maltreated. It was claimed that the juveniles were physically abused, given tranquilizing drugs improperly, and placed in isolation without proper safeguards being taken. Similarly, there have been suits against child welfare workers and their agencies when they failed to report the maltreatment of foster children.[28]

Negligence *per se*

Under the common law, the violation of a statutory duty—in this instance, the required reporting of known and suspected abuse and neglect—may be "negligence *per se*." No legislation specifically creating civil liability is needed. Failure to comply with a statutory mandate "in itself" establishes the negligence.[29]

Over the years, all legal commentators examining the question have concluded that the doctrine of negligence *per se* should apply to violations of reporting mandates.[30] Under their analysis, a specific civil liability statute is not necessary to hold would-be reporters financially responsible for the harm to children that results from not reporting. In 1967, for example, law professor Monrad Paulsen concluded that reporting laws probably "create a cause of action in favor of infants who suffer abuse after a physician has failed to make a report respecting earlier abuse brought to his attention."[31] The correctness of this analysis was soon confirmed by two California cases and decisions in other states that have followed them.

In 1970, a lawsuit, *Robinson v. Wical, M.D., et al.*, was filed against the police, two hospitals, and individual doctors who *repeatedly* failed to report a child with severe injuries indicative of abuse.[32] When the child was 5 months old, his 17-year-old mother had taken him to the hospital with a long skull fracture. The mother's explanation was that the child had "fallen off a bed." The child was treated and released three days later. The hospital record indicated that the examining physician noted contusions and many old bruises on the child's body and blood blisters on his penis, that he had questioned the mother about these injuries and did not believe her answers, that he therefore had suspected child abuse, but that he had not made a report.[33]

Eight days later, the child was readmitted with marked swelling and discoloration of the left arm from his elbow to his fingertips. The mother signed the child out and took him to another hospital where there was concern "regarding possible child abuse," but the child was "discharged in the hope that it was not so." No report was made by either hospital.

Within weeks, the child was returned to the first hospital, this time with burned fingers, puncture wounds and strangulation marks on his neck, and welts on his back. The child was not breathing at the time of admission. Before respiration was restored, the child had suffered extensive brain damage from the lack of oxygen in his blood. (At the time of the trial, when the child was 3 years old, his I.Q. was 24 and his physical development was extremely retarded.) The mother's boyfriend was convicted of child abuse; no charges were filed against the mother.

The infant's father, separated from the mother, sued, claiming that the hospital's failure to report was the proximate cause of the infant's permanent brain damage. The case was settled out of court for $600,000. The lawsuit—and the size of the settlement—received wide publicity, especially within the medical community.[34]

The second case, *Landeros v. Flood*,[35] was not settled out of court, and the California Supreme Court was called upon to decide whether the plaintiff had stated a cause of action against a doctor who failed to diagnose and report a case of the battered child syndrome. The lawsuit alleged that an 11-month-old girl had been brought to the hospital with a broken leg—a spiral fracture of the right tibia and fibula that could only have been caused by a twisting of the child's leg until it cracked.

> The child's mother had no explanation for this injury. The girl also had bruises over her entire body and a linear fracture of the skull, which was in the process of healing. Without taking full body skeletal X rays, the hospital released the child to her mother and the mother's common-law husband. The hospital made no report of suspected child abuse, as is required by California law. Within 11 weeks, the child was brought to a second hospital, having now sustained traumatic blows to her right eye and back, severe bites on her face, and second- and third-degree burns on her left hand. At this time, the battered child syndrome was immediately diagnosed and reported to the appropriate agencies.[36]

The California Supreme Court found that the plaintiff had stated a cause of action on theories of both negligence *per se* and professional malpractice. The court held that, as a matter of law, the hospital and the doctor could be liable for damages if it could be proven that the doctor had violated the state reporting law by knowingly failing to report when he actually suspected that the girl's injuries were the result of abuse.

There is widespread agreement that the *Landeros* case represents the present state of the law.[37] As one legal commentator summarized:

> The basic elements of this theory are that: (1) the physician, by failing to report a suspected case of child abuse, violated his statutory duty; (2) as a proximate result of that violation, the child suffered subsequent injuries; (3) the child was a member of the class of persons which the statute was designed to protect; and (4) the subsequent injuries were the result of acts that the statute was designed to prevent.[38]

In states where the criminal penalty provision of the reporting law requires a "knowing" or "willful" failure to report, liability under the negligence *per se* doctrine requires an intentional failure to report. On the other hand, if the reporting law or criminal penalty clause applies an objective standard of liability (that is, reasonable cause to suspect or believe), then a negligent failure to report, in itself, may create liability. But even here, courts would probably require evidence of an intentional violation of the statute, as the California Supreme Court did in *Landeros*.[39]

Whether the doctrine of negligence *per se* creates liability in a particular case depends on whether the defendant is among those required to report and whether the situation involves a reportable condition. Thus, as in the case of civil liability statutes, liability under the negligence *per se* doctrine is circumscribed by the precise provisions of the state's reporting law: (1) the defendant must be legally required to report, and (2) the situation must involve one of the forms of maltreatment for which a report is required.

The same limits do not apply to potential liability under the common law doctrines of professional malpractice and failure to warn, both of which are discussed next. (These doctrines are broader than the doctrine of negligence *per se* for another reason. Under them, liability is created by conduct that is simply negligent, while, as we have seen, the negligence *per se* doctrine, in this context, can require intentional or willful behavior.)

Professional Malpractice

The second theory under which the California Supreme Court allowed the *Landeros* case to proceed was, in essence, that of medical malpractice. The intermediate appellate court had held that there was no cause of action based on malpractice because it concluded that the ability to recognize the battered child syndrome was not part of the skill and learning of the ordinary medical practitioner, and that, for this reason, there could be no liability for the failure to do so.[40] The California Supreme Court disagreed, explaining that the question of medical ability to identify battered children was for the jury to decide. The court held that liability would be established upon proof that "a reasonably prudent physician examining the [child] in 1971 would have been led to suspect she was a victim of the battered child syndrome from the particular injuries and circumstances presented to him, would have confirmed the diagnosis by ordering X rays of her entire skeleton, and would have promptly reported his findings to appropriate authorities to prevent a recurrence of the injuries."[41]

As in the case of the court's negligence *per se* holding, legal commentators have been unanimous in concluding that the *Landeros* approach would be adopted in other jurisdictions.[42] "This theory is premised on the basic duty of a physician to possess and use reasonable skill and care in the treatment of patients and the diagnosis of their ailments. Incorrect diagnosis by a physician is as actionable as improper treatment, and the common-law malpractice theory is essentially based on the physician's failure to properly diagnose a child as physically abused."[43]

The *Landeros* case is widely interpreted as making the failure to report a form of professional malpractice for physicians only. There is nothing in the court's opinion, however, or in legal doctrine generally, that necessitates this conclusion. In fact, the basic rule applies to all professions. As Prosser and Keeton explain:

> Professional men in general, and those who undertake any work calling for special skills, are required not only to exercise reasonable care in what they do, but also to possess a standard minimum of special knowledge and ability. Most of the decided cases have dealt with physicians and surgeons, but the same is undoubtedly true of dentists, pharmacists, psychiatrists, attorneys, architects and engineers, accountants, abstractors of title, and many other professions and even skilled trades.[44]

At one time, it may have been correct to think that only physicians could be expected to possess the knowledge and ability necessary to identify maltreated children. Twenty years of professional training and public awareness campaigns, however, have significantly upgraded the diagnostic skills of many other professional groups, *including social workers*. At the same time, there has been a parallel increase in societal expectations about the ability of various professions to identify maltreated children—as reflected by the expansion of mandatory reporting laws to cover most child-serving professions. Thus, it is likely that social workers, as well as nurses, dentists, mental health professionals, and teachers, all of whom are, in fact, mandated reporters in most states, might be held financially liable for their negligent failure to identify and report maltreated children.[45]

The standard of professional negligence, of course, varies from profession to profession. Failure to report direct evidence of maltreatment, such as the student's description of sexual abuse in *Beuning*, would be strong evidence of negligence for almost any mandated profession, but the standard is considerably less uniform for circumstantial evidence, where a would-be reporter is required to weigh often conflicting, incomplete, and subtle indications of maltreatment. "Many professionals required to report presumably were selected because of their substantial opportunity for contact with children, and not because of any physiological or psychological diagnostic skills. (Teachers and religious practitioners exemplify this.)"[46]

Expert testimony is needed to determine whether a particular profession should be held responsible for failing to recognize a particular form of maltreatment (or a particular set of diagnostic indicators). "Since juries composed of laymen are normally incompetent to pass judgment on questions of [professional knowledge] or technique, it has been held in the great majority of malpractice cases that there can be no finding of negligence in the absence of expert testimony to support it."[47] "The formula under which this usually is put to the jury is that [the defendant] must have the skill and learning commonly possessed by members of the profession in good standing; and he will be liable if harm results because he does not have them."[48]

To assess the diagnostic capabilities of a particular profession, great weight is given to the practice standards established by the profession itself. The *NASW Standards for Social Work Practice in Child Protection* require that: "All social workers have professional responsibility for supplementing the efforts of CPS [Child Protective Services] in the identification, assessment, treatment, and prevention of child abuse and neglect."[49] Standards 37 and 38 seem to create the basis for establishing malpractice liability for the failure to report.

STANDARD 37. The Social worker Shall Acquire Knowledge About Child Abuse and Neglect, the Local CPS Process, and Child Welfare Services
All social workers need to have basic knowledge of the indicators of child abuse and neglect, factors contributing to the problem, and community resources to help resolve the problem. This knowledge is to be integrated into daily professional practice, and shared with other professionals to make early identification of child abuse and neglect possible and to deter misconceptions about CPS intervention.

STANDARD 38. The Social Worker Shall Comply with Child Abuse and Neglect Reporting Laws and Procedures
It is the responsibility of every social worker to obtain knowledge of the state's child abuse and neglect laws and procedures, and to share this knowledge with employers and colleagues. In addition, whenever it is necessary to report a case of suspected child abuse or neglect, the social worker shall collaborate with CPS and, as appropriate, shall explain the report and the CPS process to family members.

The doctrine of professional malpractice for failure to report requires that there be a professional relationship between the person who should have reported and the child. Often, though, the relationship is between the professional and the parent (or some other third party). For example, the professional may be a social worker seeing the parent for emotional difficulties.[50] If the parent tells the social worker about a child's maltreatment, there can be no liability under the doctrine of professional liability—because the child is not the social worker's client.

Similarly, many reporting laws require a report from professionals only when the child comes "before them in their professional or official capacity." Such reporting laws, like the doctrine of professional malpractice, do not create potential liability when a social worker learns, second hand, of danger to a child who is not a client.

There does not mean, however, that the social worker may not be held liable. There may be another basis of liability.

Violation of Duty to Warn of Danger to Third Parties

Since 1976, a line of cases has firmly established the liability of psychiatrists, psychologists, probation officers, and social workers for the failure to warn *third parties* of a clearly recognized danger. The most widely known of these cases, again from California, is *Tarasoff v. Regents of University of California*.[51] "In that case a University of California student, who was a psychiatric outpatient at a University clinic, followed through on his threat, previously expressed to his therapist, to kill a specific victim. The Supreme Court of California, in a suit by the victim's parents against the University and its therapists, ruled that a psychotherapist owes a duty of reasonable care to third persons who may be intended victims of the therapist's patient."[52] In the court's words:

> When a therapist determines, or pursuant to the standards of his profession should determine, that his patient presents a serious danger of violence to another, he incurs an obligation to use reasonable care to protect the intended victim against such danger. The discharge of this duty may require the therapist to take one or more of various steps, depending upon the nature of the case. Thus it may call for him to warn the intended victim or others likely to apprise the victim of the danger, to notify the police, or to take whatever other steps are reasonably necessary under the circumstances.[53]

The *Tarasoff* doctrine, although much criticized by mental health professionals, seems to have been adopted by almost all of the courts considering the question.[54] Furthermore, there is general agreement that the doctrine applies not only to psychiatrists but also to psychologists, social workers, and "psychotherapists" generally.[55]

The analogy between this situation and that of a therapist who learns of a clear danger to a child while treating a parent or other family member is self-evident. The failure to take protective action (here a report to the authorities rather than a warning to the victim) is as likely to result in future harm—and as likely to create liability.

Vicarious Liability

Whatever theory of liability is applied, when the person who allegedly failed to report is employed by an agency or organization, the agency or organization may also be sued—and invariably is sued. This vicarious liability is based on the legal doctrine of *respondeat superior*,[56] under which the tortious conduct of a staff member may be imputed to the employer. (Vicarious liability also attaches for the acts or omissions of volunteers.)

Conversely, since most reporting laws do not lift the reporting obligations of staff members when they notify their superiors of suspected child maltreatment, the staff members may still be liable for the damages caused by the failure to report—if they knew or should have known that no report was made. Staff members who were falsely told that a report was made will have a defense against liability unless they knew or should have known that this was untrue.

Statute of Limitations

Most nonlawyers know that there is a statute of limitations to the bringing of lawsuits. Generally, an action must be filed within three or five years of the harm done. However, in all but a few states, the statute of limitations usually does not begin to run against minor plaintiffs until they reach the age of 18.[57] Thus, the failure to report the suspected maltreatment of an infant may result in a lawsuit up to 23 years later. Of course, an action may be initiated while the child is still a minor if it is brought by a legal representative or a duly appointed guardian.

Extent of Liability

The amount of liability faced by someone who fails to report is limited to compensation for the actual harm or injury to the child proximately caused[58] by the failure to report, unless the failure was intentional or so reckless that punitive damages are appropriate.[59] The only harms or injuries that are considered are those that occurred *after* the report should have been made.[60] Potential reporters are not held responsible for maltreatment that occurred before they knew or should have known about the child's situation.[61] And, of course, there is no liability if there is no further maltreatment.

Civil Liability for Wrongful Reporting

In the past, fear of being unjustly sued for libel, slander, defamation, invasion of privacy, or breach of confidentiality was frequently cited as a deterrent to more complete reporting. This fear existed even though existing legal doctrines seemed to protect anyone making a legally mandated or authorized report in good faith. As two well-known experts on family law wrote in 1966, "there is no American case that even suggests that there may be liability for a good faith report of the kind required by battered child statutes."[62]

Nevertheless, in the experience of many states, only an explicit statutory grant of immunity from liability would erase the concerns of potential reporters. Hence, all states specifically grant immunity from civil and criminal liability to persons who report. Almost all states require that, for immunity to attach, the report must be made in *good faith* (see Chart 2-4). The absence of good faith is shown by evidence that a false report was made maliciously, because of prejudice or personal bias, or because of reckless or grossly negligent decision making.[63] To reassure potential reporters even further, in 1984, 16 states had laws that established a *presumption of good faith* (Chart 2-4).[64]

In recognition of the other responsibilities assigned to persons who report, 39 states specifically extend the grant of immunity to participation in judicial proceedings, and 24 extend immunity to the performance of other acts authorized by law, such as taking photographs and X rays, participating in the removal of a child from parental custody, and cooperating with the child protective agency's investigation (Chart 2-4). Colorado's statute is typical of the broad immunity often granted:

> Any person participating in good faith in the making of a report or in a judicial proceeding...the taking of color photographs or X rays, or the placing in temporary protective custody of a child pursuant to this article, or otherwise performing his duties or acting pursuant to this article shall be immune from any liability, civil or criminal, or termination of employment that otherwise might result by reason of such reporting. For the purpose of any proceedings, civil or criminal, the good faith...shall be presumed.[65]

In addition, federal court decisions have also granted qualified, or good faith, immunity for reporting to persons sued under the Federal Civil Rights Act.[66] (Such cases are based on the claim that a wrongful report is a violation of the parents' constitutional rights.)

The immunity provisions of reporting laws do not prevent the initiation of lawsuits claiming damages for wrongful reporting. A lawsuit can always be filed, but immunity provisions do make it almost impossible for such suits to succeed—as long as the report was made in good faith.

Furthermore, a complaint that fails to offer sufficient allegations of bad faith will be dismissed *before trial.*[67] One New York appellate court described the applicable rules:

> Where, as here, a defendant's statements are presumptively privileged, either by statutory mandate or at common law, they are actionable only if the plaintiff

Chart 2-4
State Immunity Laws

States and Territories	Any Authorized Act	Civil & Criminal Immunity in Making a Report	Immunity for Taking Photographs	Immunity for Taking X rays	Placing Children in Protective Custody	Participating in Judicial Proceedings	For Child Protective Workers[1]	Adverse Employment Actions	Requirement of Good Faith[2]	Good Faith Presumed
AL		✓			✓	✓				
AK		✓				✓			✓	
AZ		✓				✓			✓	
AR		✓	✓						✓	✓
CA		✓	✓			✓			✓	
CO		✓	✓	✓	✓	✓		✓	✓	✓
CT		✓				✓			✓	
DE		✓				✓			✓	
DC		✓				✓			✓	✓
FL	✓	✓	✓	✓	✓[3]	✓	✓		✓	
GA		✓				✓			✓	
HI		✓				✓			✓	
ID		✓			✓	✓			✓	
IL		✓	✓	✓	✓	✓	✓		✓	✓
IN		✓	✓	✓		✓			✓	✓
IA		✓	✓	✓		✓			✓	
KS		✓				✓			✓	
KY		✓				✓			[5]	
LA		✓				✓			✓	
ME		✓	✓	✓		✓			✓	✓
MD		✓				✓			✓	
MA		✓							✓[4]	
MI	✓	✓	✓[3]	✓[3]		✓			✓	✓
MN		✓					✓	✓	✓	
MS		✓				✓			✓	✓
MO		✓	✓	✓	✓	✓	✓		✓	
MT		✓				✓			✓	
NE		✓				✓			✓	
NV		✓				✓			✓	
NH		✓				✓			✓	
NJ		✓			✓	✓			✓	
NM		✓				✓			✓	✓
NY		✓	✓			✓	✓		✓	✓
NC		✓			✓	✓	✓		✓	✓
ND		✓		✓	✓	✓			✓	✓
OH		✓				✓				
OK		✓				✓			✓	
OR		✓				✓			✓	
PA		✓	✓		✓	✓		✓	✓	✓
RI		✓				✓			✓	
SC		✓				✓			✓	✓
SD	✓	✓	✓			✓	✓		✓	
TN		✓				✓		✓	✓	✓
TX		✓				✓			✓	
UT		✓	✓	✓	✓				✓	
VT		✓				✓			✓	
VA		✓			✓	✓			✓	
WA		✓			✓	✓			✓	
WV	✓	✓	✓[3]	✓[3]					✓	
WI		✓	✓						✓	✓
WY	✓	✓	✓[3]	✓[3]	✓[3]	✓			✓	✓
AS		✓	✓		✓	✓			✓	✓
GU		✓	✓		✓	✓			✓	✓
PR		✓					✓		✓	
VI	✓	✓	✓[3]	✓[3]	✓	✓			✓	

Note: This chart presents data on *state* immunity provision as of 9/1/84. Federal rules may differ, as discussed at various points in the text.

[1] All laws granting child protective workers immunity require good faith on their part.

[2] Good faith includes statutes that require the absence of malice.

[3] Immunity is not specifically granted for taking photographs and X rays and for placing children in protective custody. However, the statute authorizes such actions and extends immunity to all authorized actions.

[4] Good faith is only required for persons permitted but not required to report.

[5] The statute establishes an objective test for liability, that is, reasonable cause to report.

can prove their falsehood and that the defendant was motivated by actual malice or ill-will. Plaintiff, in support of this burden, must submit evidence; suspicion, surmise or accusations will not suffice. Similarly, malice is an essential element of prima facie tort and where a complaint fails to allege facts sufficient to support a claim of malice, it is subject to dismissal. As plaintiff has not presented any factual allegations of malice or ill-will on the part of the defendants, his complaint must be dismissed.[68]

Four recent cases illustrate the crucial importance of good faith to the enjoyment of immunity from liability. In 1982, an Alabama mother and grandmother sued a doctor and the hospital where he worked for making an incorrect report "negligently," "wantonly," and "with reckless disregard" of their rights. The Alabama Supreme Court affirmed the dismissal of the suit, but only because state law provided absolute immunity for reporting; that is, immunity was not limited to reports made in "good faith."[69]

In 1977, a Philadelphia physician was the defendant in a lawsuit claiming that she had reported in "bad faith." The four-day trial resulted in a hung jury, and, while the case awaited retrial, the judge dismissed the complaint on the ground that "the evidence clearly demonstrates that the doctor acted in good faith believing that she was confronted with a situation that involved child abuse."[70]

Most cases alleging the reporter's lack of good faith fail because of the difficulties involved in trying to prove malicious motivation or intent. Rarely is there direct evidence of knowingly false reporting, prejudice, personal bias, or grossly negligent behavior. That is what makes *Austin v. French,* and what it has to say about circumstantial evidence of bad faith potentially so important.[71] The defendant, a Virginia physician, was sued in 1980 for maliciously reporting a child who had numerous bruised knots on his body. The parents had brought their infant son to the doctor for possible blood problems. Later, it was established that the bruising resulted from the child's hemophilia. The doctor moved to dismiss the suit on the ground that he acted in good faith and, thus, was immune from liability.

The court refused to dismiss the lawsuit, ruling that the *allegations* of "grossly negligent" diagnosis were sufficient to allow the case to be considered by a jury. Although the court's decision is not explicit on the subject, it appears that allegations of the doctor's "unnecessarily irresponsible and defamatory" remarks toward the parents—on two occasions he seems to have berated them, causing them also to seek damages for his remarks, which, they claimed, caused "mental and physical stress, humiliation, and embarrassment"—helped to resolve the case in the parents' favor. In this context, the court stated:

It is clear that plaintiff's allegations are sufficient to raise this question of fact. It might not be unusual if a doctor discussed child abuse with parents in an attempt to promote the best interests of the child. It is quite another matter if a doctor berates, belittles, and verbally condemns parents in an unnecessarily excessive manner, especially if the physician's accusations are made in the absence of exercise of common diagnostic analysis. Such questions of degree are appropriately left to the jury.[72]

After the judge's ruling, the case was settled for $5,000.

In *Roman v. Appleby,* the parents alleged that Appleby, a high school guidance counselor, made an improper report to the local child protective agency "knowingly,...maliciously and...with reckless indifference to and disregard of" the parents' constitutional rights. The court's opinion is instructive because, in explaining why the parents' allegations were "insufficient to overcome the defense of good faith," it describes the care with which the decision to report the emotional needs of the child, Alexander, was made.

> Before Appleby made her referral and recommendation, she conducted approximately eight interviews with Alexander. Appleby involved the parent plaintiffs in one counseling session where she disclosed her findings and conclusions that Alexander needed professional mental health analysis and asked them to obtain that help on their own. On numerous occasions Appleby sought the advice of the school psychologist, McMullen, who attended two counseling sessions and who in his affidavit corroborates what Appleby wrote in her report. It is also undisputed that Mrs. Roman initiated a phone conversation with Mrs. Appleby during which, at the very least, family problems were discussed. Prior to contacting [the child protective agency], Appleby spoke with Alexander's parents and asked them why they had not contacted Crisis Intervention on their own, an issue which had been discussed at the counseling session when the parents, McMullen and Appleby were present....None of these factors indicates arbitrary action, gross negligence or reckless disregard of plaintiff's rights. The fact that Appleby failed, refused or declined to divulge confidential information to the parents at the counseling session which might have been relayed to her by Alexander in confidence, is consistent with careful action and inconsistent with the claim of reckless disregard for the student's rights and interests.[73]

This kind of careful decision making not only reduces legal vulnerability, it also reflects the highest standards of professional behavior.

These four cases should be reassuring to social workers considering whether or not to make a report. The immunity provisions of reporting laws (and court decisions under the Federal Civil Rights Act) fully protect persons who report in good faith; it will be all but impossible to rebut the presumption of good faith as long as the person reporting has not been reckless in deciding to report nor abusive in dealing with the parents.

Adverse Employment Actions
Social workers employed by public or private agencies sometimes are discharged or suffer other adverse employment actions for failing to report

suspected child maltreatment. Assuming that the worker had knowledge of sufficient information to make a report, and of the obligation to report, such penalties may be justified.

Greater concern arises when the adverse employment action is taken because the worker did make a report. If the report turns out to have been unfounded, *and* if it appears that the report was made maliciously or recklessly, a penalty, again, may be justified. But, too often, it appears that such actions are taken inappropriately.

The allegations in one case suggest how this can happen. A social worker in a private clinic was told by the father that he had hit his child with a belt. The worker informed the father that she would have to file a suspected child abuse report. The father happened to be vice president of a company that had a $1 million contract with the clinic to provide counseling for company employees; in fact, he was in charge of writing the contract. According to the worker, the father convinced the clinic director to tell the worker not to file a report. The worker insisted on filing the report—and was fired.[74] This case resulted in passage of Minnesota's antiretaliation law.

Retaliation

After a report is determined to be unfounded, some parents seek retaliation against the person who made the report by complaining to the agency. Sometimes, the agency improperly gives in to parental pressure, but, even when the agency does not do so, the procedure it follows in responding to the complaint can unnecessarily punish the reporter. In one case, for example, a parent filed a formal complaint with the state licensing agency, claiming that a visiting nurse had wrongfully reported. Although the parent made no substantial allegations of the nurse's bad faith, the agency took eight months to dismiss the complaint. Those eight months of uncertainty and stress—and the cost of defending the claim—were not lost on other professionals licensed to practice in the state.

By far the greatest danger of wrongful retaliation arises when social workers report the institutional maltreatment of children by their own agencies. One social worker's description of what happened to her when she tried to protect a child in her care speaks for itself:

> I was fired from my position as the only social worker at [a center for the treatment of cerebral palsy] because I was advocating for a child who attended the center. The child, an eleven year old who was fully ambulatory, was tied into a wheelchair from 9 to 3 each day for the past three years in order to prevent his acting out self abusive behavior. A helmet was placed on his head and tied to the back of the wheelchair and his upper arms were tied behind him. No motion was possible. In addition, he was heavily sedated. On the basis of my previous, extensive work with handicapped children, examination of the reports

in the child's file and discussions with my colleagues at the agency, I believed that the child had, in addition, been misdiagnosed as severely retarded and was in the wrong program at the Center. After trying, without success, for four months to convince the Center administration, the psychologist and the doctors to untie the boy, to reevaluate him and to plan a proper educational program for him, I contacted the Chairman of the Board of Trustees of our agency and asked him to intervene. Three weeks after contacting him, the child's situation was unchanged and I then notified [the state agency that had placed the child and the state agency responsible for investigating reports of child abuse].

I did not seek support from the child's parents because staff members had reported that the child was tied and kept in a closet at home. I had met the mother and believed that she could not, at that time, be helpful to the child.

I then gave information to the [state agency] and was immediately suspended from my job. I received my salary for 55 days and was then fired, with a dismissal letter containing false statements that will totally damage my professional reputation as a social worker. I asked for an evaluation of my work at the agency the day I was fired and was refused. I also utilized all of the grievance procedures that were available to me according to the agency's written Personnel Policies, but my efforts were ignored.

* * *

I was fired for properly doing my job as a social worker and advocating for a client and for my commitment to NASW Code of Ethics.[75]

The social worker accepted a $5,000 payment in settlement of her lawsuit after she realized that the legal costs for pursuing her claim might be higher than any additional payment she might receive. She also wanted to put a very unpleasant incident behind her.

There is no way of knowing how often this kind of retaliation occurs; it rarely comes to public attention.[76] But enough cases have become known so that four states have now passed specific legislation to protect employees who report in good faith from what the Tennessee statute calls "a detrimental change in employment status."[77] (See Chart 2-4.) Pennsylvania's law gives the employee an express cause of action against the agency:

Any person who...is required to report...and who, in good faith, makes or causes said report to be made and who, as a result thereof, is discharged from his employment or in any manner discriminated against with respect to compensation, hire, tenure, terms, conditions or privileges of employment, may file a cause of action in the court of common pleas of the county in which the alleged unlawful discharge or discrimination occurred for appropriate relief. If the court finds that the individual is a person who, under this section, is required to report or cause a report of suspected child abuse to be made, that he, in good faith, made or caused to be made a report...and that as a result thereof he was discharged or discriminated against with respect to...employment, it may issue an order granting appropriate relief, including but not limited to reinstatement with back pay.[78]

Even in the absence of this kind of specific legislation, the basic employment law of many states would protect employees who report in good faith.[79]

The ability of the law to protect the reporter suffers from one major limitation. To be protected, the employee must establish a connection between the report and the adverse employment action. This can be difficult. Often, there is a history of poor relations and conflict between the employee and the agency's administrators, and the adverse action is claimed to be based on this history. Or, the action is attributed to legitimate administrative or budgetary needs of the agency. The connection, thus, comes down to a question of proof, which the employee frequently cannot produce.

To meet this often insurmountable problem, Minnesota's employee protection statute creates a "rebuttable presumption that any adverse action within 90 days of a report is retaliatory." It goes on to define an "adverse action" to include, but not be limited to: "(1) discharge, suspension, termination, or transfer from the facility, institution, school or agency; (2) discharge from or termination of employment; (3) demotion or reduction in remuneration for services; or (4) restriction or prohibition of access to the facility, institution, school, agency, or persons affiliated with it."[80]

Notes

1. This is in keeping with the federal regulations implementing the Federal Child Abuse Prevention and Treatment Act (45 C.F.R. §§2340.1-2[b][3]). The requiring of reports of institutional maltreatment only if it occurs in residential facilities is based on two considerations. First, children are more vulnerable to maltreatment in foster homes, shelters, and other residential facilities because parents may be out of touch, uncaring, or deceased; only an independent agency is able to take effective action. Second, when a child has been placed in an agency or home, whether or not with the parent's consent, that agency or home is as responsible for the child's welfare as any natural parent would be.

2. For a discussion of state reporting laws, and their steady expansion, see U.S. National Center on Child Abuse and Neglect, *State Child Abuse and Neglect Laws—A Comparative Analysis* (Washington, D.C.: Department of Health and Human Services, 1983); U.S. National Center on Child Abuse and Neglect, *Child Abuse and Neglect—State Reporting Laws* (Washington, D.C.: Department of Health and Human Services, 1978, 1980); D. Besharov, "The Legal Aspects of Reporting Known and Suspected Child Abuse and Neglect," *Villanova Law Review,* 23 (1977–1978), p. 458.

3. U.S. Children's Bureau, *Juvenile Court Statistics* (Washington, D.C.: Department of Health, Education and Welfare, 1966), p. 13.

4. See S. Nagi, *Child Maltreatment in the United States: A Challenge to Social Institutions* (New York: Columbia University Press, 1977), p. 35; *Reported Child Maltreatment: 1981* (Denver, Colo.: American Humane Association, 1982).

5. U.S. National Center on Child Abuse and Neglect, *National Study of the Incidence and Severity of Child Abuse and Neglect* (Washington, D.C.: Department of Health and Human Services, 1981), Chap. 6; see especially p. 36, Table 6-3, and p. 25, Table 5-2.

6. Confidential material held by author.

7. Region VI Resource Center on Child Abuse, *Child Deaths in Texas* (Austin: University of Texas, Graduate School of Social Work, 1981), p. 26.

8. U.S. National Center on Child Abuse and Neglect, *National Analysis of Official Child Neglect and Abuse Reporting (1978)* (Washington, D.C.: Department of Health, Education and Welfare, 1979), p. 18, Table 5.

9. Cf. *Trends in Child Abuse and Neglect: A National Perspective* (Denver, Colo.: American Human Association, 1984), p. 37.

10. For example, the failure to report may be misprision of a felony. Cf. *Pope v. State,* 38 Md. App. 520, 382 A. 2d 880 (1978); modified, 284 Md. 309, 396 A. 2d 1054 (1979), dismissed because the state's child abuse law did not apply and because there was no crime of misprision of a felony in Maryland.

11. J. Downey, "Accountability for Failure to Protect Children," in D. Bross, ed., *Legal Representation of the Maltreated Child* (Denver, Colo.: National Association of Counsel for Children, 1979), p. 252.

12. See, for example, for doctors, "Doctor, Parents Charged in Death of Abused L.A. Child," *Los Angeles Times,* 3 December 1983, Pt. 1, p. 1; "MD Charged With Not Reporting Child Abuse," *Toronto Star,* 2 June 1983, p. A16; for psychiatrists, *Groff v. State,* 390 So. 2d 361 (Dist. Ct. of App., 2nd Dist., Fla., 1980); *State v. Groff,* 409 So. 2d 44 (Dist. Ct. of App., 2nd Dist., Fla., 1981), ultimately dismissed on the ground that Florida's reporting mandate was limited to "any person. . . serving children" and, therefore, did not apply to the defendant psychiatrist, who was treating the father, not the child, and, in fact, had never met her; for psychologists, *People v. Poremba* (Denver County Court, 17 December 1980), *Family Law Reporter,* 7 (31 January 1981), p. 2142; for teachers, *People v. Sok* (for punching and pushing two children) and *People v. Molitor* (for not reporting the abuse), mentioned in "Monk Seeks $60 Million Damages for Lawsuit's Allegations of Racism," *Los Angeles Times,* 23 June 1982, Pt. 2, p. 12 (according to the Los Angeles District Attorney, both cases resulted in convictions); for spouses, "Two Found Guilty of Not Reporting Child-Abuse Case," *Providence Journal,* 4 December 1981 (on appeal, the case was dismissed on procedural grounds [the case was tried in the wrong court]); *State v. Boucher and Flinkfelt,* 468 A.2d 1227 (R.I., 1983); for friends of the family, *Pope v. State, supra,* n. 10; and for social workers, *People v. Noshay, NASW News,* 29 (February 1984), p. 21, and 29 (April 1984), p. 7, a case, later dismissed, charging the social worker for failing to report "immediately" because she worked with the victim's family for five weeks before a report was made by the family.

13. "Principal Fined for Failure to Report Abuse Suspicion," *Denver Post,* 10 March 1982, p. A-1, col. 1; "PTA Backs Fine in Failure to Report Alleged Abuse," *Denver Post,* 11 March 1982, p. A-1.

14. *People v. Poremba,* p. 2144.

15. J. Hall, *General Principles of Criminal Law,* Chaps. 11 and 12 (New York: Bobbs-Merrill, 1947).

16. All information and quotations from "Doctor, Parents Charged in Death of Abused L.A. Child."

17. *Los Angeles Times,* 1 December 1984, Metro Section, p. 1.

18. *People v. Noshay, NASW News.*

19. See, for example, Ibid.; *Pope v. State; Groff v. State.*

20. There are, however, decisions denying such claims under the Federal Civil Rights Act. For example, in *Davis v. Casey,* 493 F. Supp. 117, 120 (D. Mass. 1980), the Civil Rights Act complaint for failure to report was dismissed because no "affirmative state

action played any part" in the child's maltreatment.

21. See Appendix C.

22. J. Aaron, "Civil Liability for Teacher's Negligent Failure to Report Suspected Child Abuse," *Wayne Law Review,* 28 (1981), pp. 183, 207, n. 164, citing an interview with S. Matz (22 January 1981), the attorney who brought the action against the school personnel in *Beuning v. Waun,* discussed on p. 31.

23. See, for example, *Leach v. Chemung,* No. 75-2652 (Chemung City Sup. Ct., N.Y., filed May 18, 1976), a case brought under New York's civil liability statute. It is not clear what effect, if any, these laws have on the preexisting common law tort actions for the failure to report that are described below. The primary legislative intent seems to have been to remove any ambiguity over the plaintiff's right to sue. However, these statutes, by the narrower test of liability that they set forth (and the commentary associated with them) also seem to be an attempt to limit the grounds of liability to "knowing" and "willful" failures to report. See U.S. National Center on Child Abuse and Neglect, *Model Child Protection Act,* Comment to Section 12 (1977 Draft), stating: "This standard was adopted as a *specification* and a limitation on the situations in which liability may arise."

24. W. P. Keeton and W. L. Prosser, *Prosser and Keeton on Torts,* 5th ed. (St. Paul, Minn.: West Publishing Co., 1984), p. 213. The "knowing" and "willful" standard is discussed on pp. 27–28.

25. *Beuning v. Waun,* No. 80-214188 (Cir. Ct., Oakland Co., Mich., filed 7 November 1980).

26. *Landeros v. Flood,* 17 Cal. 3d 399, 131 Cal. Reptr. 69, 551 P.2d 389, n. 13.

27. *Borgerson v. Minnesota,* Nos. 3-78-228, 4-81-14, slip opinion (U.S.D. Ct. of Minn., 3d Div., 12 June 1981). This case is cited as an example of the claims that can be made. Minnesota does not have a civil liability statute.

28. For example, *Doe v. New York City Department of Social Services,* 649 F.2d 134 (2nd Cir., 1981) *cert. denied,* 104 S. Ct. 195 (1983); *Bartels v. County of Westchester,* 76 A.D.2d 517, 429 N.Y.S.2d 906 (2nd Dept., 1980).

29. *Prosser and Keeton on Torts,* p. 220. However, jurisdictions differ over whether proof of the statute's violation is the equivalent to proof of negligence, whether it raises a rebuttable inference of negligence, or whether it is merely some evidence of negligence. Violation of the statute may raise a claim of liability under the Federal Civil Rights Act (§1983), but so far such claims have been rejected by the courts when the failure to report is not a government action or policy. See, for example, *Davis v. Casey,* 493 F. Supp. 117 (D. Mass. 1980).

30. See Appendix C.

31. M. Paulsen, "Child Abuse Reporting Laws: The Shape of the Legislation," *Columbia Law Review,* 67 (1967), pp. 1, 36.

32. Civil No. 37607, Calif. Superior Ct., San Luis Obispo, filed 4 September 1970.

33. All case details from R. Brown and R. Truitt, "Civil Liability in Child Abuse Cases," *Chicago-Kent Law Review,* 54 (1978), pp. 753, 762–763.

34. *Time,* 20 November 1972, p. 74.

35. 17 Cal. 3d 399, 131 Cal. Reptr. 69, 551 P.2d 389 (Sup. Ct. 1976).

36. U.S. National Center on Child Abuse and Neglect, *Curriculum on Child Abuse and Neglect: Resource Materials* (Washington, D.C.: Department of Health, Education and Welfare, 1979), p. 78.

37. See Appendix C.

38. Annotation, "Failure to Report Suspected Case of Child Abuse," *American Jurisprudence: Proof of Facts 2d,* 6 (1975), pp. 345, 346 (citation omitted).

39. *Supra,* n. 35, 551 P.2d at pp. 397–398. But see Annotation, *supra,* n. 38, p. 357, stating: "Thus, the reporting statutes generally require a report where there is reasonable cause to believe that child abuse has occurred. There are two possible interpretations of what constitutes a violation. Under one interpretation, the statute is violated if the reporter should have recognized child abuse but did not, whereas the other interpretation would require a willful failure to report for a violation. It has been argued that the first interpretation is preferable, since it applies a reasonable person standard, while still allowing room for judgment, and since a willful violation would be extremely difficult to prove" (citation omitted).

40. *Landeros v. Flood,* 40 Cal. App. 3rd 189, 123 Cal. Rptr. 713, 719 (1975), *vacated,* 17 Cal. 3d 399, 131 Cal. Rptr. 69, 551 P.2d 389 (1976).

41. *Supra,* n. 35, 551 P.2d at 393.

42. See, for example, *Doran v. Priddy,* 534 F. Supp. 30, 33 (D. Ken. 1981) (dicta); *Commonwealth v. Labbe,* 375 Mass. 788, 373 N.E.2d 227, 233 (App. Ct. of Mass., Barnstable, 1978) (dicta); *Commonwealth v. Cadwell,* 374 Mass. 308, 372 N.E.2d 246, 253, n. 8 (Sup. Jud. Ct. of Mass., Berkshire, 1978) (dicta). See also Appendix C.

43. Annotation, *supra,* n. 38, p. 358 (citations omitted).

44. *Prosser and Keeton on Torts,* pp. 185–186 (citations omitted).

45. For a discussion arguing that the failure to report should be considered "educational malpractice," see Aaron, "Civil Liability for Teacher's Negligent Failure."

46. Ibid., p. 203, n. 140.

47. *Prosser and Keeton on Torts,* p. 188.

48. Ibid., p. 187.

49. *NASW Standards for Social Work Practice in Child Protection* (Silver Spring, Md.: National Association of Social Workers, 1981), p. 27.

50. See, for example, *Groff v. State.*

51. 17 Cal.3d 425, 551 P.2d 334, 131 Cal. Rptr. 14 (1976).

52. D. Wexler, "Victimology and Mental Health Law: An Agenda," *Virginia Law Review,* 66 (1980), pp. 681, 682.

53. 17 Cal.3d at p. 431, 551 P.2d at p. 340, 131 Cal. Rptr. at p. 20.

54. For critical as well as supportive commentary, see Appendix A.

55. See, for example, *Hicks v. United States,* 511 F.2d 407 (D.C. Cir. 1975) (mental hospital); *Beck v. Kansas University Psychiatry Foundation,* 580 F. Supp. 527 (D. Kansas 1984) (mental health center, staff doctors, director of security services, and director of emergency room); *Hasenei v. United States,* 541 F. Supp. 999 (D. Md. 1982) (psychiatrist); *Vu v. Singer Company,* 706 F.2d 1027 (9th Cir.), *cert. denied,* 104 S. Ct. 350 (1983) (operator of job corps center); *Lipari v. Sears, Roebuck & Co. v. United States,* 497 F. Supp. 185 (D. Nebraska 1980) ("psychotherapist"); *Rodriguez v. Inglewood Unified School District,* 152 Cal. App. 3rd 440, 199 Cal. Rptr. 524 (2nd Dist., Div. 3, 1984) (school district); *Sinacore v. The Superior Court of Santa Clara County,* 81 Cal. App. 3rd 198, 144 Cal. Rptr. 893 (1st Dist., Div. 2, 1978) (applied to social worker to lift confidentiality); *Bradley Center v. Wessner,* 250 Ga. 199, 296 S.E.2d 693 (1982) (mental health hospital); *Durflinger v. Artiles,* 234 Kan. 484, 673 P.2d 86 (1983) (therapist); *Mangeris v. Gordon,* 580 P.2d 481 (Nev. 1978) (massage parlor); *McIntosh v. Milano,* 168 N.J. Super. 466, 403 A.2d 500 (1979) (psychiatrist); *Furr v. Spring Grove State Hospital,* 53 Md. App. 474, 454 A.2d 414 (Md. App. 1983) (state psychiatrist and director of admissions of state mental hospital); *Coath v. Jones,* 419 A.2d 1249 (Pa. Super. 1980) (employer). See also *Prosser and Keeton on Torts,* §32; *Restatement on Torts 2d,* §319 (St. Paul, Minn.: American Law Institute Publishers, 1965).

56. *Prosser and Keeton on Torts,* Chap. 12, "Imputed Negligence." See also Note, "Agency: Liability of a Hospital for Negligent Acts of a Physician–Employee," *Oklahoma Law Review,* 18 (1965), p. 77; Annotation, *American Law Reports 2d,* 69 (1960), p. 30.

57. In some states, there are significant exceptions to these generalizations. For example, there is sometimes a more limited tolling (suspension) of the statute of limitations in medical malpractice cases. A full discussion of these issues can be found in R. Horowitz, "The Child Litigant," in Horowitz and H. Davidson, eds., *The Legal Rights of Children,* §3.04, "Statutes of Limitation" (Colorado Springs, Colo.: Shepard's, McGraw-Hill, 1984); *American Jurisprudence 2d,* 51 (1970 and Supp. 1981), "Limitations of Actions" §§181–185. Two case examples are discussed on p. 15.

58. The questions that can arise under the concept of proximate cause are very complex and will not be discussed here. (For example, what if the subsequent injury occurs many months later—or many years later? Also, can the failure to report be considered the proximate cause of an injury to a sibling?) See N. Lehto, "Civil Liability for Failing to Report Child Abuse," *Detroit College of Law Review,* 1977 (1977), pp. 135, 161–162.

59. *Prosser and Keeton on Torts,* pp. 213 and 281.

60. Ibid., p. 281.

61. Many jurisdictions require that a report be made "immediately." Others specify 24 hours, 48 hours, and so forth. In those jurisdictions requiring "immediate" reports, courts would probably hold that there could be a "reasonable" delay while the diagnosis is confirmed and other necessary administrative procedures are followed. When a specific time frame is set forth, a court might hold a defendant responsible for damages that occurred *within* the specified time if it concluded that an ordinarily prudent person would have acted more quickly. Any delay beyond the specified time would cause presumptive liability, subject to the defendant's ability to raise a valid defense. Cf. *People v. Noshay.*

62. H. Foster and D. Freed, "Battered Child Legislation and Professional Immunity," *Journal of the American Bar Association,* 52 (1966), p. 1071.

63. *Black's Law Dictionary,* 4th ed. (St. Paul, Minn.: West Publishing Co., 1951), defines "good faith" as: "Honesty of intention, *and* freedom from knowledge of circumstances which ought to put the holder upon inquiry" (emphasis added).

64. Actually, such provisions are technically redundant, at best. Under most reporting laws, good faith is not an affirmative defense that must be raised and proved by the reporter. Rather, the plaintiff must allege and prove the reporter's bad faith. Thus, the burden is already on the person suing to disprove the reporter's good faith. Furthermore, under the so-called Thayer Rule concerning the rebuttal of presumptions, the presumption of good faith could be rebutted by some credible evidence suggesting that the report was made maliciously. Query: If the presumption is successfully rebutted, does the plaintiff still have the burden of proving bad faith by a preponderance of the evidence? Perhaps the best thing to say is that the presumption of good faith is a public relations provision, designed to soothe potential reporters, which does not take into account how presumptions operate in the law. See J. Thayer, *Preliminary Treatise on Evidence* (Boston: Little, Brown & Co., 1898), p. 336. For a discussion of the development and present statement of the Thayer Rule, see E. Cleary, ed., *McCormick's Handbook of the Law of Evidence,* 2d ed. (St. Paul, Minn.: West Publishing Co., 1972), §345, p. 821.

65. Colo. Rev. Stat. §19-10-110 (Supp. 1983).

66. See, for example, *Roman v. Appleby,* 558 F. Supp. 449 (E.D. Pa., 1983); cf.

April K. v. Boston Children's Service Association, 581 F. Supp. 711, 713 (D. Mass. 1984), stating: "Were this Court to accept plaintiffs' argument and hold that a proper ...report could be filed only after personal contact with the minor involved, then any parent could frustrate the execution of the child-protection law merely by being uncooperative. The Court refuses to read such an unreasonable requirement into [the law.]"

67. See, for example, ibid.

68. *Miller v. Beck,* 82 A.D.2d 912, 440 N.Y.S.2d 691, 692 (2nd Dept., 1981), citations omitted.

69. *Harris v. City of Montgomery,* 435 So.2d 1207 (Ala. 1983).

70. "Immunity Not Absolute for M.D. Reporting Child Abuse," *Pediatric News,* December 1977, p. 3, cited in Brown and Truitt, "Civil Liability in Child Abuse Cases," pp. 753, 769–770.

71. *Austin v. French,* Civ. Action No. 80-0114, 0115 (D), U.S. Dist. Ct., West. Dist. of Va., Danville Div., 1980.

72. Ibid., p. 4.

73. *Roman v. Appleby,* pp. 458–459.

74. Material on file with author.

75. Confidential material on file with author.

76. See, for example, "Virginia, Massachusetts Agencies Draw Sanctions," *NASW News,* 28 (October 1983), p. 18. See, generally, N. Rindfleisch and J. Rabb, "How Much of a Problem Is Resident Mistreatment in Child Welfare Institutions?" *Child Abuse and Neglect,* 8 (1984), p. 33.

77. Tenn. Code Ann. §37-1210 (Michie Supp. 1983).

78. Pa. Stat. Ann. tit. 11, §2202(d) (Purdon Supp. 1984).

79. See generally H. Perritt, *Employee Dismissal Law and Practice* (New York: Wiley Law Publications, 1984); D. Cathcart and S. Kruse, "The New American Law of Wrongful Termination," *International Business Lawyer* (February 1984), p. 73; T. Moore, "Individual Rights of Employees Within the Corporation," *The Corporation Law Review,* 6 (Winter 1983), p. 39.

80. Minn. Stat. Ann. §26.556(4a)(c) (West Supp. 1984).

3

Inadequately Protecting a Child

The Basis of Liability

Over the past 20 years, there has been an enormous expansion of programs to prevent child abuse and child neglect.[1] Almost all major population centers now have specialized "child protective agencies" to investigate reports.[2]

The actual organization of child protective agencies varies widely from state to state, and from community to community within the same state. But these differences are less substantial than they seem. All child protective agencies perform essentially the same functions. They receive and screen reports (usually called "Intake"); they investigate reports and determine whether child protective action is needed (usually called "Investigation"); they determine whether the child requires immediate protection (usually called "Emergency Services"); they determine what longer-term protective measures and treatment services are needed and then seek the parents' consent for them (usually called "Case Planning and Implementation"); when a maltreated child is left home (or is returned home after having been in foster care), they supervise the parents' care of the child and monitor the provision of treatment services (usually called "Case Monitoring"); and, finally, they close the case after it appears that the parents can properly care for the child or after parental rights have been terminated and the child has been placed for adoption (usually called "Case Closure") (see Chart 3-1). To the fullest extent possible, child protective agencies seek the parents' voluntary consent to the protective measures and treatment services deemed necessary. If the parents do not agree to the agency's plan, the agency may seek court authority to impose the plan on the parents (usually called "Court Action").

Chart 3-1
Standard Child Protective Functions

Intake

- Receive reports.

- Screen reports.

- Assign reports to individual workers.

Investigation

- Collect information.

- Verify reports.

Emergency Services

- Assess need for immediate protective measures.

- Implement emergency services (either with parents' consent or through court order).

Case Planning and Implementation

- Determine appropriate case plan (i.e., longer-term protective measures and treatment services).

- Implement case plan through direct provision of services or referral to other agencies (either with parents' consent or through court order).

Case Monitoring

- Supervise the parents' care of child.

- Continually monitor implementation of case plan (to determine whether the case plan remains appropriate, a new case plan is needed, or the case can be closed).

Case Closure

- Close case because parents can care properly for the child, *or*

- Close case because parental rights terminated and child placed for adoption.

Child protective agencies differ only in the degree to which these functions are separated and assigned to different staff units; this, in turn, is determined by the size of the agency. The larger the agency, the greater the efficiency—and hence the greater the likelihood—of specialization.

Although inadequate funding is a continuing problem, increased reporting and specialized child protective agencies have saved many thousands of children from injury and even death. In New York State, for example, after the passage of a comprehensive reporting law that also mandated the creation of specialized child protective staffs, there was a 50-percent reduction in child fatalities, from about 200 a year to under 100.[3] Similarly, Drs. Ruth and C. Henry Kempe report: "In Denver, the number of hospitalized abused children who die from their injuries has dropped from 20 a year (between 1960 and 1975) to less than one a year.[4]

Despite this progress, many children suffer further maltreatment *after* their plight becomes known to a child protective agency. Studies in a number of states have shown that about 25 percent of all child fatalities attributed to abuse or neglect involve children already reported to a child protective agency.[5] Tens of thousands of other children receive serious injuries short of death while under child protective supervision.

As this chapter will describe, a civil lawsuit, a criminal prosecution, or both, may result whenever a child suffers further maltreatment after having been reported to the authorities. The key word here is "after," for there is no liability for injuries that occur before something can be done to protect the child.[6] As of this writing, lawsuits alleging the failure to protect a child would most likely be brought in state court, because such claims have not yet been widely held to be a violation of the Federal Civil Rights Act. Should the federal courts do so, child protective workers (and their agencies) would confront a major expansion of legal vulnerability.[7]

Under state law, liability is established through proof that the agency (or worker) breached a duty owed to the child, which was the proximate cause of the child's subsequent injury. Because courts do not recognize a general duty of public agencies to act to prevent harm, the duty to the child must be established by a specific state law (or by a special relationship between the agency and the child).[8]

The detailed nature of legally mandated child protective functions, and, hence, the scope of possible liability they create, are best illustrated by the provisions of the model legislation recommended by the U.S. National Center on Child Abuse and Neglect (see Chart 3-2). Actual state laws and administrative rules are generally of equal or greater specificity.[9] On the basis of such legal mandates, lawsuits alleging inadequate protection of children have been brought in each of the following categories: (1) failure to accept a report for investigation; (2) failure to investigate adequately; (3) failure to

Chart 3-2
Model Guidelines for Child Protective Legislation

(a) The local agency shall be capable of receiving reports of known or suspected child abuse or neglect twenty-four hours a day, seven days a week. If it appears that the immediate safety or well-being of a child is endangered, the family may flee or the child disappear, or the facts otherwise so warrant, the agency shall commence an investigation immediately, regardless of the time of day or night. In all other cases, a child protective investigation shall be commenced within twenty-four hours of receipt of the report. To fulfill the requirements of this section, the local agency shall have the capability of providing or arranging for comprehensive emergency services to children and families at all times of the day or night.

(b) For each report it receives, the local agency shall perform a child protective investigation within the time limits specified in (a) to: (i) determine the composition of the family or household, including the name, address, age, sex, and race of each child named in the report, and any siblings or other children in the same household or in the care of the same adults, the parents or other persons responsible for their welfare, and any other adults in the same household; (ii) determine whether there is reasonable cause to believe that any child in the family or household is abused or neglected, including a determination of harm or threatened harm to each child, the nature and extent of present or prior injuries, abuse or neglect, and any evidence thereof, and a determination of the person or persons apparently responsible for the abuse or neglect; (iii) provided that there is probable cause determine the immediate and long-term risk if each child were to remain in the existing home environment; and (iv) determine the protective, treatment, and ameliorative services that appear necessary to help prevent further child abuse or neglect and to improve the home environment and the parents' ability to care adequately for the children. The purpose of the child protective investigation shall be to provide immediate and long term protective services to prevent further abuse or neglect and to provide, or arrange for, and coordinate and monitor treatment and ameliorative services necessary to safeguard and insure the child's well-being and development and, if possible, to preserve and stabilize family life.

(c) The local agency may waive a full child protective investigation of reports

Source: U.S. National Center on Child Abuse and Neglect, *Child Protection: A Guide for State Legislation* (Washington, D.C.: Department of Health and Human Services, 1983), §13.

The Vulnerable Social Worker

Chart 3-2 (continued)

made by agencies or individuals if, after an appropriate assessment of the situation, it is satisfied that: (i) the protective and service needs of the child and the family can be met by the agency or individual, (ii) the agency or individual agrees to attempt to do so, and (iii) suitable safeguards are established and observed. Suitable safeguards shall include a written agreement from the agency or individual to report periodically on the status of the family, a written agreement to report immediately to the local agency at any time that the child's safety or well-being is threatened despite the agency's or individual's efforts, and periodic monitoring of the agency's or individual's efforts by the local service for a reasonable period of time.

(d) The local agency shall convene one or more interdisciplinary "Child Protection Teams" to assist it in its diagnostic, assessment, service, and coordination responsibilities. The head of the local agency or his designee shall serve as the team's coordinator. Members of the team shall serve at the coordinator's invitation and shall include representatives of appropriate health, mental health, social service, and law enforcement agencies.

(e) If the local child protective service is denied reasonable access to a child by the parents or other persons and the local service deems that the best interests of the child so require, it shall seek an appropriate court order or other legal authority to examine and interview such child.

(f) The child protective service may determine that a child requires immediate or long-term protection, either through (1) medical or other health care, or (2) homemaker care, day care, casework supervision, or other services to stabilize the home environment, or (3) foster care, shelter care, other substitute care to remove the child from his parent's custody. If such a determination is made, services first shall be offered for the voluntary acceptance of the parent or other person responsible for the child's welfare. If such services are refused and the child protective service deems that the child is in imminent danger the service shall seek an appropriate court order or other legal authority to protect the child.[a]

(g) After providing for the immediate protection of the child but prior to offering any services to a family, the local agency shall forthwith notify the adult subjects of the report and any other persons alleged to be responsible for the child abuse or neglect, in writing, of the existence of

---

[a] The police and, if authorized by the optional provision in section 9(a), the child protective service may take the child into protective custody.

Inadequately Protecting a Child   **55**

Chart 3-2 (continued)

the report and their rights pursuant to this Act. This notification shall include an explanation of their right to refuse services and their right to obtain access to and amend, expunge, or remove reports in the central register of child protection cases. The local agency shall explain that it has no legal authority to compel the family to accept services; however, it shall inform the family of the obligations and authority of the local agency to petition the juvenile court to decide whether a child is in need of care and protection or to refer the case to the police or the district attorney who will then decide whether there shall be a criminal prosecution. Upon the initiation of any judicial action the parents shall be informed of their legal rights.

(h) If the local child protective service determines that there is not reasonable cause to believe that a child is abused or neglected, it shall close its protective case. However, if it appears that the child or family could benefit from other social services, the local service may suggest such services for the family's voluntary acceptance or refusal. If the family declines such services, the local service shall take no further action.

(i) If the local child protective service determines that there is reasonable cause to believe that a child is abused or neglected, based upon its determination of the protective, treatment, and ameliorative service needs of the child and family, the local service shall develop, with the family, an appropriate service plan for the family's voluntary acceptance or refusal. The local service shall comply with subsection (g) by explaining its lack of legal authority to compel the acceptance of services and shall explain its concomitant authority to petition the juvenile court or refer the case to the police, district attorney, or criminal court.

(j) If the local agency determines that the best interests of a child require juvenile court or criminal court action because the child is in need of protection, the local service may initiate a court proceeding or a referral to the appropriate court-related service, police department, district attorney, or any combination thereof.

(k) The child protective service shall give telephone notice and immediately forward a copy of reports which involve the death of a child to the appropriate district attorney [or *other appropriate law enforcement agency*] and medical examiner or coroner. In addition, upon the prior written request of the district attorney or if the local service otherwise deems it appropriate, a copy of any or all reports made pursuant to this Act which allege criminal conduct shall be forwarded immediately by the child protective service to the appropriate district attorney.

Chart 3-2 (continued)

(l) If a law enforcement investigation is also contemplated or is in progress, the child protective service shall coordinate their efforts and concerns with those of the law enforcement agency.

(m) In any juvenile or criminal court proceeding commenced by the child protective service or by any other individual or agency, the service shall assist the court during all stages of the court proceeding, in accordance with the purposes of this Act, the juvenile court act, and the penal law.

(n) The child protective service may request and shall receive from any agency of the state, or any of its political subdivisions such cooperation, assistance, and information as will enable it to fulfill its responsibilities under this section.

---

place a child in protective custody; (4) returning a child to dangerous parents; and (5) failure to provide adequate case monitoring.

It is important to note that the performance of child protective workers cannot be judged by whether the child suffered further injury after the report was made. Subsequent maltreatment, in itself, does not necessarily mean that greater protective measures should have been taken. As described in the following pages, the worker, after an adequate investigation, may have had no reason to believe that the child was in danger. The only valid way to judge the worker's performance is to determine whether the worker followed appropriate investigative procedures (as established by statutes, agency rules, professional standards, or other authoritative sources) and whether, in doing so, the worker responded appropriately to warning signals of danger. If the worker's conduct reflected good practice standards in assessing the degree of danger to children, and if the worker took the protective actions that were indicated, then a *successful* lawsuit is unlikely.

Failure to Accept a Report for Investigation

State laws generally require child protective agencies to receive reports 24 hours a day, often by means of highly publicized "hot lines." These laws also require the agencies to initiate an investigation on the same day, or shortly thereafter.[10] Violation of these statutory duties can establish the basis of a lawsuit. As Iowa's Attorney General has written: "We will never know if a report of child abuse is valid or not until the appropriate investigation is made. Failure to perform a duty imposed by statute may have serious tort consequences."[11]

Child protective agencies must accept and investigate all reports made properly to them. A reporter need not prove, on the telephone, that a child is abused or neglected. A reporter need only show a *reasonable basis* for suspecting that the child is maltreated.[12]

Even anonymous reports cannot be automatically rejected. Although there are obvious dangers to investigating reports for which no one is willing to take responsibility, many people simply will not give their name, especially since the agency cannot guarantee that the parents will not learn their identity.[13] Moreover, given the handicaps imposed on workers investigating anonymous reports, a surprising number are substantiated by the subsequent investigation. (About 25 percent of all anonymous reports are substantiated, as compared to 35 percent of reports from other nonprofessional sources.[14])

Mammo v. Arizona illustrates the potential liability for failing to accept a report of suspected child maltreatment. The facts, as described by the court, were as follows:

[When the Mammos divorced, the mother received custody of their three children: Sirgute (age 3), Tamiru (age 1), and Messeret (an infant). The father] was granted weekly visitation, which he exercised one day each weekend. He normally would visit with Messeret for only a short time at her mother's home because of her young age and would keep the two older children for a whole day.

Over the course of two weekends in late June and July of 1977, [the father] observed bruises on the bodies of the two older children. He learned from Tamiru that all three children had been beaten by their mother and her live-in boyfriend. [The father] became concerned for Messeret, whom he had not been allowed to see for the past two weeks. [He] took the two older children and reported his fears and concern for Messeret's immediate well-being to the police. The investigating officer relayed [the father's] allegations to [the Arizona Department of Economic Security (DES)] and told [the father] to retain custody of the two older children. A DES agent was to call him the next day.

The following day, [the father] called DES himself and spoke with an intake unit supervisor for Child Protective Services. DES took no action except to recommend that [the father] retain an attorney to contest [the mother's] custody of the children.

[The father] did consult with an attorney, which resulted in an action being immediately filed to restrain [Mrs.] Mammo from exercising custody over the children. Messeret, however, remained in her mother's custody. [Mrs.] Mammo did not appear for the July 15, 1977, hearing. Her counsel advised the court that she and Messeret were on a vacation in the East. The hearing was reset for July 28, 1977.

Messeret died on July 24, 1977, the victim of an apparent homicide. ...[According to the investigating police officer's testimony] the cause of Messeret's death was homicide at the hands of either [her mother] or her live-in boyfriend.[15]

The father filed a wrongful death action against the Department of Economic Security, claiming the negligence and breach of its statutory duties to accept and investigate reports. After a trial, the jury returned a verdict for $1 million. The trial judge, deciding that the verdict was excessive, reduced it to $300,000.[16] The award was affirmed on appeal.

Although it is somewhat unfair to make a judgment based only on the court's description of what happened, it appears that the child protective agency viewed Mr. Mammo's report as the exaggerated concerns of a disgruntled spouse (at best) or as a tactical maneuver in a custody battle (at worst), rather than as a sign of serious danger to the child. In effect, the father's report was being screened in accordance with a well-known fact: the vast majority of reports from noncustodial parents prove to be unfounded.

Overreacting to cases like *Mammo v. Arizona*, some agencies assume that they should not screen reports at all; that is, they must assign all reports for investigation. This is a mistake. Considering the large number of unfounded reports (from all sources),[17] social work professor Chris Mouzakitis concluded, "Much of what is reported is not worthy of followup."[18] Just as agencies have a duty to investigate reports made appropriately to them, they also have a duty to screen out inappropriate reports. Indeed, the failure to screen reports can lead to liability for unnecessarily intruding on family privacy (as discussed in the next chapter).

The proper lesson to be drawn from *Mammo* is not that screening reports is disallowed, but, rather, that decisions to reject a report must be made with great care. In *Mammo*, whether because of heavy workload or careless decision making, it appears that there was no individual assessment of the report. The father's report was simply disregarded—even though his claims were corroborated by the bruises on the bodies of the two older children and by the actions of the investigating police officer.

Thus, although child protective agencies have an affirmative obligation to screen reports, they should reject a report only if an investigation would be patently unwarranted. For example, if the caller does not provide sufficient information with which to investigate a report (if the child's name or location is not given), or if the caller's allegations simply do not amount to child abuse or child neglect (often, the family has a coping problem more appropriately referred to another social service agency), an investigation may not be warranted.

The foregoing examples are relatively easy to apply. More difficult to assess are reports that appear to be made falsely (and maliciously) by an estranged spouse, by quarrelsome relatives, by feuding neighbors, or even by an angry or distressed child. As a general rule, unless there are sufficient grounds for concluding that the report is being made in bad faith, any report that falls within the agency's legal mandate must be investigated. Even a history of past unsubstantiated reports may not be sufficient basis, on its own, for rejecting a report. There may be a legitimate explanation for the failure of previous investigations to substantiate the reporter's claims. (If the agency determines that the report is being made maliciously, consideration should be given to referring the case for criminal prosecution or to notifying the parents so that they can take appropriate action.)

The conditions under which a child protective agency should consider rejecting a report are listed in Chart 3-3. The absence of one of these conditions suggests that a report was wrongfully rejected and that the consequent violation of state law may have established liability.

Chart 3-3
Reports That May Be Rejected

- Reports in which the allegations clearly fall outside the agency's definitions of "child abuse" or "child neglect," as established by state law.

- Reports in which the caller can give no credible reason for suspecting that the child has been abused or neglected.

- Reports in which insufficient information is given to identify or locate the child.

- Reports whose unfounded and malicious nature is established by specific evidence.

Failure to Investigate Adequately

Accepting a report only fulfills the first stage of a child protective agency's legal responsibility. The report must next be investigated in accordance with the detailed provisions of state law and agency regulations.

Outright failures to investigate reports of maltreatment by parents are rare,[19] so there are few lawsuits making such a claim.[20] Reports of institutional maltreatment present a different picture. For well-documented reasons, reports of institutional maltreatment raise political and programmatic problems that most agencies have yet to resolve.[21] As a result, such reports often languish in administrative limbo because effective procedures to ensure investigative accountability have not been developed.

Brasel v. Children's Services Division was a wrongful death action brought by the parents of 18-month-old Desha, who died in a day care center certified by the Oregon Children's Services Division. The parents alleged that the Division was negligent in "(1) failing to properly investigate the day care facility in which their daughter was injured before issuing a certificate of approval for its operations. . .; (2) failing to investigate an incident of child abuse alleged to have occurred at the facility *before* plaintiffs placed their daughter there; (3) failing to halt operation of the center following the incident; (4) failing to inform plaintiffs of a previous incident; and (5) allowing them to rely upon representations that the day care facility was a safe and secure place for their child when defendant knew that it was not."[22] The Oregon Supreme Court dismissed the parents' last claim on the ground that the state law that prohibited public access to reports and records of child abuse also applied to prospective users of a day care center. Thus, under state law, the agency was "not authorized to advise the parents" of the previous reports of child abuse at the center.[23] However, the court allowed the parents' other claims to go to trial.

Promptly investigating a report can mean the difference between a child's life or death. Therefore, most child protective agencies are required to commence investigations within a short time. The precise wording of this requirement varies; common formulations are: "promptly," "immediately," "within 24 hours," "within 72 hours," and "as soon as possible."

The failure to commence an investigation within the time specified opens to door to liability and, of course, to administrative sanction. For example, one child protective worker "was suspended without pay for a month as punishment for failing to investigate a reported case of maltreatment within the mandated seven days. (The child's body was found soon after.)"[24]

The ability to comply with such mandates (even when they allow seven days) depends on the resources available to investigate new cases.[25] Staff shortages compel many agencies to ignore such time limits and to assign priorities among reports. Situations requiring emergency action are given priority status and assigned for immediate investigation. (Most child protective agencies are now able to make emergency investigations during evenings and on weekends, either by having caseworkers on call or by making special arrangements for police assistance, or both.)

In general, any situation suggesting the need for protective custody requires an emergency response (Chart 3-4). The difficulty lies in identifying such situations—on the basis of a telephone call from someone who may have an incomplete or distorted sense of what is happening to the child. As Vincent DeFrancis, director emeritus of the American Humane Association's Children's Division, has written, workers must make such decisions based only "on the information on hand and on the interpretation of these facts based

Chart 3-4
Situations Suggesting the Need for Protective Custody

- The child was severely assaulted, i.e., hit, poisoned, or burned so severely that serious injury resulted—or would have resulted but for the intervention of some outside force or simple good luck. (For example, the parent threw an infant against a wall, but somehow no serious injury resulted.)

- The child has been systematically tortured. (For example, the child was locked in a closet for long periods of time; forced to eat unpalatable substances; or forced to squat, stand, or perform other unreasonable acts for long periods of time.)

- The parent's reckless disregard for the child's safety caused serious injury—or could have done so. (For example, the parent left a very young child home alone under potentially dangerous circumstances.)

- The physical condition of the home is so dangerous that it poses an immediate threat of serious injury. (For example, there is exposed electrical wiring, upper-story windows are unbarred and easily accessible to young children, or there is an extreme danger of fire.)

- The child has been sexually abused or sexually exploited.

- The parents have purposefully or systematically withheld essential food or nourishment from the child. (For example, the child is denied food for extended periods of time as a form of punishment for real or imagined misbehavior.)

- The parents refuse to obtain (or consent to) medical or psychiatric care for the child that is needed to prevent or treat a serious injury or disease. (For example, the child's physical condition shows signs of severe deterioration to which the parents seem unwilling to respond.)

- The parents appear to be so out of touch with reality that they cannot provide for the child's basic needs. (For example, the parents are suffering from severe mental illness, mental retardation, drug abuse, or alcohol abuse.)

- The parents have abandoned the child. (For example, the child has been

Chart 3-4 (continued)

left in the custody of strangers who have not agreed to care for the child for more than a few hours and do not know how to reach the parents.)

- There is reason to suspect that the parents may flee with the child. (For example, the parents have a history of frequent moves or of hiding the child from outsiders.)

Note: In any of the above situations, the younger the child, the greater the presumable need for protective custody.

---

on experience with similar situations. One can never be sure of arriving at the correct answer."[26]

By far the greatest number of lawsuits for inadequately investigating a report allege that the agency failed to conduct a sufficiently careful or thorough inquiry. Many investigations are closed, for example, because the child or family cannot be located. *Jensen v. Conrad* illustrates the dangers involved:

> On February 28, 1980, the principal of New Prospect Elementary School informed the Anderson County Department of Social Services that the older brother of Michael Clark showed signs of child abuse. A caseworker from the Department immediately met with Michael's brother. The child was bruised about the face and told the caseworker that his father had hit him on several occasions. After conferring with teachers at the school, the caseworker concluded that a meeting with Mrs. Clark was necessary. Between March 6, 1980, and April 28, 1980, the caseworker and the Department attempted repeatedly to contact Mrs. Clark. Letters and telephone calls went unanswered, and seven visits to various addresses failed to locate the Clark family. After 60 days the Department classified the case as "unfounded" and officially closed the investigation.
> On June 23, 1980, Michael Clark was beaten to death by Mrs. Clark's boyfriend, Wayne Drawdy. Drawdy was subsequently tried and convicted for the child's murder.[27]

The suit against the agency and workers was dismissed on jurisdictional grounds.[28] Had it gone to trial, the court would have judged whether their efforts to locate Mrs. Clark were "sufficient."

Once a family is located, the investigation must be designed to gain necessary information about the child's care, not obscure it. In *Nelson v. Missouri Division of Family Services,* the noncustodial father alleged that the agency "failed to investigate adequately reports that the Nelson children were being abused by their mother and certain men, and that as a result of defendant's negligence, the children continued to suffer abuse, ultimately leading to the death of eight-year-old Tammy Nelson." The appeals court summarized his allegations:

> DFS [Division of Family Services] allegedly received several hotline calls concerning the Nelson children, but it appears that only two were investigated, one in November 1978, and the second in May 1979. The callers in both instances identified the Nelson children and gave information as to the nature of the alleged abuse and the names of witnesses. [n. 2. Appellants allege that the callers informed DFS that Tammy Nelson was being sold by her mother to an older man for the purpose of having sex, and that Audrey Nelson, the children's mother, forced her children to watch her perform sex acts with various partners and perhaps forced them to participate.] Plaintiffs assert, however, that the investigators failed to conduct a thorough investigation as required by the statute. Both investigations basically consisted of a brief interview of Audrey Nelson and a brief interview of the children, possibly within hearing distance of Audrey. The children, as well as Audrey, denied the allegations of the callers. At least one witness testified that children often deny, especially in the presence of the abuser, that they are being abused. The investigators seem not to have interviewed the children individually or apart from their mother, nor did they interview possible witnesses or request physical examinations for the children.[29]

The complaint was dismissed on the ground that Missouri's child protective statute, although containing a detailed description of required investigative procedures, did not create a legal duty to the individual endangered child, "as opposed to a duty to the general public."[30]

Most courts would take a different view of the duty that child protective agencies (and workers) have toward individual children. In assessing the adequacy of an investigation, they would look first to see whether the applicable statutory or administrative requirements were fulfilled. In *Florida National Bank v. City of Jacksonville,* the bank (acting as the guardian of the children's property) sued the city for the alleged failure of the police to respond to numerous reports of suspected abuse in violation of various state laws as well as the department's own internal procedures. Although the case involved a police investigation, it illustrates how courts use established agency procedures to judge allegedly negligent investigations:

> At all times mentioned herein the defendant City of Jacksonville, Florida, was under a duty to protect and keep minor children, residing or present within the municipality, safe from abuse and maltreatment and in the performance of that duty was obliged to respond to reports of child abuse or neglect in accordance with the following accepted and established police procedures:
>
> a. to make a prompt and thorough investigation of all reports of child abuse including:

1. a physical examination of each child in the family;
2. an interview with each child in the family;
3. an interview with each parent;
4. a complete check of the condition of the house;
5. an interview with the person who made the report or complaint; and
6. a review of the police and juvenile court records concerning prior complaints of child abuse; [and]

*   *   *

c. to take into immediate custody and bring before the juvenile court for protection, care and treatment any child with marks or bruises indicating abuse or mistreatment or whose environment was such that the welfare of the child required that the child be taken into custody.[31]

If state law or agency rules do not provide guidance about how an investigation (or a particular issue) should have been handled, courts usually look to state-of-the-art professional standards or practices for a yardstick with which to judge the agency's performance. The major professional standards relating to child welfare are listed in Appendix D.

If the failure to conduct an adequate investigation leads the child protective agency to miss important information bearing on the danger to the child, potential liability is established. This seems to have happened in a subsequent Florida case. The Florida Department of Health and Rehabilitative Services was ordered to pay $60,000 to the father of a 5-year-old boy who was beaten to death by the child's mother and stepfather. Apparently, the jury's award was based on a finding that the agency inadequately investigated numerous reports of the child's maltreatment.[32]

Although most lawsuits involved the worker's alleged failure to take adequate protective measures, sometimes the worker's conduct may actually contribute to the child's maltreatment. Wayne Holder, former director of the American Humane Association's Children's Division, gives an example of how this can happen:

Upon receiving a sexual abuse referral the worker interviews the female teenage victim and subsequently the father who is the alleged perpetrator. The worker doubts the victim and is intimidated by the father. In the presence of the father the worker admonishes the daughter, but warns the father if any such thing were to go on there would be serious consequences. The worker goes on to advise that since there seemed to be no evidence, that he would disqualify the referral. Subsequent to the worker's exit the father went into a rage over the daughter's disclosure and beat her severely.[33]

Failure to Place a Child in Protective Custody

Based on their investigations, caseworkers must decide whether children are in such immediate danger that protective custody is needed. The consequences of a wrong decision—either in favor of foster care when it is not needed, or against foster care when a child is in serious danger—make this the hardest decision that child protective workers must make and the one most likely to result in potential civil (and criminal) liability. The basis of liability was aptly stated by Lewis Carroll in *Alice's Adventures in Wonderland:*

> If I don't take this child away with me, thought Alice, they're sure to kill it in a day or two. Wouldn't it be murder to leave it behind?[34]

In 1980, a caseworker in El Paso, Texas, the caseworker's supervisor, and the agency's Director of Child Welfare were charged with criminal negligence. The agency had become involved with the family when a hospital reported that a 9-month-old child had severe scald burns on the lower back and buttocks. The agency decided that the child could remain at home while the parents received treatment services. Ten months later, the child died of apparent asphyxiation. "Although he was unable to determine the cause of death, the medical examiner testified that the child had very small, circular bruises on the right side of her head and on her chest, abdomen, thighs, and knees. Other doctors testified...that she was also suffering from malnutrition."[35] The prosecuting attorney is said to have claimed that "if the [agency] staff had been willing to admit its mistakes [in not removing the child] and cooperate in the removal of the surviving children following their sister's death, the case probably would not have been taken to the grand jury."[36] One month before the trial was to begin, on preliminary motions, the trial court quashed the indictment on the ground that "no indictable offense had been charged."[37]

In the same year, a child protective worker in Louisville, Kentucky, and the worker's supervisor were charged with official misconduct. The charges arose out of a 3-year-old's death from hot water scald burns. Hospital physicians treating the child did not make a report, but a policeman on the scene called the child protective agency because he suspected abuse. A month before, the agency had received two previous reports alleging abuse of the child's two older siblings, but it had decided that the reports were not valid, and it was in the process of closing its case on the family. A subsequent investigation revealed that, six months earlier, the dead child had suffered a broken leg, determined to be a "wringer injury" strongly suggestive of abuse. The hospital had not reported this injury either. (One physician attending the child was also indicted.) At the trial, all charges were dismissed after the prosecution presented its case and before the defense presented any evidence. In dismissing the case, the judge is quoted as saying: "It offends my sense of fairness that these three people were chosen [for prosecution] when everyone else who came into contact with the child could have been charged as well."[38]

Although there is good reason to question the propriety of these two prosecutions, some children unnecessarily suffer further maltreatment because of a worker's poor judgment. For example, children are often left at home "at the risk of further damage to a defenseless child in the mistaken belief that 'there is no such thing as a person we cannot help'," according to Kempe.[39] Research studies suggest that many fatalities are preceded by obvious warning signals of immediate and serious danger, to which decision makers should have responded more forcefully.[40]

The allegations in a civil lawsuit against a caseworker and the Missouri Department of Social Services illustrate how signs of serious danger to a child can be overlooked or ignored. According to the complaint, the caseworker, over the course of 26 visits during a five-month period, "negligently failed to recognize severe and permanently damaging neglect of the child." It was alleged that, during the period in question, the 2-year-old child "failed [sic] to thrive and in fact reduced from a weight of approximately twenty-three [23] pounds to a weight of approximately thirteen [13] pounds."[41] Damages amounting to $4 million were sought for the child's subsequent injuries. The case was settled. The terms of the agreement included the state's promise to provide extensive medical and psychiatric care for the child (even past majority), postsecondary school educational assistance to the child, and subsidy payments in the event of the child's adoption.

The warning signals that suggest the need to place a child in protective custody are listed in Chart 3-4. The presence of any one of the factors listed there is a clear indication that the child faces an imminent threat of serious injury. Unless the child's safety can be assured by some other means, the child should be placed in protective custody quickly—and kept there until the home situation is safe or until parental rights are permanently terminated.[42] The basis of liability is established by proof that a worker ignored or negligently overlooked one of these factors and thereby failed to place into protective custody a child who suffered subsequent maltreatment. If the worker noted these warning signals, the existence of liability depends on whether appropriate protective action was taken.

Returning a Child to Dangerous Parents

After a child has been removed from the home, the danger of future serious injury must be regularly assessed to determine whether the child should be returned to the parents' custody. Caseworkers must decide whether the parents' emotional condition has improved sufficiently to return the child to their custody or even to close the case entirely. For example, the precipitating cause of the parents' behavior may have disappeared or been removed, the parents may have developed the ability (either by themselves or through treatment) to care for their child, or the provision of voluntary services may sufficiently reduce the likelihood of a recurrence of the problem to obviate the need for foster care.[43] These are crucial issues, and they must be weighed carefully before returning a child to parental custody.

"Frequently children are returned home, are reinjured (or killed) and the agency cannot demonstrate sufficient accountability in terms of appropriate case planning, service provision and evidence of client behavioral change,"[44] points out Wayne Holder. The mix of subjective factors that must be considered in deciding whether to return a child make it unlikely, however, that liability will be imposed for a decision that turns out poorly—unless the decision was clearly negligent or inconsistent with prevailing professional standards.

There are at least two situations in which the child would be in obvious danger. First, a child should not be returned if the parent demonstrates a continuing inability to care properly for the child. Further abuse of the child during trial home visits is the most unequivocal evidence of continuing danger to the child. To ignore such re-abuse would be unconscionable, and yet that seems to be what happened in a case investigated by a Brooklyn Grand Jury. According to the Grand Jury's report, 7-month-old Fay had been removed from her 15-year-old mother's custody after a hospital discovered a fresh double fracture of her left arm and an older, untreated fracture of her right arm.[45] A month later, Fay was returned home on the basis of her mother's promise to attend a counseling program. Between the mother's first and second counseling sessions—a matter of weeks—Fay was again brought to the hospital. This time, she was dead on arrival. "There was a lump on Fay's forehead and new and old bruise marks on her body." The mother was later prosecuted for homicide and pleaded guilty.

Over the next two years, the mother had two more children, Kim and Tammy. At birth, each was removed from her custody. Because the mother's treatment program reported that she had "made substantial progress," however, her two children were soon returned for a 90-day trial discharge. Forty-five days into the trial discharge, a worker from the treatment program noted that "one-and-a-half-year-old Kim had a swollen jaw and a black mark under her eye. [The mother] gave a series of implausible explanations. . . . No action was taken."

Two and a half months later, the worker observed additional injuries: "Kim had several bruise marks on each cheek and swelling at her right temple." Ten days later, Kim's father twisted her arm in a struggle between him and the mother. The children were again removed from the home. A doctor's examination of Kim, who was not yet 2 years old, revealed "linear marks on her lower abdomen and buttocks resembling strap marks."

Fourteen months later, there was another 90-day trial discharge. Over the next three months, a worker "observed injuries on Kim and Tammy on three separate occasions. Despite [the mother's] known history of abuse and lying, [her] explanations of the injuries as accidental were accepted without medical verification. No child abuse reports were filed."

A month after this trial discharge was extended, Kim, now 3 years old, "sustained serious injuries—a gash under the chin, a bruise on the left side of the face, scrape marks across the forehead and two teeth knocked out." The treatment agency held a case conference and decided that the foster care agency should be contacted regarding Kim's "accident proneness." Again, Kim and Tammy stayed in their mother's questionable custody.

Two months later, the trial discharge was made final. In the same month, the children were re-injured. "Tammy's eye was injured. Kim suffered a swollen lip." Still, they remained at home.

The next month, Tammy, now 2½ years old, was "severely scalded. She had second- and third-degree burns on her feet, left hand and buttocks. Fifteen percent of her body was burned. As a result of her burns, several of Tammy's toes on both feet had to be amputated." At this point, and with the intervention of the District Attorney's office, both children were finally placed in protective custody.

Besides providing an example of the most egregiously inadequate decision making, for which civil liability would be likely, the Grand Jury's report documents numerous apparent violations of New York's reporting laws—for which a criminal prosecution would be possible.

The second situation in which a child should not be returned home is when the fundamental conditions upon which the discharge is premised are violated. For example, the return of children is often conditioned on the parents' participation in a suitable treatment program or on the departure from the home of the person responsible for the abuse (usually an unrelated adult but sometimes one of the parents). Of course, it may be impossible to ensure that the parents are successfully treated or that the wrongdoer does not eventually reappear, as agencies do not have sufficient resources for such long-term monitoring.[46] But, certainly, before placing the child back in the home, the agency should have a reasonable basis for believing that the conditions are at least initially being met; indeed, the failure to make a sufficient inquiry establishes possible liability.

The allegations in *Bailey v. County of York* illustrate the kind of liability that can be claimed.[47] According to the plaintiff, the child protective agency received a report that 5-year-old Aleta Bailey had been physically abused. After taking Aleta into custody, the agency had her examined at a hospital, where evidence of abuse was found and it was determined that she was being excessively disciplined by her mother's sometime live-in boyfriend. Aleta was placed with her aunt but was returned to her mother two days later on the condition that the boyfriend move from the home and the mother deny him access to Aleta. Five days later, Aleta was dead. Her mother and the boyfriend were subsequently convicted of her murder. The father sued the agency for its alleged failure to "ascertain" whether the boyfriend continued to live with the mother. The trial court's dismissal of the case on jurisdictional grounds was reversed by an appellate court.

Failure to Provide Adequate Case Monitoring

If a maltreated child is left in parental custody, or is returned home, regular follow-up visits are needed to see how the parents are doing—and to see whether the child has been re-abused. Inadequate monitoring of home care can be the difference between the child's life and death, and can give rise to civil and criminal liability. As Mouzakitis explains:

> One error commonly committed by child protection workers during lengthy investigations is worker inactivity. It is possible for investigators to fail to meet the urgent needs of a particular family while waiting for the case to be assigned for ongoing treatment. This in-between period from investigation to treatment sometimes may vary from a week to a month due to bureaucratic red tape, work backlog, consultations with supervisors, consultations with attorneys, and other priorities. It is a risky period. If something happens to the child during this time the worker and the agency are liable. If there is any question to insuring continuing of care, it is therefore recommended that the investigator be actively involved with the family in meeting their most pressing needs, such as making arrangements for a homemaker, day care for the child, medical checkups, employment, or food stamps to mention a few.[48]

In *Buege v. Iowa,* the noncustodial father reported to the Department of Social Services that his 34-month-old daughter had a bruise on her buttocks; he also told the agency that he believed that the bruise was inflicted by the mother's lover.[49] The agency investigated and substantiated the injury. (The lover was not interviewed, however.) At an agency staff meeting the next day (two days after the initial report), a decision was made not to remove the child from the mother's custody, but, instead, to make follow-up visits coupled with day care, counseling, and other appropriate services. *No follow-up visit was made.* Eight days later, the child was hospitalized in a comatose state, with bruises, both old and new, over most of her body. The child died after three days of unsuccessful treatment. The mother's lover was convicted of second-degree murder.[50] The father sued the agency, alleging negligent investigation and supervision of the case, failure to employ qualified employees, failure to staff the protective unit sufficiently, and failure to remove the child from the home. The case was settled for $82,500.[51]

Staff shortages and overwhelming caseloads limit the degree and duration of case monitoring that agencies can provide, of course.[52] Therefore, as with investigations, the agency only has an obligation to conduct reasonable monitoring, as determined by the danger to the child *and* by the agency's monitoring standards. Thus, the level of necessary monitoring becomes a question of professional judgment, and the plaintiff must establish, through expert testimony, the unreasonableness of the agency's conduct. Sometimes, though, the plaintiff is relieved of this burden of proof. In *Buege v. Iowa,* for example, the inadequacy of the case monitoring was established by the agency's failure to fulfill its own plan to protect the child.

In some cases, the necessary level of monitoring is established by a preexisting court order.[53] *Kevin R.* is an example of what can happen when a court order requiring close home supervision is violated:

> At two months of age, Kevin was brought to the hospital with a broken femur (the upper thigh). His father said that Kevin received the injury by falling off a bed. Five months later, Kevin suffered a fractured skull. This time the father claimed that he had accidentally dropped him. Only after this second injury did the hospital make a report of suspected child abuse.
>
> A court petition alleging child abuse was filed based on these two injuries. The attending physician testified that it was impossible for Kevin to have suffered the broken thigh in the way his father claimed. After a full hearing, the court held the father had abused Kevin. The child protective agency recommended that Kevin be placed in foster care because his home was at least temporarily unsafe. The judge decided, however, that Kevin could remain at home, if the agency made regular home visits. To protect the child, he ordered that Kevin's father was not to be left alone with him.
>
> Shortly thereafter, a protective worker made a home visit. He found the father and Kevin home alone—contrary to the judge's order. But because they were playing happily on the floor, from this brief display, he concluded that all was well. He noticed (and recorded in the case file)—but took no action about—what appeared to be a swelling of Kevin's skull.
>
> Two weeks later, Kevin was dead from repeated head beatings inflicted by his father.[54]

At all times, child protective agencies must respond to renewed evidence of danger to the child. Again, the presence of any of the factors in Chart 3-4 suggests the need to consider protective custody. In addition, the parents' failure to fulfill one of the conditions under which the child was left at home or returned there should cause the agency to reconsider its treatment plan.[55] The alleged failure to do so led to a major lawsuit in South Carolina:

> The plaintiff alleged that Sylvia Brown's plight first became known to Richland County social workers on February 28, 1979, when the then four month old child was admitted to the Richland Memorial Hospital with a fractured skull. A C.A.T. scan revealed a "healing subdural hematoma." The attending physician immediately became concerned about the possibility of physical abuse by Sylvia's parents. This suspicion, the plaintiff contends, was confirmed after Mrs. Brown and her boyfriend visited Sylvia at the hospital. Hospital social workers received a report that during the visit Mrs. Brown's boyfriend held the child by the head and neck, and slapped the child in a rough manner.

The following week, a Richland Hospital social worker reported the case to the Richland County Department of Social Services and requested a child protection investigation. After an initial review of the case, the Department of Social Services allegedly reached an agreement with Mrs. Brown requiring her to reside with Sylvia at the home of Sylvia's grandmother. Under the agreement, if Mrs. Brown returned home with her child, Sylvia would be placed in the custody of the Department of Social Services. In addition to this agreement, the Department also decided that an "intensive follow-up and in-home supervision" would be required.

According to the plaintiff, over the course of the next two months the Department caseworkers failed to supervise adequately the family and carry out the recommendations of department officials and Sylvia's attending physician. The plaintiff claims that Department caseworkers visited Mrs. Brown's house only twice, and on both of those occasions Sylvia was living alone with her mother. Despite the agreement, no action was taken.

On May 11, 1979, Sylvia was brought dead on arrival to the Richland Hospital. An autopsy revealed that brain hemorrhaging had occurred three times in the previous three weeks—the last hemorrhage apparently took place only minutes before Sylvia died. After initially disclaiming responsibility, Mrs. Brown pleaded guilty to involuntary manslaughter.[56]

A criminal prosecution for inadequate case monitoring is also possible. In 1976, a child protective worker in Pueblo, Colorado, and her supervisor were *convicted* of official misconduct. They were charged with having allowed the death of a child by their failure to respond adequately to reported maltreatment—as mandated by state law. The child had previously been placed in foster care and then returned to her parents' custody. During the time when the caseworker was on medical leave, the agency received new reports of suspected abuse from the child's school and the school nurse. In the words of the indictment against the supervisor, the reports consisted of "telephone contacts...wherein a report was made of cigarette burns on the child, wounds to arms of the child, bruises and scratches to a large portion of said child's back, scars from apparent large burns to the child's back, and other injuries...."[57] With her doctor's permission, the caseworker, who had a BSW degree and ten years of experience with the agency, returned to the office for one day to arrange a psychological evaluation of the child. No attempt was made to verify the nature or extent of the reported injuries. (The worker claimed that she was not told of the school reports.)[58] Shortly thereafter, the child died of apparent neglect. The convictions of both the caseworker and her supervisor were overturned on appeal because of legal issues not related to their guilt.[59]

Notes

1. Compare V. DeFrancis, *Child Protective Services in the United States: A Nationwide Survey* (Denver, Colo.: American Humane Association, 1956); and DeFrancis,

Child Protective Services: A National Survey (Denver Colo.: American Humane Association, 1967); with W. Hildenbrand, *Child Protective Services: Entering the 1980s* (Denver, Colo.: American Humane Association, 1981).

2. See U.S. National Center on Child Abuse and Neglect, *Annual Analysis of Child Abuse and Neglect Programs* (Washington, D.C.: Department of Health and Human Services, 1980); U.S. General Accounting Office, *Increased Federal Efforts Needed to Better Identify, Treat, and Prevent Child Abuse and Neglect* (Washington, D.C.: Government Printing Office, 1980), Chap. 3.

3. *Child Protective Services in New York State: 1979 Annual Report* (Albany: New York State Department of Social Services, 1980), Table 8.

4. R. Kempe and C. H. Kempe, *Child Abuse* (Cambridge, Mass.: Harvard University Press, 1978).

5. See, for example, Region VI Resource Center on Child Abuse and Neglect, *Child Deaths in Texas* (Austin: Graduate School of Social Work, University of Texas, 1981), p. 26; B. Mayberry, *Child Protective Services in New York City: An Analysis of Case Management* (Albany, N.Y.: Welfare Research, Inc., draft dated May 1979), p. 109.

6. See. p. 38.

7. See pp. 17–18.

8. See pp. 17–18.

9. See, for example, N.Y. Social Services Law §424 (1975 and 1984).

10. D. Besharov, "The Legal Aspects of Reporting Known and Suspected Child Abuse and Neglect," *Villanova Law Review,* 23 (1978), p. 458.

11. Iowa Attorney General, Opinion No. 78-9-12, 28 September 1978, cited in *Family Law Reporter,* 5 (7 November 1978), p. 2015.

12. Besharov, "The Legal Aspects of Reporting Known and Suspected Child Abuse and Neglect," p. 471.

13. W. Adams, N. Barone, and P. Tooman, "The Dilemma of Anonymous Reporting in Child Protective Services," *Child Welfare,* 61 (January 1982), p. 3.

14. U.S. National Center on Child Abuse and Neglect, *National Analysis of Official Child Neglect and Abuse Reporting (1978)* (Washington, D.C.: Department of Health, Education and Welfare, 1979), p. 20, Table 7. One pending lawsuit, *Covert, et al. v. Reightnour, et al.,* MCA-80-263 N.D.C. Fla. (filed 26 December 1980), challenges the authority of the Florida Department of Health and Rehabilitative Services to investigate anonymous reports of child abuse or neglect.

15. *Mammo v. Arizona,* 138 Ariz. 528, 675 P.2d 1347 (Ariz. Ct. App. 1983).

16. *Association of Trial Lawyers of America Reporter* (Washington, D.C., 1981), p. 76.

17. See pp. 24–25.

18. C. Mouzakitis, "Investigation and Initial Assessment in Child Protective Services," in W. Holder and K. Hayes, eds., *Malpractice and Liability in Child Protective Services* (Longmont, Colo.: Bookmakers Guild, 1984), pp. 71, 75.

19. U.S. General Accounting Office, *Increased Federal Efforts.*

20. One of the few on the subject, dismissed for failure to state a cause of action under the Federal Civil Rights Act, is *Davis v. Casey,* 493 F. Supp. 117 (D. Mass. 1980).

21. R. Hanson, ed., *The Institutional Abuse of Children and Youth* (New York: Haworth Press, 1982).

22. *Brasel v. Children's Services Division,* 56 Or. App. 559, 642 P.2d 696, 697 (1982) (emphasis added).

23. Ibid., 642 P.2d at p. 700.

24. J. Garbarino and S. H. Stocking, "Preface," in Garbarino et al., eds., *Protect-*

ing Children from Abuse and Neglect (San Francisco: Jossey-Bass, 1981), p. viii.

25. For a brief discussion of the defense of "impossibility" to claims that a statute has been violated, see pp. 139-140 and p. 175.

26. V. DeFrancis, *The Fundamentals of Child Protection: A Statement of Basic Concepts and Principles* (Denver, Colo.: American Humane Association, 1955), p. 19.

27. *Jensen v. Conrad,* 747 F.2d 185, 188 (4th Cir. 1984), *cert. denied,* ____ U.S. ____, No. 84-1159, *Family Law Reporter,* 11 (19 March 1985), p. 1239.

28. For a discussion of liability questions under the Federal Civil Rights Act, see pp. 17-18.

29. *Nelson v. Missouri Division of Family Services,* 706 F.2d 276, 277 (8th Cir. 1983).

30. Ibid.

31. *Florida First National Bank of Jacksonville v. The City of Jacksonville,* 310 So. 2d 19, 22 n. 8 (Fla. App. 1975), *aff'd,* 339 So.2d 632 (Fla. 1976). Another case alleging the failure of policy to investigate possible child abuse properly is *Robinson v. Wical, M.D., et al.,* discussed on pp. 32-33.

32. *Family Law Reporter,* 5 (15 December 1978), p. 2100.

33. W. Holder, "Malpractice in Child Protective Services: An Overview of the Problem," in Holder and K. Hayes, eds., *Malpractice and Liability,* pp. 5, 12.

34. L. Carroll, *Alice's Adventures in Wonderland,* Chap. 6, quoted in J. Downey, "Accountability for Failure to Protect Children," in D. Bross, ed., *Legal Representation of the Maltreated Child* (Denver, Colo.: National Association of Counsel for Children, 1979), pp. 252, 257.

35. J. Spearly, "Caseworker Indictments—A Closer Look," *National Child Protective Services Newsletter,* 3 (Winter 1981), p. 6.

36. Ibid., p. 9.

37. R. Horowitz and H. Davidson, "Improving the Legal Response of Child Protective Agencies," *Vermont Law Review,* 6 (1981), pp. 381, 384.

38. C. Gembinski, M. Casper, and E. Hutchinson, "Worker Liability: Who's Really Liable?" in C. Washburne, ed., *Looking Back, Looking Ahead: Selections from the Fifth National Conference on Child Abuse and Neglect* (Milwaukee: University of Wisconsin, School of Social Work, 1982), p. 116.

39. C. H. Kempe, "Some Problems Encountered by Welfare Departments in the Management of the Battered Child Syndrome," in R. Helfer and Kempe, eds., *The Battered Child* (Chicago: University of Chicago Press, 1968), pp. 169, 170.

40. See, for example, Region VI Resource Center on Child Abuse and Neglect, *Child Deaths in Texas,* p. 26; Mayberry, *Child Protective Services in New York City,* p. 109.

41. Complaint, *Maupin v. Maupin, et al.,* U.S. Dist. Ct. E.D. Mo., 1979.

42. See R. Helfer and C. H. Kempe, "The Child's Need for Early Recognition, Immediate Care and Protection," in Kempe and Helfer, eds., *Helping the Battered Child and His Family* (Philadelphia: J. B. Lippincott Co., 1972), p. 70.

43. See, for example, N.Y. Family Court Act S1051(c) (1983), allowing the court to dismiss a proven neglect petition if it determines that its "aid is not required...."

44. Holder, "Malpractice in Child Protective Services," p. 10.

45. Office of Kings County District Attorney, "Report of the Term V 1983 Extended Grand Jury on the Failure of New York City Child Protective Services to Protect the Abused Children of Jane Doe" (6 April 1984). All quotations are from this report.

46. If, however, agencies do gain information on unsuccessful treatment or reappearance of a wrongdoer, they have a duty to take appropriate action. Also, for a discussion of case monitoring resources, see p. 134; for a discussion of the defense of "impossibility" to claims that a duty has been violated, see pp. 139-140 and p. 175.

47. *Bailey v. County of York,* 580 F. Supp. 794 (W.D. Pa. 1984), rev'd——F.2d——, No. 84-5231 (3rd Cir. 1985), *Law Week,* 54 (23 July 1985), p. 2047.

48. Mouzakitis, "Investigation and Initial Assessment," p. 81.

49. *Buege v. Iowa,* No. 20521 (Allamakee, Iowa, 30 July 1980). See also *Fischer v. Iowa Dept. of Social Services,* No. C1664-280 (18 February 1980); but, see *Rittscher v. Iowa,* 352 N.W.2d 247 (1984), holding that there is no liability for failing to remove a child from a harmful home environment.

50. See *State v. Hilleshiem,* 305 N.W.2d 710 (Iowa 1981).

51. Jury Verdict Research, Inc., "Case Summary" (Solon, Ohio, 3 March 1982).

52. For a discussion of case monitoring resources, see p. 134.

53. For a discussion of how the existence of duty is determined, see p. 139.

54. Confidential material held by author.

55. For a discussion of such conditions, see pp. 67–68.

56. *Jensen v. Conrad, supra,* n. 27, 747 F.2d at p. 188. Footnote omitted.

57. Count 2 (of indictment).

58. W. Holder, "A Personal View of Casework Liability," in Holder and Hayes, eds., *Malpractice and Liability,* pp. 95–96.

59. The caseworker's conviction was overturned because she had been compelled to testify (against the supervisor) before her sentencing (*Steinberger v. District Court,* 596 P.2d 755 [Colo. 1979]). The supervisor's conviction was overturned on the ground that the official misconduct statute was "void for vagueness" (*People v. Beruman,* 638 P.2d 789 [Colo. 1982]).

4

Violating
Parental Rights

The Basis of Liability

As a society, we have adopted a predominantly therapeutic—or, in the vernacular, a "social work"—response to the problems of child abuse and child neglect. Almost all reports of suspected child maltreatment are made to child protective agencies. Even in states where the law still permits reporting to the police, most reports are made to these specialized agencies.[1] (If the police receive a report, they usually forward it to the child protective agency. In rare situations, they perform a parallel or joint investigation with the child protective agency.)

Usually housed within the public child welfare or social services department, child protective agencies operate in the social work tradition of helping people with their personal problems through a mixture of concrete and counseling services. (Nationwide, fewer than 5 percent of substantiated cases result in a criminal prosecution.)[2] Based on their investigation of the home situation, child protective agencies decide what kinds of social and mental health services a family needs, and then they help the family to obtain them. Many of these services, such as financial assistance, day care, crisis nurseries, and homemaker care, are concrete efforts to relieve the pressures and frustrations of parenthood. Other services, such as infant stimulation programs, parent aides, and parent education programs, are designed to give parents specific guidance, role models, and emotional support in child rearing. In addition, individual, group, and family counseling or therapy services are used to ease the tensions of personal problems and marital strife.[3]

The Vulnerable Social Worker

There is a fundamental difference, however, between classic social work and child protective practice. Social work, in its purest form, is built on the client's willing participation in the therapeutic process. If the client refuses to participate, the case is closed. This may not be desirable, and the worker may attempt to persuade the client to remain in the program, but, ultimately, the client decides. This is not how child protective workers must operate. If the parent declines services—or refuses to cooperate altogether—the worker must decide whether the danger to the child is so great that *treatment must be imposed.* (Such treatment includes counseling and other traditional social work services, but it also extends to involuntary home supervision, foster care, and, ultimately, to the termination of parental rights.) The need to investigate reports made against parents and to impose treatment services on unwilling parents sets child protective work apart from most other types of social casework, making it more difficult, more stressful, and less rewarding.

Child protective workers do not impose such "services" by dint of their casework skills alone. They do so through laws—laws that authorize courts to require parents to participate in treatment programs, to remove children from parental custody, and to terminate parental rights. Thus, child protection is a social work process set within the law's power to coerce parental cooperation. This power also increases the possibility of civil liability for violating parental rights.

Laws against child abuse and neglect are an implicit recognition that parental rights are not absolute, and that society, through its courts and social service agencies, should intervene in private family matters to protect endangered children. In seeking to protect helpless children, however, it is all too easy to ignore the legitimate rights of parents. As Supreme Court Justice Brandeis warned in a different context, "experience should teach us to be most on guard to protect liberty when the government's purposes are beneficient."[4] In the effort to protect maltreated children, traditional American values of personal freedom and due process should also be protected. If society is to intrude into family matters, it should do so with due regard to parental rights, as well as to the needs of children.

In our society, parents have the prime responsibility of caring for their children. They have broad discretion to do what they think is best for the child. Many state laws—and court decisions—recognize and seek to protect parental rights. Moreover, the U.S. Constitution protects the parental right to be free from unwarranted governmental interference. The Supreme Court's most widely quoted statement on the subject was written by Justice White in *Stanley v. Illinois:*

> It is plain that the interest of a parent in the companionship, care, custody, and management of his or her children "come[s] to this Court with a momentum

for respect lacking when appeal is made to liberties which derive merely from shifting economic arrangements." The Court has frequently emphasized the importance of the family. The rights to conceive and to raise one's children have been deemed "essential," "basic civil rights of man," and "rights far more precious...than property rights."[5]

Thus, the need to protect children from abuse or neglect does not justify violating, or ignoring, parental rights. In recent years, a number of workers and their agencies have been sued for the violation of the common-law, statutory, and constitutional rights of parents. These cases fall under five broad categories: (1) unnecessarily intrusive investigations; (2) defamation; (3) wrongful removal or withholding of children; (4) malicious prosecution; and (5) disclosure of confidential information. In the following discussion, no distinction is drawn between cases brought under state tort law and those brought under state and federal constitutions and civil rights acts because the underlying substantive issues are similar. State and federal courts do differ, however, in when they grant immunity for decisions made in good faith. This issue is discussed in a later section.[6]

Unnecessarily Intrusive Investigations

Child protective investigations are, inherently, a breach of parental and family privacy. To determine whether a particular child is in danger, workers must inquire into the most intimate of personal and family matters. The parents and children almost always must be questioned about the report. And, it is often necessary to interview friends, relatives, and neighbors, as well as schoolteachers, day care personnel, doctors, clergymen, and others who know the family.

Every day, then, child protective workers could be said to commit a host of torts: invastion of privacy, defamation, harassment, intentional infliction of mental suffering, interference with family relationships, trespass, and false imprisonment. They are not ordinarily subject to liability, though, because the law considers their behavior to be "privileged."

"Privilege" is the modern term applied to those considerations which avoid liability where it might otherwise follow. As used in this context...it signifies that the defendant has acted to further an interest of such social importance that it is entitled to protection, even at the expense of damage to the plaintiff. The defendant is allowed freedom of action because his own interests, or those of the public, require it, and because social policy will be best served by permitting it.[7]

No reported case suggests that reports of suspected child maltreatment should not be investigated aggressively. Necessary efforts to protect a child do not give rise to legal liability. As the Attorney General of Iowa concluded, "an appropriate investigation" does not constitute "an invasion of privacy."[8]

The law does not grant workers an unrestricted or absolute privilege to investigate reports, however. The need to gain quickly as much information as possible about children and the care they are receiving does not give workers free rein to ignore the family's civil rights. Workers may not perform unnecessarily intrusive investigations, and many lawsuits have been filed claiming that workers overstepped the bounds of "appropriate" investigation.

The most direct assault on the worker's privilege to invade family privacy is "bad faith" or malicious intent.[9] By definition, there is no need to protect professional discretion in such situations; in effect, the worker has forfeited the law's protection.

In *Hale v. City of Virginia Beach,* for example, two workers and the agency were sued for $100,000. The plaintiff was a father who alleged that "for the ostensible purpose of investigating and promoting the welfare and best interest of the plaintiff's children, [the caseworkers] subjected the plaintiff to a course of conduct amounting to harassment, including threats of prosecution for crimes and conduct of which the plaintiff was innocent, interference with the plaintiff's family relationships, and interference with the plaintiff's proper efforts to rear and educate his children."[10] The complaint also alleged that the workers *"maliciously and falsely addressed remarks to third persons,* the substance of which were that the plaintiff was an alcoholic; that the plaintiff was mentally unstable and was a 'very sick man'; that he was guilty of child molestation; that they were going to take his child or children away from him; and that he would be prosecuted criminally."[11] The case was settled when the city, although maintaining that the workers had conducted themselves appropriately, agreed to pay the parents $4,000.

Claiming bad faith and proving it, though, are two very different things. In fact, many lawsuits are dismissed before trial because the assertion of bad faith is not specifically explained or supported by the actual allegations in the complaint.[12]

Martin v. Weld demonstrates what can happen when the parents are unable to prove bad faith at the trial. The child protective agency had received an anonymous report of the father's sexual abuse of his 13-year-old daughter. The parents sought monetary damages for "slander, outrageous conduct, negligence, and gross negligence" arising from the ensuing investigation.[13] They claimed that the daughter was interviewed at school for 1½ hours, during which the worker "made various allegations of sexual abuse and criminal misconduct against [the father, which the daughter] denied."[14] Following that interview, both parents and another family member were interviewed. Based on its investigation, the agency determined that the anonymous report was unfounded, and it closed the case. The court rejected a motion to dismiss the complaint, effectively sustaining the parents' right to sue, because the complaint *alleged* the defendants' "lack of good faith." The court explained the following:

> First, [the plaintiffs] set out details showing that [the caseworker's] interview of the child...went beyond mere investigation and amounted to harassment and intentional infliction of emotional distress. Second, the [parents] alleged that defendants intentionally leaked information about the case to the county commissioners, with whom [the father], as a member of the county council, regularly met, and also to the press....Third, they alleged that the defendants published statements that were slanderous *per se*....[15]

Because the parents were not able to *prove* the allegations at the trial, the judge granted a motion for a directed verdict in the defendants' favor (the equivalent of a dismissal). At a subseqent hearing, the judge denied the parents' request for a new trial and, instead, levied attorneys' fees and court costs against the parents—on the ground that they had brought *their* case in bad faith and had abused court procedure. The Weld County Department of Social Services was awarded $14,794.84 plus costs, and the social worker was awarded $11,183.75 plus costs.[16] Many social workers may be comforted by this outcome, but they must remember two things: (1) it took almost five years of stress and uncertainty before the defendants were vindicated; and (2) the imposition of attorneys' fees and court costs against an unsuccessful plaintiff is extremely unusual.

Negligence in determining the need to investigate also negates the defense of "privilege." The worker's negligence is usually difficult to establish because child protective work involves ambiguous situations and the continuous exercise of subjective judgment. (Hence, the emphasis on the worker's alleged bad faith.) Nevertheless, workers expose themselves to lawsuits when they are inattentive to reasonably available information, when they do not consider all relevant factors before reaching a decision, or when they otherwise deviate from well-established legal or professional standards.[17]

Claims of overly intrusive investigations are, obviously, much more likely when it turns out that the child was not abused or neglected. Hindsight easily transforms what, at the time, seemed like a reasonable response to apparent danger into an unthinking overreaction to insubstantial suspicions. Thus, worker vulnerability in this area is magnified by the high rate of "unfounded" reports.[18]

One common claim is that the report should not have been investigated in the first place, or, at least, that better efforts should have been made to evaluate the report before commencing the investigation.[19] In effect, the child protective agencies are being blamed for not properly screening reports. but, as the section on the liability for failure to accept a report for investigation describes, state laws allow child protective agencies little discretion on the question. Iowa's Attorney General explained the rationale for limiting discretion: "We will never know if a report of child abuse is valid or not until the appropriate investigation is made."[20]

Unfounded reports from nonprofessionals are a fertile ground for lawsuits claiming that the agency should have evaluated the nature and source of the report before commencing the investigation.[21] However, for the reasons given above, agencies cannot refuse to investigate reports merely because they are made anonymously, and no court decision suggests that they should.[22] For example, in a criminal prosecution (*Wisconsin v. Boggess*), the Wisconsin Supreme Court approved a warrantless search of the defendant's home following an anonymous report. The court held that "under the totality of circumstances in this case, a reasonable person would have believed that there was an immediate need to render aid or assistance to the children due to actual or threatened physical injury."[23] The court described the anonymous report:

> On Friday. . .a social worker with the Oconto county department of social services received an anonymous telephone call around suppertime. The caller indicated that the children may have been battered and were in need of medical attention. The caller identified two children by their last names (and at least one, if not both of the children, by the first name), and indicated that they lived with Boggess, the defendant. Through this information, the caller indicated that the children had different last names than Boggess. The caller also indicated that one of the children, L.S., was limping, and that because of bruises the caller witnessed on L.S., L.S. may have further damage done to his body and should be checked by a doctor. The caller additionally stated that he knew the Boggesses fairly well and that Mr. Boggess had a bad temper.[24]

Nevertheless, it would be patently improper to investigate all reports. Chart 3-3 (see p. 60) lists the four situations in which a report should not be investigated. To fail to consider these factors, and, instead, to investigate unthinkingly all reports called in, would be to invite a lawsuit. It would also be unwise child protective policy, because the workers would be immobilized by the need to investigate tens of thousands of cases of no apparent danger to children.

There are limits, also, to permissible investigative techniques. Overzealous efforts to uncover evidence are therapeutically counterproductive and can be the basis of a subsequent lawsuit.

An important—and early—step in any investigation should be an interview with the parents. Finding out whether the parents actually abused or neglected the child is a major purpose of this interview, of course. Thus, if the child has suspicious injuries, the worker should seek the parents' explanation for them, the parents' description of what precautions were taken to prevent the injuries (if they claim that the injuries were accidental), and the parents' description of the medical care, if any, that was obtained for the child's injuries. The parents should also be asked whether the child has been injured before, and, if so, the same information should be sought concerning any previous injury. If the child shows signs of physical or emotional deprivation, the worker should seek the parents' description of the care they provide the child. If possible, the worker should seek specific information on feeding practices, personal hygiene, sleeping arrangements, medical care, supervision and babysitting, and the physical conditions of the home.

The parents' answers to such questions are often inculpatory. In effect, the parents may confess to child maltreatment or may make other inculpatory statements that can be used against them in later court proceedings. Because child protective investigations are civil in nature and have as their main purpose the protection of children and the provision of supportive social services to parents, such statements are held to be admissible even though the worker may not have given *Miranda*-type warnings.[25] As one court explained:

> To require such a warning would frustrate the State's performance of its duty as *parens patriae* to investigate and protect the welfare of children. In any event, there appears to be no precedent for the requirement of a warning in connection with a civil proceeding.[26]

Although the use of such admissions "may smack uncomfortably of betrayal of a confidence when the parent has confessed his fault only because he was desperately seeking help for the child or psychotherapy for himself, his admission against interest must, of course, be considered by the Court."[27]

Nevertheless, workers cannot use the right to interview the parents as an excuse to conduct an inquisition. Forceful interrogation is inappropriate and does not elicit as much information as subtle probing. Furthermore, situations that at first appear to be maltreatment may turn out to be something else. Thus, the interview should be conducted professionally; the worker should adhere to facts and avoid placing blame and making accusations. "It is important not to alienate the family. Regardless of the outcome of the current situation, the [agency] is likely to continue serving the family, perhaps for many years to come."[28] The exact tone of the interview will vary, depending on the setting and the nature of the relationship between the parents and the interviewer. Chart 4-1 provides some guidelines that may help the interview go more smoothly and be more productive.

Potential liability is created when workers step beyond the bounds of proper interviewing—to harass, threaten, or browbeat the parents (as suggested by the allegations in the *Hale* and *Martin* cases described above). Thus,

Chart 4-1
Guidelines for Interviewing Parents

- The parents should be made to feel as comfortable as possible. (Conduct the interview in private.)
- The interviewer should be professional, direct, and honest.
- The parents should be told that the child's physical condition or behavior is a matter of concern. In most cases, though, it is neither necessary nor appropriate to say that abuse or neglect is suspected.
- At least initially, the interviewer's questions should focus on the child's condition and its possible causes.
- Questions should be open-ended; for example, the parents should be asked if they know what happened.
- The interviewer should not try to prove abuse or neglect through accusations or demands. It rarely helps to ask: "Did you hit your child?"
- Inconsistencies should not be pressed, but they should be carefully noted.
- With rare exceptions, the interviewer should not confront the parents with the child's description of being abused or neglected, or otherwise betray the child's confidences. (One exception involves situations in which the child's statements are such outright fabrications or distortions of reality that the child's need for therapy is indicated and parental cooperation must be obtained.)
- The interviewer should not display anger, repugnance, or shock.
- The interviewer should be attentive to what the parents have to say and should pick up on nuances in the parents' statements. For example, if a parent expresses difficulty in caring for the children, the interviewer may follow up with a comment such as: "It must be difficult to keep up with things when you have five active children."
- If appropriate, the parents should be informed that a report of suspected child maltreatment will be made. In so informing the parents, however, the interviewer may wish to extend to them an offer to be of continued support and assistance during the child protective investigation.

Source: Derived from U.S. National Center on Child Abuse and Neglect, *The Nurse's Role in the Prevention and Treatment of Child Abuse and Neglect* (Washington, D.C.: Department of Health, Education and Welfare, 1979), p. 25.

in *Harris v. City of Montgomery,* the court allowed a trial on the mother's claim that a police officer "did take [her] unlawfully into custody and did unlawfully confine her in a small isolated room at Police Headquarters" and that: "By confining her in said room, by threat of physical harm, and by threat to take her eight-day-old child into custody, [the officer] did force [her] to involuntarily confess to child abuse and/or neglect."[29]

The *Harris* case involved the police, but the claims would have had equal validity if made against a child protective agency. Sometimes, though, such claims are palpably unconvincing. For example, in *Darryl H. v. Coler,* the parents alleged that the worker "coerced" them into allowing her to enter their home, but, as the court pointed out, the worker was "five feet two inches tall and was eight months pregnant at the time of the investigation, hardly an intimidating figure."[30]

Children are often the best source of information—and testimony—concerning home conditions and any possible maltreatment. They can give moving—and frequently decisive—evidence about the allegations aginst their parents. Therefore, even very young children are interviewed by child protective workers. Although what they say may not be of sufficient reliability for use in court, their answers to workers' questions may shed light on ambiguous situations or provide additional leads for exploration.

As with interviews of parents, overzealous questioning of children also raises potential liability. When a child is questioned, every effort should be made not to frighten or traumatize the child. The child may already be hurt, fearful, or apprehensive. The timing and location of the interview should be designed to make the child feel as comfortable as the circumstances permit. Whether or not sexual abuse is the issue, it is generally advisable to have someone of the same sex interview the child or at least be present during the interview.

The interview should begin with generalized, nonjudgmental, and open-ended questions. Questions that can be answered by a simple "yes" or "no" should be avoided. Leila Whiting, a staff member of the National Association of Social Workers and former director of a child abuse project for that association, recommends such questions and comments as: "Can you tell me what happened?" or, "I know that when kids get hurt, there is usually something upsetting going on at home," or, "I can see that you are upset and I am interested in hearing about it."[31] Children should be permitted to answer questions in their own way. They should not be pressed for information they seem unwilling or unable to give. (Chart 4-2 contains some useful guidelines for interviewing children.)

The child's body, tragically, often provides the most telling evidence of maltreatment. Unsatisfactorily explained injuries suggestive of physical assaults, for example, are the single most important means of detecting child

Chart 4-2
Guidelines for Interviewing Children

DO:

- Make sure the interviewer is someone the child trusts.
- Conduct the interview in private.
- Sit next to the child, not across a table or desk.
- Ask the child to indicate words or terms that are not understood.
- Tell the child if any future action will be required.

DON'T:

- Allow the child to feel "in trouble" or "at fault."
- Disparage or criticize the child's choice of words or language.
- Suggest answers to the child.
- Display shock or disapproval of the parents, the child, or the situation.
- Force the child to remove clothing.
- Conduct the interview with a group of interviewers.
- Leave the child alone with a stranger (for example, a CPS worker).

Source: U.S. National Center on Child Abuse and Neglect, *We Can Help: A Curriculum on Child Abuse and Neglect: Resource Materials* (Washington, D.C.: Department of Health, Education and Welfare, 1979), p. 71.

---

abuse. For children too young or too frightened to tell what happened to them, such injuries may be the only way to discover child abuse—and the only way to prove it, should court action be necessary.[32] Hence, all good practice manuals recommend a full examination of the child's body.[33] A number of suits have challenged the child protective worker's right to examine the child, however. (To gain judicial sympathy, they usually characterize the examination as a "strip search.") Such suits are uniformly unsuccessful[34]—unless there was insufficient rason to *suspect* maltreatment. If there was not sufficient basis to commence the investigation in the first place, a physical examination, too, would be unjustified.[35]

Authority to look for signs of maltreatment on a child's body is not license to humiliate the child. In *E. Z. v. Coler,* for example, the parents alleged that the male worker completely undressed their 2-year-old daughter in the presence of her 4-year-old brother and a neighbor. They further alleged that he "held her up to a light, spread-eagled, for visual inspection of her vaginal area. [He] then placed [her] on a couch and lifted her legs over her head to make a visual inspection of her anus."[36] It is impossible to judge whether the worker's alleged conduct was necessitated by the circumstances, but, as a general rule, such intimate examinations should be performed by medical personnel.[37] Moreover, all examinations should be performed in private, with only necessary persons present, and with great concern for the child's sensibilities. (Except for infants, the examination should be performed by a worker of the same sex.)

Home visits are an essential element of most investigations. Home conditions often reflect the quality of care being provided for the children. Also, interviews of the parents and children are usually best conducted in the family home. A number of suits have claimed that the worker's entry into the home was not legally authorized. These cases fall into one of two categories: (1) coerced consent, and (2) unjustified forcible entry.

The parents' consent, of course, is a defense against later charges of illegal entry. But parents sometimes claim that they never consented to the worker's entry or that their apparent consent was coerced.[38] Courts tend to be unsympathetic to such claims, in part because they know that most parents allow workers to enter their homes, and in part because they do not find workers to be particularly "intimidating" figures.[39]

Claims of unjustified forcible entry raise a greater chance of liability. This is not because many child protective workers would find themselves forcing their way into a home, but rather because, on being refused entry by the parents, workers routinely seek police assistance. If a search warrant is obtained,[40] liability is unlikely;[41] but the police may force entry without a warrant on the ground that there is no time to obtain a court order. If this decision is made in bad faith *or* without probable cause to believe that the child is truly in immediate danger (what the law calls "exigent circumstances"), potential liability is created.[42] And if the child protective worker has been sufficiently involved in the decision-making process, liability may well attach to the worker, too.[43]

Defamation of Parents

"Defamation" is the name given to the tort of damaging a person's "reputation and good name."[44] Prosser and Keeton describe what is meant by a "defamatory communication":

> A defamatory communication usually has been defined as one which tends to hold the plaintiff up to hatred, contempt, or ridicule, or to cause him to be

shunned or avoided. This definition is certainly too narrow, since an imputation of insanity, or poverty, or an assertion that a woman has been raped, which would be likely to arouse pity or sympathy in the minds of all decent people, have been held to be defamatory. Defamation is rather that which tends to injure "reputation" in the popular sense; to diminish the esteem, respect, good will or confidence in which the plaintiff is held, or to excite adverse, derogatory or unpleasant feelings or opinions against him.[45]

Labeling a parent as abusive or neglectful is, without doubt, "defamatory communication." In the words of Supreme Court Justice Hugo Black, the parent "is charged with conduct—failure to care properly for her children—which may be viewed as reprehensible and morally wrong by a majority of society."[46]

Defamation is divided into two separate torts: (1) "libel," generally a written statement, and (2) "slander," generally an oral statement. Thus, child protective workers can defame parents in two ways: (1) by what they write in letters, reports, and case records (libel), and (2) by what they say to others in the course of investigation, treatment, or casual conversation (slander).

The legal rules governing these two torts, though substantially similar, differ in many important ways. For example, actual damage must be proven for most forms of slander, but is often not required for libel. Within the context of child protection, however, the differences are small enough to discuss both torts together. For example, proof of actual damages is not required in slander cases involving imputations of criminal behavior (which, of course, would include child abuse and neglect).[47]

Communication of the defamatory statement to some *third person* is essential for tort liability. In a typically misleading manner, the law calls this requirement "publication." This does not mean that the statement must be widely disseminated. Publication can be to just one other person; it can be a handwritten note to a supervisor. (However, the degree of dissemination may affect the amount of damages.) Also, the publication need not be printed or written; "it may be oral, or conveyed by means of gestures, or the exhibition of a picture or statue."[48] It must, however, be to someone other than the person defamed. "Where there is no communication to anyone but the plaintiff there may be criminal responsibility, or a possible action for the intentional infliction of mental suffering,[49] but no tort action can be maintained upon the theory of defamation."[50]

Repeating someone else's allegations of possible maltreatment amounts to a publication. "Every repetition of the defamation is a publication itself, even though the repeater states the source, or resorts to the customary newspaper evasion 'it is alleged,' or makes it clear that he does not believe the imputation."[51] Even a worker's question that suggests that the parent is suspected of or is being investigated for possible child maltreatment is a form of "publication." Furthermore, "It is not necessary that anyone believe [the defendant's words] to be true, since the fact that such words are in circulation at all concerning the plaintiff must be to some extent injurious to his reputation—although obviously the absence of belief will bear upon the amount of the damages."[52]

Most laypersons believe that "truth" is a defense to claims of defamation. This was the traditional rule. Only about 38 states, however, still make truth an absolute defense. In these jurisdictions, even malicious statements are protected—as long as they are true. "It is immaterial that the defendant published the facts for no good reason or for the worst possible motives, or even that he did not believe at the time that they were true."[53]

Because such a rule can be easily abused, about 12 states now require that the statement has to have been made "for good motives or for justifiable ends."[54] Furthermore, even where truth is still a defense to defamation, a lawsuit can be brought for the intentional (and, sometimes, the negligent) infliction of mental suffering or the invasion of privacy. These were the allegations, for example, in *Martin v. Weld* and *Hale v. City of Virginia Beach,* discussed earlier. When coupled with the confidentiality imposed on child protective activities (by the laws of all states),[55] truth becomes a minimal protection to workers who wrongly disclose harmful information about the family.

The real bar to liability is "privilege." All people, for example, are accorded an absolute privilege—that is, immunity—for participating in judicial proceedings. This includes the judge, the attorneys, and any witnesses. "The privilege covers anything that may be said in relation to the matter at issue, whether it be in the pleadings, in affidavits, or in open court."[56]

> The immunity extends to every step in the proceeding until final disposition, although it does not cover publications made before commencement or after termination....Although there is some authority to the contrary, the better view seems to be that an informal complaint to a prosecuting attorney or a magistrate is to be regarded as an initial step in a judicial proceeding, and so entitled to an absolute, rather than a qualified, immunity.[57]

Thus, in *Overman v. Klein,* the court dismissed a defamation suit based on the worker's affidavit concerning the plaintiff's child care practices, a home study evaluation, and a recommendation that a change in custody would be in the best interest of the plaintiff's children.[58] Statements to court probation officers are also generally considered privileged, although a 1984 Florida lawsuit by an incarcerated father claimed defamation based on the statement of a nonlawyer guardian *ad litem* to a probation counselor that the father was a pedophile.[59]

For the child protective investigation itself, however, workers enjoy only a "qualified" privilege. This means that they can be liable for malicious or careless, negligent, or unjustified defamatory communications. "Probably the best statement of the rule is that the defendant is required to act as a reasonable person under the circumstances, with due respect to the strength of his belief, the grounds that he has to support it, and the importance of conveying the information."[60] The application of this subjective standard is illustrated by Robert Horowitz, associate director of the American Bar Association's National Legal Resource Center for Child Advocacy and Protection:

> A child protection worker responsible for intake and investigation receives a phone call from an unidentified person who claims that her neighbor, a Sally Jones, has repeatedly left her one-year-old daughter alone in the house for many hours at a time. The neighbor is now calling because she hears the infant crying and she believes no one is at the house. After giving you Ms. Jones' address she hangs up.
> ...Upon receiving the report, the worker immediately goes to Ms. Jones' house. The worker arrives at the house and rings the door bell, but no one answers; the worker does not hear a baby crying so decides to check with the two closest neighbors to see if she can locate the reporter. In talking to each neighbor, the worker identifies herself, says that someone claimed a baby was left unattended at Ms. Jones' house, and asks if they made the report or heard a baby cry. (The case is ultimately closed because abuse or neglect could not be substantiated.)
> Ms. Jones subsequently sues the worker, alleging that her inquiries with the neighbors slandered her, defaming her reputation in the community.
> * * *
> In [this] hypothetical [case], the worker seemed cautious in approaching only close neighbors who may have heard the baby scream, and eliciting their viewpoints. She did not brand Ms. Jones or broaden her inquiry to encompass distant neighbors who are unlikely to have relevant information. This circumspection should probably defeat the mother's slander charges. . . . [The] information the worker is relaying has a bearing upon the investigation, and the persons the worker talks to are "reasonably believed to be necessary and useful for the furtherance of that (investigation)."[61]

The allegations in another case demonstrate how the need to interview those who might know something about suspected maltreatment does not justify unnecessarily broad disclosure of the report's existence. A child protective agency received a report claiming that a female social worker in private practice had sexually abused two young female patients. To determine whether other patients of the social worker were abused, the agency sent out a memo to its employees requesting them to identify persons in their caseloads who were treated by her. The social worker claimed that this inquiry needlessly brought the report to the attention of agency employees; she argued that a list of her patients could have been obtained from her employer and that the list could then have been cross-checked with the agency's own computer list of clients. She sued for the consequent and, according to her, avoidable damage to her professional reputation and earnings (resulting from the loss of existing patients and new referrals).[62]

An incorrect determination that the report is "substantiated," "indicated," or even that it is "not unfounded," also raises the possibility of liability. Some courts would hold that the worker's determination is not technically a "publication" of defamatory information—because child protective records are confidential.[63] Most courts, however, would disagree on the ground that (1) there are many exceptions to the "confidentiality" established by state law and (2) central registers make the worker's determination widely available.[64] These courts would look to see whether the determination was reasonably made: whether the worker made a sufficient inquiry and made a careful, professionally competent determination based on what was known at the time.

Determinations made in accordance with accepted agency and professional practices will ordinarily be considered reasonable. However, the practice itself may be challenged by the parents. If they convince the court that the practice, although widely endorsed and adopted, is unreasonable, the worker faces possible liability for following it.[65]

Until recently, it would have been said with great certainty that a successful challenge to established agency and professional practices would be unlikely. But this has changed. Heightened public and professional concern over child abuse—especially sexual abuse—has led to the adoption of a number of questionable practices. Some agencies, for example, now authorize (or require) intervention based on the most tenuous of circumstantial evidence. Circumstantial evidence is often the only way to establish that a child has been abused. The "battered child syndrome" is actually a form of circumstantial evidence.[66] The unusual behavior of the child suffering from the syndrome is properly used to corroborate a determination of possible or likely abuse based on suspicious or unexplained injuries to the child.[67] In a misguided attempt to protect children, however, there has been a recent tendency to use these "behavioral indicators" as the *sole* basis for intervention. This is a mistake. Behavioral indicators are notoriously overinclusive; their use as the *sole* basis of decision falsely labels many innocent parents. Ignoring this reality will expose workers and agencies to recurrent lawsuits.[68]

There are two ways to reduce legal vulnerability for possibly incorrect and unreasonable determinations. First, disclosure of the finding, and any other information about the family, should be kept to the minimum needed to fulfill the agency's mission.[69] Besides avoiding liability in many situations, this will almost always limit the amount of damages that can be claimed. Second, the parents should be accorded the opportunity to challenge the determination. About 17 states have laws that expressly require that parents be told of the record about them.[70] Many of these laws give parents a right to request that the record be amended, sealed, or expunged; often, the parents are guaranteed an administrative hearing if their request is denied. But even in the absence of such specific legislation, child protective agencies should recognize the wisdom of allowing parents to correct misleading or inaccurate information in agency records. The parents' right to do so was the basis of the dismissal of *Bohn v. County of Dakota*, a suit by a couple claiming that an erroneous finding of abuse caused irreparable harm to their family relationships and reputation.[71]

Wrongful Removal (or Withholding) of Children

The great majority of maltreated children need not be removed from parental custody—especially not on an emergency basis. Most forms of maltreatment do not pose the threat of immediately serious injury. The danger they pose, though great, arises from the *long-term consequences* of inadequate child care. There is usually time to work with parents so that they can care adequately for their children.[72] Hence, less than 15 percent of all substantiated reports result in the child's placement.[73]

Many maltreated children, however, are in immediate danger, and only protective custody can safeguard their safety and well-being. To deal with such situations, most states have adopted statutory schemes similar to that recommended by the U.S. National Center on Child Abuse and Neglect (Chart 4-3).

Chart 4-3
Model Guidelines for Protective Custody

(a) A police or law enforcement official [, *a designated worker of a child protective service,*]† and a physician treating a child may take a child into protective custody without the consent of parents, guardians, or others exercising temporary or permanent control over the child when he has reasonable cause to believe that (1) there exists an imminent danger to the child's life or safety, (2) the parents are unavailable or have been asked and do not consent to the child's removal from their custody, and (3) there is not time to apply for a court order.

(b) In the event there is not time to seek a court order the person in charge of any hospital or similar medical institution may retain custody

---

Source: U.S. National Center on Child Abuse and Neglect, *Child Protection: A Guide for State Legislation* (Washington, D.C.: Department of Health and Human Services, 1983), §9.

†Optional.

Chart 4-3 (continued)

of a child reasonably suspected of being abused or neglected, when he believes the facts so warrant, whether or not additional medical treatment is required and whether or not the parents or other person responsible for the child's welfare request the child's return.

(c) The child shall be taken immediately to a place previously designated for this purpose by the juvenile court or the local agency. Such place may include a foster home; group home; shelter; hospital, if the child is or will be admitted to the hospital; or other institution; but it shall not be a jail or other place for the detention, incarceration, or residential care of criminal offenders or juveniles either alleged or adjudicated as delinquents or status offenders.

(d) No child shall be kept in protective custody under this Act for more than twenty-four hours unless authorized by a judge of a court of record. If after 24 hours there has been no protective custody order from the court, the person having custody of the child shall return the child to his parents.

(e) Any person taking a child into protective custody shall immediately notify the appropriate local child protective service. Upon such notification, the service shall immediately see to the protection of any other children in the home, commence a child protective investigation in accordance with Section 13 of this Act, and make every reasonable effort to inform the parent or other person responsible for the child's welfare as to where the child has been taken. Parents shall be informed of where and when the case will be heard; their right to legal representation as well as the provision of legal representation if indigent; and their visitation rights. The service shall make a reasonable attempt to return the child to his home, whenever it seems safe to do so. At the next regular session of the juvenile court [or family court or similar civil court],* the service shall (i) commence a child protection proceeding in the court, or (ii) recommend to the court [court intake service or other initiating authority]** that one not be commenced. The court may order commencement of a proceeding even if the service recommends against doing so, if it finds that such a proceeding would be in the best interests of the child. If a proceeding is commenced, the service shall recommend whether or not the child should be returned to his parents or other person responsible for his welfare pending further court action.

---

*As appropriate.
**Optional.

Parental consent is always the preferred method of removing a child, because resort to unnecessary legal coercion can be detrimental to later treatment efforts. In a surprising number of cases, the parents will consent to a request from the police or a child protective agency to place a child in substitute care. Some parents recognize their problems and understand the need to move the child. Others have highly ambivalent feelings about their child (or children) and may welcome the relief that placement provides. If the child is to be placed with relatives or friends, parental agreement is more likely. Recognizing the importance of parental consent, many states have specific laws or administrative regulations requiring that the parents' agreement be sought before involuntary protective custody is invoked.[74]

No one should deny the coercive element in "voluntary" placements. The parents may sense that failure to consent may result in formal court action. In fact, many authorities recommend telling the parents about the possible consequences of not cooperating. The National Center on Child Abuse and Neglect, for example, suggests the following statutory provision:

> The local agency shall explain that it has no legal authority to compel the family to accept services; however, it shall inform the family of the obligations and authority of the local agency to petition the juvenile court to decide whether a child is in need of care and protection or to refer the case to the police or the district attorney who will then decide whether there shall be a criminal prosecution.[75]

But there is an enormous difference between allowing parents to make an informed decision about how to proceed[76] and pressing them by threats or other forms of intimidation. The latter opens the door to liability. So does consent gained under false pretense, for example, by making inaccurate or misleading statements about the parents' ability to withdraw the consent. One federal appeals court, for example, recognized a damage claim by a mother who was told that the temporary care of her three children could be arranged only if she signed a six-month, voluntary placement agreement. She signed, based on "assurances," apparently later ignored by the agency, "that her children would be returned whenever she found suitable housing."[77]

Frequently, however, a child must be removed from his or her home against parental wishes. In those cases, whenever conditions permit, prior judicial review and authorization should be sought. As in all situations in which individual discretion is preeminent, there is always the danger of careless or automatic, though well-meaning, exercise of the power to place a child in protective custody.[78] Court-ordered removal lessens this danger by ensuring that a judge, an outsider, reviews the administrative decision to place a child in custody. Indeed, police and child protective agencies having authority to remove a child against the parents' wishes are often reluctant to do so without a court order. On nights and weekends, some will go so far as to seek a judge's approval by telephone.

A major reason for seeking a judicial authorization, of course, is to avoid liability for a wrongful removal. However, although the existence of a court order makes a successful lawsuit unlikely, it does not rule one out.[79] First, the violation of statutory or established constitutional mandates for the issuance of a removal order—even if inadvertent and in good faith—may establish liability. For example, in *McGhee v. Moyer,* the federal court recognized potential liability for an emergency removal because, although the state law provided that only a judge could order a child's emergency placement, the order had been signed by a deputy clerk of the court.[80] Second, going beyond the terms or conditions of the removal order may create liability, because it is the same as acting without a court order. In an unusual case, a mother was allowed to sue various local officials who sent her son to his grandparents in Germany pursuant to a court order that had been stayed.[81]

Finally, a court order obtained through false, distorted, misleading, or unnecessarily incomplete information does not prevent liability; indeed, it can create liability, especially when the conduct was malicious or in reckless disregard of the parents' rights. This was the claim in *Doe v. Hennepin County,* in which the parents alleged that the child protective agency had filed a "Petition for an Emergency Warrant" that contained "distorted and false" statements leading to their children's removal.[82] According to the parents, the agency violated state law by failing to conduct an appropriate investigation before seeking the removal order. (The only contact with the family was when the mother called to say that the report was unfounded.) The parents attributed the agency's conduct, in part, to its *"policy of treating as true all allegations of abuse,* regardless of source and [the fact] that the Hennepin County Child Protection's procedures manual has no reference to the possibility that the maker of a report may have improper motives. This results in a failure to investigate, contrary to statutory duty. . . ."[83] The court ruled that the parents had made a "sufficient showing that fact questions exist concerning whether defendants' actions were reasonable and in good faith."[84]

Sometimes it appears that the child must be removed before court review is possible, because, in the time it would take to obtain a court order, the child might be further harmed or the parents might flee with the child. In all states, the police are authorized to take a child into protective custody *without a court order.* In about 12 states, child protective agencies also have this power.[85] However, as a practical matter, child protective agencies normally do not attempt a *forcible* removal of the child without police assistance, because of the potential danger to the worker.

If authorized officials remove a child in good faith—and in accordance with state laws—a successful claim for damages is unlikely.[86] In *Griffin*

v. *Pate,* for example, the court dismissed a lawsuit against police officers who, "as the result of proper investigation [mistakenly] felt that for the child's protection she should be removed from her mother. . . ."[87] Although the question of good faith is ultimately a subjective one, the presence of one or more of the factors listed in Chart 3-4 is at least presumptive evidence of good faith. Conversely, the absence of a sufficient inquiry before removing the child is strong evidence of unreasonable behavior.[88]

In keeping with the guidelines of the National Center, many states have adopted a prohibition against removing a child without a court order unless there is no time to obtain one.[89] A number of suits have been filed claiming liability for the violation of this requirement.[90] These cases are hard for parents to win, however, because, for there to be real damages, they must prove that the court would have refused to order the child's removal.[91]

Whatever the initial basis for placing a child in protective custody, there is a real need for a court to review the initial administrative decision. It may have been wrong; it may have been based on incomplete or misunderstood facts; or the situation may have changed since the decision was first made—for example, counseling, homemaker, day care, or housing services may have succeeded in making the child's home safe for his or her return. Therefore, the correctness of such decisions should be reviewed by a court as soon as possible. Although some states put no time limit on protective custody before court review,[92] most provide a time limit—usually from 24 to 72 hours or "the next court day."[93] In this time, according to the National Center's guidelines and the laws of many states, "Parents shall be informed of where and when the case will be heard; their right to legal representation as well as the provision of legal representation if indigent; and their visitation rights."[94] Court decisions have imposed similar requirements.[95]

Even if the original emergency removal was valid, the failure to obey a statute mandating court approval of the child's *continued placement* raises potential liability—unless the parents have consented. Furthermore, an actual statutory mandate is not needed to establish liability. Parents have a constitutional right to a judicial review of agency removals.[96]

Thus, regardless of the circumstances of the original removal, agencies and individual workers can be held liable for the wrongful failure to return a child.[97] One of the best known of these cases is *Duchesne v. Sugarman.* The day after the mother was unexpectedly hospitalized for emotional problems, the agency took custody of her two children, one 7 years old and the other 6 months old. The mother refused to sign a consent form authorizing the agency to continue caring for the children. The caseworker reported the mother's refusal to his supervisor, who advised that no consent was necessary at that point. Five days later, the mother was released from the hospital and she "immediately. . .demanded that her children be returned.

However, the children were not relinquished."[98] For the next 27 months, the mother unsuccessfully sought to have the agency return her children, but the agency continued to rebuff her—and never sought a court order legalizing the situation. The court described what happened over those 27 months:

> Several days later, Perez [the mother] voluntarily returned to the hospital where she remained until February 1970. Upon her release at that time, requests for return of her children were made to the Bureau and the two institutions; the requests were again rejected. An explanation for these refusals may be found in St. Joseph's conclusion that Perez was "sweet," but "not mother material."
>
> In succeeding months, Perez repeatedly requested the return of her children; but all of these requests were denied. During this entire time, the children were never able to visit each other.
>
> The records reveal that at least as of November 10, 1971, B.C.W., St. Joseph's and the Foundling Hospital were all aware that Perez had never signed any consent or commitment papers. The three discussed the absence of consent, but decided that they would take no action unless Perez initiated legal proceedings on her own. Indeed, the records reveal that "[s]ince obtaining [Perez]'s signature at this point seem[ed] an impossibility, [they] agreed not to attempt it." Finally, the Foundling Hospital's records demonstrate that it informed Perez of her legal right to institute an action if *she* thought the children should be with her.
>
> Finally, on February 22, 1972, some 27 months after the family had been separated, Perez filed a petition in the New York Supreme Court seeking a writ of *habeas corpus*.[99]

The court held that the absence of any prior parental consent established potential liability for monetary damages under the federal Civil Rights Act.[100] This factual situation was distinguished from that in which parents originally consent to foster placement. In such cases, courts have held that it is constitutionally permissible to require the parent to file a *habeas corpus* petition to obtain custody.[101]

When a court "commits" a child to a child protective agency, many statutory schemes allow the agency to return the child to the parents without a subsequent court order. Sometimes, children are "committed" to the agency without ever being removed from parental custody. In the past, it was possible to claim that such "commitments" effectively divested parents of legal custody over their children and transferred it to the agency, so that the agency could remove the child whenever removal seemed "advisable." Recent court decisions indicate that this legal artifice no longer avoids the need for judicial review. The removal from parental custody of children "committed" to the agency is governed by the same standards as any other removal.[102]

Finally, whatever the reasons for the removal, it must be carried out in a reasonable manner. Unnecessary force, household disruption, or publicity can create potential liability. A 53-year-old Vermont grandfather, for instance, suffered a heart attack when a worker, her supervisor, and a security guard took his granddaughter from him. Seeking $7.5 million dollars in damages, he claimed that he was threatened with a fist, verbally assaulted, restrained by having his arms twisted, and held in a chair for 20 minutes.[103]

Malicious Prosecution

Child protective agencies seek to avoid formal court action whenever possible. Nationally, fewer than 20 percent of all reported cases reach court.[104] Instead, child protective agencies seek to gain the parents' voluntary participation in treatment by offering a range of services designed to help them meet their child-rearing responsibilities. In most cases, court action is commenced only because (1) the parents have refused to accept treatment services (including an agreement to have the child placed in foster care) voluntarily, and (2) the child protective agency decides that, to protect the child, it needs the court's authority either to remove the child from the home or to impose treatment services.

Sometimes, initial parental cooperation is not enough to keep a family out of court. The parents' care of the child may not improve or may even worsen during the period of contact with the child protective agency, yet they may refuse to place their child in foster care "voluntarily," thereby necessitating court action. The legal sufficiency of the evidence must also be considered. Does the agency have admissible and persuasive evidence that establishes parental responsibility for the child's abuse or neglect? In short, the decision to commence court action is a subjective weighing of competing and often inconsistent factors.[105]

In most large communities, when it appears that court action is appropriate, the child protective worker contacts an agency lawyer, county attorney, attorney general, or other public law officer. It is up to the lawyer to initiate the necessary proceeding. Lawyers performing this function are considered "prosecutors"[106] who, in almost all jurisdictions, enjoy *absolute* immunity from lawsuits claiming the improper initiation of court action.[107] Absolute immunity protects them even from claims of recklessness, bad faith, and personal malice. The U.S. Supreme Court recognized the importance of prosecutorial immunity in *Imbler v. Pachtman,* where it explained how, if prosecutors were exposed to liability, their performance would be hampered by the fear of future lawsuits and by the need to divert their energy to the defense of such suits. Justice Powell, writing for the Court, said:

> The common law immunity of a prosecutor is based upon the same considerations that underlie the common law immunities of judges and good jurors acting within the scope of their duties. These include concern that harassment by unfounded litigation would cause a deflection of the prosecutor's energies from

his public duties, and the possibility that he would shade his decisions instead of exercising the independence of judgment required by his public trust. One court expressed both considerations as follows: "The office of public prosecutor is one which must be administered with courage and independence. Yet how can this be if the prosecutor is made subject to suit by those whom he accuses and fails to convict? To allow this would open the way for unlimited harassment and embarrassment of the most conscientious officials by those who would profit thereby. There would be involved in every case the possible consequences of a failure to obtain a conviction. There would always be a question of possible civil action in case the prosecutor saw fit to move dismissal of the case. . . .The apprehension of such consequences would tend toward great uneasiness and toward weakening the fearless and impartial policy which should characterize the administration of this office. The work of the prosecutor would thus be impeded and we would have moved away from the desired objective of stricter and fairer law enforcement."[108]

There is no juvenile court "prosecutor" in many communities. Unrepresented child protective workers decide whether to initiate court action. They prepare and file the necessary legal papers (often with the assistance of court personnel). A 1983 case suggests that child protective workers might some day be granted absolute immunity for their decisions to initiate court action. In *Whelehan v. County of Monroe,* the parents claimed that the juvenile court proceeding against them had been brought in bad faith.

> Plaintiffs claim this proceeding was commenced and continued with knowledge of its groundlessness and characterize this conduct both as a deprivation of due process and as malicious prosecution. Plaintiffs also claim that, in the course of these proceedings and the preliminaries thereto, defendants deliberately and wrongfully refused and neglected to furnish plaintiffs and the court with exculpatory evidence to which plaintiffs were entitled and also negligently or deliberately supplied plaintiffs' attorneys and the court with false and misleading information.[109]

Equating the child protective worker's decision to commence court action with that of a prosecutor, the court reasoned that inasmuch as prosecutors enjoy absolute immunity, so should workers. (The worker's possible liability for other aspects of the child protective process, such as investigations and removals, is unaffected.)

As of this writing, however, the great weight of authority holds that workers have only *qualified* immunity for their decisions to commence court action.[110] A lawsuit—and liability—can be based on evidence that the decision was made recklessly or in bad faith. These were the allegations in *Doe v. County of Suffolk,* in which the mother sued for malicious prosecution, alleging that the worker and the agency initiated a court child protective proceeding "knowing full well that they could not successfully prosecute the peti-

The Vulnerable Social Worker

tion against said plaintiff..., and knowing full well that ultimately the said petition must be dismissed."[111] The worker had filed a petition against both the mother and the father after the *mother* called and told the police that her husband had sexually abused their child. Apparently, there was no reason to suspect that the mother had in any way been abusive or neglectful, and the county attorney withdrew the petition against her before the trial. The court allowed the mother's lawsuit to continue.

Doe is a powerful reminder that although workers have broad discretion in deciding whether to initiate court action, in doing so, they cannot be reckless, indiscriminant, or preemptory.

Disclosure of Confidential Information

Child protective agency records contain information about the most private aspects of personal and family life. Whether or not the information is true, its improper disclosure can violate the sensibilities of all those involved and can be deeply stigmatizing.

> Once an agency...labels a parent as abusive, other agencies tend to accept this label and treat the family accordingly. Consistency across agencies occurs even though initially a second agency may not have labelled the family as abusive by its own criteria. Similarly, informal communication of the label through the family's court appearances or social worker visits may promote adoption of the abuse tag by friends and relatives....[112]

To safeguard family privacy, *all* states have laws making child protective records confidential. Most of these laws make unauthorized disclosure a crime; some, such as those in Iowa, Mississippi, and West Virginia, also impose civil liability for unauthorized disclosures.[113] A specific civil liability provision is not necessary, however. In most states, the violation of a criminal statute against disclosure establishes a sufficient predicate for civil liability.[114] And, of course, there can always be a claim of defamation.

No state makes child protective records totally confidential. The information in records must be available to those who make crucial case-handling decisions. Thus, although states differ, access is usually authorized for law enforcement officials, physicians, parents or guardians, foster care agencies, treatment programs for children and parents, grand juries, courts, relevant state officials, and researchers.[115]

Not many lawsuits seem to be filed claiming the improper disclosure of confidential information. In one case, the agency released an obituary on a foster child. The biological parents threatened to sue the agency, claiming that although only the names of the foster parents and the child were mentioned, readers might somehow connect them to the child, but no lawsuit was ever filed.[116] A few suits have been brought claiming that the child protective worker breached confidentiality during court proceedings. Such cases typically involve the worker's testimony in a separate custody case. Because of the absolute immunity all witnesses enjoy for testimony concerning matters before the court, however, the worker's motion to dismiss (or for summary judgment) is usually granted.[117]

Ironically, confidentiality seems to be more often used as a shield by agencies seeking to hide their own malfunctioning than to protect the privacy of individuals. Clients and advocacy groups are frequently denied access to case records on the false ground of confidentiality—even when the records are sought to document a pattern of bias or discrimination.[118] Similarly, in *Hanson v. Rowe*, a foster care agency sought to deny a mother access to the names of the other children placed in a foster home where the foster father had murdered her daughter and injured her son. She wanted to find out whether the father had previously abused other children placed in the home and whether the agency knew or should have known about any such prior abuse. Because this information was a crucial element of the mother's lawsuit claiming money damages against the agency, the appellate court ordered the agency to provide it.[119]

Confidentiality is also used against workers seeking to expose agency weaknesses. In 1981, administrative disciplinary proceedings were initiated against Irwin Levin, a New York City worker, who released case records to the press. He claimed that he wanted to prove that many child abuse deaths "stemmed from...staff incompetence and irresponsibility in handling clients."[120] Unfortunately, in doing so, he apparently released client-identifying information. The agency first sought to fire Levin. In a compromise agreement, he agreed to a demotion and reduction in salary. It took three years, a harshly critical report from the agency's own Inspector General, and personal intervention by the mayor before Levin was vindicated—and reinstated with back pay.

Even more unsettling was the reason given for firing another worker. According to the court, Arlene Fracaro was dismissed as an Eligibility Supervisor in a public welfare agency "on the ground that she publicly revealed confidential information about clients...." The letter of dismissal referred to two instances in which Mrs. Fracaro appeared on news broadcasts of a local TV station.[121] In its opinion, the court set out the transcripts of the two offending broadcasts, dated June 23 and June 26, 1978:

June 23
NEWSWOMAN:
      Veno and Constance Hutchins live in a Stokes County subdivision with their four children and a niece. The Hutchins have been charged with child abuse. Mrs. Hutchins says she received a Court summons yesterday to appear for an immediate custody hearing next Monday requested by Social Services;

but, she says the family has not had any home conferences with social workers on the matter, and she had no idea the Department wanted to remove two of her children from the home until a subpoena was delivered last night. Today a social worker and the Director of Social Services did pay a visit. Mrs. Hutchins and her husband were at work at the time.

Barbara Taylor, the worker assigned to the case, told us she had attempted to make home visits on at least four other occasions but found no one at home. Mrs. Taylor also said she had not left a note to say she had been by, nor had she called to say she was coming at any of those times. Neither she nor the Department Director, Paul Priddy, would do an on camera interview. Priddy said he had no comment today but said we could call him next week. Meanwhile, Mrs. Hutchins says the department has treated her unfairly.

MRS. HUTCHINS:
Everybody would be in for child abuse if they didn't investigate it. Its odd and they ain't going to take your children from you and serve you with a subpoena? Because, the police officer told me that this subpoena was issued about 3:00 yesterday afternoon and was served on me around 6:00.

NEWSWOMAN:
Arlene Fracaro, the Social Services Eligibility Supervisor, charges that the Hutchins' case is a good example of the way social workers mishandle many child abuse cases.

MRS. FRACARO:
She was reported for a suspected child abuse and neglect; but, no home call was ever made, no follow up. She was told to go—her solution was to go to Florida.

NEWSWOMAN:
We talked with several Social Services employees who confirmed Mrs. Fracaro's allegations. Those employees told us of a number of suspected child abuse and neglect cases which were never investigated. One case reportedly involved a six month old baby weighing less than seven pounds. Workers say the baby died several months later. Meanwhile, those who talked with us refused an on camera interview saying that they had been warned that if they talked they'd be fired.

June 26
NEWSWOMAN:
Last week Mrs. Constance Hutchins received a summons to appear in District Court today on an immediate custody hearing requested by the Stokes County Department of Social Services. The Hutchins have been charged with child abuse. On Friday, Mrs. Hutchins told News Center 12 that the case had not been investigated by Social Services, that no social worker ever visited her home or talked with her children or neighbors about the case. Mrs. Hutchins contended that she and her husband were innocent. Today District Court Judge Foy Clark dropped the child abuse charge and the Hutchins said justice had been rendered at last.

MR. HUTCHINS:
The Judge said that he had no doubt in his mind that we were not guilty of it.

MRS. HUTCHINS:
He completely dismissed it. He said there was no doubt in his mind at all, that I was just a person trying to seek help and got took advantage of.

NEWSWOMAN:

The Eligibility Supervisor for Social Services had backed Mrs. Hutchins in her fight against the agency. Arlene Fracaro told us many child abuse cases are mishandled in Stokes County. Today Mrs. Fracaro said she had been told her comments to the news media last week had cost her her job.

MRS. FRACARO:

A rumor through the grapevine is that I probably will be fired for speaking in this client's behalf, of trying to uncover in the Department of Social Services the misuse and just dereliction of duty by the Services, AFDC Services.[122]

Notes

1. U.S. National Center on Child Abuse and Neglect, *National Study of the Incidence and Severity of Child Abuse and Neglect* (Washington, D.C.: Department of Health and Human Services, 1981), p. 16.

2. U.S. National Center on Child Abuse and Neglect, *National Analysis of Child Neglect and Abuse Reporting (1978)* (Washington, D.C.: Department of Health, Education and Welfare, 1979), p. 36, Table 28.

3. U.S. National Center on Child Abuse and Neglect, *Annual Analysis of Child Abuse and Neglect Programs* (Washington, D.C.: Department of Health and Human Services, 1980).

4. *Olmstead v. United States,* 277 U.S. 438, 479 (1928) (Brandeis J., dissenting).

5. *Stanley v. Illinois,* 405 U.S. 645, 651 (1972), citations omitted.

6. See pp. 151–156.

7. W. P. Keeton and W. L. Prosser, *Prosser and Keeton on Torts,* 5th ed. (St. Paul, Minn.: West Publishing Co., 1984), p. 109.

8. Iowa Attorney General, Opinion No. 78-9-12, 28 September 1978, cited in *Family Law Reporter,* 5 (7 November 1978), p. 2015.

9. For various definitions of "bad faith," see pp. 38–42 and p. 155.

10. *Hale v. City of Virginia Beach,* U.S. Dist. Ct., E.D. of Va., Norfolk Div., Civ. SO-151-N. Complaint, ¶6.A.

11. Ibid. at ¶9, emphasis added.

12. See pp. 39–42.

13. *Martin v. Weld,* 598 P.2d 532, 533 (Colo. Ct. App. 1979).

14. Ibid., p. 534.

15. Ibid., p. 535.

16. National Association of Counsel for Children, *The Guardian,* 5 (Spring 1983), p. 5.

17. For a listing of the most relevant standards, see Appendix C.

18. See pp. 24–25.

19. See, for example, *Marrone v. New York State Department of Social Services,* cited in *National Law Journal,* 3 October 1983, p. 7, col. 1.

20. *Supra* n. 8.

21. See, for example, *Covert v. Reightnour,* MCA 80-263 (U.S. Dist. Ct., N.D.C. Fla., filed 12-26-80); *Ehret v. New York City Department of Social Services,* 80 Civ. 2042 (LDW) (U.S. Dist. Ct., E.D. N.Y.); *Wisconsin v. Boggess,* 340 N.W.2d 516 (Wisc. 1983); *Martin v. Weld; Marrone v. New York State Department of Social Services.*

22. See pp. 57–60.

23. The court was referring to the "totality of the circumstances" test established by the U.S. Supreme Court to judge the reliability of informers. See *Illinois v. Gates,* 462 U.S. 213, 103 S. Ct. 2317, 2330 and 2332 (1983); *Aguilar v. Texas,* 378 U.S. 108, 114 (1964).

24. *Wisconsin v. Boggess,* 340 N.W.2d at p. 519. Footnote omitted.

25. If the police perform the investigation, they are subject to the rules established in *Miranda v. Arizona,* 384 U.S. 436 (1966). Cf. *Harris v. City of Montgomery,* 435 So.2d 1207 (Ala. 1983).

26. *In the Matter of Diana A.,* 65 Misc. 2d 1034, 1040, 319 N.Y.S.2d 691, 697 (Fam. Ct., N.Y. Co., 1971). Cf. *People v. Yanus,* 92 A.D.2d 674, 460 N.Y.S.2d 180 (3rd Dept. 1983).

27. N. Dembitz, "Child Abuse and the Law — Fact and Fiction," *Record of the Bar Association of the City of New York,* 24 (1969), pp. 613, 616–617.

28. U.S. National Center on Child Abuse and Neglect, *The Educator's Role in the Prevention and Treatment of Child Abuse and Neglect* (Washington, D.C.: Department of Health, Education and Welfare, 1979), p. 25.

29. *Supra* n. 25, 435 So.2d at p. 1210.

30. *Darryl H. v. Coler,* 585 F. Supp. 383, 388 (N.D.Ill., 1984).

31. U.S. National Center on Child Abuse and Neglect, *We Can Help: A Curriculum on Child Abuse and Neglect: Resource Materials* (Washington, D.C.: Department of Health, Education and Welfare, 1979), p. 116.

32. See D. Besharov, *Proving Child Abuse: A Guide for Practice under the New York Family Court Act* (Ithaca, N.Y.: Cornell University College of Human Ecology, 1984).

33. See, for example, Illinois Department of Children and Family Services, *Child Abuse and Neglect Investigation Decisions Handbook* (Washington, D.C.: American Bar Association, 1982), p. 66; *Darryl H. v. Coler, supra,* n. 30, 585 F. Supp. at p. 387.

34. *Darryl H. v. Coler.* Similar claims were made, but, at this writing, not resolved, in: *Stone v. Holt,* No. 84-C-351-D (U.S. Dist. Ct., W.D. Wisc. 8-20-84); *E. Z. v. Coler,* 603 F. Supp. 1546 (N.D.Ill., 1985); cf. *Del Valle v. Taylor,* A2-83-148 (U.S. Dist. Ct. N.D., N.W. Div. 9-29-83), a case involving an alleged detention facility strip search by male guards of a 17-year-old who claimed to have been sexually abused by her grandfather.

35. See *Darryl H. v. Coler,* 585 F. Supp. at p. 390, stating: "There is no evidence in the record to suggest that alleged child abuse investigations are being conducted in an arbitrary manner."

36. *Supra* n. 34, Complaint ¶9(c). However, the court's opinion suggests that there is reason to question the accuracy of this claim, 603 F. Supp. at pp. 1551–1552, n. 7.

37. See Illinois Department of Children and Family Services, *Child Abuse and Neglect Investigation Decisions Handbook,* p. 66.

38. See *Darryl H. v. Coler.*

39. Ibid.

40. Some states have legislation empowering juvenile court judges to authorize a child protection search of the home: N.Y.Fam. Ct. Act §1034(2) (1984); see *In the Matter of Marcario,* 119 Misc.2d 404, 462 N.Y.S.2d 1000 (Fam. Ct., Suffolk Co., 1983).

41. There may be liability, for example, if they intentionally or negligently mislead the court; see pp. 7–8.

42. Compare *Dennison v. Vietch,* 560 F. Supp. 435 (D. Minn., 4th Div. 1983) (finding no exigent circumstances because police were given no information suggesting that the child was in immediate danger); with *People v. Sutton,* 134 Cal. Rptr. 921, 65 Cal. App. 3d 341 (1976) (approving an entry based on a report of "small children left alone").

43. See, for example, *Darryl H. v. Coler; Wisconsin v. Boggess.*

44. *Prosser and Keeton on Torts,* p. 771.

45. Ibid., p. 773. Footnotes omitted.

46. *Kaufman v. Carter,* 402 U.S. 954, 949 (1971) (Black J., dissenting from a denial of *certiorari*).

47. *Prosser and Keeton on Torts,* pp. 786 and 788.

48. Ibid., p. 797.

49. See pp. 78–79.

50. *Prosser and Keeton on Torts,* pp. 797–798. Footnotes omitted.

51. Ibid., p. 799. Footnotes omitted.

52. Ibid., p. 780. Footnotes omitted.

53. Ibid., pp. 840–841. Footnotes omitted.

54. Ibid., p. 841.

55. See pp. 99–100.

56. *Prosser and Keeton on Torts,* p. 817. Footnotes omitted. See, for example, *Black v. Sacramento Clinical Labs, Inc.,* 131 Cal. App. 2d 386, 182 Cal. Reptr. 438 (1982).

57. *Prosser and Keeton on Torts,* pp. 819–820. Footnotes omitted.

58. *Overman v. Klein,* 103 Idaho 795, 654 P.2d 888 (1982).

59. Material on file with author.

60. *Prosser and Keeton on Torts,* p. 835. Footnotes omitted.

61. R. Horowitz, "Improving the Legal Bases in Child Protective Work—Let the Worker Beware," in W. Holder and K. Hayes, eds., *Malpractice and Liability in Child Protective Services* (Longmont, Colo.: Bookmakers Guild, 1984), pp. 17, 18, and 21, quoting W. L. Prosser, *Prosser on Torts* (St. Paul, Minn.: West Publishing Co., 1971), p. 792.

62. *Johnson v. Shea, et al.,* File No. 83-1234 (Hennepin Co. Dist. Ct., 4th Judicial Dist., Minnesota, 1983), mentioned in "Court Cases Have Serious Implications," *NASW News,* 29 (February 1984), p. 21.

63. See *Whelehan v. County of Monroe,* 558 F. Supp. 1093 (W.D. N.Y. 1983).

64. Cf. *DeSpain v. Johnson,* 731 F.2d 1171 (5th Cir. 1984); *Sims v. State Department of Public Welfare of the State of Texas,* 438 F. Supp. 1179 (S.D. Tex., Houston Div. 1977), *rev'd* on abstention grounds, *sub nom.; Moore v. Sims,* 442 U.S. 415 (1979).

65. *Prosser and Keeton on Torts,* p. 194.

66. Besharov, *Proving Child Abuse,* p. 21ff.

67. Ibid., p. 43ff.

68. See *Doe v. Hennepin County,* No. 4-84-115 (U.S. Dist. Ct. Minn. 4th Div. 1984), *Family Law Reporter,* 10 (27 June 1984), p. 1504.

69. See p. 99.

70. U.S. National Center on Child Abuse and Neglect, *State Child Abuse and Neglect Laws—A Comparative Analysis* (Washington, D.C.: Department of Health and Human Services, 1983), p. 61, col. 43, Table "1980."

71. *Bohn v. County of Dakota,* No. 4-83-733 (U.S. Dist. Ct. Minn. 4th Div. 1984), *Family Law Reporter,* 10 (29 May 1984), p. 1414.

72. See D. Besharov, "Protecting Children from Abuse and Neglect: The Need to Narrow the Grounds for State Intervention," *Harvard Journal of Law and Public Policy,* 8, No. 3 (1985), p. 539.

73. American Humane Association, *Trends in Child Abuse and Neglect: A National Perspective* (Denver, Colo.: American Humane Association, 1984), p. 41, Table V-3.

74. Besides the guidelines in Chart 4-3, see Conn. Gen. Stat. Ann. § 17-38a(e) (West Supp. 1984); N.J. Stat. Ann. § 9:6-8.27 (West 1984); N.Y. Fam. Ct. Act § 1021 (1983).

75. U.S. National Center on Child Abuse and Neglect, *Child Protection: A Guide for State Legislation* (Washington, D.C.: Department of Health and Human Services, 1983), § 9(g).

76. *Hatfield v. Williams,* 376 F. Supp. 212 (N.D. Iowa 1974), on letting stand uncounseled articles of surrender.

77. See, for example, *McTeague v. Sosnowski,* 617 F.2d 1016, 1017 (3rd Cir. 1980). Compare with pp. 95–96.

78. A well-explained example of a court's refusal to grant an agency request for a child's removal is *In the Matter of Adrian J.,* 119 Misc.2d 900, 464 N.Y.S.2d 61 (Fam. Ct., Omondaga Co., 1983).

79. See *Anthony v. White,* 376 F. Supp. 567 (D. Del. 1974), where parents brought an action against a social worker seeking damages on the ground that the defendant had caused them to be illegally arrested, detained, and imprisoned for the "abduction" of their own child. A summary judgment was granted for the defendant on the ground that the social worker's action was done in "good faith" as she had relied on a state judge's advice.

80. *McGhee v. Moyer,* 60 F.R.D. 578 (W.D. Va., Roanoke Div., 1973). To succeed, a damage claim for the removal of a child under a statute subsequently found to be unconstitutional requires proof that the relevant officials acted in bad faith. Cf. *Gibson v. Ginsberg,* Civ. Action No. 78-2375 (S.D. W. Va. 1978).

81. *Morrison v. Jones,* 607 F.2d 1269 (9th Cir. 1979); apparently the violation of the court stay was inadvertent.

82. *Doe v. Hennepin County,* ⸺F. Supp. ⸺, ⸺(Dist. Ct. Minn. 1984), *Family Law Reporter,* 10 (24 July 1984), p. 1504.

83. Ibid. Emphasis added.

84. Ibid., p. 1505. Compare with *Dick v. Watonwan County,* 562 F. Supp. 1083 (D. Ct. Minn., 4th Div. 1983) *rev'd,* 738 F.2d 939 (8th Cir. 1984); cf. *Re Catholic Children's Aid Society and Pamela M.,* (1982) 36 Ontario Reports 2d 451.

85. As of 1979, the states giving child protective workers the power to remove a child without a court order were Alabama, Alaska, Arizona, Arkansas, Connecticut, Florida, Maryland, Massachusetts, Montana, New York, Texas, and Virginia, as well as American Samoa. U.S. National Center on Child Abuse and Neglect, *Child Abuse and Neglect: State Reporting Laws* (Washington, D.C.: Department of Health and Human Services, 1980), p. 24, n. 39.

86. See, for example, *Roe v. Borup,* 500 F. Supp. 127 (E.D. Wisc. 1980); *Brooks v. Richardson,* 478 F. Supp. 793 (S.D.N.Y. 1979); *Anthony v. White; LaBelle v. County of St. Lawrence,* 85 A.D.2d 759, 445 N.Y.S.2d 275 (3rd Dept., 1981); *Griffin v. Pate,* No. 70 CA1168, Div. 1, Colo. Ct. of Appeals, *Colorado Lawyer,* 11 (January 1982), p. 152; *Wayne S. v. County of Nassau,* 83 A.D.2d 628, 441 N.Y.S.2d 536 (2d Dept. 1981); *McBride v. Magnuson,* 282 Or. 433, 578 P.2d 1259 (1978); cf. *People v. Sutton,* 134 Cal. Rptr. 921, 64 Cal. App. 3d 341 (2nd Dist. 1977), approving police entry, without a warrant, into defendant's apartment to investigate report of "small children left alone." In a few states, there is absolute immunity for discretionary acts (good faith not being required); see *Tango v. Tulevech,* 61 N.Y.2d 34, 471 N.Y.S.2d 73, 459 N.E.2d 182 (1983).

87. *Griffin v. Pate,* p. 155.

88. Cf. *Doe v. Hennepin County; Mabry v. Board of County Commissioners of the County of Adams,* Civ. Action No. 82-M-2246 (1982), a pending case.

89. See N.Y. Fam. Ct. Act § 1024(a)(ii) (1983).

90. See, for example, *Wayne S. v. County of Nassau; Ehret v. New York City Department of Social Services,* a pending case.

91. See *Lossman v. Pekarske,* 707 F.2d 288 (7th Cir. 1983) (failure to notify father of emergency removal hearing).

Violating Parental Rights   **105**

92. For example, Ill. Ann. Stat. Ch.23, § 2055 (Smith-Hurd Supp. 1984); Minn. Stat. Ann. § 260.165 (1982); Utah Code Ann. § 55-10-90 (1974).

93. Ala. Code tit. 26, § 14-6 (1977) (72 hours), Ariz. Rev. Stat. § 8-546.01(D) (West Supp. 1984) (48 hours); Conn. Gen. Stat. Ann. § 17-38a(e) (West Supp. 1984) (96 hours); MD. Cts. & Jud. Proc. Code Ann. § 3-815(c) (Supp. 1977) (next court day); N.Y. Fam. Ct. Act § 1021 (McKinney 1983) (3 days).

94. U.S. National Center on Child Abuse and Neglect, *Child Protection,* at § 9(e).

95. See *Ormsby v. Blum,* No. 78-531, U.S. Dist. Ct., W.D. of N.Y. (1981), stipulation of settlement.

96. See *White v. Minter,* 330 F. Supp. 1194 (D. Mass. 1971), holding that failure to initiate a judicial review hearing, whether or not required by statute, is a violation of parental rights that creates a cause of action for damages.

97. See, for example, *Lester v. Brezenoff,* 548 F. Supp. 616 (E.D. N.Y. 1982), *aff'd without opinion,* 722 F.2d 728 (2nd Cir. 1983), an alleged failure to return child after expiration of placement order, dismissed for failure to name proper defendants; *McEntee v. N.Y. Foundling Hospital,* 194 N.Y.S.2d 269 (Supp. Ct., Kings Co. 1959).

98. *Duchesne v. Sugarman,* 566 F.2d 817, 823 (2nd Cir. 1977); *Perez v. Sugarman,* 499 F.2d 761 (2nd Cir. 1974), an earlier decision in the same litigation.

99. Ibid., pp. 823–824. Footnotes deleted.

100. The same considerations seem to have been involved in *Thorn v. New York City Department of Social Services,* 523 F. Supp. 1193 (S.D. N.Y. 1981), in which the defendants removed a child from the mother without her consent, after they had returned the child to her following three years of voluntary foster care. Cf. *Hatfield v. Williams,* uncounseled surrender.

101. See *Boone v. Wyman,* 295 F. Supp. 1143 (S.D. N.Y. 1969), *aff'd,* 412 F.2d 857 (2nd Cir. 1969).

102. See, for example, *Siereveld v. Conn.,* 557 F. Supp. 1178 (E.D. Ky., Covington Div. 1983); *Lester v. Brezenoff.*

103. "Monroe Grandparents Ask $7.5M in Damages," *Manchester Union Leader,* 6 May 1984, p. 116.

104. U.S. National Center on Child Abuse and Neglect, *National Analysis of Official Child Neglect and Abuse Reporting (1979)* (Washington, D.C.: Department of Health and Human Services, 1980), p. 38.

105. See D. Besharov, "Representing Abused and Neglected Children: When Protecting Children Means Seeking the Dismissal of Court Proceedings," *Journal of Family Law,* 20 (1982), p. 217; Besharov, *Juvenile Justice Advocacy* (New York: Practising Law Institute, 1974), Chap. 2 and § 6.4.

106. See *Walden v. Wishengrad,* 573 F. Supp. 1115 (W.D. N.Y. 1983), *aff'd* 745 F.2d 149 (2nd Cir. 1984).

107. *Prosser and Keeton on Torts,* at § 132.

108. *Imbler v. Pachtman,* 424 U.S. 409, 422-424 (1976), quoting *Pearson v. Reed,* 6 Cal. App. 2d 277, 287, 44 P.2d 592, 597 (1935). Footnote omitted.

109. *Whelehan v. County of Monroe,* 558 F. Supp. 1093, 1096 (W.D. N.Y. 1983). Footnotes omitted.

110. See, for example, *Doe v. Hennepin County; Roman v. Appleby,* 558 F. Supp. 449 (E.D. Pa. 1983); *Dick v. Watonwan County; Anthony v. White;* cf. *Madison v. Gerstein,* 440 F.2d 338 (5th Cir. 1971) (police); *Angel v. Kasson,* 581 F. Supp. 170 (N.D.N.Y. 1983) (police).

111. *Doe v. County of Suffolk,* 494 F. Supp. 179, 180, n. 1 (E.D.N.Y. 1980).

112. R. Parke, "Socialization into Child Abuse: A Social Interactional Perspective,"

J. L. Tapp and F. Levine, *Law, Justice, and the Individual in Society* (New York: Holt, Rinehart and Winston, 1977), pp. 184–185.

113. U.S. National Center on Child Abuse and Neglect, *State Child Abuse and Neglect Laws,* p. 47.

114. See pp. 32–34.

115. See D. Besharov, "Putting Central Registers to Work: Using Modern Information Management Systems to Improve Child Protective Services," *Chicago-Kent Law Review,* 54 (1978), pp. 687, 733ff.

116. Material on file with author.

117. See, for example, *Overman v. Klein; Block v. Sacramento Clinical Labs, Inc.*

118. See *Wilder v. Sugarman,* 385 F. Supp. 1013 (S.D.N.Y. 1974), in which a court order was needed for clients to gain access to records, which, they claimed, would prove a pattern of religious and racial discrimination by foster care agencies.

119. *Hanson v. Rowe,* 18 Ariz. App. 131, 500 P.2d 919 (1972). For a discussion of how this information could establish liability, see pp. 112–113.

120. Quoted in "Legal Defense Fund Aids in Test Case in Confidentiality," *NASW News,* 27 (June 1982), p. 22.

121. *Fracaro v. Priddy,* 514 F. Supp. 191, 193 (M.D.N.C., Winston-Salem Div. 1981).

122. Ibid., pp. 193–194. n. 1.

5

Inadequate Foster Care Services

The Basis of Liability

The expansion of child protective programs has led to a concomitant increase in the number of children in foster care. Each year, about 400,000 children are placed in foster care.[1] This is a sharp increase from 1960, when about 100,000 children were placed outside their homes.[2]

Many children must be placed in foster care to protect them from serious injury, and many children benefit from foster care.[3] Nevertheless, foster care has well-known hazards.[4] Over the past 20 years, hundreds of thousands of children have been left adrift in foster care, shifted from foster home to foster home with no real plan for their future. Even with recent progress, tens of thousands of children are in foster care limbo. Moreover, many children are placed in homes or institutions that are unable to meet their needs for special physical or emotional care. Worse, some children are neglected, abused, and even killed by their foster parents. Other foster children are themselves dangerous. They sometimes assault or kill their foster parents or others, and they destroy their property.

Recent years have seen a substantial increase in the number of lawsuits claiming money damages from child welfare agencies and individual workers who, it is claimed, were responsible for the serious harm suffered by a foster child, a birth parent, or a foster parent. Possible suits fall within five categories: (1) dangerous foster children, (2) dangerous foster parents, (3) failure to meet the foster child's needs for special care, (4) failure to treat foster parents, and (5) failure to arrange the foster child's adoption. There is strong reason to believe that this trend will continue—and that it will grow in momentum—as foster care services are subjected to greater public and professional scrutiny and, perhaps more importantly, as more parents and children are represented by independent legal counsel.

Alleged liability is grounded on general state law rules as well as a number of federal statutes.[5] Courts usually hold that, by assuming custody of a child—either pursuant to a court order or with the parents' consent—and by making decisions about the child's care, agencies and workers accept a degree of legal responsibility for the child's health, safety, and well-being, and for the child's behavior.[6] The imposition of liability is not automatic, of course. Courts require that the agency or worker must have violated a specific duty of care toward the child. Nevertheless, neither intentional nor negligent conduct is required when liability is alleged under state and federal statutes that impose specific duties on child welfare agencies. In addition, courts often use the failure to follow written agency procedures for the supervision of foster placements as the basis for finding an agency or worker liable.[7]

Dangerous Foster Children

Agencies and workers are often sued for the harm caused by the children they have placed.[8] For example, in *Snyder v. Mouser*, the foster mother sued to recover damages for the death of her husband, who was killed by a child placed in their home.[9] The Supreme Court of Indiana allowed the suit to proceed because the agency had failed to warn the foster parents of the child's *known* homicidal tendencies. Similarly, in *Kreuger v. Louise Wise Services*, a 16-year-old foster child allegedly killed his 18-year-old foster brother and his foster mother.[10] Lawsuits involving less serious assaults are relatively common occurrences.[11]

Foster parents and others frequently sue because a foster child has damaged or destroyed their property—usually by setting fire to it.[12] One agency sent an emotionally disturbed foster child to a summer camp for disturbed children. The child started a fire that burned the camp to the ground, and the camp sued for $100,000, claiming that it had not been informed of the girl's tendency to set fires.[13]

The child need not be violent or misbehaving to pose an actionable danger to the foster parents. Thus, in *Vaughn v. North Carolina Department of Human Resources* liability was imposed on the agency for the placement of a child because the agency knew that the foster mother intended to become pregnant and that the child suffered from a cytomegalo virus, a disease likely to cause birth defects.[14] The foster mother sued for damages when she was forced to have an abortion after contracting the virus. In another case, an agency was sued after a tubercular foster child infected two other children in the household.[15]

As the foregoing cases suggest, for liability to attach, the agency or worker must have been negligent in the placement process. That is, the agency or worker must have known (or had sufficient reason to know) that the child posed a danger to the foster parents or others and yet took no action to protect or to warn the foster parents. Thus, liability in the *Kreuger* case was predicated on the claim that the agency "knew or should have known of the [child's] prior imbalance, emotional and psychiatric problems."[16]

If, on the other hand, the plaintiff had knowledge of the danger posed by the child, whether or not that knowledge was gained from the agency, there is usually no liability. In technical legal terms, the plaintiff is considered to have "assumed the risk."

Cairl v. Minnesota is an unusual example of how prior knowledge can prevent liability. The birth parents were suing the agency for improper release of their mentally retarded and potentially dangerous son who, during a holiday visit with his family, set fire to their apartment, killing one sister and severely burning another. One of the court's reasons for dismissing the suit was that "if a duty to warn exists at all, it is a duty to warn of latent dangers. In this case, [the son] was released to his mother who was well aware of her son's history of setting fires."[17]

Social workers may also be attacked by foster children. One social worker described what happened to her while she was transporting a 14-year-old child from his foster home to court:

> [The boy] became very belligerent and was using vulgar language because I would not allow him to smoke in my car.
>
> I do not smoke and do not allow anyone to smoke in my car. [The boy] is well aware of my feelings on this, having been in my car on numerous occasions. . . .
>
> I stopped the car and warned [the boy] that if he persisted and insisted on attempting to light a cigarette, I would take his cigarettes away from him. He continued, so I took the pack of cigarettes from his hand.
>
> [The boy] then hit me twice in the face—once on my right cheekbone next to my eye resulting in slight swelling, and once on my right cheek. At this point, I started to drive and warned him that if he hit me again, I would file assault charges. He flew into a rage and his language became worse. He punched me quite hard in my right arm while I was driving on the winding, narrow road and threatened to. . .push my. . .head through the. . .windshield and other similar threats. Then he started to throw everything in my car out of the window, including my registration, insurance documents, briefcase, and some wires from under the dash.
>
> When I stopped to retrieve my possessions, he climbed out of the window and across the roof and hood of my car. While I was continuing to pick my things up from the side of the road, he forced my front, right-hand side door open and pulled it forward as far as he could, and kept pulling on it. After I told him that if he wrecked my door, he would pay for it, he forced it shut and kicked it on the outside. He stated that if he was going to have to pay for it, he would wreck it good. He challenged me to a fight and when I

didn't react he said, "If I can't do this side, I'll do the other side," and he walked around to the other side and began pulling that front door forward for a while.

By this time, I had picked up my things which he had thrown out of the window and put them in the trunk of the car. I got into the driver's seat and was able to pull the door away from him and close it. I was able to persuade him to get back into my car so that we could proceed to court.

As we were traveling along the road, he opened the door, which would only open part-way and kicked and pushed at it with his foot. I asked him to stop doing that. When he continued, I stopped the car and told him to either stop it or get out. He said, "Okay, but remember that you told me to get out." He got out and again pulled the door forward with all of his strength for several moments. I slowly drove the car forward to extricate the door from his grasp. He then took off in the direction of the foster home. I did not feel that it would be safe to attempt to get him back into my car. I had to wire the front door on the passenger side to the rear door in order to hold it even partially closed so that I could drive my car.[18]

The social worker's personal insurance policy did not cover the damage caused by the foster child. The agency eventually reimbursed her, but it took more than a year. The agency subsequently established a formal procedure for the reimbursement of employees for damages incurred in the course of employment.

The agency's failure to warn is, in general, essential to the creation of tort liability, but because most social workers employed by an agency will be familiar with a child's condition and history (or should be), they are unlikely to succeed with a claim of failure to warn. Nevertheless, there are times when a worker will have a solid reason for not knowing about a child's dangerous propensities. For example, while making a home visit, a social worker from a private treatment agency was allegedly raped at knife-point by a "mentally disturbed" youth. The court allowed her to sue the city agency that had released the youth from an institution on the ground that it had failed to warn her that the child was "prematurely" released "from confinement despite his previous mental and psychiatric condition and sexual proclivities."[19]

Dangerous Foster Parents
More often than we would like to admit, children are abused or neglected while in foster homes, shelters, or residential institutions.[20] Foster parents and institutional staff can be criminally prosecuted for such conduct,[21] and, except in states that apply the doctrine of parent-child tort immunity to substitute care situations,[22] they are also subject to civil suits for damages.[23]

A criminal prosecution is possible against the workers who placed the child or monitored the home, their supervisors, and (under certain circumstances) agency heads and directors—if there is criminal culpability. In fact, as far back as 1894, county directors of the poor were criminally prosecuted for binding a youthful pauper child to the service of a master whom they knew to be cruel and for continuing the child in the placement, where he eventually died.[24]

A civil lawsuit against the agency or staff, however, is much more likely (because criminal intent is usually lacking and because of the higher standard of proof required in criminal cases). Historically, the doctrines of charitable and governmental immunity limited potential liability.[25] However, the demise of these doctrines in most states has made claims for injuries to foster children the most active area of litigation against social workers and their agencies.[26] Furthermore, even when state law precludes liability, a suit may be brought in federal court. A number of cases hold that a foster child has a constitutional right to a safe placement.[27] One judge wrote:

> A child who is in the custody of the state and placed in foster care has a constitutional right to at least humane custodial care. . . . It would be ludicrous if the state, through its agents, could perpetrate the same evil the [foster care] sought to prevent.[28]

The foster child's injury does not, by itself, create liability. For liability to attach, the agency or the worker must have been negligent in the selection of foster parents or in the supervision of the foster placement. That is, the child's abuse or neglect must have been the reasonably foreseeable consequence of conditions the agency or worker knew about or should have known about.[29] For example, in *Bartels v. County of Westchester,* a foster child less than 3 years old was severely scalded when, it was alleged, the foster parent carelessly bathed her. The child "sustained extensive second- and third-degree burns, causing permanent scarring to 40 percent of her body, webbing of the fingers of the right hand, and a deformity known as 'clam toe.' "[30] The court explained how the agency and individual workers could be held liable for the child's burns:

> If, as has been asserted, the [county child welfare agency] knew of the incompetence of the foster parents or the indifferent discharge by them of their duties, [it] might be held liable for an ensuing injury to the child, dependent on the evidence at the trial.[31]

To avoid liability, child welfare agencies must be extremely careful in selecting foster parents. The failure to investigate homes adequately before placing the children can lead to egregious consequences:

> In the fall of 1980, . . . [a] forty-year-old former pediatric nurse, Mrs. Q, was tried for the murder of her nine-month-old son, Baby Q, who had bled to death internally from stomach punches inflicted before he was put to bed. Astonished investigators discovered an almost unbelievable history of abusive behavior which was pieced together only after the child's death. Baby Q was the fourth child *adopted*

by Mrs. Q. The first child, who lived with Mrs. Q until the trial, had been treated by a local hospital a few years earlier after an attempt to smother her was nearly successful. A second child was returned to the adoption agency after one month because Mr. Q felt he was "too dark." A third child was removed from Mrs. Q's home by a third adoption agency in August of 1980, one month before Baby Q's death, for failure to thrive (a possible indication of neglect) and symptoms of physical abuse. Her husband, who testified that he "only cared about drinking," was the initial suspect after the child's body was discovered. However, he was exonerated when hospital records proved that he had been hospitalized before Baby Q's death with a leg broken by Mrs. Q in a fit of rage. In all, Mrs. Q had been in contact with one public adoption agency, two private adoption agencies, the public welfare department from which she fraudulently collected Aid to Dependent Children, and various hospitals. Yet none of these agencies knew of her history of violent behavior until her trial and subsequent conviction for murder.[32]

In response to such cases, a number of states have passed legislation that requires agencies to screen prospective foster parents through child abuse central registers.[33]

Child welfare agencies also must monitor the quality of care provided to children by their foster parents. Agencies have an affirmative obligation to supervise foster care placements and to remove children from unsuitable or dangerous environments.[34] Adequate supervision of foster placements requires periodic home visits (during which the children are interviewed) and periodic medical examinations of the children.[35] The failure to follow written agency procedures or well-established professional standards concerning foster care supervision is often considered *prima facie* evidence of negligence.[36] A South Dakota court summed up the attitude adopted in such cases:

> Although some discretion in its literal sense is involved in foster care, social workers do not make policy decisions involving foster care placement. The criteria for placement and *standards for follow-up of foster children* are already established. Social workers are merely required to carry out or administer these previously established standards.[37]

Adequate supervision also requires that the agency be aware and responsive to reports or other indications of possible maltreatment in the foster home. The most widely known case on the subject is *Doe v. New York City Department of Social Services*. In 1964, when Anna Doe was 2 years old, she and her sister were placed in a foster home. Two more girls were placed in the same home in 1965. According to the court,

> ...the record discloses a pattern of persistent cruelty to Anna at the hands of her foster father. Anna and her foster sisters testified that starting when she was about ten years of age, she was regularly and frequently beaten and sexually abused by Senerchia [the foster father]. Plaintiff testified that he beat her with his hands and belt all over her body, threw her down the stairs, and on one

occasion lacerated her with a hunting knife, that he confined her to her room for days at a time, and ultimately forced her to have intercourse and oral sexual relations with him.[38]

A $225,000 jury verdict against the agency was sustained on the ground that the agency had inadequately monitored her 13-year foster placement. Most telling was the agency's failure to act on information strongly suggesting that Anna was being abused—which was bad practice and a violation of state law. For six months (between January and June 1975), Anna did not attend school. Her foster father claimed that he had removed Anna from school because she had

> engaged extensively in group sex with the other children at school, that this had gone on since the first grade, and had included full sexual intercourse, even between first-graders. The children's sexual congress, [he said,] took place in empty classrooms, hallways and [the] cafeteria, and occurred four or five times a day. Senerchia claimed that Anna had told him she would be forced to resume sexual activities when she returned to school, and for that reason he was enrolling Anna in a parochial school.[39]

To "assess [Anna's] learning skills and determine appropriate school placement," the agency had her seen by a psychiatrist, Dr. de Alvarado.[40]

> On March 19, [1975,] Anna met with Dr. de Alvarado, an expert in child abuse, who, based on Anna's responses and the other information she had received, concluded that Anna was sexually involved with her foster father and should be immediately removed from the foster home. That same day Dr. de Alvarado met with agency officials and "related that she felt the foster father was sexually involved" with Anna, and she should be immediately removed from the home through legal action if necessary. Dr. de Alvarado testified at the trial that Anna did not admit to having sexual relations with her father but became unresponsive and began crying when the question was asked.
>
> The Bureau responded by holding an administrative review on April 10, 1975. Present were agency administrative personnel and the case worker. It was decided that Senerchia's "involvement with Anna should be further investigated." However, no action appears to have been taken other than to have Dr. de Alvarado revise her report, *deleting the references to sexual involvement with Senerchia.* On April 14, 1975, the caseworker spoke to the truant officer, who said he thought the stories of orgies in Anna's former school were unfounded. On April 16, 1975, the principal of the school informed the caseworker that he had checked the records and found that Anna had not missed any of her classes prior to being removed from school. That day the worker called Senerchia to discuss this new information, but he said he was ill, and the meeting was put off. He was not seen until May 12, 1975, when the Bureau conducted its first home visit since December, 1974. On that visit Senerchia related to the social worker a version of Anna's sexual activity that varied greatly from what the Bureau had been told previously. Although with this additional information the

agency may have had growing reason to doubt the veracity of Senerchia's original charges, it chose not to follow or act upon Dr. de Alvarado's professional recommendation. It continued to allow Anna to remain in the foster home and neglected to file a report of suspected child abuse with the Department of Social Services as was required by state law.

On May 17, 1975, the Board of Education had Anna evaluated by one of its psychiatrists. The agency sent the Board a copy of Dr. de Alvarado's edited report from which *all references to suspected sexual abuse had been deleted.* No information was supplied about Senerchia or his problems, and the psychiatrist was not asked to, and did not investigate the possibility of Anna's sexual abuse.

In June, 1975, the agency submitted its annual report to the Department of Social Services. Neither in this report nor at other times thereafter did the Bureau inform the Department of Anna's six-month absence from school, her supposed sexual proclivities, the problems in the foster home or Dr. de Alvarado's report and recommendations, although defendant's supervisory personnel admit that it was mandated that such information be shared with the Department.[41]

For the next two years, in the face of yet further indications of serious problems in the placement, the agency took no action. "Even when Senerchia told the agency that he planned to divorce his wife to marry his pregnant, teenage girlfriend, the agency did not act. Finally, Mrs. Senerchia, distraught over the impending divorce, reported that she had seen her husband and Anna in bed together. At that point, Anna and all other foster children in the Senerchia home were removed."[42] As mentioned earlier, in the subsequent federal lawsuit, the court awarded damages of $225,000.

Similarly, in *Vonner v. State,* the Louisiana Supreme Court allowed a lawsuit against the placing agency to proceed on the basis of allegations that 3½ months before a 5-year-old was beaten to death by his foster mother, the agency had received reports that the child's two older siblings were being beaten.[43] Instead of investigating these allegations, the agency placed the two children, who had run away, in a detention facility. In *Bradford v. Davis,* the plaintiff foster child received $90,000 in settlement from the state of Oregon based on allegations that the Children's Services Division negligently failed to supervise, screen, and monitor his foster placement. One of the allegations was that the agency failed to investigate reports by neighbors that the child was being beaten.[44]

Most lawsuits claiming dangerous foster care conditions are brought in the name of individual children seeking compensation for harm done to them. But recent years have seen the emergence of class actions seeking systemwide reforms. *G. L. v. Zumwald,* for example, challenged the basic operations of the Kansas City, Missouri, foster care system.[45] The plaintiffs claimed that "the manner in which the foster care system is run violates plaintiffs' constitutional and federal statutory rights [under Title IV-B of the Social

Security Act] to appropriate care and treatment and freedom from harm."[46] As examples of the harm inflicted by the system, the plaintiffs alleged that "one five-year-old girl was repeatedly sexually abused by her foster father; a seven-year-old child was beaten by his foster mother; a three-year-old boy had been in five foster homes in three years and was becoming increasingly emotionally disturbed; and a 17-year-old girl whose white mother was living with a black man was placed with a bigoted foster mother who turned the girl against her mother and her inter-racial half-brother on racial grounds."[47] The case was settled with a consent decree that required the agency to revamp its foster care system completely. Set forth were detailed procedures concerning: licensing of foster homes; training of foster parents; proper matching of foster children with foster parents; preplacement processes and supervision of foster homes; investigations of suspected maltreatment and unsuitable care; elimination of overcrowding in foster homes; reimbursement rates; caseload size; social worker training; medical care; psychological, emotional, and educational services; permanency planning; a uniform case record system; and reporting and monitoring. In addition, the defendants agreed to pay $40,000 in attorneys' fees. As part of the consent decree, the plaintiffs withdrew their claim for money damages.

Failure to Meet the Child's Needs for Special Care

While in foster care, children are supposed to receive the treatment services that they may need to remedy the effects of past maltreatment or other special problems, but few do.[48] However, courts have been reluctant to translate this basic need into a broad constitutional "right to treatment."[49]

Courts cite the lack of incarceration or secure institutionalization as reasons why the constitution does not require appropriate services for foster children.[50] In *Sinhogar v. Parry,* for example, a New York appeals court distinguished the rights of foster children from those of juvenile delinquents and persons in need of supervision who, because they are deprived of their liberty, have a right to treatment.[51] According to the court, foster children "do not have a constitutional right to a particular kind of care from the state and what rights they do have are limited by the facilities and funds made available by the legislature."[52] (As of this writing, the few successful claims based on the constitutional rights of foster children have involved cases of alleged racial discrimination.[53])

Until recently, claims of negligent or careless provision of diagnostic or treatment services have been equally unsuccessful. Thus, one California court dismissed a complaint alleging that an agency's mistaken—and negligent—diagnosis of a foster child's mental retardation resulted in the child's placement in classes for the mentally retarded and discouraged potential adoptive parents from adopting the child, who was in foster care for almost

17 years.[54] One senses, though, the beginnings of a move away from this extreme position. A growing number of courts seem willing to consider claims of negligently provided services.[55] *Little v. Utah State Division of Family Services* illustrates this trend. A 2½-year-old autistic child, Jennifer Little, was placed in foster care because, in the words of the juvenile court's order, she was "in need of specialized assistance which the parents are emotionally unable to provide."[56] The Utah Supreme Court described what happened next:

> Family Services obtained custody and guardianship of Jennifer and placed her with therapeutic foster parents for handicapped children and children with special problems. Arrangements were made for medical and psychological treatment to begin at some future date as openings became available. Shortly after placement, the foster mother noticed that Jennifer would periodically bang her head against the floor, furniture and walls and pull out hair from her scalp. She notified the Family Services caseworker of this behavior and attempted to shield Jennifer from injury by holding her until she stopped and by keeping her away from sharp objects as much as she could. She was told by the caseworker that Jennifer definitely had problems but was never given any explanation of her autism nor instructions on remedying her behavior. No medication was prescribed and no physical shield was provided to protect the child against injury. Jennifer manifested facial bruises which were brought to the attention of the caseworker by both her foster mother and Mrs. Little, her mother. Mrs. Little was told that it was natural for children to bruise. The Orientation to Therapeutic Child Care, a workbook for child care parents distributed by Family Services to the foster parents, contained a short paragraph on autism but made no reference to head banging and other acts of self-mutilation. Family Services expected the foster parents to monitor and report unusual behavior, but provided no specific instructions.
>
> Jennifer died on June 4, 1977 of a massive hemorrhage of the right half of the brain. A post mortem examination revealed symptoms resembling the battered child syndrome. The exterior autopsy disclosed that her body was covered with bruises suffered at intervals. An interior examination revealed areas of hemorrhage scattered from the forehead to the parietal region, again of varying colorations, ergo of different ages. The medical expert concluded that the aggregate trauma sustained by Jennifer over an extended period of time was a significant contributing factor to the child's death. He was unable to attribute death to a single incident, as he could not ignore the fact "that there were various areas of injury on the same area of the body, and various stages of healing and various intensities." A police report made on the day of Jennifer's death divulged that the child was left for several hours with another foster child, a mildly retarded boy of 17 years of age, who apparently slapped her in the face when she fussed about going to the bathroom. Testimony revealed that the boy was a trusted babysitter with neighbors and had no history of aggressive behavior. No charges were ever preferred against him.[57]

The trial court found the Division of Family Services responsible for Jennifer's death and entered a judgment against it of $20,000 damages plus funeral expenses and costs. The court explained that Family Services violated its duty of care to Jennifer in the following ways:

a. Failure to adequately train Jennifer's foster parents or whoever would take care of the child when the foster parents were gone.
b. Failure to make timely evaluations of her condition to prevent potential serious harm and injury.
c. Failure to provide inexpensive headgear for her which would have reduced the risk of possible serious harm and injury.
d. Lack of proper supervision at all times as indicated by allowing the child to be left under the supervision and care of. . . , a seventeen (17) year old child who was in the custody of the. . . because of his own special problems and who slapped the child around during said care, triggering cerebral hemorrhaging that brought about Jennifer's untimely death. . . .[58]

There is also a discernible trend toward imposing liability for the violation of the state and federal statutes that create or regulate treatment services.[59] Thus, although they dismissed the constitutional claims in *Sinhogar v. Parry,* the New York courts allowed the plaintiff's statutory claims under the federal Social Security Act to go to trial.[60]

Similarly, in *Patton v. Dumpson,* the federal court allowed claims under Section 504 of the Federal Rehabilitation Act,[61] which provides in part:

No otherwise qualified handicapped individual in the United States. . .shall, solely by reason of his handicap, be excluded from the participation in, be denied the benefits of, or be subjected to discrimination under any program or activity receiving Federal financial assistance.[62]

The court explained that, under this provision, "the plaintiff, a handicapped child, is seeking to hold public and private agencies liable for damages for discrimination against him because of his handicap. The complaint alleges that, due to the plaintiff's physical and mental handicaps, agency employees denied him the benefit of educational services (while he was in foster care)."[63] Other federal courts have adopted the same position.[64]

Failure to Treat Patients

The array of treatment services now routinely available to child protective agencies—such as Parents Anonymous, homemaker care, patient aid and parent education programs, multidisciplinary treatment teams, community mental health and counseling programs, therapeutic day care, respite care and crisis nurseries, and infant stimulation programs—were largely unheard of in 1960; some had not yet been invented. These treatment services, however, are only successful with parents who are motivated or who can easily be motivated to accept help. They do not work for parents who have more serious, deeply ingrained problems.[65] Such parents require intense, sustained, and skilled casework. Based on the clinical experience of programs such as the Bowen

Center in Chicago, successful treatment of such parents requires weekly casework visits for long periods of time—often for years—combined with an array of sophisticated and expensive supportive services.[66] In fact, an evaluation of the first round of federal child abuse demonstration projects found that, to reduce "re-incidence" at all, parents must be "in treatment for at least six months" and must be seen "on a weekly basis at least during the first six months of treatment."[67]

This kind of intensive treatment is simply not available for most parents whose children are in foster care. Child protective agencies cannot provide it, because of high caseloads and deployment patterns that stress the prompt investigation of newly reported cases. The closest they come are sporadic home visits by workers who are often inexperienced. (Although there are wide variations, the average case receives four or five home visits—after which it is closed or ignored unless another report is received.)[68] Parents who need more intensive therapy are referred to other community agencies, such as mental health clinics and family service agencies. Although these agencies are increasingly willing to provide counseling and family supportive treatment to maltreating parents, without additional funding, they, too, are unable to provide the level of intensive care needed by these parents.

The lack of intensive treatment for parents is widely cited as a reason why children are removed from their parents and why they remain in foster care "limbo."[69] However, a lawsuit for the failure to provide adequate treatment services to parents is unlikely to succeed because the courts refuse to find that parents have a constitutional right to treatment.[70] In *Dixey v. Jewish Child Association,* for example, a mother sought money damages for the agency's failure to provide treatment. She claimed that the "family was deprived unlawfully of its constitutional right to remain together as a result of defendant's failure to make diligent efforts to assist, develop and encourage a meaningful relationship between plaintiff and her child as required by New York law."[71] Indeed, as quoted by the federal court, the family court judge had found that: "Although several caseworkers were involved with this mother, there was a total lack of coordination in their efforts. Hardly the kind of diligent effort that the Agency is legally required to make in order to promote the parent-child relationship."[72] Nevertheless, the federal court refused to allow the parents to proceed with their lawsuit. First, it found that "deliberate indifference to the plaintiffs' constitutional rights" had not been alleged.[73] Second, the court held that even if agency actions contributed to the child's remaining in foster care, parents "do not have a constitutional right to rely on an agency to strengthen and reunite their families even if that agency has a statutory duty to do so."[74] Such decisions probably reflect an underlying judicial recognition that funds for treatment services are limited, and that a court order cannot achieve the major expansion of services needed to realize a parent's "right to treatment."

Judges respond differently, however, when they conclude that the failure to provide appropriate treatment services was caused by poor judgment or negligent administration rather than lack of funds. This apparently happened in *Cameron v. Montgomery County Child Welfare Services.*[75] The foster child, as plaintiff, alleged that "the agency which placed the child in foster care pursuant to a (court's) dependency finding had: prevented parental visitation; failed to provide any services to the mother which were designed to facilitate the child's speedy return home; transferred the child to another foster home fifty miles from the mother's residence; and had not informed the child of his right to counsel or to a placement review."[76] After the federal court refused to dismiss the suit, the case was settled when the defendants agreed to pay $5,000.

Similarly, in *Burgos v. Department of Children and Family Services,* Spanish-speaking parents (with limited ability to speak English) claimed that their constitutional rights were violated by the agency's failure to have Spanish-speaking caseworkers and foster parents. (It is hard to see how *any* service could have been provided if agency personnel could not communicate with their clients.) After the federal court recognized the potential validity of the parents' claim, the case was settled based on a "consent order setting forth specific time frames in which the state was to review each Hispanic case to insure that each such child's and family's rights were protected."[77]

Social workers and agency officials are sometimes held in contempt for failing to comply with a trial court judge's dispositional order. In one Kansas case, the judge found the Secretary of Social and Rehabilitative Services in contempt of court for failing to obey its order "to hold a joint meeting [between agency staff and the mother] to openly exchange views and attempt to arrive at a plan for the natural mother to follow."[78] A meeting had, indeed, been held; but at that meeting an agency representative had advised the mother that "the agency's goal was permanent placement of the children with someone other than the mother."[79] The Supreme Court of Kansas reversed the order because of procedural deficiencies: the Secretary had not received personal notice of the proceeding at which he was to be held in contempt.

A recent class action in a Massachusetts federal court suggests another approach that future suits for money damages may follow. In *Lynch v. King,*[80] a group of parents and foster parents alleged that Massachusetts state officials, including employees of the Department of Social Services, had violated their right to family integrity through the administration of the state's child welfare system. The complaint claimed that the defendants failed to comply with the due process guarantee of the U.S. Constitution, provisions of the Social Security Act, and regulations requiring service plans and in-home services where possible (Aid to Families with Dependent Children–Foster Care Program).[81] Specifically, the complaint alleged that, among other things, the defendants: (1) failed to provide ongoing staff training programs; (2) failed to complete a full evaluation of every child referred to foster care; (3) failed to develop and periodically review a service plan for each case; (4) failed to assign a worker to each case; and (5) failed to maintain contact between the child and his or her family.

The district court affirmed the plaintiffs' cause of action relating to the agency's alleged violation of federal law by its failure to develop and periodically review service plans to determine when children could be returned to their parents. In what many predict could be an opinion of far-reaching consequences, the district court issued a preliminary injunction requiring that, in order for Massachusetts to continue to receive federal funds under Title IV-E of the Social Security Act, it must, among other things:

- provide written case plans for children in care within 60 days of assuming responsibility for providing services or placing the children;
- provide a periodic review meeting for each child in care; and
- limit the social worker caseloads so that they can "fulfill their obligations...to provide case plans and periodic reviews."[82]

In 1983, the district court's decision was affirmed by the First Circuit Court of Appeals.[83] Thereafter, in a related state court case, the Department entered into a settlement agreement that

contains goals and minimum requirements for workload control, social worker and foster parent training, health care, and attention to the needs of ethnic and language minorities. It also requires [sharing] of information with [the plaintiffs for monitoring purposes]... and provides for a Professional Advisory Committee and full-time Monitor. But the single most important provision, according to Associate Director Helen Patterson [of the plaintiff Massachusetts Committee for Children and Youth] is the staff ratio requirement which mandates no more than three ongoing investigations and no more than eighteen other protective service cases per social worker.[84]

Failure to Arrange the Child's Adoption

In theory, foster care is a short-term remedy—to protect children from harm while parents have time to respond to treatment or until the child can be freed for adoption—but the reality is far different. More than 50 percent of children in foster care are in this "temporary" status for over two years; over 30 percent are away from their parents for over six years.[85] As the U.S. Supreme Court has recognized, these children are lost in the "limbo" of the foster care system.[86]

Long-term foster care can leave lasting psychological scars. Foster care is an emotionally jarring experience; it confuses young children and unsettles older ones.[87] Over a long period, it can be irreparable damage to the bond of affection and commitment between parent and child. The period of separation may so completely tear the fragile family fabric that the parents have no chance of being able to cope with the child when he or she is returned. Furthermore, children who stay in foster care for more than a short time (especially if they are older) tend to be shifted through a sequence of ill-suited foster homes—a situation that denies them the consistent support and nurturing that they so desperately need.[88] Increasingly, the graduates of the foster care system evidence such severe emotional and behavioral problems that some thoughtful observers believe that foster care is often more harmful than the original home situation might have been.[89]

Some children cannot be returned to their parents, either because their parents do not want them or because their parents cannot care properly for them. The inability to identify such children and to move promptly to arrange for their adoption is a major reason why so many children remain in foster care limbo.[90]

Until now, at least, courts have been unwilling to hold that children in foster care have a constitutional right to be adopted.[91] But, as in the case of liability for failing to provide services to a foster child,[92] if the failure to arrange an adoption was caused by racial discrimination, potential liability is established.[93]

Negligence in failing to arrange a child's adoption can create liability under state tort law. In *Bradford v. Davis,* a 17-year-old child filed suit claiming that "the agency had failed to take reasonable actions to find [him] an adoptive home."[94] The child had been placed in foster care shortly before his fourth birthday, and his parents had signed adoptive release forms when he was eight. The Oregon court allowed the case to proceed to trial. Before the trial, the case was settled for $90,000.[95] In a similar situation, however, a California court dismissed the lawsuit. In *Smith v. Alameda County Social Services Agency,* another 17-year-old sought damages from a public child welfare agency for its failure to take reasonable action to bring about his adoption. This child had been in custody since shortly after his birth, when "his mother relinquished him to the custody of the agency for the purpose of adoption."[96] The court held that the alleged neglect was not actionable, because, among other things, the failure to arrange for the child's adoption did not create reasonably foreseeable harm. In a passage that many might find to be an inaccurate description of foster care realities, the court stated:

> We may take it for granted that, other things being equal, adoption is a desirable goal and it is preferable to have a child reared by a single set of parents rather than a succession of foster parents. But it does not follow that a foster child will probably or necessarily suffer greater emotional or developmental or other damage than an adopted one. This is especially so where a child receives competent and stable foster care. (A claim of inadequate foster care would present different problems not embraced by this litigation.)[97]

The Vulnerable Social Worker

To reduce the number of children caught in foster care limbo, the federal government and most states have adopted specific requirements concerning individual case plans, periodic case reviews, appropriate staffing, and other administrative safeguards.[98] *Joseph and Josephine A. v. New Mexico Department of Social Services* illustrates how the violation of these federal requirements opens another line of potential liability for failure to arrange for an adoption.

> Joseph and Josephine A., a seven- and eight-year-old brother and sister, have been in the custody of the local social services department since they were six months and one-and-a-half years old, respectively, when the court took them from their mother because of severe abuse. Their mother lives in another state, where another of her childen had died under unexplained circumstances. She has not seen Joseph or Josephine for a five-year period and legal grounds exist to terminate her parental rights. In seven years Joseph and Josephine have not been freed for adoption, nor have they ever been referred for adoption.[99]

The complaint, filed by the ACLU's Children's Rights Project, "alleged that the defendants have failed and refused to establish procedures to determine whether children should continue in foster care, whether the rights of the biological parents should be terminated or whether a child should be placed for adoption. It [was] also alleged that the Department [did] not even have an accurate count of the children in their custody."[100] Although the court did not find a "constitutional right to a permanent, stable adoptive home," it nevertheless held that "monetary relief for [violations of Titles IV and XX of the Social Security Act] is available in an action brought under 42 U.S.C. § 1983...."[101] Thus, the absence of periodic case reviews and other administrative safeguards required by federal law can be another basis for liability.[102]

After the court decision in *Joseph and Josephine A.,* a consent decree was entered with the following requirements:

- permanent plans must be developed for foster children within six months after the child enters care;
- "permanent foster care" must be eliminated as a category of permanent plans considered appropriate;
- case plans must include highly specific recommendations and timetables;
- caseloads must be limited to no more than 20 cases per worker;
- child welfare workers and supervisors must meet more stringent qualifications;
- extensive training programs must be provided for child welfare workers and supervisors;
- detailed guidelines for enhancing children's opportunities for adoption must be followed;
- Detailed, computerized information and tracking systems must be implemented;
- Citizen review boards must be formed to monitor the progress of foster children and have access to their case files.

In addition to these specific substantive requirements, to ensure adequate implementation of its provisions, the decree provides for hiring a compliance monitor and for the court retaining jurisdiction of the action for five years.[103]

State law also provides a possible cause of action for the failure to have adequate permanency planning procedures. *Matter of P.,* another ACLU case, was heard in Kentucky state courts:

> The court removed Michael and Michelle P. from their father's and stepmother's home because the children were afraid to go home and their stepmother had made it clear that she did not want the children. Very shortly thereafter the children's father surrendered them for adoption; their natural mother's whereabouts had long been unknown. These children, four and seven years old when they became the responsibility of the local social service department, were subjected to delays, administrative mishaps, and continuing evaluations for almost two years rather than being placed for adoption.[104]

After class action status was granted, the parties entered into a consent judgment that required the Department of Human Resources to comply with "stringent, mandated time periods and procedures to facilitate and expedite adoption for children in the Department's custody."[105] The department was also required "to report to the ACLU and County Attorney on a quarterly basis concerning many details of its operations," and to provide for "community review of individual cases."[106]

Social workers should find such cases heartening for two reasons. First, although they usually begin with a claim for money damages from the individuals involved, the damage claim is usually withdrawn as part of the settlement. Second, such consent decrees often result in improved services for children and families, although the process can be long and agonizing.[107] In the P. case, for example, the department was later held in contempt of court for its failure to implement the conditions of the consent judgment.[108]

Notes

1. There is great controversy over the exact number of children in foster care at any one time, with estimates varying from 200,000 to 500,000. Cf. U.S. Children's Bureau, *Child Welfare Research Notes #1* (Washington, D.C.: Department of Health and Human Services, 1983); with U.S. Children's Bureau, *National Study of Social Services to Children and Their Families* (Washington, D.C.: Department of Health, Education and Welfare, 1978), p. 109 and p. 117, Tables 5-3.

2. U.S. Children's Bureau, *Juvenile Court Statistics* (Washington, D.C.: Department of Health, Education and Welfare, 1966), p. 13.

3. See, for example, D. Fanshel and E. Shinn, *Children in Foster Care: A Longitudinal Investigation* (New York: Columbia University Press, 1978).

4. See L. Murray, "A Review of Selected Foster Care—Adoption Research from 1978 to Mid-1982," *Child Welfare*, 63 (March–April 1984), p. 113.

5. See Annotation, "Governmental Tort Liability for Social Service Agency's Negligence in Placement, or Supervision After Placement, of Children," *American Law Reports 3d*, 90 (1979), p. 1214; S. Donnella, "Safe Foster Care: A Constitutional Mandate," *Family Law Quarterly*, 19 (Spring 1985), p. 81; M. Kieffer, "Child Abuse in Foster Homes: A Rationale for Pursuing Causes of Action Against the Placement Agency," *Saint Louis University Law Review*, 28 (1984), p. 975; Opinion of Attorney General of Alaska, "Liability in the Context of Foster Care," 1977 Op (Inf.) Atty. Gen., 11 October 1977.

6. Even the arrest of the parents may raise the possibility of liability for inadequate placement of the child. See *White v. Rochford*, 592 F.2d 381 (7th Cir. 1979), allowing a lawsuit against police officers who, upon arresting the children's uncle (who had custody of the children), allegedly left the children without adult supervision in an automobile on the side of the road on a cold evening.

7. See, for example, *Doe v. New York City Department of Social Services*, 649 F.2d 134 (2nd Cir. 1981) and 709 F.2d 782 (2nd Cir. 1983), *cert. denied*, 104 S.Ct. 195 (1983); *Vonner v. State*, 273 So.2d 252 (La. 1973).

8. Annotation, "Governmental Tort Liability."

9. 149 Ind. App. 334, 272 N.E.2d 627 (1971).

10. N.Y.Sup.Ct., #83-13467; *National Law Journal*, 29 August 1983, p. 17, col. 1.

11. See, for example, *Johnson v. State*, 69 Cal.2d 782, 73 Cal. Rptr. 240, 447 P.2d 352 (1968); *Staruck v. County of Ostego*, 285 App.Div. 476, 138 N.Y.S. 2d 385 (1955), *move for leave to appeal denied*, 309 N.Y. 1032, 130 N.E.2d 749 (1955).

12. See *Seavy v. State*, 21 A.D.2d 445, 250 N.Y.S.2d 877 (1964), *aff'd* 17 N.Y.2d 675, 269 N.Y.S.2d 455, 216 N.E.2d 613 (1966).

13. Material on file with author.

14. 296 N.C. 683, 252 S.E.2d 792 (1979).

15. *Marsh v. Brooklyn Bureau of Community Services*, New York Law Journal, 12 July 1983, p. 12, col. 5 (Kings Co. Sup. Ct.).

16. *National Law Journal*, p. 17.

17. 323 N.W.2d 20, 26 (Minn. 1982).

18. Material on file with author.

19. *Davidowitz v. City of New York*, No. 13024/82, *Family Law Reporter*, 9 (30 November 1982), p. 2139 (Queens Co. Sup. Ct. 1982).

20. See U.S. National Center on Child Abuse and Neglect, *Preventing Child Abuse and Neglect: A Guide for Staff in Residential Institutions* (Washington, D.C.: Department of Health and Human Services, 1980); *Child Abuse and Neglect in Residential Institutions: Selected Readings on Prevention, Investigation and Correction* (Washington, D.C.: Department of Health, Education and Welfare, 1978).

21. See *Regina v. Isaac*, (1979) 48 C.C.C. (2d), 481 (Y.T.C.A.); "Foster Mother Guilty of Killing Boy," *Newsday*, 27 April 1979, p. 7.

22. See, generally, Annotation, "Liability of Parent for Injury to Unemancipated Child Caused by Parent's Negligence—Modern Cases," *American Law Reports 4th*, 6 (1981), p. 1066.

23. See, for example, *Zalak v. Carroll*, 15 N.Y. 2d 753, 257 N.Y.S.2d 177, 205 N.E.2d 313 (1965) ("Even without compensation, when defendants undertook to control a young child and provide care for her, they became responsible for her injury through their negligence."); *Goller v. White*, 20 Wisc. 2d 402, 122 N.W.2d 193 (1963); cf. *New Jersey Property Liability Insurance Guaranty Association v. State of New Jersey*, 195 N.J.

Super. 4, 477 A.2d 826 (1984) (seeking to disclaim insurance coverage); *Merchants Mutual Insurance Company v. Hoffman,* 56 N.Y.2d 799, 452 N.Y.S.2d 398, 437 N.E.2d 1155 (1982) (seeking to disclaim insurance coverage); *contra Mayberry v. Pryor,* 134 Mich. App. 826, 352 N.W.2d 322 (1984) (holding that Michigan parental immunity rule applies to foster parents); *Headrick v. Tennessee,* slip opinion, 5 October 1984 (Ct. of App., Knoxville) (foster parents, as state employees, are immune to liability).

24. *Commonwealth v. Coyle,* 160 Pa. St. 36, 28 A.634 (1894).

25. See, for example, *Headrick v. Tennessee; Boyd v. Norris,* 107 Wisc. 2d 747, 322 N.W. 700 (1982).

26. See, for example, *Doe v. New York City Department of Social Services; Brooks v. Richardson,* 478 F. Supp. 793 (S.D.N.Y. 1979); *National Bank of South Dakota v. Leir,* 325 N.W.2d 845 (S.D. 1982); *Andrews v. County of Ostego,* 112 Misc.2d 37, 446 N.Y.S.2d 169 (Sup. Ct. Ostego Co. 1982); *Bradford v. Davis,* 290 Or. 855,626 P.2d 1376 (1981); *Bartels v. County of Westchester,* 76 A.D.2d 517, 429 N.Y.S. 2d 906 (2nd Dept. 1980); *Koepf v. County of York,* 198 Neb. 67, 251 N.W.2d 866 (1977); *Vonner v. State; Hanson v. Rowe,* 18 Ariz. App. 131, 500 P.2d 916 (1972); *Elton v. County of Orange,* 3 Cal.App.3d 1053, 84 Cal. Rptr. 27 (Ct. of App. 1970); *Fox v. Mission of Immaculate Virgin for Protection of Homeless and Destitute Children,* 202 Misc. 478, 119 N.Y.S.2d 14 (Sup. Ct. Kings Co. 1952), *rev'd* 285 App. Div. 898, 138 N.Y.S.2d 17 (2nd Dept. 1955); *Cf. Chancellor v. Lawrence,* slip opinion #78-C-4496 (U.S.D. Ct. N.D. of Ill., E. Div., 9 July 1982); *Morales v. Turman,* 364 F. Supp. 166 (E.D. Tx., Sherman Div., 1973); *Davis v. St. Joseph's Children's Services,* 99 A.D. 2d 960, 472 N.Y.S.2d 655 (1st Dept. 1984); *M. v. State,* 649 P.2d 425 (Mont. 1982); *Parker v. St. Christopher's Home,* 77 A.D.2d 921, 431 N.Y.S.2d 110 (2nd Dept. 1980); *Walker v. State,* 104 Misc.2d 221, 428 N.Y.S.2d 188 (Ct. of Claims 1980); *Pickett v. Washington County,* 31 Or. App. 1263, 572 P.2d 1070 (1977). See, generally, Annotation, "Governmental Tort Liability"; Donnella, "Safe Foster Care"; Kieffer, "Child Abuse in Foster Homes."

27. See Donnella, "Safe Foster Care"; Kieffer, "Child Abuse in Foster Homes."

28. *Brooks v. Richardson,* 478 F. Supp. 793, 795–796 (S.D.N.Y. 1979).

29. See *Parker v. St. Christopher's Home* (no liability when foster child accidentally knocked over a cup of coffee and spilled it on herself).

30. *Bartels v. County of Westerchester,* 429 N.Y.S.2d 908.

31. Ibid., p. 909.

32. U.S. National Center on Child Abuse and Neglect, *Impact of Federal Law on Provision of Child Protective and Related Services* (Washington, D.C.: Department of Health and Human Services, 1981), pp. 2–3. Emphasis added. See also *Hanson v. Rowe.*

33. Dist. of Col. Bill No. 4-164, 2 March 1981, reported in *Family Law Reporter,* 8 (3 August 1982), p. 2567.

34. See, for example, *Gill v. Smith,* 86 Misc.2d 428, 382 N.Y.S.2d 626 (Sup. Ct. N.Y. Co. 1976); *In the Matter of Adoption of Doe,* 74 Wash. 2d 396,444 P.2d 800 (1968).

35. See *Vonner v. State.*

36. See *Doe v. New York City Department of Social Services.*

37. *National Bank of South Dakota v. Leir,* 325 N.W.2d 850. Emphasis added.

38. *Doe v. New York City Department of Social Services,* 649 F.2d 137.

39. Ibid., p. 138.

40. Ibid., p. 139.

41. Ibid., p. 139. Emphasis added.

42. Kieffer, "Child Abuse in Foster Homes," p. 985. Footnotes omitted.

43. *Supra* n. 7.

44. See *supra* n. 26. For reviews of this case, see National Center for Youth Law,

Youth Law News, 2, No. 6 (1982), p. 5; *Clearinghouse Review,* 15 (July 1981), p. 288.

45. *G.L. By and Through Shull v. Zumwald,* 564 F. Supp. 1030 (W.D. Mo., W.D., 1983).

46. American Civil Liberties Union, "The Children's Rights Project: A Report on the First Three Years" (New York: ACLU, 1982), p. 21. (Photocopied.)

47. Ibid.

48. See U.S. Children's Bureau, *National Study of Social Services to Children and Their Families;* Children's Defense Fund, *Children Without Homes: An Examination of Public Responsibility to Children in Out-of-Home Care* (Washington, D.C.: Children's Defense Fund, 1978).

49. See P. Piersma et al., "Right to Treatment," in *Law and Tactics in Juvenile Cases,* 3d ed. (Philadelphia: American Law Institute–American Bar Association, 1977), Chap. 23.

50. See, for example, *Nelson v. Heyne,* 491 F.2d 352 (7th Cir. 1974) (right to treatment of juvenile delinquents); *Medly v. Ginsberg,* 492 F. Supp. 1294 (S.D. W.Va., Charleston Div. 1980) (right to treatment of mentally retarded children); *Wyatt v. Stickney,* 325 F. Supp. 781 (M.D.A1. N.D. 1971) (right to treatment of mental patients).

51. 74 A.D.2d 204, 427 N.Y.S.2d 216, 227 (1st Dept. 1980), *aff'd* 53 N.Y.2d 424, 442 N.Y.S.2d 438, 425 N.E.2d 826 (1981).

52. 427 N.Y.S.2d at p. 223, citing, among others, *Black v. Beame,* 419 F. Supp. 599 (S.D.N.Y. 1976), and *Child v. Beame,* 412 F. Supp. 593 (S.D.N.Y. 1976).

53. See, for example, *Gary W. v. Louisiana,* 437 F. Supp. 1209 (E.D. La. 1976); 429 F. Supp. 711 (1977); 441 F. Supp. 1121 (1977); 622 F.2d 804 (5th Cir. 1980); *Wilder v. Sugarman,* 385 F. Supp. 1013 (S.D. N.Y. 1974); see, generally, M. Davidson, "Civil Rights and Child Welfare" (Paper presented at the National Symposium of the National Association of Social Workers, Washington, D.C., 20 November 1983).

54. *Smith v. Alameda County Social Services Agency,* 90 Cal.App.3rd 929, 940, 153 Cal. Rptr. 712, 718 (1st Dist. Ct. of App. 1979). See also *Torres v. Little Flower Children's Services,* 64 N.Y.2d. 119, 485 N.Y.S.2d 15, 474 N.E.2d 223 (1984).

55. See *James H. v. State Department of Mental Health and Mental Retardation,* 1 Ohio App.3d 60, 439 N.E.2d 437 (1980); cf. *B.M. v. State,* 649 P.2d 425 (Mont. 1982).

56. 667 P.2d 49 (1983).

57. Ibid., p. 49–50.

58. Ibid., p. 53.

59. See pp. 120–121 and 123–124.

60. *Supra* n. 51.

61. 498 F. Supp. 933 (S.D. N.Y. 1980).

62. 29 U.S.C. Section 794.

63. *Patton v. Dumpson,* 498 F. Supp. 936.

64. See, for example, *Timmy S. v. Stumbo,* 537 F. Supp. 39 (E.D. Ky., London Div. 1981); *Bobby D. v. Barry,* C.A. No. Misc. 16–77 (D.C. Superior Ct., 18 August 1980).

65. See, generally, N. Polansky et al., *Damaged Mothers: An Anatomy of Child Neglect* (Chicago: University of Chicago Press, 1981), p. 39.

66. M. Sullivan, M. Spasser, and G. L. Penner, *Bowen Center Project for Abused and Neglected Children* (Washington, D.C.: U.S. Public Services Administration, Department of Health, Education and Welfare, 1977).

67. U.S. Department of Health, Education and Welfare, *Evaluation of Child Abuse and Neglect Demonstration Projects, 1974–1977* (Washington, D.C.: Government Printing Office, 1978), Vols. I and II, p. 123.

68. See p. 134.

69. See, for example, Children's Defense Fund, *Children Without Homes.*
70. See *Black v. Beame,* 419 F. Supp. 599 (S.D. N.Y. 1976), *aff'd* 550 F.2d 815 (2nd Cir. 1977); but see *McTeague v. Sosnowski,* 617 F.2d 1016 (3rd Cir. 1980).
71. 522 F. Supp. 913, 915 (S.D. N.Y. 1981).
72. Ibid.
73. Ibid., pp. 915–916.
74. Ibid., p. 916.
75. 471 F. Supp. 761 (E.D. Pa. 1979).
76. R. Horowitz and H. Davidson, "Improving the Legal Response of Child Protective Agencies," *Vermont Law Review,* 6 (1981), pp. 381, 388.
77. 75 C3974 (N.D. Ill. 1976), *Family Law Reporter,* 2 (1976), p. 2185, described in M. L. Leahy and M. Barnes, "Private Social Welfare Agencies: Legal Liabilities Facing Employees," *Public Welfare,* 35 (Fall 1977), p. 42.
78. *In re Seelke,* 235 Kan. 468, 680 P.2d 288, 289 (1984).
79. Ibid., p. 289.
80. 550 F. Supp. 325 (D. Mass. 1982), *aff'd sub nom., Lynch v. Dukakis,* 719 F.2d 504 (1st Cir. 1983).
81. 42 U.S.C. Sections 608, 625, and 45 C.F.R. Section 220.1 et seq.
82. 550 F. Supp. at 356. The court went on to hold that compliance would be rebuttably presumed if the agency maintained an "average ratio, in each DSS area, of twenty 'generic' or 'mixed' cases per caseworker."
83. See *supra* n. 80.
84. A. Bussiere, "Sweeping Settlement in Massachusetts Foster Care System," *Youth Law News,* 5 (November–December 1984), p. 10.
85. U.S. Children's Bureau, *National Study of Social Services to Children and Their Families,* p. 120.
86. *Smith v. Organization of Foster Parents,* 431 U.S. 816, 833–838 (1977).
87. See E. Weinstein, *The Self-Image of the Foster Child* (New York: Russell Sage Foundation, 1960).
88. U.S. Children's Bureau, *National Study of Social Services to Children and Their Families,* pp. 117–118, Table 5–4.
89. See J. Goldstein, A. Freud, and A. Solnit, *Before the Best Interests of the Child* (New York: Free Press, 1979), p. 13.
90. See, generally, Children's Defense Fund, *Children Without Homes.*
91. See *Child v. Beame.*
92. See *supra,* n. 53.
93. See *Child v. Beame,* and *"Child" v. Beame,* 425 F. Supp. 194 (S.D. N.Y. 1977) (finding that the plaintiffs failed to prove a pattern of racial discrimination).
94. 290 Or. 855, 626 P.2d 1376, 1378 (1981).
95. R. Walker, "Abused Foster Child Sues State Agency, Obtains Damages," *Youth Law News,* 2 (October 1982), p. 5.
96. 90 Cal. App. 3d 929, 153 Cal. Rptr. 712, 714 (1st Dist. Ct. of App. 1979).
97. Ibid., p. 716.
98. See M. Hardin, ed., *Foster Children in the Courts* (Austin, Tex.: Butterworth Legal Publishers, 1983), especially Chaps. 5, 6, 9, 18.
99. M. Lowry, "Legal Strategies to Facilitate Adoption of Children in Foster Care," in Hardin, ed., *Foster Children in the Courts,* p. 264.
100. *Family Law Reporter,* 8 (4 January 1982), p. 2188 (U.S. Dist. Ct., N.M. 1982).
101. Ibid., p. 2190.
102. See *Lipp v. Henry,* CA No. F. 80-245 (N.D. Ind., 28 May 1981) (certifying

a class of foster children with respect to the claim that the defendant child welfare agency failed to develop "written standards for the creation of individual service plans"). See, generally, Lowry, "Legal Strategies"; A. English, "Litigating Under the Adoption Assistance and Child Welfare Act of 1980," in Hardin, ed., *Foster Children in the Courts,* p. 612.

103. A. English, "Federal Courts Issue Important Orders In Two Major Foster Care Cases," *Youth Law News,* 5 (January–February 1984), pp. 6–8.

104. Lowry, "Legal Strategies," p. 264.

105. American Civil Liberties Union, "The Children's Rights Project," p. 5.

106. Ibid., pp. 30–31.

107. For a description of the difficulties in implementing one consent agreement, see P. J. Johnson and B. J. Fried, "Implementation Dilemmas in North Carolina's Willie M. Program," *Child Welfare,* 63 (September–October 1984), p. 419.

108. *Family Law Reporter,* 11 (23 April 1985), p. 1299.

6

Blaming Social Workers: The Wrong Social Policy

Liability as an Avenue for Reform?

Extreme cases of parental brutality and neglect make society anxious to do something to protect endangered children. Child protective proceedings are confidential, and relatively few of these cases reach the news media. But enough do so that all communities have had their share of news stories about children who have been mercilessly beaten, cooked in boiling hot water, sexually brutalized, or left in locked closets to die—*after* having been reported to the authorities. Until recently, such horror stories were seen as evidence of inadequate staffing and poor administrative procedures; as a result, they often sparked major administrative and legislative reforms.

  In New York State, for example, complacency over the plight of maltreated children came to an abrupt end in 1969, when the brutal murder of a young girl gained intensive media publicity. For more than a month, New York City newspapers ran numerous front-page stories about Roxanne Felumero's death and the tragic mistakes that made it possible.[1] After repeated beatings, Roxanne had been removed from her parents, who were drug addicts. Subsequently, in the face of clear evidence that her parents were extremely disturbed individuals, Roxanne was returned home—where the beatings resumed. Because agency follow-up was so poor, no one noticed the bruises all over Roxanne's body. Eventually, Roxanne died from these beatings, and her parents dumped her body into the East River. A subsequent investigation performed by the judicial authorities found that: "If the Family Court and the complex of public and private agencies operating within it had functioned more effectively, Roxanne Felumero would probably not have met her tragic death."[2] As a result of the attention this one case received, the New York State Legislature completely revamped the state's child protective system.[3]

It has become increasingly difficult, however, for the public—and politicians—to see inadequate funding as the main reason for such failures of protection. Twenty years of effort have resulted in an enormous expansion of child protective programs. With about 400,000 families under the supervision of child protective agencies and about 400,000 children placed in foster care because their home situations were deemed dangerous or otherwise unsatisfactory,[4] there has been a growing tendency to blame the child's subsequent maltreatment on the agency's or caseworker's inadequate or improper performance. Hence, the lawsuits recounted in this book.

> [T]he more bizarre or sensational the child trauma may be the more likely repercussion will occur. Fatalities, serious physical injury, torture or sexual abuse stimulate feelings of repulsion, anger and revenge. Someone has to answer. If agencies have had any previous knowledge of the child then the potential for litigation is great. In these circumstances there will more likely be a media hype which fans community emotion and affects community politics.[5]

After reading the preceding chapters, no one could reasonably deny that social workers and their agencies are often guilty of egregious and inexcusable malpractice. A 1977 official investigation of child abuse deaths in Massachusetts, mirroring findings made in state after state, concluded that "the murder and dismemberment of a two year old girl and the permanent physical and emotional maiming of a four year old boy were. . .'a direct result of institutional ineffectiveness and individual error.' "[6]

Our's is commonly called the most litigious society on earth. Whether or not this is so, it is true that we believe that people who have been harmed through carelessness or negligence have a right to sue for damages. We also believe that such suits serve as a deterrent to all sorts of wrongdoing—including professional malpractice. Thus, liability becomes the avenue for needed systemic reform. As one would expect, this is an argument often made by lawyers. Richard Levine, for one, writes that " 'malpractice' actions seeking compensatory and punitive damages from child care professionals who seriously breach their personal responsibilities can be the awaited catalyst to 'systemic' change."[7] Seeing great benefits to using the tort law to hold professionals accountable and thus to improve the quality of services they provide, some observers have gone further, arguing that notions of fault and negligence should be discarded, and that professional services should be held to the same standard of strict liability as are consumer goods.[8]

So deep-seated is this view of the beneficial effects of liability that it is shared by many social workers. Leroy Schultz, a social work professor at the University of West Virginia, has written: "For the aggrieved client, an immovable social service agency must be challenged in his 'court of last resort.' Thus, court test cases, while destructive of a worker or two, have benefit for all future children, and in some cases, for other workers as well."[9]

Many social workers, deeply concerned about the rights and well-being of their clients, have turned, in frustration, to litigation as the only way to protect their clients. José Nazario, a social worker with Mobilization for Youth Legal Services in New York City, was active on the plaintiff's side of *Doe v. New York City Department of Social Services,* a case that resulted in an award of $225,000 for physical and sexual abuse in foster care.[10] "The importance of such a cash award, says Nazario, is that agencies anxious to avoid similar penalties will institute better monitoring in the future and provide better ongoing service after placement of a child in foster care." Nazario is willing to sue agencies on behalf of his clients because, frequently, "The only language they understand is, 'I'll see you in court.' "[11]

Fear of liability undoubtedly has some beneficial effect on professional behavior. One psychiatrist concluded that malpractice suits have prompted professionals "to question their own competency to do the things we are licensed to do. The prevailing atmosphere has, perhaps, pushed more private practitioners to attend professional meetings than ever before and has forced us into a greater realization of our responsibilities as professional people."[12] Perhaps so, but it is hard to identify more concrete improvements in services that result. The *Doe* case, for example, has had no real impact on New York's foster care system. Other factors, such as the level of funding, the degree of political interest, and the quality of state and local administrative leadership, shape the system and determine its effectiveness.

The little empirical research that there is on the effects of social worker liability focuses on the impact of the *Tarasoff* decision.[13] Although far from definitive, the research suggests that therapists make "more careful and deliberate attempts to predict patient violence."[14] But the research suggests substantial negative effects as well; therapists seem to respond by adopting defensive practices that "may injure psychotherapy."[15] Research on the effects of medical malpractice liability is more extensive, although it is also not definitive. The research, too, suggests the same mixture of beneficial and adverse effects.[16]

Few would deny that social workers should be held accountable for careless or slothful conduct. Everyone should be deeply troubled, for example, when a child dies because a worker overlooked or ignored signals of great —and obvious—danger. Civil and criminal liability might well deter the most egregious forms of professional malpractice. But for the fear of liability to

The Vulnerable Social Worker

deter wrongful conduct, the imposition of liability must bear some reasonable relationship to culpability. The culpable must be held accountable, and the faultless protected. In the area of services for children and families, neither is happening. As a result, the deterrent impact of liability is, at best, deflected and, at worst, misdirected toward defensive social work. The next two sections elaborate on these two points.

Unfair Blame

Many of the cases described in this book document shockingly poor casework practices. No one should attempt to defend the reckless and insensitive conduct of some social workers and their agencies, but this sad truth should not obscure the larger reality. In most of the cases, the workers were being blamed for situations simply beyond their control, for performing their professional and official responsibilities under the most difficult conditions. And, in some cases, the workers were being scapegoated for failures at higher levels of government.

First, child maltreatment is inherently difficult to detect or predict. In many cases, no one is at fault. No one, not even the most dedicated and competent caseworker, could have prevented the child's subsequent maltreatment. Child protective decisions must often be based on incomplete and misleading information as important facts go undiscovered or are forgotten, concealed, or distorted. Child maltreatment usually occurs in the privacy of the home; unless the child is old enough (and not too frightened) to speak out, or unless a family member steps forward, it is often impossible to know what really happened.

In addition, some home situations deteriorate sharply—and without warning. It is easy to see the need for protective intervention if the child has already suffered serious injury. Often, however, a decision must be made before serious injury has been inflicted. Under such circumstances, assessing the degree of danger to a child requires workers to predict the parents' future conduct. The worker must predict that the parent will engage in abusive or neglectful behavior and that the child will suffer serious injury as a result. The unvarnished truth is that *there is no way of predicting,* with any degree of certainty, whether a particular parent will become abusive or neglectful. Even setting aside the limitations imposed by large caseloads and poorly trained staff, such sophisticated psychological predictions are simply beyond our reach.

Moreover, sometimes no decision is clearly correct. "There will always be borderline cases. . . ."[17] As long as child protective decisions must be made by human beings, the chances for human error will always be present. Thus, social workers and agencies cannot guarantee the safety of all children known to them. Even if workers placed into protective custody all children who appeared to be in possible danger—a degree of overintervention that few would support—some children would continue to suffer further injury and even death, because the danger they face would go undetected—or unpredicted.

Second, many child protective tragedies are the inevitable result of inadequate funding. The past 20 years' expansion and improvement of child protective programs, though remarkable, is too easily exaggerated. There has never been enough money to attract the most qualified workers; preservice and inservice training has been largely nonexistent or superficial; the size of investigative staffs has never kept pace with the rapid—and continuing—increase in reported cases; and there has always been a chronic shortage of the mental health and social services needed to treat both parents and children.[18]

Recent budget cuts at the federal level have only aggravated these problems. Past expansions of services were facilitated by federal financial support provided under Title XX of the Social Security Act. Until the late 1970s, most states had not yet reached the ceiling in their Title XX allotments, the major federal social service funding program, and therefore they were able to obtain 75 percent federal reimbursement for their increased expenditures.[19] Thus, federal expenditures just for "child protective services" rose from a few million dollars a year in 1960 to over $325 million in 1980.[20] These funds are now under great pressure, as states and localities are called upon to shoulder an increased share of social service expenditures. As a result, even communities that had developed strong child protective systems are having difficulty keeping up with constantly increasing caseloads.

With more cases than they can handle, poorly trained caseworkers do not have enough time to give individual cases the attention required.[21] In the rush to clear cases, many key facts go undiscovered as workers are forced to perform abbreviated investigations. Moreover, protective agencies are rarely able to monitor dangerous home situations with sufficient intensity and duration to ensure a child's safety. The average family under home supervision receives about five visits over a six-month period, after which the case is closed or forgotten in the press of other business.[22]

Unfortunately, these two realities are often ignored in the rush to criticize social workers who have "allowed" a child to suffer further abuse. One Canadian case illustrates how far groundless charges can be taken. *Regina v. Leslie, Simpson and Fenemore* was a criminal prosecution of a caseworker in a local Children's Aid Society, her supervisor, and the Society's director.[23] At 7 weeks of age, Jeffrey Disotell was viciously assaulted by his mother, who was convicted at trial and placed on three years' probation. Jeffrey spent the rest of his first two years in foster care. When he was returned to his mother, the judge ordered "close supervision of the home." Over the next 250 days, the Society's worker made "approximately 30 visits to the home..., plus numerous telephone conversations" with the mother. During this time, the worker noted numerous bruises and marks on Jeffrey but, based on medical opinions she sought and the mother's explanations, she concluded that the child was not being abused. Sixteen days after the doctor's last examination, Jeffrey "was again seriously assaulted by his mother and suffered a ruptured stomach. [The mother] was charged again with assault..., pleaded guilty and was sentenced to seven days in [jail]."

After a full trial, the judge dismissed the charges against the agency supervisor on the ground that there was "no evidence against her that her conduct in any way contributed to this unfortunate incident." The charges against the director were likewise dismissed, because there was "no evidence *whatever* against him." In dismissing the charges against the caseworker, Mary Jane Leslie, the judge uttered these important words:

> ...A Children's Aid Society worker, such as Mary Jane Leslie, must make decisions that are risky, use her common sense in so doing and use such other assistance as is available. In short, she must do the best she can with the tools she has available and, in so doing, may often feel isolated and vulnerable. This she must do in spite of a heavy caseload described in this case by a co-worker and Crown witness, as being between 52 and 53 cases at the time she was involved in this case. Contrast this caseload on the part of Mary Jane Leslie with the evidence of Thomas O'Brien, a Crown witness and Director of the Children's Aid Society in Cornwall, whose evidence was that, in his opinion, 35 cases is a reasonable caseload but, as a matter of fact, 15 cases could be too many if the cases involve high risk. It would certainly appear on the Crown evidence, that Mary Jane Leslie's caseload was a very heavy one at the time in question.

> * * *

> ...I cannot find any acts of commission or omission on her part that even approach the requirement of [intent] required in this case.... She was on the firing line, to put it bluntly; she had to make her own decisions with whatever assistance she could get and hope that her decisions were correct and, to my mind, she did the best she could under the circumstances, and I so find. I also find that she followed the guidelines laid down by the Ministry to the best of her ability. Certainly there is no evidence that any omissions on her part amounted to wilful conduct amounting to a reckless or callous disregard for Jeffrey Disotell's safety.[24]

Scant consolation can be gained from the fact that so many suits against social workers end up being dismissed. Although winning is better than losing, defending a lawsuit is expensive. Even if the worker's agency or insurance pays the legal expense, there is still the emotional cost:

> No man sued for malpractice ever wins completely....You can't know what it's like to go through such an ordeal—until you do it. One day you're a respected,

confident professional man. The next day your ability is being debated in court, with all your friends and patients looking on—and wondering.[25]

Blaming social workers for conditions beyond their control is simply unfair. In child protective work, most workers "are just government employees doing a difficult, often unpleasant job, and because they deal with volatile, unpredictable family situations, injuries are sometimes unavoidable."[26] Unjustified criticism of social workers is also deeply unfair to the children and families in the child protective system because it leads to social work practice that is defensive.

Defensive Social Work

The harmful effects of unfairly blaming social workers go far beyond the individuals involved. Cases like those in this book are well known in the field. They—and the media coverage that surrounds them—have convinced social workers that the imposition of liability is a haphazard and unpredictable lottery having little to do with individual culpability. Ordinarily, the deterrent impact of civil and criminal liability might improve child protective practices. In the present atmosphere, however, with workers and agencies being unfairly blamed, the prospect of such liability worsens practices, because it causes defensive social work.

The first manifestation of defensive social work is overintervention. Workers feel that they will be blamed if there was *any* reason, however minor, for thinking that the child was in danger. Hence, they are under great pressure to take no chances, and to intervene whenever they might be criticized for not doing so. The dynamic is simple enough: negative media publicity and a lawsuit are always possible if the child is subsequently killed or injured; but there will be no critical publicity if it turns out that intervention was unneeded, and much less chance of a lawsuit. Joanne Selinske, formerly director of the American Public Welfare Association's child abuse project, characterized this approach as the " 'better safe than sorry' attitude that permeates the child protection system."[27]

A fair analogy to this process is the defensive medicine practiced by many physicians these days. The ease with which former patients seem to be able to win large cash judgments makes most physicians fearful of malpractice lawsuits. To minimize the possibility of a subsequent lawsuit, many physicians routinely order more medical procedures, x-rays, and other tests than are reasonably needed.[28]

As in the case of defensive medicine, no one knows exactly how much defensive social work goes on. There is no denying, however, that it affects all aspects of child protective decision making. Many of the great number of unfounded reports now flooding the system, for example, reflect the "better safe than sorry" syndrome. Educational materials that emphasize liability for failure to report, as well as immunity for incorrect reporting, foster this process.

Removal decisions are also distorted by liability concerns. Most observers would agree with Yale Law School Professor Peter Schuck that: "Social workers may more quickly—but prematurely—remove children from troubled families rather than risk being sued on behalf of an abused child."[29] Schultz found in his survey of child protective workers at least one worker who "tries to get state custody of all suspected abused children just to protect herself from liability."[30] In another state, a program director described what happened after he was indicted for "allowing" a child to be killed:

> Upon learning of the indictments, caseworkers and their supervisors became aware of their own vulnerability. As a result, paperwork increased to account for everyone's actions and for a while more children were removed from their homes. Supervisors told me that these removals seemed unnecessary but that caseworkers were afraid.[31]

Until recently, overintervention was the major form of defensive social work. Now, however, we are beginning to see another form of defensive social work: immobilized decision making.

Doctors face minimal liability for performing unwarranted treatment. Because the physician-patient relationship is a voluntary one, the patient's ability to obtain damages is generally limited to situations in which the patient's consent to treatment was obtained through duress, fraud, or inaccurate or misleading information. Social workers face similar liability, of course, when they improperly gain a client's consent to treatment. Because they are authorized, however, to act without the client's consent—in seeking the client's institutionalization, in reporting suspected child abuse, in providing child protective services, and so on—social workers are much more vulnerable to claims of unnecessary action. That is the lesson of Chapter 4. As child protective intervention occurs in increasingly questionable circumstances, there are more claims of violating parental and family rights. Remember, for example, that one of the claims in *Doe v. Hennepin County* was that the agency had a "policy of treating as true all allegations of abuse, regardless of source. . ." and a procedural manual that did not mention "the possibility that the maker of a report may have improper motives."[32]

In individual cases, the violation of the client's rights may clearly require legal redress, but from a distance, workers see such cases as further examples of the legal system unfairly blaming social workers for merely doing their job. The law seems more unpredictable and their legal responsibilities more confusing. Scholars describe the situation as follows:

> Child protection personnel are uncertain about the professional standards to which they and their agencies are held accountable. There is concern that there

is no avenue of action or decision that can be made that is not objectionable in the eyes of the law.[33]

Line workers are more basic in their description; they say, "You are damned if you do, and damned if you don't!"

This two-edged liability creates a classic double bind.[34] Child protective work is not easy. Workers are well aware of the consequences of a wrong decision. Failure to act may lead to a child's serious injury or, as we have seen, death. On the other hand, intervening when a child is not in danger can leave lasting psychological scars on the child as well as the parents.[35] Fears of liability raise this inherently stressful responsibility to an unattainable, and morale-destroying, level of accountability.

"I think we can create paranoid workers. Workers must perform their duties with care but must not be afraid to take action," warns Thomas Czelusta, an Assistant Attorney General for the State of Virginia.[36] But that is just what is happening. Hear what one Massachusetts social worker says:

> When the administrator hands the case to a social worker it becomes that worker's sole responsibility. And whose fault is it if the foster home is not sufficient and the child gets hurt? It's the social worker's. . . .
> Everything is on our backs. We are expected to provide the best for the child and our resources don't even allow that half the time. It is getting to the point where social workers are very reticent about making decisions in extreme cases.[37]

Child protective work consists of decisions: decisions to report suspected cases; decisions to investigate and validate reports; decisions to remove children from parental custody, or to leave them at home; decisions about the adequacy of foster parents; decisions to initiate court action; and decisions to seek the termination of parental rights and the child's adoption.

> Workers. . .are called upon to make a variety of judgments daily. The worker's ability to make these judgments is at the heart of quality CPS work. Policies, standards, educational materials and simple advice are useful tools employed by the workers in making such judgments. Nonetheless, it is the worker who must ultimately decide the relevance and importance of various facts of a family situation and act accordingly.[38]

If liability concerns preclude responsible decision making, then the whole system will collapse. Recruiting qualified people for children's services is hard enough. Salaries are low, working conditions poor, and positive feedback from clients minimal. There are many more rewarding areas of human services work. Continued, and rising, levels of liability could lead to the ultimate defensive social work: The best people may simply avoid the field.

Lowering Expectations

Underlying all successful lawsuits against social workers is one central element: the worker's deviation from a legally recognized standard of conduct or performance.[39] Although it sometimes seems that liability-creating standards are plucked out of the air by courts, they are invariably based on statutory mandates, agency rules, and standards of professional practice. Vincent DeFrancis, a former director of the American Humane Association's Children's Division, describes the progression from the existence of a statute establishing a child protective program to the use of the statute to establish a standard for liability:

> Though the exact wording may vary, the intent expressed in the statutory language of most states is to require the child protective service to: investigate reports of neglect and abuse; and to provide services to stabilize the home and, where possible, maintain the intactness of the family.
>
> This expression of legislative intent becomes a charge upon the agency. It defines specific service objectives and goals. In turn, these goals become clear expectations of outcomes to be achieved to benefit the client served. For the clients served this is tantamount to a delineation of what they have a *right to expect and receive*.
>
> When these goals are not achieved, the child protective service client (the child victim and sometimes a parent) has a right to hold the agency accountable for the failure. That this is so is rapidly being established by successful challenges directed against agencies and workers. In these challenges, accountability is emerging as an enforceable liability.
>
> More accurately, failure to live up to mandated service objectives exposes the agency and/or workers to liability in terms of money damages for the harmful consequence of such failure.[40]

Unwittingly, existing statutes, agency rules, and professional standards raise social worker vulnerability beyond what is necessary or fair. Some recent history is important here. Faced with enormous weaknesses in child protective efforts, reformers, from the mid-1960s on, attempted to "mandate" programmatic improvement through detailed laws, administrative procedures, and professional guidelines.[41] Thus, these materials are usually written as if agencies had unlimited resources and workers had unlimited time to handle individual cases. Moreover, in a well-meaning attempt to protect as many endangered children as possible, these materials are usually written as if child maltreatment were easily detected (or predicted), and as if case decision making were clear-cut. In effect, they are written to describe what *should be*, not what *is*—nor what *can be*.

The practical impossibility of meeting legal and professional standards is a well-recognized defense to tort liability. However, to be excused from liability, the defendant must prove "reasonable diligence [in attempting] to obey the statute."[42] This defense is difficult to establish and usually requires a full trial before the defendant may be exonerated—a reality that has led one indicted program director to warn:

> [T]ake those state regulations and laws which mandate you to save all children and families in your state and develop strategies to change them. To paraphrase one attorney, to have legal mandates by law and regulations requires that we live up to them to the letter. Not to do so places us in severe jeopardy of civil or criminal suit. I have threatened to burn the Social Services Handbook of Texas, and I may just do so if our own state office does not take serious steps to change what needs to be changed. Unfortunately handbooks are written by social workers who are concerned with their own ideals and not by policy-makers who are concerned with establishing law and regulations which meet the intent of law and are possible to accomplish. I am truly sorry, but the administrative mandate placed on me and my staff to elicit cooperation of all clients will never be met in every case. It contradicts reality and sets up those of us involved in administrating or performing direct practice for civil and criminal suit. Where is the law or state regulation that mandates doctors cure every case of cancer?[43]

Therefore, statutory, administrative, and professional materials should be rewritten to reflect their pivotal role in establishing standards for liability. Provisions that articulate goals to be sought should be clearly identified as such; those that establish true minimum standards of acceptable performance should be carefully reviewed to ensure that they are realistic.

It may be hard for social workers to achieve modifications of state laws and agency procedures, but there is no excuse for not correcting professional standards. As social work professor George Sharwell has written:

> [S]ince courts commonly look to the standards of practice developed by professional societies as a guide to the standards to which a given professional shall be held, we can, in effect, develop our own standards—standards that can have the force, if not the status, of law. In brief, we can place ourselves in the position of almost totally writing the rules that will be applied to our practice. We can write the principles that courts can incorporate as legal standards, and we should prefer to write our own standards than having the courts do this for us. If we do not clarify our standards, the courts surely will do it for us. . . .[44]

Vague Laws

As a priority, definitions of "child abuse" and "child neglect" must be improved. These definitions help establish eligibility for an array of voluntary social and mental health services; hence, they have been called a "diagnostic door" through which services are made available to a family.[45] More important, they authorize public agencies to intervene to protect a child, even against parental wishes. Definitions describe the situations that professionals and private citizens must report to the authorities. Definitions authorize child protective agencies to investigate a home situation. Definitions establish civil, child protective court jurisdiction to impose treatment, to remove a child from the home, and, often, to terminate parental rights. And definitions authorize the imposition of criminal sanctions.

The expansion of child protective efforts over the past 20 years has not been accompanied by a concomitant development of reasonably precise definitions of "child abuse" and "child neglect," which, as explained, establish the legal standards for determining when child protective intervention is needed—and when it is not needed. Giovannoni and Becerra have noted the following:

> Many assume that since child abuse and neglect are against the law, somewhere there are statutes that make clear distinctions between what is and what is not child abuse and neglect. But this is not the case. Nowhere are there clear-cut definitions of what is encompassed by the terms.[46]

Most state laws authorize child protective intervention with conclusory phrases such as: when the child's "environment is injurious to his welfare,"[47] when the child "lacks proper parental care,"[48] or when the parents are "unfit to properly care for such child."[49] Other statutes are blatantly tautological, authorizing intervention when a child has been "abandoned or physically, mentally, or emotionally abused or neglected or sexually abused,"[50] without further defining these terms.

In an attempt to be more specific, some recent statutes speak in terms of the failure to provide "adequate" or "necessary" or "proper" food, clothing, shelter, medical care, education, supervision, or guardianship.[51] But, again, such statutes do not define the key—but ambiguous—words: "adequate," "necessary," or "proper." Furthermore, even definitions that contain lists of relatively precise examples of child abuse or neglect also contain a catch-all phrase such as "any other acts of similarly serious nature requiring the aid of the court. . . ."[52] Such open-ended provisions are usually defended on the ground that it is "unwise, if not impossible to catalog all the various kinds of abuse and maltreatment that occur; even a long list of specific examples might overlook many situations that are unusual or unique, yet harmful to children. It is imperative that protective workers be able to take action when the facts warrant it."[53] Based on their popularity, such catch-all provisions seem to have a legitimate place in statutory construction. But one is reminded of the preacher who began a sermon by saying that there were 15 sins. In his sermon, he described only 14. After the service, a parishioner went up to the preacher and asked what the fifteenth sin was. In a hushed tone came the answer: "Miscellaneous."

State and local agencies with child protective responsibilities have developed a wide array of materials designed to give more precise meaning to child abuse laws. So have many hospitals, school systems, and other service agencies, as well as professional organizations. But there is little uniformity among these materials, and issues are often treated in a generalized fashion, using pat phrases and ambiguous indicators. The noted authority Dr. C. Henry Kempe reflected the feelings of most child protective professionals when he asserted: "Child abuse is what the courts say it is."[54]

The absence of more specific standards for intervention reflects, and increases, the general confusion about what is and what is not child maltreatment. Based on a national survey of local programs, Nagi found:

> ...evidence of uncertainty regarding decision making throughout the system.... Respondents from protective agencies representing 56 percent of the population served and from police departments representing 84 percent agreed that "it is difficult to say what is and what is not child maltreatment." Higher proportions of judges and physicians indicated similar uncertainty....[55]

Laws, agency manuals, and professional guidelines should set the ground rules for decision making. They should specify when child protective intervention should occur and when it should not occur. By doing so, they would help protect social workers from unfair criticism and thus help social workers to withstand the pressures toward defensive social work.

But existing standards for intervention do just the opposite; they feed unfair criticism and, consequently, defensive social work. Schultz explains:

> [T]here exists an inherent difficulty in the application of broad, inclusive laws and policies to a breadth of situations defying neat categorization. Policies, laws and standards do not provide adequate guidelines for the worker in all possible situations, yet require action in all. This is the breeding ground for malpractice.[56]

The vagueness and overbreadth of existing standards for intervention have been widely criticized. Goldstein, Freud, and Solnit, for example, have written that existing laws "delegate to administrators, prosecutors, and judges the power to invade privacy almost at will."[57] But the problem is not that existing standards vest too much discretion in social workers. Rather, they place too much responsibility on social workers.

Existing standards—and the decision-making confusion they foster—are a direct reflection of society's overambitious expectations about the ability of social agencies and courts to identify and protect endangered children. As a society, we have been unwilling to accept that some children cannot be protected from abuse and neglect, that, no matter what we do and how hard we try, as long as parents raise their children in the privacy of their own homes, some children will continue to suffer serious injuries—and some will die—before anything can be done to protect them. This failure to be realistic about child protective capabilities has prevented the development of practical decision-making standards that balance the need to protect children with the need to prevent unwarranted state intervention.

This desire to give courts and social agencies preventive jurisdiction explains the open-ended nature of existing standards. Laws that authorize intervention if a child "lacks proper parental care," or is "without proper guardianship," or has parents "unfit to properly care" for him or her, or is in an "environment injurious to his welfare" are intentionally phrased to give social workers broad authority to intervene on a *preventive* basis. These laws authorize intervention before the child has been injured in order to *prevent future maltreatment.* In fact, they authorize intervention even before the child has been either abused or neglected.

The variations are endless, but, without exception, such provisions come down to one simple proposition: past child abuse or neglect is *not a prerequisite to intervention.* Children are to be protected from "threatened harm."

Even those who are deeply critical of the present level of child protective intervention advocate preventive action. Goldstein, Freud, and Solnit, for example, would authorize intervention to protect children who face an "imminent risk of death or serious bodily harm."[58] Wald, another critic of the present level of intervention, explains why he concluded that preventive jurisdiction is needed:

> [I]t would be unwise to allow intervention only after a child has been seriously injured as a result of inadequate living conditions or supervision. For example, a court must be able to protect a 5-year-old child left unattended for several days even if the child has avoided injury.[59]

As a general principle, there is nothing wrong with this prevention orientation. Indeed, it is commendable. Society should not wait until a child is seriously injured before taking protective action. However, by giving social workers such broad and unfettered authority to intervene preventively, existing laws greatly overstate the ability of social workers to identify children "threatened with harm." Existing laws suggest that workers can protect *all* the children in their care. In effect, these provisions imply that workers can do the impossible—predict future parental behavior. Agency policies and public pronouncements encourage this belief by instructing workers to make sophisticated psychological assessments intended to do just that.[60]

Expecting decision makers to predict future child maltreatment is totally unrealistic and ultimately counterproductive. Despite years of research, there is no psychological profile that accurately identifies parents who will abuse or neglect their child in the future.[61] Based on his own work on the subject, and after reviewing the work of others, Dr. Ray Helfer concluded that "the ability to separate out a distinct group of parents (or future parents) who will *physically* abuse or serious[ly] neglect one or more of their children will probably never be possible."[62] Unless the parent is suffering from a severe and demonstrable mental disability,[63] not even the best clinicians can make a reliable assessment of a parent's propensity to become abusive or neglectful. Furthermore, in many cases, the home situation deteriorates sharply—and without warning.

By greatly overstating the ability of social workers and judges to predict future maltreatment, existing laws and the agency policies that implement them fail to give practical guidance on when intervention is needed and when it is not needed. Instead, they encourage reliance on an array of "high risk" indicators that make sound decision making unlikely.

Moreover, by overstating the ability to predict future maltreatment, existing laws foster harsh public and media criticism whenever a child dies. Because there are no articulated limits to their preventive jurisdiction (and powers), social workers are more easily criticized for having "allowed" a child to die. Hence the defensive social work described above. Fear of criticism (and possible civil or criminal liability), coupled with an honest desire to protect children, leads workers to view *all* minor assaults and *any* marginally inadequate child care as signs of a parent's *future* propensity to abuse or neglect a child. Richard Bourne was merely expressing the prevailing view in the field when he wrote that "without appropriate intervention, minor injuries are likely to increase in severity over time. A minor injury thus forewarns of more dangerous trauma...."[64] As a result, reports of suspected maltreatment are made in many minor situations that simply do not amount to child maltreatment. A child is hit by a parent and, whether or not the assault was serious, he or she is considered "abused." Children living in dirty and disorganized households, whether or not their basic needs are being met, are labeled "neglected." The National Study of the Incidence and Severity of Child Abuse and Neglect found that over 50 percent of all the reports *substantiated* by child protective agencies involved nothing more than such minor situations.

Although such situations may reflect poor or inappropriate child rearing, they are not of sufficient gravity to justify coercive state intervention. Furthermore, by themselves, they do not signal future child maltreatment. Almost all parents have physically or verbally lashed out at their children during times of unusual stress; all parents have at least some moments when they neglect to meet the needs of their children. If actual harm results, it is usually minor; if it is more serious, it is usually transitory. According to data collected by the National Incidence Study, less than one in five minor assaults or other examples of poor child care will ever grow into anything resembling child abuse or child neglect.[65] Unfortunately, there is no way of knowing which situations will become more serious with the degree of assurance needed to justify involuntary child protective intervention.

At the same time, by not focusing on children who have already been abused or neglected and who are thus in clear danger of further maltreatment, existing laws make it less likely that these children will receive the protection they so desperately need. These children get lost in the press of minor cases flooding the system.

For the peace of mind of social workers who must make critical life-and-death decisions, as well as to protect the well-being of children and the rights of parents, child protective policies should be reformulated to reflect the realities of decision making. They should make it clear that, subject to the relatively rare exceptions described below, social workers and judges cannot predict future maltreatment, and thus it is unfair—and unwise—to expect them to do so.

Seriously Harmful Behavior

Laws and agency policies should be redrafted so that child protective intervention is authorized only when the parents have already engaged in abusive or neglectful behavior. Children who have already been abused or neglected are in clear danger of further maltreatment. As the Supreme Court of California said in the landmark case of *Landeros v. Flood:*

> Experiences with the repetitive nature of injuries indicate that an adult who has once injured a child is likely to repeat. . . . [T]he child must be considered to be in grave danger unless his environment can be proved to be safe.[66]

Limiting state action to situations of past wrongful conduct is the criminal law's posture, and it has equal validity for child protective intervention. There are only two exceptions to this general proposition. First, parents suffering from *severe and demonstrable* mental disabilities (such as an overt psychosis so severe that the parent is detached from reality)[67] are simply incapable of providing adequate care for children.[68] Second, intervention is needed when parents of infants or very young children report that they feel themselves slipping out of control and that they fear they may hurt or kill their children.[69] However, there are many degrees of mental disability, and a prediction of future serious injury to the child is justified only at the extremes of parental incapacity. To ensure proper application of the policy, it is essential to emphasize that the parent's mental disability must be "severe and demonstrable."

There is a way to reflect society's legitimate preventive concerns— and this is the key to reforming decision-making standards. The parent's behavior need not have already seriously injured the child for it to be considered "abusive" or "neglectful" and for it to be the basis of child protective intervention. Intervention should be authorized if the parent did something that was *capable of causing serious injury.*[70] By having engaged in seriously harmful behavior once, parents demonstrate that they are a continuing threat to their children, for it is reasonable to assume that unless there is a change in circumstances, what the parents did in the past, they will do again in the future. The mere fact that the child did not suffer or has not yet suffered serious injury[71] does not reduce the need for protective action. As Alfred Kadushin, Professor of Social Work at the University of Wisconsin, asks: "Do we sit by impassively if a parent shoots a child but misses?"[72] Of course not. Society should adopt a preventive orientation toward protecting such children. It just should not use the kind of open-ended and unregulated approach that laws now permit.

Therefore, child protective intervention should be authorized if the parent's behavior *could* have seriously injured the child. The criminal law would call such behavior an "attempt" or "reckless endangerment." However, such terms are not applicable to child protection because they imply a higher level of intent than is necessary and because they seem to exclude situations of child neglect.[73] Hence, to encompass all the situations that should be the subject of child protective intervention, this section calls such behavior "seriously harmful behavior." (See Chart 6-1, which describes the two categories of "seriously harmful behavior.")

The harmfulness of the parents' past behavior is the unspoken— and unspecified—basis of many child protective decisions. But because it is not articulated, there is a great deal of unnecessary confusion about the differences between this concept and the existence of actual, serious injuries. This confusion was described by Holmes:

> In some communities the use of any object which leaves marks on a child's body is considered abuse; in other communities this depends on the age of the child, so that a strapping of a 12-year-old may be defined as nonabusive whereas the strapping of an infant is ipso facto evidence of abuse. Similarly, some programs take into account the location of the injury and are most likely to apply the label "abuse" in cases of physical marks to the face and genitalia than to marks on other areas of the body.[74]

Laws based on the parents' "seriously harmful behavior" would provide all the preventive jurisdiction that agencies and courts should have. They would authorize intervention to prevent a child from being seriously injured— but only after there is clear evidence of the need to do so. (See Chart 2-1 for a listing of "seriously harmful behaviors" for which preventive child protective intervention should be authorized.)

Basing intervention on the "harmfulness" of past parental behavior

Chart 6-1
Seriously Harmful Behavior

Immediately Harmful Behavior
    Parents demonstrate that they are a continuing threat to a child if they
have done something that could have caused an *immediately serious* injury, but serious injury was averted by the intervention of an outside
force, or perhaps simple good luck. A parent shoots at a child but
misses; a parent throws an infant against a wall, but, by some good fortune, the child is not injured; a parent begins to beat a child brutally,
but a relative or neighbor intervenes; a parent leaves a young child home
alone in a hazardous environment, but the child is found before he injures himself. Although, through some good fortune, such children did
not suffer serious injury, it is fair to predict that what the parents did
once, they will do again.

Cumulatively Harmful Behavior
    Parents demonstrate that they are a continuing threat to a child if they
engage in a course of conduct that will cause *cumulatively serious* harm
to the child if it continues for a sufficient length of time. A parent provides a nutritionally inadequate diet for the child, which, over time, will
cause serious health problems; a parent inflicts repeated, but otherwise
minor, assaults on the child, which, over time, will make him into an
easily frustrated, violence-prone individual; a parent provides grossly inadequate emotional support and cognitive stimulation, which, over time,
will lead to severe developmental disabilities. Again, although such
children have not yet suffered serious injury, it is only a matter of time
until they will do so.

---

would be directly at variance with the arguments of those reformers who have
insisted that standards for intervention should be based on harm to the child.
For example, Wald argues: "Neglect statutes should be drafted in terms of
specific harms that a child must be suffering or extremely likely to suffer,
not in terms of desired parental behavior."[75] But, as this section has described,
statutes that authorize intervention if a child is "extremely likely to suffer"
harm are open-ended invitations to overreact to situations of limited danger
to children. The only way to provide fair guidelines for decision making is
to limit the grounds upon which predictions of future maltreatment can be

based. And the only way to do that is to base intervention on the "harmfulness" of past parental behavior.

It is important to note that minor assaults and marginally inadequate child care are not what is meant by "seriously harmful behavior." To be "seriously harmful," and, hence, a ground for intervention, the behavior itself must have been capable of causing serious injury. (The behavior must be relatively recent; ordinarily, intervention should not be based on behavior from the distant past.)

Heartfelt concern for children leads many people to believe that all inadequate or poor child-rearing situations—whether or not they are "seriously harmful"—should be grounds for intervention. This is a mistake. Even though its purpose is to protect endangered children, child protective intervention is a major intrusion into parental rights and can often do more harm than good. It should be limited to situations in which the need for intervention is supported by clear and sufficient evidence.

This does not mean that situations of less damaging child care do not merit social action. Many such situations would benefit from specific social and community services. But these services should be offered for the parents' voluntary acceptance—or refusal.[76]

Child protective intervention in response to the parents' *past* "seriously harmful behavior" is based on the reasonable assumption that what the parents did once, they will do again. It is possible, however, that circumstances have changed, and that the presumption of continued harmful behavior should not be applied (or, in technical legal terms, is "rebutted"). For example, the precipitating cause of the parents' behavior may have disappeared or been removed; the parents may have developed the ability to care for the child (either by themselves or through treatment); or the provision of voluntary services may sufficiently reduce the likelihood of a recurrence to obviate the need for coercive intervention. These are crucial issues in determining whether intervention should actually occur—and how long it should last.[77] Therefore, standards for intervention must also require decision makers to determine whether the parents' emotional condition has improved or whether the factors that led to the parents' past behavior have been nullified.

The Foster Care Decision

This kind of definitional improvement will naturally lead to more useful standards for the removal of children from parental custody. At the present time, there are no legal standards governing the foster care decision. Juvenile court acts, for example, give judges unrestricted dispositional authority.[78] Once initial court jurisdiction is established, they set no limits—and hence provide no guidance—on which situations require foster care and which do not. Consequently, "decision-making is left to the ad hoc analysis of social workers and judges."[79] The absence of standards cuts both ways. Many children who need immediate protection are not placed in foster care, and many other children are taken away from their parents even though there is no pressing need.

The approach to standards for intervention proposed in this section provides a simple and practical basis for building standards to determine whether a child should be placed in foster care. As described above, all forms of "seriously harmful behavior" can be divided between those that are "immediately harmful" and those that are "cumulatively harmful." Standards governing the foster care decision should reflect this distinction. Children whose parents have engaged in "immediately harmful behavior" continue to face an imminent threat of serious injury. Unless their safety can be ensured by some other means, they should be placed in protective custody quickly— and kept there until the home situation is safe or parental rights are permanently terminated.

Child protective laws should establish a rebuttable presumption that children whose parents have engaged in "immediately harmful behavior" require foster care. This presumption would be rebutted only by specific evidence that the parents' emotional condition has improved sufficiently or that other services short of removal can adequately protect the child.[80] Furthermore, if, during treatment, the parent again engages in "immediately harmful behavior" toward the child, the presumptive need for foster care would be revived.

On the other hand, children whose parents engage in "cumulatively harmful behavior" do not need foster care on an emergency basis. The danger they face, though great, derives from the longer-term (and cumulative) consequences of the inadequate care they are receiving. Regardless of how upsetting their present situation seems to be, they have already endured within it for some time, and there is ordinarily no need that they be immediately rescued from it. Instead, there is much more time to help the parents to care adequately for the child without removing him or her from the home. There are, however, some exceptions: Children in "cumulatively harmful" situations require *emergency* foster care when (1) the parents may flee from the jurisdiction, taking the child with them, or (2) the child's condition has deteriorated so much that irreparable injury is imminent.

Even if treatment efforts for "cumulatively harmful" situations are unsuccessful, the need for foster care can often be obviated through in-home, child-oriented services that "compensate" for parental deficiencies. "Compensatory" services include infant stimulation programs, Head Start, therapeutic day care, homemaker care, early childhood or child development programs, nutritional services, and youth counseling programs.

According to data from the American Humane Association, as many as 50 percent of the children in foster care are removed from "cumulatively harmful" situations.[81] Many children are placed in foster care because their parents have inflicted unreasonable corporal punishment. But in most cases, the punishment posed no danger of serious physical injury to the child, and there is no evidence that it would have grown into severe beatings. The harmfulness of such punishment stems from the long-term effect of this assaultive behavior on the child's developing personality.[82]

Similarly, many children are placed in foster care because of the low quality of physical care they receive. Often, however, the physical conditions, though poor, pose no real *physical* threat to the child. The physical conditions are used as a proxy indicator for the parents' general inability to meet the emotional needs of the child. Sometimes consciously, but usually not, the system concludes that because the parents are unable to maintain the household, they can hardly be able to meet the child's emotional needs. This conclusion may or may not be valid. The point is that the danger to the child, if there is any, is of a cumulative, nonemergency nature.

In part, the failure to recognize that the harm to the child is cumulative in nature stems from the system's unwillingness to admit that the reason for intervention in most "cumulatively harmful" situations is emotional harm to the child. Emotional maltreatment is seen as a vague and amorphous concept, upon which coercive intervention should not be based. Putting aside the merits of this concern, repressing the real reason for intervention makes sound decision making unlikely. When parental functioning fails to improve, as it so often does, the system overreacts, concluding that placement is needed to safeguard the child's health and well-being. If standards compelled decision makers to recognize the absence of immediate danger to the child, they would be more willing to forestall foster care while additional treatment efforts were made with the parents, or while compensatory services were provided to the child.

Child protective laws should prohibit even non-emergency removal of children from a "cumulatively harmful" situation unless: (1) the parents refuse to accept or cooperate with efforts to provide needed compensatory services; (2) the child needs specific diagnostic or remedial services that are available only through residential care; (3) the foster care is used in response to an otherwise irreconcilable conflict between the parent and an adolescent child; or (4) the foster care is a planned precursor to the termination of parental rights and a subsequent adoption. (In the latter situation, foster care still might not be needed, unless there was a danger that the parents might flee with the child before their rights could be terminated.)

This section has proposed a new approach to legal standards that, by minimizing unreasonable expectations about what social workers can accomplish, will help relieve the unfair tensions under which they operate, and, at the same time, will help them to make more appropriate decisions. This more realistic approach to what can be accomplished will help ensure that more children who need lifesaving protection will receive it, while, at the same time, the legal vulnerability of social workers is reduced.

Improved legal standards, however, are only a partial solution to unfair liability. Even if the approach to standards proposed in this section is entirely correct, adopting standards in conformity to it will not provide sufficient protection for social workers. Only legislation creating qualified immunity will do that.

"Good Faith" Immunity

Indefensible social worker misconduct and shockingly weak agency administration led to many of the tragedies described in this book. It is easy to get angry at these horror stories—and to demand a legal remedy. Most Americans believe in individual accountability, and we are justly proud that our legal system provides an avenue for the legal redress of harmful conduct, whether at the hands of private persons or government officials. Social work professor George Sharwell, for example, has written: "Malpractice actions exist because they should exist in any system that claims to seek equity; it is not unfair that those who err should compensate those they injure."[83]

But what about the much larger number of cases in which neither the individual worker nor the agency was at fault? One lesson above all others should stand out from the cases described in this book: the legal system does a disgracefully poor job in protecting innocent social workers from unwarranted liability. In each chapter, we have seen examples of apparent miscarriages of justice.

Even when social workers win in court, they lose. Legal vindication comes at a high price. Newspapers carry stories about the suit (usually focusing on the untested allegations), about the pretrial maneuvering, and about the trial testimony. Workers employed in agencies are often suspended, placed on administrative leave, or transferred, pending resolution of the case. Workers in private practice usually lose clients and new referrals. A trial —and all that goes with it—is confusing, stressful, and time-consuming.

> Whether or not a social worker is ultimately found liable, the time spent in preparation of pleadings, depositions, interrogatories, briefs, and courtroom testimony can be both financially and emotionally taxing....[T]ime lost can never be regained.[84]

Legal fees have to be paid, whether one wins or loses. Lawyers' bills can range from $5,000 (when the case is dismissed quickly) to over $50,000 (when a trial and appeal are necessary). In the El Paso prosecution described earlier, for example, before the charges were dropped, the indicted child protective workers incurred legal fees of $15,000—for which they were solely responsible.[85] Rarely are unsuccessful plaintiffs required to reimburse the innocent defendant for these costs, although the worker's agency or an insurance policy may do so. And, for long after, friends, colleagues, and clients remember that the social worker's conduct, judgment, and ability were challenged in court.

The best way to protect social workers from the high costs of unwarranted litigation would be to reform the entire tort system, because may other professions also face problems similar to those plaguing social work. Real reform would mean a comprehensive reformulation of the rules concerning attorneys' fees, standards of liability, court procedures, evidence, and so forth. However, such extensive changes are, for the present, not realistically contemplated; the complexity of the issues and the strong objection of entrenched interests require a much more intensive and broadly based effort than has heretofore been made.

Nevertheless, for publicly employed social workers and for those required to report suspected child maltreatment, protection is possible through more modest reform. They should be given immunity for their *good faith* efforts to serve children and families. The *Restatement of Torts* describes good faith immunity as meaning that "the officer is not liable if he made his determination and took the action that harmed the other party. . . in an honest effort to do what he thought the exigencies before him required."[86]

Reflecting the need to protect public officials who must exercise their best judgment in performing their duties, state and federal law grants public officials good faith immunity for their "discretionary" actions.[87] Some court decisions go further and grant public officials absolute immunity.[88] But these cases are decidedly in the minority—and they seem to go too far. Absolute immunity precludes liability even when the official's misconduct results from actual malice or a reckless disregard of legal requirements. As the cases in this book sadly demonstrate, there are times when civil and even criminal liability may be justified.

For either good faith or absolute immunity to be granted, the official's act must have been "discretionary." All other acts are "ministerial," for which there is no immunity. The following description of the difference between the two was given by the New York Court of Appeals: "Discretionary or quasi-judicial acts involve the exercise of reasoned judgment which could typically produce different acceptable results whereas a ministerial act envisions direct adherence to a governing rule or standard with a compulsory result."[89]

If the existence of immunity were solely determined by applying such word formulations, all child welfare workers would be protected, because no one could reasonably disagree with the description of child protective work provided by James Cameron, executive director of the New York State Federation on Child Abuse and Neglect: "Protective workers are called upon to make extremely difficult decisions which can have an enormous impact in often unpredictable ways upon the welfare of children and the continued viability of a family unit. Field workers must examine their best judgment in each case."[90]

Most courts, however, refuse to apply the discretionary-ministerial dichotomy mechanically, because they realize that if they did so, it "could be invoked to establish immunity from liability for every act or omission of public employees...."[91] In most jurisdictions, deciding whether an act is "discretionary" or "ministerial" is, as the *Restatement of Torts* explains, "a legal conclusion whose purport is only somewhat incidentally related to the definitions of the two words composing it. Instead of looking at a dictionary, therefore, the court must weigh numerous factors and make a measured decision...."[92] The *Restatement* goes on to state the factors that are considered:

(1) The nature and importance of the function that the officer is performing....
(2) The extent to which passing judgment on the exercise of discretion by the officer will amount necessarily to passing judgment by the court on the conduct of a coordinate branch of government....
(3) The extent to which the imposition of liability would impair the free exercise of his discretion by the officer....
(4) The extent to which the ultimate financial responsibility will fall on the officer....
(5) The likelihood that harm will result to members of the public if the action is taken....
(6) The nature and seriousness of the type of harm that may be produced....
(7) The availability to the injured party of other remedies and other forms of relief....[93]

Whatever their theoretical validity, these factors are inherently subjective and invite idiosyncratic application. As a result, for all forms of official conduct, judicial decision making is confused and unpredictable.[94] In regard to various aspects of child welfare work, some courts have held that decision making is "discretionary"; others have concluded that it is "ministerial." People familiar with child welfare services, but unfamiliar with how judges reason, will be surprised to learn that some courts have found no discretion involved in the decision to accept a report for investigation,[95] the decision to initiate court action,[96] and the decision to place a child with particular foster parents.[97]

To be fair, certain child welfare decisions are, in fact, "ministerial." No real discretion is needed, for example, to decide that an apparently abandoned infant should be placed in protective custody. In addition, courts are sometimes misled by the overambitious mandates of statutes, agency policies, and professional standards. Mandates to "investigate immediately," "protect endangered children," and "supervise foster care" are taken as literal absolutes, rather than as general descriptions of programmatic responsibility. Moreover, the truth is that many of these court decisions are outcome-oriented.[98] That is, the judge, believing that there should be liability, decides that the activity was "ministerial." Unfortunately, certain extreme cases get translated into a general rule of no good faith immunity. Thus, to create liability for placing a child with foster parents known to be dangerous, courts have labeled the placement decision itself "ministerial," rather than more accurately holding that the particular decision was unreasonably careless.

Case-by-case granting of immunity is supposed to lead to decisions more precisely tailored to the situations before the court. But such fine tuning is really not possible. As Schuck has convincingly shown, court rulings are usually made "on the basis of distinctions that bear little relationship to protecting vigorous decisionmaking."[99] Moreover, because these distinctions do not lead to predictable results, no one knows which activities will be granted immunity and which will not. This increases litigation against workers—as lawyers test the outer bounds of liability. This constant testing tends to wear down judicial reluctance to impose liability. But even when such suits are ultimately unsuccessful, they increase workers' fears about their legal vulnerability. These are legitimate fears because, as described above, "defending any suit, even those that predictably will fail, is costly and subject to out-come-uncertainty."[100]

Dissatisfaction with the case-by-case approach has already led nine states, Puerto Rico, and the Virgin Islands to pass legislation granting child protective workers blanket good faith immunity for all their official actions.[101] All states should do the same. In fact, similar laws should be passed to protect all child welfare workers. (See Chart 6-2[1] for suggested statutory language.)

A parallel reform of child abuse reporting laws is also necessary. Reporting laws put too much emphasis on reporting—even under questionable circumstances. They do this by imposing criminal and civil liability for failing to report suspicions while also granting "good faith" immunity for incorrect reporting. In this context, defensive decision making leads to reports even when the would-be reporter believes—in good faith—that a report is not justified. To right this imbalance, six states now limit civil liability to "knowing" or "willful" failures to report.[102] All states should incorporate this type of good faith standard into their reporting laws. (See Chart 6-2[2] for suggested legislative language.)

Substantial precedent for overruling the judicial, case-by-case application of good faith immunity exists in other areas of the law.[103] For example, there are laws giving good faith immunity to guardians *ad litem* who appear in child protective proceedings, to psychiatrists who institutionalize

Chart 6-2
Recommended Immunity Legislation

(1) All employees of the [insert name of public agency here] required or authorized by the laws of this state to perform child protective or child welfare functions shall, if acting in good faith, be immune from any civil or criminal liability that might otherwise result from the performance of their official duties.

(2) Any person or institution required by this act to report known or suspected child abuse or neglect, or required to perform any other act, who knowingly and willfully fails to do so or who knowingly and willfully prevents another person acting reasonably from doing so shall be guilty of a misdemeanor and shall be civilly liable for the damages proximately caused thereby.

---

patients, and to public officers who release dangerous individuals from custody.[104]

Good faith immunity does not give child welfare workers *carte blanche* to act wrongfully. They are still subject to liability when they act in callous or reckless disregard of their official duties. Some courts also hold that the unreasonable failure to follow legal mandates is a form of bad faith. For claims under the federal Civil Rights Act, the U.S. Supreme Court has held that a claim of good faith is defeated if the defendant *"knew or reasonably should have known* that the action he took within his sphere of official responsibility would violate the constitutional rights of the [plaintiff], *or* if he took the action *with the malicious intention* to cause a deprivation of constitutional rights or other injury. . . ."[105]

Thus, good faith immunity does not prevent the filing of lawsuits. The plaintiff can always allege bad faith, so long as there is a sufficient basis for doing so. But good faith immunity does make groundless or unwarranted suits much less likely—and much more easily dismissed at an early stage. The establishment of good faith immunity would, then, be a major reform.

State immunity legislation does not affect lawsuits under the federal Civil Rights Act or other federal statutes—major avenues of litigation against child welfare workers. Therefore, barring congressional action, which is unlikely, federal courts will continue to determine whether worker activities are "discretionary" on a case-by-case basis. One can only hope that federal judges will become more aware of the realities of child welfare work and, hence, be more willing to grant workers good faith immunity;[106] and that state court judges, in jurisdictions that do not adopt immunity legislation, will do the same.

Good faith immunity does not protect workers from criminal prosecutions, because the heart of a criminal charge is the individual's intentional or willful conduct. The relatively limited steps that can be taken to protect workers from wrongful prosecution are discussed in the next chapter.

Holding Agencies Responsible

The preceding section recommended giving individual social workers good faith immunity. But what about the agencies for which they work? As one social worker put it: "You don't sue an assembly-line worker when a car's wheel falls off. You sue the company."

Under present law, it is often difficult to sue the agency, especially if it is a public one.[107] A surprisingly large number of commentators have argued that agencies should be made financially liable for inadequate and harmful child welfare services.[108] Vincent DeFrancis, long an advocate for improved services, has written:

> [Sometimes] the failure to provide adequate service is truly agency failure for not providing workers with the professional tools required....Any harmful consequences to the client resulting from that failure should, and must be, charged against the agency whose mandated objectives the worker sought to carry out despite less-than-complete administrative support.[109]

Agency liability is needed, says Schuck, because "much official wrongdoing is ultimately rooted in organizational conditions and can only be organizationally deterred."[110]

Poor agency administration is certainly a greater cause of the poor social work services described in this book than is worker negligence. Preservice training and inservice training are largely nonexistent, or sporadic and superficial. "Child Protective Services rendered to abusive families may do more harm than good unless adequate training qualifications are established," points out Leila Whiting, a senior staff associate for the National Association of Social Workers. "We will say that we will offer help and support, but in reality we will give them an overworked, underpaid, untrained, but well-meaning person who will not really know what to do."[111]

Management and supervision of social worker practices are haphazard so that, for example, most agency records are, at best, chaotic. Most agency administrators do not know what their employees actually "do."[112] So inadequate is administration that agency regulations and manuals—when they exist—often do not conform to statutory requirements. In *Duchesne v. Sugarman,* for example, the agency's manual failed to instruct workers to determine whether there was time to obtain a court order before removing a child without parental consent, as required by state law.[113] It further failed to mention the need for judicial review of emergency removals, also required by state law. Should it surprise anyone that the workers involved failed to follow these statutory mandates? Six years later, workers from the same agency were again being sued for illegal removal practices and, again, the agency's manuals still inaccurately described the statutorily required procedure.[114]

High caseloads, inappropriate staffing patterns, and minimal casework supervision permeate child welfare programs. From Massachusetts comes this story:

> [A] report of abuse [was] filed with DSS [Department of Social Services] on June 5, 1981, a year after the agency began to function. The report, which DSS designated as an emergency, was assigned to a supervisor who found that the father had come home one evening intoxicated and repeatedly stabbed the mother in front of her six children. The supervisor found blood on the walls and floor, in addition to poor health conditions, lice, and a strong stench of urine.
>
> This family had been the subject of previous reports to DSS dating back to the agency's inception in July 1980. Nevertheless, no worker had ever been assigned to the family. Even after the crisis, no worker was assigned; instead, a technician, who is not a social worker, was assigned because the workers were already carrying too many cases.[115]

"Agencies cannot defend themselves," concludes James Codega, director of a Child Abuse Treatment Program in Attleboro, Massachusetts, "(1) if they possess a lack of administrative commitment and informed understanding of the child protection casework process; (2) if they continue to assign generic caseloads which fail to take into consideration the unique nature of child protective services; (3) if they condone poor supervision; (4) if they allow for insufficient initial training; and (5) if they allow inadequate overall staff capability and staff preparedness."[116]

One writer summarized the benefits that are commonly assumed to follow the imposition of liability on government agencies:

> The government employer rather than the individual child protection worker should be subject to liability. Holding the employer liable would properly focus the deterrent effect on the administrative structure. In order to protect itself from liability, the state would improve its selection, training, and supervision of child protection workers. The state would have the incentive to confine the individual worker's discretion through detailed standards of conduct. Moreover, making the state employer instead of the individual employee liable would given parents greater assurance that damage judgments will be satisfied.[117]

If these analysts are correct, agency liability would be a real boon to society. Services would improve, injured clients would be compensated, and individual workers would be protected. But, despite its superficial attraction, agency liability has the same drawbacks as individual liability.

Agencies can no better afford extensive liability than can individual workers. Most private agencies carry insurance, but, as liability expands, sufficient coverage becomes more expensive to purchase and, ultimately, impossible to obtain. In the wake of widespread but largely unsubstantiated allegations of sexual abuse in day care, most centers found their insurance costs ballooning. Many are being forced to "go bare," that is, to carry no insurance. A large and uninsured award can do long-term damage to any social service agency; small or precariously funded ones could be forced to close their doors.

Even when the agency is victorious, being forced to defend a suit can be financially devastating (just as it can be for an individual worker). Legal fees are always sizable. One small private agency spent $110,000 defending itself and its workers before its case even reached trial. Because of negative publicity, private agencies often lose clients, contracts to provide services, grants, and private contributions.

Awards against government agencies, of course, come out of general tax revenues. Thus, there is no question about these agencies being forced out of business. But massive amounts of new liability will not go unnoticed by government leaders and budgetary officials. Some observers think that the government's response will be to recognize the need for improvement, followed by the infusion of more funds and programmatic support. Past experience does not support this optimistic scenario, however. At best, an agency will lose its credibility when seeking its annual appropriation; at worst, it will see its program sharply curtailed.

Thus, like individual workers, agencies have a great stake in avoiding lawsuits, even unfounded ones. And, like individual workers, they are under great pressure to resort to defensive practices. Agencies, "through the use of rules, incentives, and discipline, may explicitly or implicitly rely on the same risk-aversion techniques that individual officials currently use. . . . Inaction, delay, formalism, and changes in the character of decision, albeit to a lesser degree, can all be prescribed by the agency or administrator as well as individual officials."[118] Agency responses to reports of suspected child maltreatment are the best evidence that defensive administrative practices are likely. After cases like *Mammo v. Arizona,* in which the agency was held liable for failing to accept a report for investigation,[119] many child protective agencies have abandoned their obligation to screen reports. To protect themselves from possible lawsuits, they accept the most questionable reports without assessing their propriety. The great damage this does to the families wrongly investigated and to the system's ability to protect endangered children has already been discussed.

Furthermore, expanded agency liability would be dangerously misleading. Lawsuits claiming agency negligence do not educate the public about the complexity of child welfare problems and the need for a broad-scale improvement in services. Rather, by suggesting that agency administrators have been somehow negligent, they deflect attention from the real issues. Selinske warns:

> Newspaper headlines flash scathing indictments of the shortcomings of the public CPS system. In part, such criticism clouds the issue; it prevents careful examination of the circumstances that have hampered timely or effective responses. The ready availability of officials and systems as scapegoats soothes the consciences of communities outraged by the prevalence of child neglect and abuse. Unfortunately, this concern is wasted if its sole purpose is to criticize rather than to facilitate solutions.[120]

Of course, administrators could do a better job, a much better job, in running their agencies. Many programmatic changes could make existing resources more effective in meeting the needs of clients. But the real reason for the shortcomings of child welfare services is more basic: inadequate financial and political support.

The plain truth is that we have the kind and quality of child welfare services for which society is willing to pay. Adequate services would be enormously expensive. Consider only the costs associated with one program component—supervisory home visits. Increasing the number of home visits for the 200,000 or so families needing them from the present four to the needed 40 a year (at an average cost of $50 for each visit) would add about $350 million to the nation's annual bill for child protective services.[121] As one adds the costs of enriched counseling and psychiatric/psychosocial services, the additional investment needed quickly reaches over $800 million—almost tripling present expenditures.

If people were serious about using the tort law to obtain better child welfare services, they would not sue agencies. They would sue state budget officials, governors, state legislatures, the President, and the Congress. Merely saying this demonstrates its absurdity. No lawsuit, or slew of lawsuits, will cure the system's weaknesses. Only sustained community and political advocacy will do so.

Law, however, can be one tool of advocacy. A distinction should be drawn between *tort actions* seeking money damages and *reform or injunctive actions* seeking particular changes in agency policy or procedure. Although substantial problems have been encountered in structuring and enforcing remedial court orders, such litigation shows much promise.[122] Equally important, it focuses attention on the systemic nature of problems plaguing child welfare.

Unhappily, though, one notes a growing tendency to name individual social workers as defendants in these injunction actions and to seek money damages from them. In part, this is a necessary accommodation to changing legal rules that make it easier to sue individual employees than to sue agencies.[123] But doing so is also a lawyer's strategy designed to raise the stakes in the litigation. Whatever the motivation, this practice presents all the dangers of suing workers separately. It makes the need to give individual workers blanket good faith immunity all the more pressing.

Notes

1. See *N.Y. Times,* 29 March 1969, p. 36.

2. Report of the Judiciary Relations Committee of the Appellate Division of the First Department, quoted in *New York Law Journal,* 30 June 1969, p. 1.

3. N.Y.S. Assembly Select Committee on Child Abuse, *Report* (1972), pp. ii–v, reprinted in R. Helfer and C. H. Kempe, eds., *The Battered Child,* 2d ed. (Chicago: University of Chicago Press, 1974).

4. See pp. 70–72 and p. 108, respectively.

5. W. Holder, "Malpractice in Child Protective Services: An Overview of the Problem," in Holder and K. Hayes, eds., *Malpractice and Liability in Child Protective Services* (Longmont, Colo.: Bookmakers Guild, 1984), p. 5.

6. Quoted in Massachusetts Committee for Children and Youth, *Jane Doe and Richard Roe et al. v. England: Synopsis of Case* (undated memorandum), p. 4.

7. R. Levine, "Social Worker Malpractice: A New Approach Toward Accountability in the Juvenile Justice System," *Journal of Juvenile Law,* 1 (1977), p. 102.

8. See J. Mallor, "Liability Without Fault for Professional Services: Toward a New Standard of Professional Accountability," *Seton Hall Law Review,* 9 (1978), p. 474, collecting various references on the subject.

9. L. Schultz, "Preface," *Malpractice and Liability in West Virginia's Child Protective Services: A Social Policy Analysis* (Morgantown: West Virginia University School of Social Work, 1981), p. 10.

10. For a discussion of this case, see pp. 113–115.

11. "Confronting the System: How Social Workers Can Challenge—and Change—the Laws," *Practice Digest,* 7 (Fall 1984), p. 9.

12. R. Cohen, *Malpractice: A Guide for Mental Health Professionals* (New York: Free Press, 1979), p. 284.

13. This case is discussed on pp. 37–38.

14. T. Wise, "Where the Public Peril Begins: A Survey of Psychotherapists to Determine the Effects of *Tarasoff,*" *Stanford Law Review,* 31 (1978), pp. 163, 186. See, generally, the references in Appendix A.

15. Ibid., p. 187.

16. Cf. Committee on Government Operations, Subcommittee on Executive Reorganization, 91st Cong., 1st Sess., *Medical Malpractice: The Patient Versus the Physician,* p. 22 (Comm. Print 1969) (testimony of E. Bernzeig), with J. O'Connell, "An Alternative to Abandoning Tort Liability: Elective No-Fault Insurance for Many Kinds of Injuries," *Minnesota Law Review,* 60 (1976), p. 501; R. Brook, R. Brutuco, and K. Williams, "The Relationship Between Medical Malpractice and Quality of Care," *Duke Law Journal* (1975), p. 1197; D. Mechanic, "Some Social Aspects of the Medical Malpractice Dilemma," *Duke Law Journal* (1975), p. 1179.

17. J. Giovannoni and R. Becerra, *Defining Child Abuse* (New York: Free Press, 1979), p. 260.

18. See U.S. General Accounting Office, *Increased Federal Efforts Needed to Better Identify, Treat and Prevent Child Abuse and Neglect* (Washington, D.C.: U.S. Government Printing Office, 1980), especially Chap. 3.

19. See W. Benton, T. Field, and R. Miller, *Social Services: Federal Legislation vs. State Implementation* (Washington, D.C.: Urban Institute, 1978), p. 72, stating that: "The majority of [state administrators and federal staff surveyed] agreed that Title XX had the greatest positive impact on the children's protective service category."

20. U.S. Department of Health and Human Services, *Technical Notes: Summaries and Characteristics of States' Title XX Social Services Plans for Fiscal Year 1980* (Washington, D.C.: undated report), p. 126.

21. See J. Brady, "Grand Jury Hits Backlog of Child Abuse Reports," *Washington Post,* 6 March 1984, p. B3.

22. U.S. General Accounting Office, *Increased Federal Efforts Needed,* pp. 39–40.

23. *Regina v. Leslie, Simpson and Fenemore,* County Court for the United Counties of Leeds and Grenville, Oral Judgment (29 April 1982).

24. Ibid., pp. 7 and 14–15.

25. Cohen, *Malpractice,* p. 260, quoting G. Balliet, "13 Ways to Protect Yourself Against Malpractice Suits," *Resident and Staff Physician,* 20, No. 4 (1974), pp. 70, 73.

26. R. Horowitz, "Improving the Legal Bases in Child Protection Work—Let the Worker Beware," in Holder and Hayes, eds., *Malpractice and Liability in Child Protective Services,* pp. 17, 24.

27. J. Selinske, "Protecting CPS Clients *and* Workers," *Public Welfare,* 41 (Summer 1983), p. 31.

28. See P. Deleon and M. Borreliz, "Malpractice: Professional Liability and the Law," *Professional Psychology,* 8 (August 1978), pp. 467, 471–472; Z. Lebensohn, "Defensive Psychiatry or How to Treat the Mentally Ill Without Being a Lawyer," in W. E. Barton and C. J. Sanborn, eds., *Law and the Mental Health Professions: Friction at the Interface* (New York: International Universities Press, 1978), p. 19.

29. P. Schuck, *Suing Government: Citizen Remedies for Official Wrongs* (New Haven: Yale University Press, 1983), p. 75.

30. Schultz, "Preface," p. 10.

31. C. Gembinski, M. Casper, and E. Hutchinson, "Worker Liability: Who's Really Liable?" in C. Washburne, ed., *Looking Back, Looking Ahead: Selections from the Fifth National Conference on Child Abuse and Neglect* (Madison: University of Wisconsin School of Social Work, 1982), p. 118.

32. This case is discussed on p. 94.

33. W. Holder and K. Hayes, eds., "Preface," *Malpractice and Liability in Child Protective Services,* p. xi.

34. J. Fleming and B. Maximov, "The Patient or His Victim: The Therapist's Dilemma," *California Law Review,* 62 (1974), p. 1025.

35. See M. Wald, "State Intervention on Behalf of 'Neglected' Children: A Search for Realistic Standards," *Stanford Law Review,* 27 (1975), pp. 985, 998.

36. "Update on Worker Liability," *Virginia Child Protection Newsletter* (James Madison University, June 1985).

37. P. Pruneau, "Area Social Workers Fear Loss of Jobs," *Worcester Telegraph,* 12 September 1984, p. 3.

38. Schultz, *Malpractice and Liability,* unnumbered page.

39. For a fuller discussion of this and the other elements of tort liability, see pp. 32–38.

40. V. DeFrancis, "Guest Editorial," *National Child Protection Services Newslet-*

ter, 2, No. 8 (Denver, Colo.: American Humane Association, Winter 1979), p. 2. Emphasis in original.

41. For a further explanation of this approach, see D. Besharov, "The Legal Aspects of Reporting Known and Suspected Child Abuse and Neglect," *Villanova Law Review,* 23 (1977-1978), pp. 458, 499.

42. W. P. Keeton and W. L. Prosser, *Prosser and Keeton on Torts,* 5th ed. (St. Paul, Minn.: West Publishing Co., 1984), p. 228.

43. Gembinski, Casper, and Hutchinson, "Worker Liability," p. 119.

44. G. Sharwell, "Learn 'Em Good: The Threat of Malpractice," *Journal of Social Welfare* (Fall-Winter 1979-1980), p. 47.

45. J. Giovannoni, *What is Harmful to Children?* (Washington, D.C.: Community Services Administration, U.S. Department of Health, Education and Welfare, 1977), pp. 36-37.

46. Giovannoni and Becerra, *Defining Child Abuse,* p. 2.

47. Col. Rev. Stat. § 19-1-103(20) (1978).

48. Utah Code Ann. § 78-3A-2(17) (Supp. 1983).

49. Ark. Stat. Ann. § 45-403(4) (1977).

50. Kan. Stat. § 38-802(g) (Supp. 1978).

51. N.Y. Fam. Ct. Act § 1012(f)(i) (1983).

52. N.Y. Fam. Ct. Act § 1012(f)(i)(B) (1983).

53. U.S. National Center on Child Abuse and Neglect, *Draft Model Child Protection Act,* Commentary to Section 4(c)(v) (August 1977).

54. C. H. Kempe, *Child in Peril,* Xerox Films (Media Concepts, 1972).

55. S. Nagi, "Child Abuse and Neglect Programs: A National Overview," *Children Today,* 4 (May-June 1975), pp. 13, 17.

56. Schultz, *Malpractice and Liability,* unnumbered page.

57. J. Goldstein, A. Freud, and A. Solnit, *Before the Best Interests of the Child* (New York: Free Press, 1980), pp. 16-17.

58. Ibid., p. 190.

59. Wald, "State Intervention," p. 1014.

60. U.S. National Center on Child Abuse and Neglect, *Child Protective Services: Inservice Training for Supervisors and Workers,* Module III, "Investigations" (Washington, D.C.: Department of Health and Human Services, 1981).

61. U.S. National Center on Child Abuse and Neglect, *Review of Child Abuse Research: 1979-1981* (Washington, D.C.: Department of Health and Human Services, 1981), pp. 42-105. See, generally, J. Cocozza and H. Steadmen, "The Failure of Psychiatric Predictions of Dangerousness: Clear and Convincing Evidence," *Rutgers Law Review,* 29 (1976), p. 1084.

62. R. Helfer, "Basic Issues Concerning Prediction," in Helfer and C. H. Kempe, eds., *Child Abuse and Neglect: The Family and the Community* (Cambridge, Mass.: Ballinger Publishers, 1976), p. 363.

63. As defined by *Diagnostic and Statistical Manual of Mental Disorders (DSM III)* (Washington, D.C.: American Psychiatric Association, 1980).

64. R. Bourne, "Child Abuse and Neglect: An Overview," in Bourne and E. Newberger, eds., *Critical Perspectives on Child Abuse* (Lexington, Mass.: Lexington Books, 1979), p. 3.

65. U.S. National Center on Child Abuse and Neglect, *National Study of the Incidence and Severity of Child Abuse and Neglect* (Washington, D.C.: Department of Health and Human Services, 1981), p. 18, Table 4-1.

66. *Landeros v. Flood,* 17 Cal. 3d 399, 412, n. 9, 131 Cal. Rptr. 69, 551 P.2d 389, 395 (1976).

67. As defined in *Diagnostic and Statistical Manual of Mental Disorders (DSM III).*

68. The same is true for parents who suffer from *extreme* forms of mental retardation. If suitable arrangements have not been made to ensure that their children's needs are met, state intervention is essential. To wait until the parents demonstrate their inability to care for the child properly would require that the child be left in the parents' care until the inevitable injury occurred. See *Roberts v. State,* 141 Ga. App. 268, 233 S.E.2d 224 (1977): a baby born to a mentally retarded 14-year-old mother was placed in foster care immediately after birth; despite the absence of any "history of deprivation," the court held that, under the circumstances, parental rights could be terminated on the ground that the child would suffer deprivation if the mother were given custody of him. Likewise, alcohol or narcotic abuse, to the extent that the parent suffers an extreme impairment of judgment and coping ability *(DSM III* calls these extremes of alcohol and drug abuse "alcohol psychoses" and "drug psychoses"), are other forms of parental disability for which preventive intervention is justified. See, for example, N.Y. Fam. Ct. Act § 1046(a)(iii) (McKinney 1983).

69. Parental threats to kill or otherwise to harm a child "must trigger swift and immediate action from those charged with the protection of children." *In re Jason B.,* 117 Misc. 2d 480, 458 N.Y.S.2d 180, 181–182 (Fam. Ct., Richmond Co. 1983). D. Besharov, *Proving Child Abuse: A Guide for Practice Under the New York Family Court Act* (Ithaca, N.Y.: Cornell University, 1984), p. 20, states:

> However, a distinction must be drawn between parental threats to kill or harm a child and parental descriptions of feelings of anger or loss of control. Parental expressions of anger toward a child and of fears of losing control...require further assessment. Many parents have "angry thoughts" about their children; some find themselves thinking about beating, and even killing, their children. That the parents have summoned the courage to tell an outsider about such feelings is a reflection of how real—and disturbing—these feelings can be. In parents of young children, especially newborns and infants, such feelings are a signal of serious danger that cannot be ignored. But in parents of older children, such verbalized feelings are an all too common symptom of dysfunctional parent/child relationships. Although they are destructive and may benefit from treatment, they probably will not deteriorate into actual abuse or neglect. Thus, for parents of older children, "angry thoughts" warrant a finding only if there is sufficient additional reason to believe that they signal future maltreatment.

70. "Harmful," after all, means "causing *or* capable of doing or causing harm," according to the *Random House Dictionary,* Unabridged (New York: Random House, 1973). Emphasis added.

71. This does not mean that the degree of actual harm a child suffers is not an important decision-making concern; but, instead of creating a separate reason for intervention, the degree of actual harm should be used as an indicator of a heightened need to intervene.

72. A. Kadushin, "Emotional Abuse" (Unpublished paper presented at a joint U.S. National Center on Child Abuse and Neglect and National Institute of Mental Health Workshop on Emotional Maltreatment, Houston, Tex., April 1976).

73. Child protective intervention is needed whenever a parent cannot adequately care for a child, regardless of whether the failure is intentional or not.

74. M. Holmes, *Child Abuse and Neglect Programs: Practice and Theory* (Washington, D.C.: National Institute of Mental Health, U.S. Department of Health, Education and Welfare, 1976), p. 115.

75. Wald, "State Intervention," p. 1004.

76. Goldstein, Freud, and Solnit, *Before the Best Interests of the Child,* p. 64.

77. N.Y. Family Court Act § 1051(c) (1983), allowing the court to dismiss a proven petition if it determines that its "aid is not required...."

78. See N.Y. Fam. Ct. Act § 1052 (1983).

79. Wald, "State Intervention," pp. 1001–1002. Footnotes omitted.

80. See R. Helfer and C. H. Kempe, "The Child's Need for Early Recognition, Immediate Care and Protection," in Kempe and Helfer, eds., *Helping the Battered Child and His Family* (Philadelphia: J. B. Lippincott Co., 1974), p. 70.

81. Author's estimate, based on U.S. National Center on Child Abuse and Neglect, *National Analysis of Child Neglect and Abuse Reporting: 1979* (Washington, D.C.: (Department of Health and Human Services, 1979), p. 47, Table 17.

82. See Goldstein, Freud, and Solnit, *Before the Best Interests of the Child,* p. 73.

83. Sharwell, "Learn 'Em Good," p. 46.

84. B. E. Bernstein, "Malpractice: An Ogre on the Horizon," *Social Work,* 23 (March 1978), p. 110.

85. Texas Public Servant Standards of Conduct Advisory Committee, "Background Report for the State Employee's Tort Liability Act," p. 4 (undated). The case itself is described on p. 66.

86. American Law Institute, *Second Restatement of Torts* (Philadelphia: American Law Institute, 1979), p. 414.

87. See *Prosser and Keeton on Torts,* p. 1059 ff.

88. See, for example, *Whelehan v. County of Monroe,* 558 F. Supp. 1093 (W.D. N.Y. 1983); *Bauer v. Brown,* Civ. No. 82-0076-L (U.S. D.Ct.W.D. Vir., 30 August 1983); *cf. Tango v. Tulevech,* 61 N.Y.2d 34, 471 N.Y.S.2d 73, 459 N.E.2d 182 (1983).

89. *Tango v. Tulevech,* 471 N.Y.S.2d 77.

90. Letter from J. Cameron to A. Campriello, 31 January 1985, p. 2.

91. *Elton v. County of Orange,* 3 Cal. App. 3d 1053, 84 Cal. 27, 29 (Ct. App. 1970).

92. American Law Institute, *Second Restatement of Torts,* p. 416.

93. Ibid., pp. 416–417.

94. See, for example, L. Jaffe, "Suits Against Governments and Officers: Sovereign Immunity," *Harvard Law Review,* 77 (1963), pp. 1, 218.

95. *Mammo v. Arizona,* 138 Ariz. 528, 675 P.2d 1347 (Ariz. Ct. App. 1983); see pp. 57–60.

96. *Doe v. County of Suffolk,* 494 F. Supp. 179 (E.D. N.Y. 1980); see pp. 97–99.

97. *Elton v. County of Orange;* see pp. 111–115.

98. See Jaffe, p. 218, stating: "The dichotomy between 'ministerial' and 'discretionary' is at the least unclear, and one may suspect that it is a way of stating rather than arriving at the result."

99. Schuck, *Suing Government,* p. 89.

100. *"Suing Government,"* Book Review, *Michigan Law Review,* 82 (1984), pp. 1036, 1037–1038.

101. See Chart 2-4.

102. See Chart 2-2.

103. See, generally, Annotation, "Validity and Construction of Legislation Con-

ferring Personal Immunity on Public Officers or Employees for Acts in the Course of Duty," *American Law Reports,* 163 (1946), p. 1435.

104. See, for example, for guardian's *ad litem,* Fla. Stat. Ann.§ 415.508 (Supp. 1985); for psychiatrists, Cal. Government Code § 820.2 (1980); and for public officers, Annotation, "Immunity of Public Officer from Liability for Injuries Caused by Negligently Released Individual," *American Law Reports 4th,* 5 (1981), p. 773.

105. *Harlow v. Fitzgerald,* 457 U.S. 800, 815 (1982), quoting *Wood v. Strickland,* 420 U.S. 308, 322 (1975). Emphasis added.

106. See, for example, *Whelehan v. County of Monroe.*

107. See *Prosser and Keeton on Torts,* p. 1032ff.

108. See, for example, J. Codega, "Is Your Child Protective Program Liable?" p. 49, and M. Corey, "Treatment and Standards Which Protect the Child Protective Worker," p. 85, both in Holder and Hayes, eds., *Malpractice and Liability;* DeFrancis, "Guest Editorial"; M. Kieffer, "Child Abuse in Foster Homes: A Rationale for Pursuing Causes of Actions Against the Placement Agency," *Saint Louis University Law Journal,* 28 (1984), p. 975; Note, "A Damages Remedy for Abuses by Child Protective Workers," *Yale Law Journal,* 90 (1981), p. 657. Other commentators have made the same recommendation for public agencies in general; see, for example, Schuck, *Suing Government;* P. Lansing and J. Zieser, "The Liability of "Street-Level" Officials [sic] Societal Objectives, Congress and The Supreme Court," *Southern University Law Review,* 8 (1982), p. 231.

109. DeFrancis, "Guest Editorial," p. 2.

110. Schuck, *Suing Government,* p. 98.

111. "Training Is Key To Child Abuse Services," *NASW News,* 25 (November 1980), p. 10.

112. See D. Besharov, "Putting Central Registers to Work: Using Modern Management Information Systems to Improve Child Protective Services," *Chicago-Kent Law Review,* 54 (1978), p. 687.

113. 566 F.2d 817, 823 (2d Cir. 1977), discussed on pp. 95–96.

114. *Ehret v. New York City Department of Social Services,* 80 Civ. 2042 (LDW) (U.S. Dist. Ct., E.D. N.Y.), 1980.

115. "Mistreating Child Abuse," *Boston Globe,* 14 October 1982, p. 16.

116. Codega, "Is Your Child Protective Program Liable?" p. 59.

117. See Note, "A Damages Remedy," at pp. 697–698.

118. *"Suing Government,"* Book Review, pp. 1040–1041.

119. See pp. 58–59.

120. Selinske, "Protecting CPS Clients *and* Workers," p. 33.

121. See, generally, D. Besharov, "Child Protection: Past Progress, Present Problems, and Future Directions," *Family Law Quarterly,* 17 (1983), p. 151.

122. See, for example, P. J. Johnson and B. J. Fried, "Implementation Dilemmas in North Carolina's Willie M. Program," *Child Welfare,* 63 (September–October 1984), p. 419.

123. See *Prosser and Keeton on Torts,* p. 1032ff.

7

Reducing Legal Vulnerability

Build Professional Awareness

This chapter will describe some steps that social workers should take to reduce their legal vulnerability (Chart 7-1). Before social workers can be expected to take such steps, however, they must be made aware of their vulnerability and they must be motivated to make the necessary changes in their professional conduct to reduce it. "Every practicing social worker should have a basic knowledge of the elements of negligence and malpractice,"[1] explains Barton Bernstein, a lawyer and member of the adjunct faculty of the University of Texas School of Social Work.

Supervisors should be aware of the personal liability they face for the acts or omissions of those under their supervision, including outside consultants, students, and volunteers.[2] One article lists nine areas of potential liability:

1. the supervisor fails to provide information necessary for workers to obtain consent;
2. the supervisor has failed to catch supervisee's errors in all phases of contacts;
3. the supervisor fails to detect or stop a negligent treatment plan or treatment is carried out beyond its effectiveness, or the CPS worker has failed to terminate treatment when indicated;
4. the supervisor fails to determine that a specialist is needed for treatment;
5. the supervisee is involved sexually with the client or exerts unnecessary influence on client and conceals it from supervisor;
6. the client's record is not adequate and the supervisor does not improve it;
7. the supervisor fails to meet regularly with supervisee;

8. the supervisor has failed to review and approve of supervisee's decisions; and
9. the supervisor fails to provide adequate coverage in supervisee's absence.[3]

In addition, of course, agency officials should be aware of their potential personal liability for the negligent performance of their duties and of the agency's vicarious liability for the acts of its staff, including students and volunteers.[4] In addition, of course, agency officials should be aware of their potential personal liability for the negligent performance of their duties and of the agency's vicarious liability for the acts of its staff, including students and volunteers.[4]

Chart 7-1
Eight Steps to Reduce Legal Vulnerability

- Be aware of the existence and nature of professional liability;
- Adhere to legal and administrative requirements;
- Maintain agency and professional standards of conduct and performance;
- Keep complete records;
- Ensure financial protection;
- Involve law enforcement agencies in child protective efforts;
- Be sensitive to high-risk situations; and
- Advocate for improved services and legal reform.

This book seeks to aid in the process of professional education, but much more needs to be done. Information about professional liablity must be provided at all levels of social work education—undergraduate, graduate, and continuing professional education. George Sharwell, a professor at the University of South Carolina School of Social Work, has written:

> What social work educators do not know about malpractice can hurt us. What is more, our ignorance of this nasty yet very real legal concept also can cause injury to social work students, to social work practitioners, and to their clients. Moreover, the reluctance of social work educators to examine malpractice in the library, the courtroom, and the agency, and our failure to bring this data into the classroom, the workshop, or the scholarly or professional journal, retard [sic] the growth of social work knowledge. It also demonstrates that social work educators have abdicated their responsibility to take the lead in demonstrating how scholarship can be applied to benefit social work practitioners or their clients.

Examination of malpractice is important both because of its potential usefulness in saving the skin (or pocketbook) of the social work educator, student, or practitioner and because of the seemingly obvious relationship of malpractice to questions related to competent social work practice. Because they are opposite sides of the same coin, to learn about malpractice is to learn about competent practice as well.[5]

In 1985, the Massachusetts chapter of the National Association of Social Workers issued a policy statement on social worker liability. On the subject of professional awareness and education, it said:

All workers need some understanding of malpractice and the ways in which practice may expose them to suit. Schools should take leadership in offering training for students in liability prevention....NASW chapter should take leadership in informing practitioners about their vulnerability to malpractice. Many are fearful of the risk and desire better information. Chapters can publish articles in newsletters, conduct conferences and workshops, and distribute materials and pamphlets available through national NASW.[6]

Professional education about potential liability should have three purposes. First, for reasons of basic fairness, social workers should be warned of the legal vulnerability they face. This is especially important for students about to enter the field, but all social workers should be given "the sobering facts about malpractice," to use Sharwell's phrase.[7] Second, social workers should be given clear guidance about how liability is created and what can be done to reduce vulnerability. Particularly hazardous areas of practice and types of decisions should be identified, good practice responses suggested, and the need for adequate insurance emphasized. Finally, legal vulnerability should be placed in an appropriate perspective. Despite the very great increase in suits against social workers, the plain truth is that the vast majority of social workers will not be sued and that, for most of those who are, the legal system—and insurance—can provide reasonable protection. Thus, professional education should also seek to calm the unjustified fears of practitioners. An informed profession will understand that although liability is an important concern, there is no reason to panic. This understanding will reduce the stress under which social workers must operate and should enable them to focus on the central issue: providing high quality service for their clients.

Good Practice Is the Best Defense

As this book has repeatedly illustrated, many successful lawsuits are based on the social worker's failure to adhere to applicable state laws, administrative procedures, or professional standards of practice. Thus, a keen awareness of these liability-creating materials and a thorough knowledge of their requirements is not only good practice—it is critical to any effort to reduce personal vulnerability. (Appendices D and E contain a listing of some of the relevant professional standards.)

Agencies should provide adequate orientation, training, and supervision for all their employees. Workers should have a clear understanding of what is expected of them; they should know the essential elements of their responsibility and authority. For example, they should know what actions they can take on their own initiative (and the considerations involved) and what actions require supervisory or administrative approval. Record-keeping obligations should be specified and monitored. Staff training is an ongoing process that seeks to reinforce employees' familiarity with legal rules and agency policies and to keep them current with any changes that are made.

Ultimately, though, all social workers, whether on their own or working in agencies, "must take the responsibility to learn their business."[8] This means reading professional literature, seeking and taking advantage of educational opportunities, consulting with others, and maintaining membership in professional groups and organizations.

Many social work decisions entail a complex weighing of social, psychological, medical, and legal considerations. Joint decision making and second opinions should be sought for all difficult or unusual situations. Decision making becomes easier—and more accurate—when it is done in consultation with other mental health professionals whose skills and experience can help assess the situation. Consultation in case decision making often requires legal advice as well.

> Legal consultation should be available to staff on a regular and continuing basis. The relationships between lawyers and social workers are often tense, but workers need access to legal opinions as they make case decisions. Ongoing training from lawyers should be provided on new laws or important court decisions that alter procedure. New employees should receive training in the legal context of practice.[9]

"Agencies have an obligation to provide staff with clear policy statements that implement the agency's goals and obligations."[10] The primary purpose of an agency statement of policy or guidelines for practice is educational; such statements or guidelines inform staff members of their responsibilities. Of equal importance, though, is the way in which such formal policies serve as administrative support to front line staff. They represent an implicit commitment by the agency to back up staff members who follow prescribed policies. Moreover, the very process of drafting a written document can clarify previously ambiguous or ill-conceived agency policies.

A broad cross-section of agency officials, staff, and relevant outsiders should be consulted in drafting the policy. This will help make the document more effective and more broadly acceptable to all those bound by it. Great care should be taken to ensure that the agency policy does not ask workers to do the impossible. The policy should be written within the context of the agency's resources and competency. In addition, a lawyer's input should be sought to help "assure initial compliance with both federal and state statutes and with local interpretations of these laws. The legal advisor's recommendations should also have shaped the development of an adequate record-keeping system that monitors and records the day-to-day implementation of guidelines and procedures."[11]

The particulars of a policy depend on the agency's mission; its size, staffing, and mode of operation; and the governing state and federal law. As an example of the mix of practice, administrative, and legal issues a policy should address, Chart 7-2 presents an outline of a formal policy statement on reporting suspected child abuse and neglect. Agency policies should also have provisions concerning supervision, record keeping, confidentiality of records, ongoing staff training, staff participation in multidisciplinary teams, and case consultation and decision making generally.

Chart 7-2
Outline of Formal Policy Statement on Reporting
Suspected Child Abuse and Neglect

Element	Sample Wording
Statement of Support	In order to protect children from abuse and neglect, this agency supports the identification and reporting of such endangered children to the proper governmental authorities.
Legal Mandate	The laws of this state require the following persons to report a child if they have reasonable cause to suspect that a child is abused or neglected....
Reportable Conditions	In this state, "child abuse" is defined as.... "Child neglect" is defined as.... "Sexual abuse" is defined as....
Who Should Report	All staff members having reasonable cause to suspect that a child is abused or neglected should report. Or:....should contact the head of this agency, who shall make the report.
How to Report	As soon as possible, a report should be made by calling the local child protective agency at:... A written report must be submitted within 48 hours.* (Reporting forms may be obtained from:....)
Dangerous Circumstances	If the child appears to require immediate protection, such as emergency medical care or protective cus-

---

*This is a requirement in some states.

Chart 7-2 (continued)

	tody, bring this to the immediate attention of the child protective agency (or the head of this agency).
	If it appears that the parents may become violent or attempt to forcibly remove the child, consider calling the police at:....
Information Required	The person reporting need not prove that the child has been abused or neglected, only that there is reasonable cause for suspecting maltreatment.
	When reporting, be prepared to give the following information: name, address, and age of child; name and address of parent or caretaker; nature and extent of injuries or description of maltreatment; any other information that might help establish the cause of the injuries or condition.
Protections for Reporting	Anyone making a report in good faith is immune from civil or criminal liability for reporting.
Penalties for Not Reporting	Under state law, persons failing to report when they have reasonable cause to suspect that a child is abused or neglected are subject to criminal prosecution and civil lawsuit.
	In addition, failure to report may result in a disciplinary action by this agency.
Informing the Child and/or Parents	The decision to inform the child and/or the parents about the report should be made by the following persons:....
Record Keeping	A careful record should be kept of the report, the conditions that led to it, and its outcome. A copy of the written report should be included in this agency's records.
Confidentiality	To protect the family's privacy, all records concerning the report shall be kept confidential. Staff members should discuss the report only with persons who have a "need to know" about it.
Consultation	Advice on reporting requirements and procedures, as well as consultation on particular situations, is available from:....
	This person also serves as the liaison with the child protective agency.

Reducing Legal Vulnerability

A well-received and clearly written policy can greatly upgrade an agency's functioning. But, to be effective, a policy must be known. Copies of the policy should be distributed to all staff members. In addition, copies or appropriate summaries should be posted in key locations, such as staff lounges or cafeterias. Furthermore, the policy should be "buttressed with practice manuals and reinforced through training. It is not sufficient to simply promulgate rules and standards without providing an opportunity for staff to integrate them into their practice."[12]

Finally, agencies and social workers in private practice should regularly conduct a "risk assessment." This risk assessment should not be of their clients, but, rather, of the services they provide—their strengths and weaknesses, the degree to which they may create legal vulnerability, and the means by which they can be improved. No agency and no individual worker, however, should rely solely on the results of a self-evaluation. At appropriate intervals, agencies should arrange for an outside evaluation of their performance.[13] Similarly, a worker in private practice should have an ongoing consultative or quasi-supervisory arrangement with another clinician (it need not be overly formal).[14] At regular intervals, the worker should review the legal implications of his or her private practice with a lawyer familiar with the issues involved.

Keep Complete Records

Careful record keeping is always good social work practice. In the context of potential liability, "good case record maintenance, proper use of the case record and professional recording is essential for the agency and caseworker concerned with being adequately defended against malpractice suits."[15]

Many months often elapse between the events in question and the initiation of a lawsuit. A written record of what transpired at the time will help refresh memories of events long past and may be used, under certain circumstances, as evidence to bolster a worker's testimony. In addition, records are a form of institutional memory that can usually be introduced into evidence if the original maker of the record is unavailable to the court. This can be especially important for those institutions, such as public social service agencies, having high staff turnover.

> When caseworkers leave an agency they take with them the things they experienced, remembered, planned and perhaps wrote somewhere in their notes, sometimes undecipherable to anyone else. Only the record is permanent, and what was not documented may be lost forever, even when it could make a serious difference in diagnosis and planning in the hands of the worker who next has the responsibility. Such potential for error is a disservice to the children and families who come into child protective services, to the next worker who may be "flying blind," and to the agency's intent.[16]

Most important, "Good records imply competent practice and allow for service accountability. Inadequate records too easily can suggest substandard practice."[17]

> Carefully documented records may well mean the difference between a court judgment for you and a court judgment against you. Clear, concise statements summarizing your contacts with the patient are looked upon favorably by judges and juries. Conversely, the professional who comes into court with a confused jumble of notes and who testifies in a like manner (e.g., "On that day we talked about....No, wait now. I think it was two weeks before we got into something like that....") will certainly not make a very convincing witness. Slawson (1970) has advised that "good clinical records are the keystone" of a defendant's case and that "in those cases that go to trial, sloppy and incomplete records count heavily against the litigant who relies upon them."[18]

Unfortunately, few social work case records meet professional standards of thorough and timely preparation. No one familiar with record-keeping practices would deny the general applicability of the following comments about child protective records:

> Experience from various program evaluations involving record review demonstrates that record keeping is a general and pervasive problem within child protective service agencies. Poor record keeping can be found to be apparent in various forms: no recording, insufficient recording, inappropriate recording, too much recording and even recording which is damning....[19]

Many agencies have carefully formulated record-keeping requirements, together with forms and instructional materials. If they have not, they should. Social workers in private practice should develop an appropriate system of record keeping and adhere to it diligently.

Because this book is designed for a national audience of social workers practicing in a variety of settings, it is impossible to specify the form or content of records that should be maintained. The general approach to appropriate record keeping is most succinctly stated in an NASW publication:

> Keep current, written records which include clear, objective statements upon which any interpretations are based. Adhere to administrative policies and procedures when actions are taken and assure a completed record, free of erasures, which would be available for legal perusal.[20]

Chart 7-3 contains an outline of a useful approach to clinical records. For further guidance, readers should consult any of the fine works available on this subject.[21]

Two specific points, though, can be made in the context of liability concerns. First, special care should be taken to document the nature and basis

Chart 7-3
Outline of Model Clinical Record

Formulation

I. Intake/Opening/Diagnostic Summary
  A. Reason for service request or referral, including initial goals, needs, resources
  B. Description of the client and the relevant environment
    1. Personal (e.g., developmental, behavioral, cognitive, and emotional) factors
    2. Interpersonal (e.g., family, work) relationships
    3. Social (e.g., cultural, community, role) factors
    4. Institutional (e.g., school, governmental agency) relationships
    5. Physical (e.g., housing, transportation) environment
  C. Psychosocial history
    1. Personal
    2. Interpersonal
    3. Social
    4. Institutional
  D. Organization-specific information (e.g., work history, health status)
  E. Worker's assessment of A–D
II. The plan
  A. Purpose(s) of the service transaction, evolving goals
  B. Modalities of intervention
  C. Tasks, roles, responsibilities
  D. Time factors
  E. Means of assessing progress
  F. Possible barriers to achieving goals
  G. Contract, when applicable

Implementation

I. Progress notes (repeated at regular intervals)
  A. Description of relevant personal, interpersonal, social, and institutional factors
  B. Assessment of current client-in-situation
  C. Description of service and worker activity
  D. Systematic measurement of service effects, when relevant
  E. Assessment of progress
  F. Transactive information
  G. Reformulation of plan, when relevant

Evaluation

I. Closing/Transfer/Discharge Summary
  A. Reason for closing
  B. Description of client-in-situation at close
  C. List of services delivered
  D. Evaluation of service impact
    1. Worker's assessment of client-in-situation at beginning and end of service transaction
    2. Client's assessment of service
    3. Evaluation of systematic measures of service effects
  E. Analysis of factors that enhanced or impeded goal achievement
II. Follow-up: Description of the client-in-situation after a designated period of time has elapsed after service termination

Source: J. D. Kagle, "Restoring the Clinical Record," *Social Work,* 29 (January–February 1984), pp. 46–47.

The Vulnerable Social Worker

of any decision or action that creates a greater-than-average possibility of suit. For example, whenever a report of suspected child abuse is being made, or whenever a child is being removed from parental care, the record should include a full and specific description of the child's condition; any statements by the child, parents, or other witnesses (direct quotations are preferable); any other evidence; and the diagnostic or assessment process that led to the decision. The record should be equally specific about the precise actions that were taken.

Second, the record should explicitly reflect all situations in which legal or agency requirements or professional standards must be compromised because of inadequate time or service resources. This information should be forcefully—but not abrasively—brought to the attention of the supervisors and other responsible agency officers. Should there be a subsequent lawsuit, such documentation will go a long way toward establishing the worker's freedom from fault and, hence, from liability. Also, regularly reminding those in charge of the inadequacy of agency services might even result in their improvement.

Ensure Financial Protection

Most social workers still do not carry professional liability insurance. This is a serious mistake, given their steadily increasing legal vulnerability. Although insurance cannot compensate for the emotional costs of being sued, it provides vitally needed financial protection. A successful lawsuit could drive a social worker into bankruptcy.

> Some therapists go "bare," feeling that, without coverage, they are less attractive targets for a suit. This is a risky practice because an outraged client still might bring suit, and then one would have to pay sizable legal fees and possibly a settlement. Even if less than the six-figure insurance coverage, a settlement of $5,000 or $10,000 is still a substantial windfall. If it were to be taken out of a therapist's savings, or if his income were garnished, the effects could be devastating.[22]

The provision of legal representation—a component of almost all insurance policies—is as important as indemnification for payment of a court award or settlement. Almost all suits are expensive to defend—even when they are groundless, false, or fraudulent. Carrying insurance means that legal costs —which can sometimes exceed the amount being claimed as damages—will also be reimbursed.

Thus, for the self-employed social worker, professional liability insurance should be considered a necessary cost of practice. Moreover, considering its low price (as of this writing, adequate coverage can still be purchased for well under $100), going without coverage seems to be a needlessly dangerous gamble.

Social workers employed by public or private agencies usually do not purchase insurance because they think that they are protected by their status as employees. This is not necessarily true. Most private agencies now carry insurance, and so do a growing number of public agencies. Other agencies have formal indemnification programs, under which the agency will "indemnify" (reimburse) workers for the losses they sustain as the result of lawsuits.[23] But many public or private agencies have neither, or, if they do provide protection for individual workers, the type of protection provided is often inadequate.

Thus, it behooves all agency social workers to find out whether their agency carries insurance or has an indemnification program. Actually, the agency should make a point of giving this crucial information to all staff. The charts in Appendices F, G, and H identify state laws relating to insurance, indemnification, and legal representation for *publicly employed* social workers. The charts present a reasonably accurate general view of state laws, but inaccuracies in individual state law provisions are possible, and no attempt was made to list local laws or particular agency policies. As an example of a local law, on January 27, 1976, the Hennepin County, Minnesota, Board of Commissioners resolved that:

> The County of Hennepin will defend, save harmless and indemnify any officer, agent or employee, whether elective or appointive, against any tort or professional liability claim or demand, whether groundless or otherwise, arising out of an alleged act or omission occurring in the performance of duty; ...the County will compromise and settle such claim or suit and pay the amount of any settlement or judgment rendered thereon....[24]

It should also be pointed out that this is a rapidly changing area of the law, and specific state descriptions could quickly become out of date. Moreover, many of the state laws identified are permissive in nature, that is, they authorize but do not require the provision of insurance, indemnification, or legal representation.[25] Therefore, the charts should be used for initial reference only. Definitive information about the financial protection afforded by a public agency should be obtained from the agency—preferably in writing. Obviously, the same is true for private agencies. Chart 7-4 presents an example from Massachusetts of the written statements of protection often available to social workers.

The social worker's inquiry should not be limited to finding out whether there is an insurance or indemnification program. Some agencies provide unreasonably low dollar limits of coverage; others do not cover all areas of possible liability. For example, some agencies purchase $10,000 automobile accident coverage; a few do not purchase any. Coverage for constitutional violations is often absent, or at least not explicitly set forth. Chart 7-5 lists the basic questions that social workers should ask their agencies about insurance and indemnification coverage.

Chart 7-4
Massachusetts Policy on
Social Worker Indemnification and Protection

In the event that a DSS social worker is named as defendant in a lawsuit, he/she can receive certain protections. These protections may vary depending upon the nature of the lawsuit.

In the event that a social worker is sued for the negligent performance of his/her job, Massachusetts General Laws 258 Section 2, provides that the person bringing the lawsuit *must* choose to sue either the Commonwealth or the social worker but *not* both. Since the Commonwealth has more money than any defendant social worker, people generally choose to sue the Commonwealth.

However, there is one exception to this general rule. A person may sue *both* the Commonwealth and the social worker where he alleges that the social worker has committed "willful and wanton" conduct rather than negligence. The term "willful and wanton" conduct is difficult to define and even more difficult to distinguish from negligence. It has been defined as a reckless disregard for the rights of others. It is conduct which is much more severe than ordinary negligence and usually is an intentional act. The important thing to remember is that "willful and wanton" conduct is very difficult to prove. Regardless of what a lawyer might label a social worker's conduct for the purposes of a lawsuit, most social worker conduct which would form the basis for a lawsuit falls in the category of negligence rather than "willful and wanton" conduct.

According to the Attorney General's Office, in Massachusetts willful and wanton conduct is considered an "intentional tort". An intentional tort is a wrongdoing which was committed intentionally. The Commonwealth can indemnify a social worker for up to one million dollars for an intentional tort including court costs and attorney fees, provided that the social worker has been acting within the scope of his/her employment when the intentional tort occurred.

In the event that a social worker is sued for either negligence or for an intentional tort, the Attorney General may elect to represent him/her. Presently there is no criteria which the Attorney General follows to determine whether to represent a social worker. The Attorney General has the option to decide on a case-by-case basis. In the event that the Attorney General declines to provide representation, DSS attorneys are not permitted to represent individual social workers and the social worker thus must secure private counsel....

Source: Massachusetts Department of Social Services, Boston, undated.

- If the agency has an insurance policy, does it provide personal coverage for individual workers? Are there any special limitations? For example, is there a narrow definition of "scope of employment"?

- If the agency has an indemnification program, is reimbursement mandatory or discretionary? If it is discretionary, who decides? How is the decision made?

- What amount of financial coverage is provided? Is there a deductible?

- What types of claims are included? Excluded? For example, is there coverage for personal injuries caused by accidents on the premises or while in the worker's car? Is there coverage for professional decision making? For civil rights violations? For other intentional torts?

- Are punitive damages covered? (In about half the states, it is illegal to issue insurance for punitive damages.)

- Does the insurance cover all claims arising for situations that occurred when the policy was in force? Or is coverage limited to claims actually filed when the policy was in force? (If the latter, insurance is needed even after retirement.)

- Are the plaintiff's attorney's fees for claims involving the violation of constitutional and federal statutory rights covered?

- Is separate legal representation mandatory or discretionary? Who decides? How is the decision made?

The most serious shortcoming of many agency insurance policies is their failure to cover claims made against individual workers, as opposed to claims against the agency as an employer and corporate entity. This can put the individual worker in even greater jeopardy.

> [T]he therapist and his [or her] supervisors and the agency head may *all* be named as codefendants in a suit. [When the policy only covers agency liability, it] may be to the insurance company's benefit to attempt to show that the employee's behavior fell outside the scope of the insurance policy's coverage, or to break the chain of responsibility and locate the negligence solely within one employee and thereby avoid liability for the agency.[26]

Thus, only a personal policy provides employees with full coverage. "A personal policy ensures the therapist that an attorney will argue strenuously for the therapist's own interests."[27] If an agency does not provide employees with personal coverage—and cannot be convinced to do so through reason or labor-management negotiation—then they should purchase their own.[28] Should there be a suit, employees will need legal advice about their personal exposure to liability, their rights in the litigation, and any protective actions they should take. The cost of such a consultation alone easily exceeds the cost of many years of premiums for a personal policy.

Indemnification programs, by definition, cover individual employees. But they, too, can place the agency in an adversarial position against an individual employee. As Appendix G suggests, besides other serious limits in coverage, most programs deny indemnification for "willful," "wanton," or "intentional" conduct or conduct that is "outside the scope of employment." Consequently, even workers covered by indemnification programs should seriously consider purchasing personal liability insurance.

Before insurance is purchased, comparison shopping is necessary. The costs of premiums can vary by as much as 150 percent. One variable is the amount of coverage, of course. The greater the amount of coverage, the more expensive the policy. In this matter, it is wrong to be penny-wise and pound-foolish. The first few dollars of coverage are generally the most expensive. For example, in 1984, the price difference between $100,000 and $1 million of coverage under the NASW policy was $16 (from $33 to $49).

In comparison shopping, one should also see what levels of claims are included. Some policies cover premiums for legal bonds, such as appeal bonds and bonds to release property that is being used to secure a legal obligation or to guarantee that there are funds to pay a potential award. In addition, some policies include premises coverage, that is, coverage for slips, falls, and other injuries in the office. Likewise, coverage for automobile accidents is important, because many workers use their cars to transport clients (especially children).

Most policies exclude intentional wrongdoing, such as, for example, sexual involvement with clients. The NASW policy covered claims of sexual involvement until April 1985, but the staggering increase of such claims (up from two in 1970 to 165 in 1980) led the insurance company to exclude them from coverage. The company, however, will pay a maximum of $25,000 in legal fees to defend such claims.[29]

Other policies exclude or are ambiguous about claims based on the violation of the client's constitutional rights, an area of substantial vulnerability in child welfare work. All these and other factors noted in Chart 7-5 should be considered before choosing a policy.[30]

The National Association of Social Workers sponsors a Professional and Office Liability Insurance Program under which its members may purchase insurance through the American Professional Agency. The American Orthopsychiatric Association and the American Psychological Association sponsor similar programs with the same firm. American Professional also issues policies for designated mental health professionals, including those with a master's or bachelor's degree in a mental health field, marriage and family counselors, licensed mental health professionals, master's level hypnotists, school guidance counselors, and clergy and pastoral counselors. Therapists and caseworkers who do not qualify for these policies will find it all but impossible to obtain reasonably priced insurance. If they want coverage, they will have to purchase it from a general insurance broker (the same person who sells car, home, and life insurance). Denied the efficiencies and leverage of group coverage, individual policies can be extremely expensive. (At this writing, they cost three to five times as much as the NASW policy.) This is what makes employer-purchased insurance so important—and an increasingly common element of salary and fringe benefit negotiations.

What should workers do when an agency refuses to provide insurance? One union came up with an innovative solution. Local 509 of the Massachusetts Service Employees International Union (AFL-CIO) has arranged a Group Personal Liability Insurance Plan under which employees of the Department of Social Services may purchase low-priced insurance through a voluntary payroll deduction. One hopes that other unions and organizations will adopt this creative response.

This section has not discussed the important question of legal representation because, in general, if a worker is covered by insurance or an indemnification program, a lawyer will be provided. The problem of financing legal representation when it is not provided by insurance or the agency—for example, in criminal cases—is discussed in Chapter 8.

The Special Problem of Criminal Prosecutions

Some social workers, like anyone else who breaks the law, belong in jail. In 1979, a New York City social worker was convicted of murdering his 68-year-old client after stealing her life savings. (He had been charged with throwing her weighted body into the East River after persuading her to withdraw more than $13,000 from a bank.) He was sentenced to a minimum of 25 years in prison.[31] Other social workers have been convicted of assault, rape, larceny, and fraud. Social workers who intentionally or recklessly ignore their legal duty to report an endangered child or to take necessary protective action perhaps also deserve prosecution, but there must be a clear violation of legal or ethical standards.

Besides the express penalty provisions of most child abuse reporting laws,[32] social workers can be charged under a number of statutes for a variety of crimes, including criminally negligent homicide, rape, or assault; accessoryship before or after the fact; and, if they are government employees, official misconduct.

This book has described a number of prosecutions against social workers in private practice, as well as publicly employed child protective workers, but rarely has it seemed that the indicted social workers were criminally culpable. Rather, it seems that they were being blamed—and prosecuted—for situations beyond their control. One case that almost resulted in a criminal prosecution illustrates this tendency:

> A neighbor reported that a six year old boy had been locked out of his house without shoes or socks on. It was nearly Spring and, although the worker felt that the mother needed some counseling on how to handle her son, there were no other indications that the child was in serious danger. Six weeks later, the child was dead—as a result of a brutal beating from his mother. No one, but no one, could have predicted that this would happen. The mother had never before physically assaulted the boy; she had never given any indication of having a serious emotional problem. And yet, for weeks, the local papers were filled with stories and editorials criticizing the worker and the agency for mishandling the case. The local prosecutor investigated and brought the case before a Grand Jury—calling as witnesses the caseworker, his supervisor, and his supervisor's supervisor. Thankfully, cooler heads prevailed, and the prosecution was dropped.[33]

Generally speaking, the truth appears to be that most criminal prosecutions against social workers are attempts to find a scapegoat for a child's death or, worse, to be blatant attempts by prosecutors to gain publicity. "I believe it was a political game," concluded one indicted social worker. "Because a child has died, the DA saw an opportunity to get an advantage. You know that always raises controversy in a community."[34]

Wrongful prosecution is not limited to actions against social workers. A 1984 American Bar Association committee report concluded: "Trial misconduct is increasing and threatens the defendant's right to a fair trial, the public's interest in the fair administration of justice, and the integrity of the legal profession."[35] Two former prosecutors explain why the problem seems to be growing:

> Theory dictates that the prosecutor seeks justice, not merely convictions. Yet the conviction psychology of many experienced prosecutors tempers their role as ministers of justice and emphasizes their role as advocates. Combined with the increasing use of investigating grand juries and the targeting of individuals against whom any violation is sought, this role shift presents opportunities for abusive conduct.[36]

Unhappily, the media play into the abuse of prosecutorial discretion. When indictments are first handed down, newspapers are filled with the sensational details of the unproven charges, editorials about accountability and helpless children follow, and the workers are all but convicted before their first hearing. Many months later, when the charges are thrown out by a judge, or a jury acquits the worker, the press pays almost no attention. Little more than a squib on the back pages is likely.

On the other hand, there is no denying that criminal prosecution, and the extensive media coverage that accompanies it, increase public awareness of child abuse and neglect and of the problems facing child protective agencies. Perhaps real reform sometimes results. Two workers from Louisville, Kentucky, concluded: "In retrospect, the grand jury indictments of June, 1980, though shown to have been poorly conceived and wrongly targeted, did provide a good opportunity to overhaul the CPS system."[37]

More common, however, is a less positive outcome: a spate of committee meetings, a new TV spot calling on people to report suspected maltreatment, a new brochure for professionals describing their legal responsibility to report, and a small (but not sufficient) increase in staffing. The main result of this little flurry of activity is an increased number of unfounded reports and an increased number of children unnecessarily placed in foster care, as described earlier. When things settle down, the child protective system goes back to business as usual, and the media and political leaders do not try to find out whether the situation has actually improved.

The possible positive effects of liability on the child protective system are, however, almost irrelevant. The incalculable costs of an unfounded public accusation against a worker—the fear, uncertainty, stigma, and financial expense—are simply too high a price to pay. There are other, better ways to achieve systemic reform.

When it is appropriate to consider prosecuting a social worker for a child protective failure? The decision to prosecute should not be based on the child's subsequent injuries, however tragic. Subsequent abuse does not necessarily mean that greater protective measures should have been taken. As described earlier, there may have been no reason to believe that the child was in danger. The only way to judge the need for criminal prosecution is to assess the worker's conduct within the context of established legal and agency procedures, coupled with what the worker knew at the time and seasoned with a mature realization that unintentional errors in judgment do not warrant criminal punishment.

Prosecuting social workers for the "failure" to prevent a child's further maltreatment is justified only when the three conditions listed in Chart 7-6 are satisfied. In most of the prosecutions described in this book, one or more of these three elements seem to be missing. Their absence explains why so many workers feel unfairly prosecuted and why most prosecutions are dismissed before trial.

What can be done to reduce social worker vulnerability to unwarranted—and improper—prosecutions? Unfortunately, the possibilities are limited. Because of the absolute immunity granted to prosecutors in most

Chart 7-6
Essential Conditions for the Criminal
Prosecution of Social Workers

- *First,* the child's further maltreatment must have been the proximate result of the social worker's failure to perform necessary child protective functions. That is, there must have been adequate warning signals of serious danger to the child that would have been discovered if the worker had complied with statutory and administrative requirements concerning the reporting, investigation, assessment, or monitoring of cases. Or, if such warning signals were discovered, the worker must have failed to respond to them in an appropriate manner.

- *Second,* the social worker's failure to perform necessary child protective functions must have been criminally culpable. That is, the failure must have been caused by an intentional or reckless disregard for the child's welfare. There should be no prosecution, for example, when the worker's failure was the consequence of an overwhelming caseload; poor training; or the unwise, but nevertheless good faith, exercise of legally authorized discretion.

- *Third,* no decision to prosecute should be made without a careful assessment of the sufficiency of the evidence and the social desirability of imposing criminal penalties.

---

states, it is next to impossible to sue them in state courts for malicious prosecution.[38] Likewise, prosecutorial immunity makes a federal Civil Rights Act claim equally unavailable.[39] Moreover, neither insurance nor immunity legislation, so useful in reducing vulnerability to civil suits, can help social workers. One cannot insure against the possibility of a prosecution, and insurance for attorneys' fees in such cases is not available to social workers. Furthermore, immunity legislation usually excludes "willful," "intentional," or "reckless" conduct, the key allegations in most criminal prosecutions.

Some protective steps can be taken, however. First, agency social workers should find out whether their agency has a policy of providing counsel for employees accused of crimes committed in the course of employment. Many private agencies have formal or informal policies that provide counsel on a discretionary basis. As Appendix H indicates, about 11 states have legislation that permits the provision of counsel in criminal cases. Any agency or state that has not adopted this policy should be urged to do so.

Second, police and prosecutors should be made a part of ongoing child protective efforts. Over the last 20 years, society's response to child maltreatment has been largely decriminalized. Building a therapeutic response has been a major reform, for which the field feels justly proud. However, it is equally true that some abusive parents belong in jail, and that there has been a tendency to exclude law enforcement agencies from what must be a more balanced social response to child maltreatment. Police and prosecutors should be encouraged to join community task forces on child abuse, multidisciplinary diagnostic and case planning teams, and interagency activities in general. Recognizing the important role of law enforcement agencies, a growing number of states have passed legislation that routes selected types of reports directly to prosecutors. New York, for example, requires the child protective agency to:

> give telephone notice and forward immediately a copy of reports...which involve the death of a child to the appropriate district attorney. In addition, a copy of any or all reports...shall be forwarded immediately by the child protective service to the appropriate district attorney if a prior request in writing for such copies has been made to the service by the district attorney.[40]

Involving law enforcement agencies in child protective efforts is sound practice, because they have much to offer in the way of advice and resources. This will also help prevent future prosecutions based on angry misunderstandings or unrealistic expectations. Remember how, in the El Paso case, the prosecutor is quoted as saying that: "if the [agency] staff had been willing to admit its mistakes [in not removing the child] and cooperate in the removal of the surviving children following their sister's death, the case probably would not have been taken to the grand jury."[41] After cooperating with social workers and others in planning, coordinating, and providing child protective services, police and prosecutors are much less likely to attack "the system" of which they are now a part and for which they now share responsibility.

Similarly, there should be sustained attempts to educate the media about the realities of child protective work *before* a tragic case sends reporters scurrying around to find someone to blame. Agencies should seek to provide such education, but when they fail to do so, the job falls to workers. In many communities, child protective workers have aggressively sought to explain the realities of their jobs to the press. In New York and Massachusetts, for example, they took to the streets, conducting informational picketing to get their point across. The revisions in state laws and agency procedures described earlier would be another important educational device.[42]

Finally, the social worker's response to a grand jury or district attorney's subpoena is often the most crucial determinant of whether there will be a prosecution. This important topic is discussed in Chapter 8.

Be Sensitive to High-Risk Situations

Although almost any client contact can result in a lawsuit, certain ones create a higher risk of being sued. Chapter 1 described the areas of greatest vulnerability for social workers in general, and Chapters 2 through 5 described the areas of greatest vulnerability in child welfare work. In addition, some clients present a higher-than-normal risk of suit. Clients who have already sued a professional, particularly another therapist, are in this category. So, too, are clients who are overly critical of a previous therapist or who have unreasonably high expectations about treatment.

Fee disputes are all-too-common precipitators of malpractice claims. Harsh reminders of unpaid bills and aggressive collection attempts (by the therapist, social service agency, or a collection agency) may push a former client already thinking about a lawsuit into contacting an attorney. This does not mean that therapists should allow their fees to go unpaid, but it does mean that they should be judicious in how they proceed.

Workers should be sensitive to such high-risk situations and should respond to them with due care. Added attention should be paid to the contents of case records; supervisors and colleagues should be consulted; and, if appropriate, a lawyers's advice should be sought.

Finally, it is well to remember the advice that lawyers give other lawyers about minimizing the chances of a lawsuit: stay on good terms with your clients (and former clients). For social workers providing often involuntary child welfare services, this advice may be of little practical utility; but for all other social workers, it is well worth remembering that an angry client is much more likely to sue. If a client's dissatisfaction is sensed, the social worker should consider talking through the client's feelings, either on the phone or in person. An ounce of prevention could be worth a pound of litigation.

Advocate for Legal Reform and Improved Services

The need for more realistic laws and professional standards, insurance and indemnification programs, provision of legal representation, immunity legislation, and supportive agency policies has been described in this book. Social workers concerned about the high level of legal vulnerability faced by their profession should join in efforts to achieve these and other reforms.

Equally important, social workers should examine all "reform" proposals to make sure that they do not promise too much. Many new laws and procedures are sold on the claim that they will eradicate a problem. In doing so, they create unreasonably high expectations about what social workers can do—and, when tragedies occur, as they inevitably must, such overambitious standards increase the legal vulnerability of social workers. Thus, in addition to advocating for "better" laws and procedures, social workers should advocate in favor of more honest, reasonable, and attainable standards.

This writer is a lawyer, and, as a result, this book focuses on legal responses to liability, but it would be wrong to leave the reader with the impression that reduced vulnerability lies solely in legal reform. Inadequate social and therapeutic services are the breeding ground for lawsuits. They increase the likelihood that a client will suffer real harm, that the client will seek out a lawyer to obtain redress, that the lawyer will accept the case, and that the court will impose liability. Therefore, even those few social workers who are insensitive to their clients' needs have a stake in improved services.

The NASW *Code of Ethics* articulates a professional obligation to seek improved services: "The social worker should act to ensure that all persons have access to the resources, services, and opportunities which they require."[43] Applying this general obligation to child welfare services, NASW's *Standards for Social Work Practice in Child Protection* include the following provision:

> **STANDARD 40. The Social Worker Shall Advocate for Community Services to Protect Children, Strengthen Families, and Prevent Child Abuse and Neglect.**
> All social workers have responsibility for participation in activities that can help protect children and strengthen families. These activities may include: testifying at public hearings in support of the CPS agency's budget and staff requests; showing support for needed legislative changes in behalf of children and families; participating on community task forces concerned with human service delivery; and encouraging the development of community resources and programs to meet the needs of children and families.[44]

Advocacy efforts should also be made within one's agency. Another NASW publication urges social workers to:

> Persist in efforts to have agency adopt realistic caseload standards as defined by national standard setting bodies. Raise issues for discussion at case conferences, supervisory conferences, interdisciplinary team meetings, and make citations in all appropriate agency records regarding such advocacy where decisions and outcome may be influenced by unrealistic expectations.[45]

No one should harbor any illusions about advocacy efforts. They fail more often than they succeed. They can take a large amount of the worker's time. And, they make few friends for the social worker. Sadly, most agencies—and most colleagues—are hostile to criticism and any suggestions for change, however needed. Remember, the major cases in which social workers have been punished for violating confidentiality were those in which they sought to expose programmatic weaknesses.

Thus, any advocacy efforts—and especially internal ones—should be pursued with tact and a clear appreciation of the agency's likely initial response. Allies—colleagues, a professional organization, a union, or an outside advocacy group—may not only increase the chances of success, but also reduce the likelihood of unfair retaliation. If the worst happens, and an agency punishes an employee for good faith efforts to protect clients, these allies may be crucial to the ultimate resolution of the charges against the employee.

In addition, the grievance procedure of the National Association of Social Workers is a widely overlooked avenue of protection and redress. A complaint may be filed claiming: (1) a violation of the *Code of Ethics* by a member; (2) a violation of personnel practices by an agency; or (3) that an agency imposed limitations on or penalties for professional action on behalf of clients.[46] In 1983, for example, NASW imposed sanctions against Western State Hospital, in Staunton, Virginia. According to the *NASW News:*

> The original grievance against Western State Hospital was filed in July 1981 by Brendan Buschi and Wanda Scott, former employees who were fired by the hospital after well-publicized actions raising questions about the quality of patient care at the institution.
>
> The complaint filed with NASW charged that the hospital had violated its own personnel standards in disciplining Buschi and Scott and that the penalties were imposed because of the complainants' actions on behalf of their client patients. The complainants were among nine social workers fired by the hospital in 1981 after they alleged patient abuse and subsequently refused to testify at an investigatory hearing. The report of the Staunton-area local Human Rights Committee in July 1981 confirmed that patients were being abused by other patients and that other inadequate conditions existed in the hospital.
>
> NASW found that in firing the workers the hospital had violated its own personnel rules, but that these violations were more technical than substantive in nature. The Virginia Chapter emphasized that Buschi's professional behavior was not evaluated; the National Committee on Inquiry found that the hospital had acted to impose penalties against Buschi and Scott because of their "sustained and vigorous actions to focus attention on conditions viewed as harmful to patients, and correctable by the hospital administration."
>
> NASW recommended that the complainants be reinstated and compensated for the actions taken against them, and that the hospital take steps to ensure adherence to its personnel policies and to address the patient care issues that had been raised.
>
> Because there was no response to these recommendations by Western State Hospital or the state Department of Mental Hygiene, the NASW Board of Directors has approved the imposition of sanctions against Western State and the release of publicity on the matter. The Virginia Chapter appointed two special committees to work on the recommendations concerning personnel matters and the quality of patient care.
>
>   *   *   *
>
> NASW is also asking schools of social work to refrain from using Western State Hospital as a student field placement until such time as satisfactory actions have been taken by the hospital on these recommendations. Accrediting organizations and state agencies responsible for Western State Hospital are being notified of NASW's finding and actions.[47]

Notes

1. B. Bernstein, "Malpractice: Future Shock of the 1980's," *Social Casework,* 23 (March 1981), p. 175.

2. See, for example, R. Slovenko, "Legal Issues in Psychotherapy Supervision," in A. Hess, ed., *Psychotherapy Supervision: Theory, Research, Practice* (New York: John Wiley & Sons, 1980); A. Zaphiris, "Criminal and Civil Vulnerability and Liability of Supervisors in Child Protective Services," in W. Holder and K. Hayes, eds., *Malpractice and Liability in Child Protective Services* (Longmont, Colo.: Bookmakers Guild, 1984), p. 61.

3. "Malpractice: Growing Liability for CPS Workers," *Virginia Child Protection Newsletter,* 7 (James Madison University, Spring 1983), pp. 10, 11.

4. See, generally, W. P. Keeton and W. L. Prosser, *Prosser and Keeton on Torts,* Chap. 12, "Imputed Negligence," 5th ed. (St. Paul, Minn.: West Publishing Co., 1984).

5. G. Sharwell, "Learn 'Em Good: The Threat of Malpractice," *Journal of Social Welfare,* 6 (Fall-Winter 1979-1980), pp. 34-40.

6. S. Antler, *Policy Statement on Social Worker Liability. Child Welfare at the Crossroads: Professional Liability* (Boston: Massachusetts National Association of Social Workers, 1985), pp. 41-42.

7. Sharwell, "Learn 'Em Good," p. 46.

8. W. Holder, "Malpractice in Child Protective Services: An Overview of the Problem," in Holder and Hayes, eds., *Malpractice and Liability,* p. 14.

9. Antler, *Policy Statement,* p. 36.

10. Ibid., p. 34.

11. B. Corder et al., "Legal Issues Affecting Residential Child Care Workers," *Child Welfare,* 63 (May-June 1984), pp. 217-218.

12. Antler, *Policy Statement,* pp. 34-35.

13. See, for example, T. Lewis, "A Suggested Model for the Child Protective Services Program Review," and J. Solheim, "Independent Assessment of Child Protective Casework as Malpractice Prevention," Chaps. 13 and 12, respectively, in Holder and Hayes, eds., *Malpractice and Liability.*

14. See *NASW Standards for the Practice of Clinical Social Work* (Silver Spring, Md.: National Association of Social Workers, 1984), Standard 7.

15. M. Romero, "The Case Record: A Major Source of Liability Protection for the Worker," in Holder and Hayes, eds., *Malpractice and Liability,* p. 105.

16. K. Hayes, "Commonly Identified Program Weaknesses in Child Protective Services," in Holder and Hayes, eds., *Malpractice and Liability,* pp. 113, 117.

17. Ibid., pp. 117-118.

18. R. Cohen, *Malpractice: A Guide for Mental Health Professionals* (New York: Free Press, 1979), pp. 265-266, quoting P. Slawson, "Psychiatric Malpractice: A Regional Incidence Study," *American Journal of Psychiatry,* 136, No. 5 (1970), p. 126.

19. Romero, "The Case Record," p. 106.

20. L. Whiting and M. Daniels, *Legal Vulnerability and Liability: A Guide for Social Workers* (Silver Spring, Md.: National Association of Social Workers, 1982), p. 2.

21. See, for example, J. D. Kagle, "Restoring the Clinical Record," *Social Work,* 29 (January-February 1984), p. 46.

22. B. Schultz, *Legal Liability in Psychotherapy: A Practitioner's Guide to Risk Management* (San Francisco: Jossey-Bass, 1982), p. 18.

23. See, generally, R. del Carmen and C. Venezano, "Legal Liabilities, Representation, and Indemnification of Probation and Parole Officers," *University of San Francisco Law Review,* 17 (1983), p. 227; R. Crane and G. Roberts, *Legal Representation and Financial Indemnification for State Employees: A Study* (College Park, Md.: American Correctional Association, 1977); Annotation, "Validity and Construction

of Statute Authorizing or Requiring Governmental Unit to Indemnify Public Officer or Employee for Liability Arising out of Performance of Public Duties," *American Law Reports 3d,* 71 (1976), p. 90. Recent child welfare cases on the subject include: *New Jersey Property-Liability Insurance Guaranty Association v. New Jersey,* 195 N.J. Super. 4, 477 A.2d 826 (1984); *Kern v. Steele County,* 322 N.W.2d 187 (Minn. 1982); *Vaughn v. North Carolina,* 296 N.C. 683, 252 S.E.2d 792 (1979).

24. Board of Commissioners Resolution, author's files.

25. See, generally, for insurance, Annotation, "Validity and Construction of Statute Authorizing or Requiring Governmental Unit to Procure Liability Insurance Covering Public Officers or Employees for Liability Arising out of Performance of Public Duties," *American Law Reports 3d,* 71 (1976), p. 90; for indemnification, *supra,* n. 23; and, for legal representation, Annotation, "Payment of Attorney's Services in Defending Action Brought Against Officials Individually as Within Power or Obligation of Public Body," *American Law Reports,* 130 (1941), p. 736.

26. Schultz, *Legal Liability in Psychotherapy,* p. 19.

27. Ibid.

28. The charts in Appendices F, G, and H, which describe state laws on the subject, can be used to help guide public sector negotiations.

29. " 'Sexploitation' by Therapists Condemned," *NASW News,* 30 (May 1985), p. 15.

30. See, generally, J. Brownfain, "The APA Professional Liability Insurance Program," *American Psychologist,* 26 (1971), p. 651.

31. "Social Worker Ordered to Prison for 25 Years in Murder of Client," *New York Times,* 11 September 1979, p. B3, col. 5.

32. See pp. 25–29.

33. Case mentioned in author's files.

34. W. Holder, "A Personal View of Caseworker Liability," in Holder and Hayes, eds., *Malpractice and Liability,* pp. 95, 101.

35. Standing Committee on Professional Discipline, "The Judicial Response to Lawyer Misconduct" (Chicago: American Bar Association, 1984), p. I. 3.

36. J. Lawless and K. North, "Prosecutorial Misconduct: A Battleground in Criminal Law," *Trial Magazine,* October 1984, p. 26.

37. E. Hutchinson and M. Casper, "CPS Indictments in Kentucky and Their Aftermath," *National Child Protective Services Newsletter,* 4, No. 6 (Denver, Colo.: American Humane Association, 1981), p. 9. The case is described on p. 66.

38. See *Prosser and Keeton on Torts,* § 132. The major exception to prosecutorial immunity is when liability is claimed for the prosecutor's investigatory acts, made independently or in aid of the police. Even here, though, good faith is a defense. See, for example, *Guerro v. Mulhearn,* 498 F.2d 1249 (1st Cir. 1974).

39. See, for example, *Imbler v. Pachtman,* 424 U.S. 409 (1976).

40. N.Y. Social Services Law § 424(4) (1983).

41. See p. 66.

42. See pp. 139–156.

43. National Association of Social Workers, *Code of Ethics* (Silver Spring, Md.: NASW, 1980), Vl.P, ¶A2, p. 9.

44. *NASW Standards for Social Work Practice in Child Protection* (Silver Spring, Md.: National Association of Social Workers, 1981), p. 28.

45. Whiting and Daniels, "Legal Vulnerability and Liability," p. 2.

46. A description of the Adjudication of Grievances procedure together with the necessary complaint forms may be obtained from the NASW National Office. NASW's Legal Defense Service, described in Chapter 8, may be able to provide support.

47. "Virginia, Massachusetts Agencies Draw Sanctions," *NASW News,* 28 (October 1983), p. 18.

8

Obtaining Legal Representation

First, Get a Lawyer

Tempting as it would be to provide a detailed set of recommendations on how to handle a lawsuit, only the following three pieces of advice can be given responsibly.

First, on learning of a lawsuit, *immediately* make all the appropriate notifications. If you carry an insurance policy, notify the insurance company. Many policies contain a provision excusing the company from responsibility for claims not referred to it within a specified time period (usually a very short one). If you are employed by a private agency, notify your superiors and make sure that they notify the agency's insurance company or legal counsel. If you are employed by a public agency, again, notify your superiors and make sure that they, in turn, make the required notifications, usually to the county attorney or state attorney general. In some jurisdictions, you may be under a *personal* obligation to make such notifications.[1] Find out whether you will be provided with legal representation by your agency. If so, determine whether such representation will adequately protect your interests, as described in the next section.

Second, *never* alter case records or other documents once you know of the lawsuit. Some social workers foolishly try to "tighten up" or otherwise alter records so that they will look better, but it is all too easy to discover that records have been "doctored"—and that is certainly what the opposing lawyer will call it. This will put you in the worst possible light, because it will suggest that there was something to hide. In criminal cases, if you haven't previously committed a crime, this would probably be one. When, for whatever reason, appropriate records have not been kept, write a memorandum to the file, bringing it up to date, filling in any gaps, and correcting any inaccuracies—and date it correctly.

The third piece of advice is: *Get a lawyer.* Coming from a lawyer, this advice may seem self-serving, but it is honest. No real guidance can be given here about the intricacies of legal rules and procedures. They vary too widely from state to state, and from community to community. For example, in some states, going before a grand jury without signing an explicit waiver creates absolute immunity. In most states, however, the effect is just the opposite; if a grant of immunity has not been given, the appearance by the social worker waives any objection, and the testimony may be used against the worker in a subsequent prosecution.[2]

Lawyers are highly trained professionals who specialize in helping others understand and negotiate the legal system. Just as we do not expect a lawyer to provide psychotherapy, so, too, we should not expect a social worker to handle a lawsuit.

Moreover, the old proverb is correct: "He who is his own lawyer has a fool for a client." For social workers attempting to represent themselves, a little knowledge is a dangerous thing, to cite another old saying. Besides wasting valuable time in trying to break through the legal thicket, laypersons are likely to do major damage to their cases because of lack of appropriate knowledge. When they finally do engage a lawyer, as many inevitably will, they are likely to have to spend extra money to have their lawyer try to undo whatever damage has been done—if, in fact, it can be undone.

Early representation by a lawyer, for example, can be crucial to avoiding criminal liability. It is many times easier to convince a prosecutor not to seek an indictment before the press learns of the case, for example, than afterward. Many workers are indicted because of a simple breakdown in communication.[3] For instance, some social workers have found themselves being prosecuted for failing to give a grand jury what they believed was confidential information.[4] Unfortunately, professional confidentiality is rarely a valid reason for withholding information from a grand jury.[5] A lawyer could explain the worker's rights and obligations and thus prevent him or her from taking a commendable but ultimately self-destructive stand.

Thus, the basic advice is simple: Get a lawyer. Your lawyer should tell you the rest of what you need to know: how to respond to the press, what motions to make, how to handle depositions, how to testify, how to dress for trial, when a settlement seems advisable, and so forth.

The problem is knowing *when* you need a lawyer. In civil cases, you should see a lawyer whenever you hear from a client's lawyer. When a client threatens to sue or when there are other high-risk indicators of possible litigation, more careful assessment is needed.[6] If the likelihood of a suit is small, you can safely wait, though you should take other steps to reduce your legal vulnerability.[7]

Criminal cases are more difficult to judge. Of course, if the police come and arrest you, it is clear that you need a lawyer. But what if the prosecutor asks you to come to the office, or even to testify before a grand jury? Each year hundreds of social workers are called to testify before grand juries (or to discuss pending cases with prosecutors). Almost always, the investigation is focusing on someone else: a parent in a child abuse case, for example. In a significant number of cases, though, the focus is on the worker's possible malfeasance—or it turns in that direction, quickly and without warning. Hear how one convicted social worker described what happened to her:

> CASEWORKER: "...I was subpoenaed to appear before a Grand Jury called by the District Attorney. He assured our agency attorney that no action was to be taken against the agency. The DA told the agency that the reason I was subpoenaed was to testify about any tendencies the parents showed toward violence and their parenting abilities. Well, I went to the Grand Jury. It met at night. The agency attorney assured me there would be no problems, and therefore he was not there. I testified from 7:00 p.m. to midnight, and it got to the point where it wasn't questioning anymore, but people from the DA's office yelling at me!"
>
> QUESTION: "Did you have any idea if this was a "set-up"? Was there an agenda, or did it just happen?"
>
> CASEWORKER: "I really don't know. I feel the DA worked himself up to the point where he didn't care. It was a nightmare!"[8]

Given this reality, what should social workers do when served with a subpoena to appear before a grand jury? Consulting with a lawyer whenever one is called before a grand jury is ordinarily good advice, but not really practical for those who, like child welfare workers, are regularly involved with criminal matters (or matters that could be of interest to prosecutors). The vast majority of the cases about which they are called to testify involve the possible criminal behavior of others, for example a parent's possible abuse of a child. It would be silly and prohibitively expensive if workers were to run to a lawyer every time their work brought them into contact with the criminal justice system.

Yet social workers must be wary lest they be called to testify about their own alleged malfeasance. They should be sensitive to high-risk situations[9] or to prosecutorial behavior suggesting that they are the focus of the investigation. For example, if the prosecutor asks the social worker to waive any rights, it is time to see a lawyer. On a more subtle level, if the prosecutor is vague about the purpose of the social worker's testimony or seems overly interested in the social worker's conduct, the worker should realize that there could be a problem. At this point, the worker should either see a lawyer or request an unequivocal assurance from the prosecutor that the investigation concerns another person. Only if such an assurance is immediately forthcoming should the worker agree to testify without talking to a lawyer.

Once in the grand jury room, without a lawyer to provide advice, the social worker must continually assess the situation. *"Be alert to any obvious changes in focus or direction,"* caution Bernstein and McCutchan. "Ask for a recess if defensive or hostile feelings are kindled. Call a lawyer during the recess. Get answers to any legal questions before proceeding."[10]

Following this advice requires that you be able to reach a lawyer qualified to provide the needed guidance, that is, one who specializes in criminal matters. Do not depend on an agency lawyer who usually handles juvenile court matters; and do not depend on your Uncle Joe, who usually handles real estate cases. If you do not have access to a lawyer qualified to advise you, ask for a longer recess. Do not allow yourself to be pressured into continuing. It is better to be safe than sorry. Any responsible prosecutor should appreciate your concerns and your need for legal advice. The prosecutor's failure to do so would be an added reason to feel vulnerable—and to talk to your own lawyer.

Under no circumstances should you sign a waiver of immunity without the advice of a competent attorney. One indicted agency administrator gives this warning:

> [I]f ever called to appear before a grand jury investigation, find out your rights before appearing. If when appearing your rights are read to you, do not waive them and [instead] seek advice from an attorney. In Texas I recently heard an attorney attribute the following statement about grand jury to Racehorse Hanes: "You can talk your way to jail or you can go to jail for not talking." If you offer to testify, then the grand jury, which has probably already been primed to indict someone, will use your statement against you no matter how innocent you are. The risk of going to jail for not talking is preferable because it puts the burden clearly on the state, where the U.S. Constitution clearly placed it. This is fraught with danger in community relations, but unless you feel almost certain indictment is worth it, your own self-preservation must come first. Indictments even without convictions have destroyed many people in the past. Don't be one of them.[11]

After a lawyer has been engaged, the social worker should place the handling of the case in the lawyer's hands. *All* inquiries should be referred to the lawyer. This, of course, requires that the worker have confidence in the lawyer, and this, in turn, brings us to two important questions: (1) how to determine the adequacy of representation supplied by an employer, and (2) how to select your own lawyer.

When Representation Is Supplied

Social workers who have been foresighted enough to purchase insurance are assured of being represented in a civil suit. (As a rule, insurance is not available to finance the defense of criminal charges.) Similarly, workers protected by a formal agency indemnification program will also be provided representation.

Even in the absence of insurance or an indemnification program, public and private agencies often provide counsel to represent employees who are sued; and, contrary to popular misconception, most agencies are not prohibited from providing legal representation in criminal cases.[12] Representation can be mandatory or, more likely, discretionary, pursuant to the employment contract or state law.[13] For public employees, representation is usually discretionary, as described in Appendix H. Many states have formal policies that elaborate on the general provisions of state laws. One state's formal policy on the representation of employees is set forth in Chart 8-1. In the absence of a preexisting policy, private and public agencies may still provide or pay for legal representation.

Whether or not the agency has a formal policy, actually obtaining legal representation may require intensive advocacy on the part of the worker who is sued, as well as by the worker's colleagues, union, and professional organization. Sometimes community groups must become involved. Also, an initial decision against providing counsel may be reversed later, and the worker may be reimbursed for the lawyer's fees, especially if the worker is vindicated by the outcome of the litigation.

Social workers cannot blindly rely on the lawyers supplied by their agencies. They must determine: (1) whether the lawyer is properly qualified by training and experience to handle the case, and (2) whether there is a conflict of interest.

When *your own* insurance company provides counsel, no real issue arises. Your insurance company has a large stake in the outcome of the suit: it will be paying any award up to policy limits. Ordinarily, this is sufficient to ensure adequate representation of your interests. Hence, it is always reassuring to have high policy limits that place the entire risk on the company.

Greater care is required when the agency's insurance company or the agency itself supplies legal representation, whether through house counsel, the attorney general's office (or similar legal officer), or outside counsel. To determine whether the attorney is qualified to handle your case, you should ask the same questions as you would ask when selecting your own lawyer, discussed in the next section.

To determine whether there is a possible conflict of interest, you should be direct about asking whether the lawyer is *your* lawyer—whether the lawyer represents *you* and *your* interests. If the lawyer says yes, ask for this assurance in writing. More probably, the lawyer will say something like

Chart 8-1
New Jersey Policy on Representation of Public Employees
by the Attorney General

Generally there are two types of legal action that may be instituted against a DYFS employee. A civil action is usually brought by a private citizen seeking money or "damages" as compensation for injury or loss resulting from an intentional or negligent act or omission on the part of a DYFS employee. Criminal action results from a criminal complaint or a grand jury indictment based upon alleged criminal conduct on the part of the employee. All references to "employee" also apply to a former employee against whom a criminal or civil action occurs because of acts or omissions which happened during employment by DYFS and to volunteers who perform services for the State of New Jersey and are duly authorized to perform these services, even though uncompensated.

Civil Action
Representation
Under New Jersey law (N.J.S.A. 59:10A-1) the Attorney General *shall* provide representation, upon request, for any employee against whom a civil action is brought on account of an act or omission in the scope of his employment. The Attorney General may refuse to represent the employee if he determines that any one of the following circumstances exists:

- the act or omission was not within the scope of employment;

- the act or the failure to act was because of actual fraud, willful misconduct or actual malice;

- the defense of the action or proceeding by the Attorney General would create a conflict of interest between the State and the employee.

When representation is provided, it may be by a member of the Attorney General's staff or by private counsel selected by the Attorney General.

Indemnification (payment of damages)
When the Attorney General provides representation for an employee in a civil action, the State will indemnify the employee. This means that any money judgment rendered against the employee will be paid by the State except for punitive or exemplary damages. These are damages awarded to the plaintiff over and above actual compensation for his loss, which may be levied as punishment against the defendant. The State will not pay any damages resulting from the commission of a crime. See *Recourse Upon Refusal to Provide Representation* for other circumstances in which indemnification may be provided.

Chart 8-1 (continued)

The employee's entitlement to indemnification is lost ". . .unless within 10 calendar days of the time he is served with any summons, complaint, process, notice, demand or pleading, he delivers the original or a copy thereof to the Attorney General or his designee." It is imperative that employees promptly follow the procedures below for notifying ORLA of legal actions and requesting representation.

Acceptance of Service
When an attempt is made to serve a summons and complaint upon an employee, the employee must look at the portion of the papers that identifies the parties who are being sued or "named" in the action. Only if the employee is named (singly or with other defendants such as the State or DYFS) may he accept service. No employee is authorized to accept service on behalf of DYFS or the State.

If there is confusion about the action (civil or criminal) or if the employee should accept service, the employee should contact the assigned Deputy Attorney General.

Procedure for Requesting Representation
Upon receiving a summons or other legal papers, the employee must notify his supervisor and the Office of Regulatory and Legislative Affairs (ORLA). The following materials should be forwarded immediately to ORLA, with a copy to the appropriate Regional Administrator:

- a request for representation (in memo form) by the employee;

- the originals of all documents served on the employee; and

- a brief description of the events involved.

The employee should keep copies of this material.

ORLA will make an initial determination whether the action is based upon an act or omission within the scope of employment. If it appears that the action is not job-related and that a request for representation may not be appropriate, ORLA will contact the employee and/or supervisor to discuss the matter. If the employee continues to believe that he is entitled to representation, his request will go to the Attorney General.

Recourse Upon Refusal to Provide Representation
When the Attorney General has refused to provide for the defense of a civil action for one of the reasons noted under *Representation* the employee may later receive reimbursement for the costs of defending the action and the amount of any bona fide settlement, agreement, or award of damages if the employee establishes that he was entitled to a defense. This will occur if:

Chart 8-1 (continued)

- the employee establishes that the incident in question occurred within the scope of employment, and

- the State fails to establish that the employee acted or failed to act because of actual fraud or malice or willful misconduct.

The payment by the State of judgments or damages is limited to actual damages as discussed in *Indemnification (payment of damages).*

Criminal Action
Representation
Under New Jersey law (N.J.S.A. 10A-3) the Attorney General *may* represent an employee against whom criminal charges are brought if he concludes that such representation is in the best interests of the State. This representation may be provided by the Attorney General's office directly or by outside counsel selected by that office. The Attorney General is responsible for deciding whether to supply representation and has issued the following statement in this regard:

"Although the facts of each individual case may be examined to determine whether the State should provide representation to an employee accused of a criminal or disorderly persons offense, the State ordinarily will provide representation in the following cases:

- Where the complaint was filed in bad faith or is totally lacking in substance; or

- Where the complaint was filed as a means of harrassing the State official in the performance of his official duties; or

- Where the subject matter of the complaint calls a fundamental interest of the State of New Jersey into question which must be defended; or

- Where the criminal or disorderly complaint or proceeding is filed or initiated by a citizen and not an enforcement official; or

- Where other special reasons or circumstances exist to warrant representation."

Request for Representation
The procedure for requesting representation in criminal matters is the same as that for civil action, with written request for representation, all legal papers served, and a full description of the events being sent to ORLA with copies to the appropriate Regional Administrator. ORLA will make an initial evaluation for the DYFS Director and, if appropriate, submit a request for representation to the Attorney General.

Chart 8-1 (continued)

Representation in criminal matters is discretionary with the Attorney General and the Attorney General has delegated some discretion to the DYFS Director by instructions to forward only those requests that are endorsed. The DYFS Director's decision is final. A decision not to forward a request to the Attorney General will be made by ORLA only with the written approval of the DYFS Director.

Fines and Penalties
The indemnification in civil actions is not available in criminal cases. Any employee convicted of a crime is solely responsible for payment of any penalty or fine imposed.

After-hours Coverage
The Attorney General's Office does not provide representation on any type of emergency basis for employees who are arrested or threatened with arrest after hours. This is because representation in criminal matters is discretionary on the part of the Attorney General and certain questions regarding the case (outlined under *Representation*) must be answered prior to any determination to defend the employee. In emergencies, employees are advised to make any necessary private arrangements with lawyers or bailbondsmen and contact their supervisor and ORLA the next working day. State statutes and policies do not guarantee reimbursement of the costs of such private arrangements. However, the Attorney General has issued the following statement:

"A public employee who has himself retained private counsel in a criminal matter where an acquittal or dismissal has occurred may request the State to pay for all or a part of the cost of his private counsel. Such a request must be approved by the Attorney General personally and by the head of the employing agency before payment will be made."

While not specifically stated in the Attorney General's guidelines, it is unlikely that this reimbursement will be approved if the employee did not request representation from the Attorney General at the outset. Since reimbursement under this provision is not automatic and would not occur until some time after the conclusion of the criminal matter, employees must assume responsibility for the costs of private counsel in these situations.

Cooperation with the Attorney General
When the Attorney General provides for the defense of a civil or criminal matter on behalf of an employee, the Attorney General has the right to control the defense and the employee has an obligation to cooperate fully with the defense.

---

the following: "I will represent you fully—but only for so long as there is no apparent conflict of interest between you and the agency [or the state]." The problem with this forthright statement is that if a conflict develops, it will generally be discovered from what you say or from your records—both of which can usually be used against you in later litigation. It is perfectly appropriate for you to ask also whether a conflict of interest is foreseen. Unfortunately, the candid answer is that, even if unlikely, a conflict of interest is always possible and the agency's lawyer cannot guarantee to protect your rights. This is why many insurance companies engage separate counsel for you and for the agency.

If you are being supplied with legal representation, it is wise to consult with your own lawyer before accepting agency-appointed counsel. In fact, one should consult with one's own lawyer before having any substantive discussions with the agency's lawyer. In addition, depending on your situation, it may be appropriate to have your personal lawyer monitor the case as it proceeds.

Selecting a Lawyer

Basically, selecting a lawyer is like selecting a doctor or a therapist. Personal recommendations from friends and colleagues are the best way to identify a qualified professional. Ask around. Find social workers or others who have been sued, find out who represented them, and ask whether they were satisfied with the representation they received. Do not be shy. Ask what the result was, and ask how expensive the lawyer was. Even workers who were represented by counsel provided by insurance companies can provide helpful leads. Most lawyers who handle insurance cases also handle individual clients.

Lawyer referral services can also help, but they must be used with care. The quality of referral services varies widely. Although some maintain minimum standards for listing, such as a specified amount of experience in an area, most do not. Referral services sponsored by local bar associations (which can be found in local telephone directories) are usually more reliable than commercial ones.

Legal directories that contain information about lawyers, their areas of specialization, and their fees can be found in most public libraries. The major ones include: *Martindale-Hubbell Law Directory, The Lawyer's Register by Specialists and Fields of Law,* the *Attorney's Register,* and the *Directory of the Legal Profession.*

Be wary of legal advertising. A television commercial or print advertisement may make the lawyer seem impressive, but it cannot provide an accurate picture of the lawyer's qualifications.

As potential lawyers are being identified, the social worker will have to decide whether to hire a general practitioner or a specialist. Many lawyers still maintain general practices, handling a variety of commercial, tax, financial, real estate, and torts cases. In smaller communities, there may be no choice but to hire a general practitioner. In larger communities, though, there will be a wide choice of specialists. (In fact, some lawyers specialize in plaintiff's tort work, while others specialize in defense work.)

A specialist is more likely to do a satisfactory job handling the case than is a generalist unfamiliar or only marginally familiar with the relevant area of the law. This is crucial in the area of criminal law. *Under no circumstances should a lawyer with no experience in criminal matters be retained to handle a criminal case.* A lawyer who has never before handled a criminal case—or who has insubstantial experience—is simply incompetent to do so. In fact, an ethical lawyer conscious of this reality should decline to represent a person charged with a crime. The stakes are too high to have the lawyer learn while doing.

Specialists usually charge more per hour than do generalists, but their greater experience should mean that they take less time to do the same tasks. Ultimately, the expense may be about the same. This important consideration is often overlooked as social workers recoil from fees of $100 to $150 or more per hour. In larger communities, it usually makes most sense to search out a specialist.

It is generally wise to hire a local lawyer—one who knows the judges, prosecutors, court personnel, and procedures in the court house where your case will be decided. Some people see the apparent friendships among local lawyers as an indication that their lawyer will not zealously represent their interests. Naturally, there is a tendency for people who work together regularly to want to get along and not to anger colleagues by taking overly aggressive stances.[14] However, this is a two-way street: prosecutors will want to maintain cordial relations with the defense bar. Only in the rarest of cases is there any real danger that "political" considerations will prevent zealous representation. This vague possibility is totally outbalanced by the great advantage of having someone who knows the "local scene."

The size of the firm, its resources, and its general reputation are also important considerations. A large firm can bring to bear greater resources and expertise than can a small one. Naturally, this comes at greater expense to the client. Fancy research and word-processing facilities, like elegant furniture in the waiting room, cost money—money that comes from clients. Small firms tend to give clients more personal attention and are usually more flexible about fee arrangements. You have to decide what kind of firm best meets your needs.

Your major focus, though, should be on the lawyer who will personally handle your case. The outcome of the case is more dependent on this individual's work than it is on the total size of the firm. Therefore, act as if you are hiring one lawyer, not the whole firm. He or she will be your main contact with the firm. No matter how good the rest of the firm is, if this basic relationship is not satisfactory, you will not be happy.

Comparison shopping is important. After developing a list of possible candidates, check their credentials with friends, colleagues, and other lawyers. Then, arrange interviews with the top two or three candidates. Use the interview to get a feel for the lawyer—you have to *like* your lawyer—and to gain basic information about the lawyer's practice, approach to cases like yours, and fees. The following passage will give you a flavor of what you should be looking for:

> If you have to hire a lawyer to try a case, how can you tell a good one from a bad one? First of all, don't pay too much attention to the certificates on the reception-room wall; they can be obtained for a lot of things besides trial work. Question the lawyer. Ask him how many cases he's actually tried in the past year. If he says, "Oh, a couple or so," he's probably not the man for you. If he says he's tried 50, he's spouting hot air; no trial lawyer who does his homework properly can try that many cases in 52 weeks. If he tells you he tries 10 to 14 significant cases a year, it's likely that he's properly experienced.
> But cases vary. Ask him about the types he's tried; make sure your sort is included.[15]

Prepare for the interview by drawing up a list of questions you want to ask. Chart 8-2 contains a checklist of questions to ask prior to and during the interview. Generally, the interview will be more fruitful, more revealing, and a more efficient use of everyone's time if you give the lawyer a description of your problem before the interview. Bring any legal papers or other relevant documents to the interview. Take notes at the initial interview and throughout the case. Cases often drag on for some time, and your records may prove invaluable as memories dim about what was said and agreed to.

Most lawyers offer to hold such exploratory interviews for free; some, though, will charge. Before arranging the interview, ask if there will be a charge. This may help you decide whether this is an attorney you would be interested in hiring.

During the interview, try to get a sense of what it would be like to work with the lawyer. Discuss the details of your case. Does the lawyer listen well? Does he or she ask probing questions? Are you comfortable with the lawyer's style and approach? Lawsuits often go badly for long periods; the two of you will probably have some tense moments. It is important that you begin your relationship with a sense of rapport.

Be sure to discuss fees. It should be unnecessary to say this, but most potential clients and a surprising number of lawyers are uncomfortable talking about this fundamental issue. After the lawyer's first bill for services arrives is the wrong time to discuss fees.

Ask for an estimate of what it would cost to defend your case. Although the lawyer cannot provide more than a general idea of total costs, the answer will help you evaluate your situation and the lawyer. Also ask the lawyer to describe the various ways that billing and payments can be handled.

Chart 8-2
Questions to Ask in Selecting a Lawyer

Prior to the initial interview:

- Do you ordinarily handle this type of case?
- Are you currently available to handle this case?
- Do you perceive a possible conflict of interest? If so, what is it?
- How quickly should I retain an attorney?
- Will there be a charge for the initial, exploratory interview?

During the initial interview:

- What kind of practice do you have? What kind of clients?
- What kind of experience do you have with cases like mine? (For criminal prosecutions, this means criminal defense work. For civil suits, this means defending professional malpractice cases.) How many have you handled? How many do you handle each year? Could you give me some examples? What was the outcome, and about how much did you charge? Could I have the names and telephone numbers of these clients and your permission to call them?
- Is there anyone else you would like me to call for a reference?
- What other background or experience makes you particularly qualified to handle my case?
- How would you handle my case? At this point, what legal and procedural approaches do you think advisable?
- Would you be doing all of the work? If not, will you introduce me to the other people who might be working on my case? What kind of supervision would you provide?
- How long do you think my case might take to be resolved? What do you think will be the likely result?
- What would be your fee arrangement for handling my case? Can you give me an estimate of total legal costs?
- What is your billing procedure? Do your bills itemize legal work done?
- How will you keep me apprised of the progress of my case?
- Would you provide me with a contract or letter of engagement describing the fee and billing arrangements to which we have agreed?

Source: Adapted from E. Krasnow and J. MacNeice, *101 Ways to Cut Legal Fees and Manage Your Lawyer: A Practical Guide for Broadcasters and Cable Operators* (Washington, D.C.: Broadcasting Publishers, Inc., in press), Appendix A. Used with authors' permission.

You will find that most lawyers bill either on an hourly basis or at a flat rate for specific steps in the litigation (such as the taking of depositions and other forms of pretrial discovery), or a combination of both. Find out whether the lawyer charges more for time spent in court; many do. Typically, specialists and lawyers practicing in urban areas will charge more than their generalist or rural counterparts.

Feel free to question the amount the lawyer wants to charge. Many lawyers are not so busy that they can afford to turn away clients who are unwilling to pay their maximum rate. They will negotiate fees.

There are few hard-and-fast rules about how to decide which lawyer is best for your needs. The decision, ultimately, is a personal one. Nevertheless, there are some lawyers you should avoid:

- Avoid a lawyer who seems too busy to give your case the requisite time and attention;

- Avoid a lawyer who guarantees a favorable outcome—even the strongest cases can unexpectedly go badly;

- Avoid a lawyer who is vague on the subject of fees;

- Avoid a lawyer who refuses to provide a contract or letter of engagement that spells out billing arrangements;

- Avoid a lawyer who tries to impress you with legal jargon; and

- Avoid a lawyer who refuses to give you references.[16]

Social workers trying to lower their legal expenses sometimes consider hiring the same lawyer who is representing other defendants in the same case. Spreading the basic costs of litigation is often sensible—as long as there is an identity of interests among the various defendants. But, as explained in the preceding section, if there is a possible conflict of interest, a separate lawyer should be retained.

The ultimate decision about selecting a lawyer is an intensely personal one. Not only are there differences in types of cases, but different clients need lawyers with different styles. Based on everything that you have learned—and your "feelings" about the lawyer—only you can decide whether this is the lawyer for you.

Your new lawyer will ask for a retainer. In this area of practice, there are two types of retainers. A "case retainer" is a nonreturnable fee paid at the beginning of the lawyer's handling of the case. In effect, it is the lawyer's minimum fee for handling the case. After a predetermined number of hours or at the next specified stage of the proceeding, the lawyer will request further payment. The second type of retainer, an "advance against costs," is more like a deposit. At the close of the case, the lawyer will return the unused portion of the advance. Whenever legal fees and expenses exceed the retainer, the lawyer will require a further advance.

Controlling Legal Costs

Any litigation is expensive. Nevertheless, there are a number of simple steps that clients can take to keep legal costs down.

One expense is particularly within the client's control: discussions with the lawyer. Lawyers, like taxicabs and therapists, always have the meter going. That pleasant half-hour you spent with the lawyer after your first court hearing will probably show up on your next bill. If you think that you are merely socializing, make sure your lawyer agrees.

Office visits should also be minimized. What with interruptions and pleasantries, they tend to take much longer than do telephone calls to accomplish the same amount of business. Even when your lawyer asks you to come in, which may in itself be a burden to you, ask if the matter can be handled on the phone. Of course, if the lawyer still asks you to come in, you should do so. But you will be surprised at how many matters can be taken care of by phone.

Similarly, if you have questions that you want to ask the lawyer, try to use the phone. You should not call your lawyer, however, each time some minor thought or question comes to mind. To make the most efficient use of your lawyer's time (and therefore, your legal fees), keep a list of nonurgent questions or comments and bring them up when you have sufficient reason to call.

Another way to help minimize legal costs is to see what you can do yourself, either on your own or under your lawyer's supervision. For example, you could collect the relevant professional standards or publications that would be helpful in determining the standard of conduct or competency that will be applied in the case. This will help to keep down legal fees, may turn up materials that legal researchers would have difficulty finding, and may be a helpful distraction from the stresses of litigation.

Your case may involve substantial out-of-pocket expenses, such as those for travel and expert witnesses. Make sure that such expenses are not incurred without your prior approval. "Since there is a wide variety of ways in which law firms charge for such expenses, ask for a schedule of charges and discuss any charges which you regard as unreasonable. Insist that your bills contain an itemized listing of disbursements."[17]

The method of billing can affect ultimate legal costs. "Find out the minimum billing time under your lawyer's system. Some lawyers bill for a quarter of an hour while others may bill for as short a period as one-tenth of an hour. The same two-minute telephone conversation may cost you 15 minutes of one lawyer's time and only six minutes of another lawyer's time. (Some lawyers will not charge you for telephone conversations of less than five minutes in duration involving questions such as the status of a pending matter.)"[18]

The format of the lawyer's bill may also help you control costs. A "summary bill" merely states the total amount charged for legal services and out-of-pocket expenses during a specified period; in effect, it says to the client: "Trust me, you do not need to know more about the costs associated with your case."

A "descriptive bill" contains a narrative description of the services rendered, such as "investigation," "reply brief," or "depositions." It ordinarily does not indicate the amount of time spent on the tasks or who performed them. This type of bill is most appropriate when a flat fee for specific services has been negotiated.

A "detailed bill" is just that; it indicates what was done and how much time it took. Although detailed bills cost more to prepare, they provide an important insight into where legal fees are going and a certain discipline on the lawyer's charges; they also allow the client to seek ways to reduce costs. For example, if the client has been calling the lawyer heavily, the cost of what seemed like merely shooting the breeze will become apparent to the client. Also, a detailed bill is a good basis for discussing how legal costs can be contained and, actually, for discussing how the case is going.

The schedule of billing is also important. Krasnow and MacNeice explain:

> Ask to be billed on a monthly or perhaps quarterly basis. This type of regular billing will put you in a much better position to control the manner in which your interests are being handled. It is much more difficult for both you and your lawyer to discuss a bill that covers work performed many months ago. Also, monthly or quarterly billing places you in a better position to spot developing patterns, to correct an undesirable course of action or to review the reasonableness of costs.[19]

Feel free to ask questions about your bill. You have a right to know where your money is going, and to ask why certain expenses were incurred, why certain tasks were performed, or why they took so long. For example, a bill for days of research and legal writing suggests either that your case raises unusually novel questions of law, or that your lawyer is not sufficiently knowledgeable in the particular area involved. Your lawyer should not hesitate to give you a more detailed explanation of costs.

Find out who has been doing most of the work on your case. Partners charge more than associates, because of their experience and the greater demand for their services. Paralegals, used by many firms for various tasks that do not require a lawyer's skills, are billed at an even lower hourly rate. Do not assume, however, that it is more economical to take advantage of these lower billing rates. The partner's higher cost usually reflects greater expertise and greater efficiency at getting the work done.

> Also, watch out for "handoffs." Don't let your lawyer substitute another lawyer in his firm for one who already has gained substantial familiarity with your case, unless there is a good reason. You might be billed for the hours the new lawyer spends learning about your case. If your lawyer concludes that a substitution cannot be avoided, ask him to write off the hours the new lawyer spends learning about your case.
> Make sure that your lawyer has not assigned too many other lawyers in the firm to work on your case. This practice is known as "pyramiding." If several lawyers are working on the same project, ask for a justification. If more than one attorney attends a meeting or hearing on your behalf, find out why the extra lawyer or lawyers were necessary.[20]

Many clients feel that they are paying too much for the results achieved, but remember (1) billable hours quickly mount up, and (2) lawyers are expensive, especially good ones whose services are in demand. If you are seriously concerned after talking to your lawyer, discuss your bill with someone else who has had to pay for similar legal services, but do not rely on the comments of friends who have never had to pay for the services of a lawyer. They will not know how expensive quality representation can be. You could also talk to another lawyer, but here, be careful. This lawyer may be reluctant to criticize the billing practices of a colleague or may unfairly do so in hopes of obtaining your business.

If, after the lawyer's explanation and after talking to others, you still feel that the charge is excessive, it is entirely appropriate for you to suggest the need to renegotiate the lawyer's fees. This is never easy to do, and, if not handled well, can raise tensions between the two of you. It is one reason why a lawyer should always be asked for an initial estimate of costs. Although such estimates cannot be made with precision, they give you a benchmark, provided by the lawyer, from which to judge the bill.

If you cannot resolve a billing question with your lawyer, you may want to discuss the problem with a more senior lawyer in the same firm, assuming that there is one. If there is not one, or if this does not work, you may decide to terminate your relationship with the lawyer, as discussed in the following section. There will still be the bill to pay, however. Krasnow and MacNeice offer the following good advice when the dispute reaches this extreme point:

> If these avenues fail *and* the dispute involves a significant amount of money or is otherwise important to you, ask your lawyer to submit the fee dispute to

informal arbitration. Suggest that the two of you select a neutral person, such as the dean of a law school or a retired lawyer, to decide the matter.

Or you can submit the dispute to a bar association for resolution. Many state and local bar associations have established procedures for the resolution of lawyer/client fee disputes. In some states and communities, lawyers are obliged to submit the dispute to arbitration if the client requests it.

As a last resort, you might refuse to pay the bill and face the possibility of a lawsuit by your lawyer for the unpaid amount. Keep in mind that if you do not pay your lawyer, he may have an "attorney's retaining lien," the right to keep all documents and records in his possession in order to protect any fee that is unpaid. Many lawyers will include a clause in the lawyer-client agreement providing for liens on files, records and monies collected from a settlement or court award. Those liens are valid, but there are limitations. They do not authorize the lawyer, for example, to dispose of client documents in his possession. A lawyer can only withhold the fruits of his own labor. Your lawyer cannot ethically refuse to release documents or research produced by another lawyer or by you or your company. Even the lawyer's own work may have to be released to you if you would suffer irreparable harm without it. Furthermore, a lawyer does not have the right to appropriate to himself monies paid to a client account, even when the lawyer's bills are unpaid. Instead, the disputed portion must be kept in the client's trust account until the dispute is resolved.

Even if you have a good chance of winning, try to avoid a lengthy dispute over your files at a critical stage in your matter. Again, withholding payment of an unreasonable fee may be unavoidable in some cases, but you should consider this tactic only as a last resort.[21]

If You Are Dissatisfied with Your Lawyer

Fewer marriages are made in heaven these days, and the same is true for attorney-client relationships. "The lawyer/client relationship is a business relationship, and accountability and solid performance should be expected. The basic point is that your lawyer works for you, not vice versa."[22] Laypersons often expect too much from their lawyers, but you have a right to be dissatisfied if your lawyer fails to meet professional standards of competence and courtesy, as outlined in Chart 8-3.

Discuss with your lawyer any dissatisfactions you may have. The lawyer may allay your concerns or may change his or her behavior. If you are not sure that your criticisms are valid, discuss them with friends and colleagues, but before taking their advice, be sure that they know what they are talking about. Few people who have not gone through a lawsuit have an accurate understanding of the unpleasant realities of litigation. You may, therefore, want to talk to another lawyer before deciding to fire your current one.

If you are ready to consider firing your lawyer, you should keep some factors in mind. There are certain inherent advantages to staying with the same lawyer. Changing lawyers is expensive and time consuming. Unless you are firing your lawyer for sufficient legal cause, you will still have to pay for services already performed and for expenses already incurred. You will

Chart 8-3
Evaluating Your Lawyer

- Is your case going poorly *and* is this attributable to your lawyer's failings?

- Is your lawyer accessible? Are your telephone calls returned promptly, i.e., usually within 24 hours?

- Does your lawyer keep you informed about developments in your case?

- Are you given copies of all documents that you request? Are you allowed access to the lawyer's case file when you ask for it?

- Does your lawyer meet all court deadlines? Or does he or she regularly seek extensions without what seem to be good reasons for this lateness?

- Does your lawyer give you clear and practical advice? Are alternative courses of action laid out and explained, with their probable consequences described?

- Does your lawyer seem committed to your case? Has an apparent conflict of interest developed?

- Does your lawyer seem to understand the legal *and social work* issues raised by your case? If not, have the appropriate experts been consulted?

- Does your lawyer seem to keep careful and accurate records concerning your case?

- Does your lawyer seem sensitive to the need to keep legal expenses down? Are you billed in accordance with your agreement? Is the lawyer hostile when you ask for an explanation of your bill?

Source: Adapted from E. Krasnow and J. MacNeice, *101 Ways to Cut Legal Fees and Manage Your Lawyer: A Practical Guide for Broadcasters and Cable Operators* (Washington, D.C.: Broadcasting Publishers, Inc., in press), pp. 133–141. Used with authors' permission.

then have to go through the whole process of finding a new lawyer and you will have to pay that lawyer to learn all about your case—something you already paid your first lawyer to do.

Moreover, lawyers view with suspicion clients who seem to be lawyer-hopping. Even though lawyers know that there are often good reasons to switch representation, they tend to blame the client. They assume that the client is hard to please, has unrealistic expectations, and will be an unrewarding client to represent. Hence, they are often unwilling to take on such a client.

There are times, though, when a change in lawyers is advisable. (The middle of a trial is *never* one of those times.) If, after considering the disadvantages, you still feel that your interests require a new lawyer, you might consider staying with the same firm but switching to another lawyer in it whom you have gotten to know and like. Otherwise, you should begin the process of lawyer selection all over again—using the same care, but, one hopes, with a better idea of your needs and preferences. Finally, unless you are forced to do so by the circumstances, do not fire your lawyer until you have found a satisfactory replacement.

Financing Legal Representation

Social workers without reimbursed legal counsel are in for a rude shock when they discuss fees with their lawyers. Sued for violating parental rights, one publicly employed social worker was told that defending her case could cost $25,000 to $50,000 over the five years that it would probably take for a final resolution.[23]

Despite the things that social workers can do to minimize legal costs, the bills will still be large—and they will have to be paid. The best way to finance legal representation is to have someone else pay for it—either your agency or an insurance company.

Many agencies will agree to pay for legal representation even in the absence of a preexisting policy on this matter. Moreover, initial decisions against reimbursement are often reversed if the worker is subsequently vindicated. That is what happened in a Texas criminal prosecution:

> Along with the notice of their suspensions, the indicted employees were advised that the agency would neither provide nor pay for legal counsel for them. If the action had been a civil one, legal representation would have been provided. However, since the action was criminal in nature, provision of legal counsel by DHS or by County Government would be considered tantamount to condoning criminal behavior if in fact the employees had been found guilty. Because of this decision, the employees were left no option but to engage legal counsel at their own expense.
>
> *　　*　　*
>
> After the employees were found innocent of all charges, the County decided to cover the balance of the legal fees not paid for by the legal defense fund.[24]

Although some agencies reimburse legal expenses out of a high-minded sense of obligation to their employees or out of a deep commitment to professional values, many others do so only after intense lobbying from within and outside the agency. Like the decision to bring the suit or prosecution, the decision to defend the social worker is often a political one. The worker and the worker's allies must act accordingly.

For the social worker who must pay legal expenses, there are no easy answers. If the worker does not have sufficient savings, a loan may be necessary. Some law firms will agree to deferred billing, or to spreading out payments so that they can be made without taking out a loan. In the past, most firms would do this without charging interest. However, recent bar association opinions have authorized them to charge interest—if the client agrees *in advance* to the payment of interest—and, therefore, a growing number of firms are asking for interest payments. Some firms will also accept major credit cards. The advantage of using a credit card is that it provides, in effect, instant and no-questions-asked credit. The disadvantage is that it is very expensive credit; interest rates will be from two to ten points higher than those on a bank loan, for example. Moreover, in a few states, it is illegal for law firms to accept credit cards.

Colleagues and community groups are often a surprisingly effective —and heartwarming—source of support. In response to many lawsuits, legal defense committees have been formed to help persuade agencies to support their employees and to raise funds to help defray legal expenses. One committee, made up of social workers and friends from a church congregation, raised $40,000 to help finance a social worker's successful defense to charges that he strangled his wife. (Unfortunately, there remained another $40,000 in expenses that he had to pay on his own.)[25] Similarly, in response to the Kentucky criminal prosecutions described earlier in this book, "a supervisor and a CPS worker established a legal defense fund, and fellow employees collected donations throughout the agency. The contributions received compensated for approximately one-fourth of all legal fees incurred."[26] Potluck dinners, by the way, are a popular and effective fund-raising technique.

Legal defense committees provide more than just money, although that would be an important enough reason for encouraging them. They also build much-needed personal and community support for the worker.

The National Association of Social Workers is also an important source of support. In 1971, NASW established its Legal Defense Service (LDS) to provide assistance to members who find themselves engaged in legal proceedings as a result of actions taken against them as professional social workers. The LDS was a response to "increasing attacks on the social work profession and a growing need for legal aid and consultation for NASW members."[27] Over the years, LDS has given approximately $30,000 to 30 social workers to help defray legal expenses.

One case in which an NASW member, aided by the LDS, successfully challenged an apparently unfair grand jury investigation of a child abuse death was reported in the *NASW News:*

> [A] child protective service worker found herself the scapegoat of a community upset by the death of an abused child. The worker voluntarily cooperated with a grand jury investigation, but claimed afterward that she was denied due process in the course of that investigation. Not given the opportunity to respond to questions about her conduct on the job, the member took legal action to stop publication of the grand jury's report, which recommended her dismissal from employment.
>
> After several rounds of litigation and thousands of dollars in legal fees, the court of appeals judge granted her request because the grand jury followed irregular procedures and presented insufficient or contradictory evidence to support its recommendation. In addition, the court found the worker was "held to standards of conduct that were not established by statute, rules or departmental policy [and] criticized for wrongdoing in making decisions which clearly involve matters of judgement."
>
> The decision means the report will not be made public or forwarded to the county social services department for action....
>
> "I have been especially grateful for the support NASW has given me," the worker wrote in a letter to the Legal Defense Service, "both in terms of financial help but also the moral support which I feel it reflected."
>
> The trustees of the Legal Defense Service, although unable to fairly judge the merits of the situation, shared the social worker's concern for the way in which the investigation was handled, and acted to support her right to due process.[28]

The Service is administered by five trustees appointed by the NASW Board of Directors. The trustees (NASW members who serve without compensation) consider requests for assistance based on two criteria: (1) the need for assistance in legal proceedings stemming from actions taken as a professional social worker; and (2) the significance of the case to the social work profession and its principles, including the NASW *Code of Ethics.*[29]

An applicant for LDS assistance must be a current member, in good standing, of NASW. Members requesting financial aid should be aware that the LDS is funded entirely through voluntary contributions, and its ability to given financial assistance is accordingly limited.[30] Thus, it is unlikely that the service would be able to assume all legal expenses. (In recent years, the average grant has been about $750.) In appropriate circumstances, however, a loan from LDS might be arranged.

The relatively small size of LDS grants belies their importance. They provide much-needed moral support and professional legitimation. In effect, the grants signify organized professional approval of the social worker's conduct. Many social workers reported that agency and community support— and additional financial aid—quickly followed upon their receipt of the grant from the LDS.

Notes

1. See Appendix H.
2. Compare B. E. Bernstein and B. McCutchan, "The Grand Jury vs. the Social Worker: Friends or Enemies?" *Social Work,* 28 (May–June 1983), p. 224, with New York Criminal Procedure Law §§ 50.10, .20, 190.40, and .45 (1984).
3. See, for example, the El Paso case discussed on p. 66.
4. Material on file with the author.
5. See, generally, S. Wilson, *Confidentiality in Social Work: Issues and Principles* (New York: Free Press, 1978).
6. See p. 185.
7. See p. 185.
8. W. Holder, "A Personal View of Caseworker Liability," in Holder and K. Hayes, eds., *Malpractice and Liability in Child Protective Services* (Longmont, Colo.: Bookmakers Guild, 1984), pp. 95, 97.
9. See p. 185.
10. Bernstein and McCutchan, "The Grand Jury vs. the Social Worker," p. 226. Emphasis in original.
11. C. Gembinski, M. Casper, and E. Hutchinson, "Worker Liability: Who's Really Liable?" in C. Washburne, ed., *Looking Back, Looking Ahead: Selections from the Fifth National Conference on Child Abuse and Neglect* (Madison: University of Wisconsin School of Social Work, 1982), pp. 116, 119.
12. For an example of this misunderstanding, and how it was ultimately corrected, see pp. 209–210. See also Holder, "A Personal View of Caseworker Liability," pp. 98–99.
13. See, generally, R. del Carmen and C. Venezano, "Legal Liabilities, Representation, and Indemnification of Probation and Parole Officers," *University of San Francisco Law Review,* 17 (1983), p. 227; R. Crane and G. Roberts, *Legal Representation and Financial Indemnification for State Employees: A Study* (College Park, Md.: American Correctional Association, 1977); Annotation, "Payment of Attorney's Services in Defending Action Brought Against Officials Individually as Within Power or Obligation of Public Body," *American Law Reports,* 130 (1941), p. 736.
14. See D. Besharov, *Juvenile Justice Advocacy: Practice in a Unique Court* (New York: Practising Law Institute, 1974), p. 53ff.
15. R. Cohen, *Malpractice: A Guide for Mental Health Professionals* (New York: Free Press, 1979), p. 274, quoting Horsley, "How to Protect Yourself Against *Legal* Malpractice," *Medical Economics,* 4 September 1978, p. 154.
16. Adapted from E. Krasnow and J. MacNeice, *101 Ways to Cut Legal Fees and Manage Your Lawyer: A Practical Guide for Broadcasters and Cable Operators* (Washington, D.C.: Broadcasting Publishers, Inc., in press), Sec. 18.
17. Ibid., p. 84.
18. Ibid., pp. 24–25.
19. Ibid., p. 78.
20. Ibid., p. 138.
21. Ibid., pp. 82–83.
22. Ibid., p. 133.
23. Personal correspondence with author.
24. Gembinski, Casper, and Hutchinson, "Worker Liability," pp. 122–123.
25. "Member Wins Fight in Manslaughter Case," *NASW News,* 29 (September, 1984), p. 9.
26. E. Hutchinson and M. Casper, "CPS Indictments in Kentucky and Their Aftermath," *National Child Protection Newsletter,* 4, No. 6 (1981), p. 9. Case discussed on p. 66.

27. "Legal Defense Service's Birthday: A Decade and $25,000 of Help," *NASW News*, 28 (January 1983), p. 13.

28. "Legal Defense–Supported Social Worker Captures Victory in Child Abuse Case," *NASW News*, 26 (February 1981), p. 15.

29. Copies of all applications for LDS grants are sent to the appropriate local NASW chapters, which are given 30 days for review and recommendation. Chapter approval, though important, is not required. When a chapter's comments are received, the LDS trustees review the entire case before making a decision. The trustees make awards to just under half of all applicants. Further information and applications for financial assistance may be obtained from the Legal Defense Service, located at NASW's national office.

30. The Legal Defense Service is funded solely by contributions made to the Legal Defense Fund. To allow financial assistance to individual members, LDS was established *without* tax-exempt status, and donations to it are not tax-deductible.

9

Reducing Agency and Personal Stress

The Stress of Litigation

Being sued can be a major professional and personal crisis. Most social workers—and their agencies—do not expect to become embroiled in litigation and, so, are usually unprepared for the stress that results. This section describes the severe stresses, both professional and personal, that can accompany a lawsuit; it is not intended to alarm social workers but, rather, to help those who are sued to deal with the stresses that they will inevitably face.

This chapter is largely based on interviews with social workers who have been criminally prosecuted or sued. These workers and administrators were almost always willing to share their painful experiences so that others could learn from them and feel less alone with their problems. By describing what happened to those who have been sued and how they and their agencies tried to cope, this section seeks to assist others who may be sued to feel less helpless and to develop useful stress-reducing strategies.

Agency Stress and Worker Morale

For the agency, a lawsuit can present a major crisis. An agency caught up in litigation suffers many stresses, not the least of which can be financial. Legal fees and a court judgment can weaken the financial viability of even the largest private agency, and, to the extent that the agency's reputation suffers, it will find it more difficult to obtain financial support as grants, con-

---

This chapter was written by Susan H. Besharov.

tributions, and referrals decline. Public agencies, too, may lose financial support from legislative and budgetary officials.[1]

For both public and private agencies, the litigation process itself can impose an enormous drain on staff resources. From the head of the agency on down, staff members must undergo repeated interviews with their own lawyers, submit to interrogatories and depositions from opposing counsel, prepare for court testimony, and, of course, testify in open court.

The greatest threat to the agency, however, is to staff morale, and, hence, the agency's overall functioning. As is well documented in the growing literature on worker burnout, low morale is a common problem, even without the added stress of civil and criminal liability. High caseloads and poor working conditions intensify the stress felt by workers assigned to the frequently frustrating task of helping deeply troubled and uncooperative families.[2]

The initiation of a lawsuit increases the danger of agencywide worker burnout. The suit is often perceived as an attack on the agency's integrity, regardless of individual or institutional fault. Staff morale falls, especially if there is sustained and negative publicity about the case. Staff become further demoralized if they believe that the accused are being scapegoated for more general problems endemic to the child welfare system.[3] Individually and as a group, workers begin to feel that they, too, are vulnerable to a suit. They see their friends and associates in legal jeopardy for doing the same things they do and wonder, "Who is next?"

There is much an agency can do to reduce the stresses inherent in major litigation. Sadly, the response of many agencies aggravates the stresses of a major suit, rather than reducing them. Too often, they all but abandon the worker (or workers) who have been sued, disclaiming any responsibility for what happened or for the worker's defense. Too many agencies jump to the conclusion that the worker is guilty simply because a lawsuit has been filed. Some agency heads have rushed to issue public statements promising to "clean house," or to hold "guilty" parties responsible without knowing whether there actually was any wrongdoing. Some workers have been dismissed, downgraded, or reassigned without any real inquiry into what happened and without any attempt to hear their version of the facts. Unfortunately, the following example is an all too common indication of how agencies respond to a lawsuit.

> Immediately following the issuance of the indictments, all three CPS workers were advised by DHS that they were suspended with pay pending the final outcome of the legal proceedings. Some felt that the suspensions occurred because the administration determined that allowing the indicted staff to continue their regular work functions would increase the agency's vulnerability to liability and criticism.

Along with the notice of their suspension, the indicted employees were advised that the agency would neither provide nor pay for their legal counsel. . . .

Approximately two weeks after the suspensions, the staff members were informed that they were to return to work but not to their previous positions. The CPS supervisor returned to the agency in an administrative capacity without supervisory responsibilities, and the two line workers were assigned to the Financial Assistance unit of the agency. The less experienced line worker accepted the transfer. The more tenured employee, with seven years experience, had strong reservations about the transfer and requested several days to make a decision. He was informed that if he did not report as directed his employment would be terminated. He resigned from the agency and was simultaneously fired. This process was handled entirely by telephone and mail. The employee later remarked: "I can't believe I worked there for seven years and was not even afforded the opportunity to discuss the matter in person to tell my side."[4]

Subsequently, all charges against the workers were dismissed.[5]

When an agency is unsupportive to sued employees, the rest of the staff become further disheartened, and their sense of loyalty to the agency is further weakened. They fear that they, too, will not be supported in the good faith performance of their duties. This is how one group of 17 social workers expressed its concerns about an agency's response to a child abuse tragedy:

We, as social workers, have accepted the responsibilities of our mandated tasks as well as the agency's stated mission of strengthening and keeping families together. We accept the extremely difficult position of working with families who are "at risk". We constantly assess this risk, that is the risk of further harm to children. This, however, is an extremely imprecise science. We are vulnerable in each judgment, for the unanticipated must be reckoned with each day. In order to fulfill our responsibilities we must feel the agency will support us at every level. Unfortunately, many facets of this case prove exactly the opposite.

1. The manner in which the media has been utilized [by the agency in question] has implicated workers long before the results of the internal investigation have been finalized. Specifically, [the newspaper quotes an agency official as stating that] "the action to reassign the two employees was taken 'to make certain that children in our care are protected and services are professionally delivered. [sic] The worker and supervisor were not informed personally of this decision, but read it in the [newspaper]. The implicating statements from the Central Office [of the agency] were reiterated in the internal memo. . .which each [regional] office received statewide. In addition, the release of the social worker's name and address [to the newspaper] under "Freedom of Information" further implicated the individual before the investigation was completed.

2. The new Standards of Practice have been developed to insure thorough investigations and social worker accountability. The new requirements necessitate a great deal of time spent on paperwork alone. We are working toward adhering to the time lines, number of visits, filling out computer forms, doing complete dictation, and case reviews. However, our caseload sizes make strict adherence to these requirements impossible, which leaves us feeling helpless and professionally vulnerable. We ask that the Administration listen to our documentable inability to fulfill all the expectations of our job and provide us with some guidelines for handling that predicament.[6]

The Vulnerable Social Worker

A failure to support workers jeopardizes the commitment of all staff to the agency and to their work. It increases the likelihood of defensive social work, and, as a result, further adds to the stresses felt by the workers. In another agency:

> Because of the anxiety created by the indictments, more emphasis was placed on increasing case documentation and filling out forms immediately. Frequently, case decisions were colored by perceptions of how the administration, the media, the community, or the legal system might respond. Staff morale was negatively affected as staff members reacted to the lack of formal support from the agency. In addition, the increase in caseload and paperwork produced a higher than usual level of stress in a normally high-stress line of work.[7]

Altogether, then, a civil damage claim—let alone a criminal prosecution—can cause low morale, paranoia, and panic, leading valued workers to leave the agency. Nonetheless, an agency cannot simply deny all allegations of malfeasance and blindly support its employees. They may, in fact, have been at fault. Moreover, if the agency is perceived as being unwilling to examine its own performance, it will lose further credibility in the community.

Agency Coping Strategies

Any agency response to a lawsuit must be carefully balanced to meet the sensitivities of the agency's divergent constituencies. For the general public and professional community, the agency cannot be seen as countenancing poor performance by workers. But to the workers who have been sued, and to agency staff in general, it must seem sufficiently supportive to innocent workers. In other words, the agency must find a way to support its staff without compromising either its public image or professional integrity.

How, then, should responsible and caring agencies respond to the initiation of a lawsuit? The following suggestions are based on the experiences of agencies caught up in litigation.

1. *Agencies should prepare for the possibility of a lawsuit.* They should train workers in the elements of legal liability to minimize the likelihood of a suit. And, of course, they should obtain adequate insurance to reduce the financial pressure should there be a suit.

Moreover, agencies should develop policies for responding to a lawsuit before it happens. None of the coping strategies described in this chapter require that agencies wait for an actual lawsuit before developing a planned response. At least for larger agencies in which it is reasonable to expect litigation, it is best to develop these plans ahead of time so that the agency will be prepared to respond if lightning strikes. If the agency does so, it will not be forced to figure out what to do in a crisis atmosphere.

2. *Agencies should avoid substantive comment about the suit—and they should not take any adverse personnel actions—until sufficient infor-*

mation is available. The agency should not jump to the conclusion that the worker is guilty, nor, for that matter, that the worker is faultless. The agency should make its own investigation of the situation, or arrange for an impartial one to be conducted, before taking any substantive actions. A good model of a formal agency policy to find out what happened before acting was adopted by the Massachusetts Department of Social Services (see Chart 9-1). Of course, even when the agency concludes that the charges are unfounded, it must cooperate with the legal process and strive to avoid the appearance of a cover-up.

3. *Agencies should provide appropriate support to their workers who are sued.* As previously mentioned, sued social workers are often under great stress. Their agencies should recognize this reality and, to the fullest extent feasible, provide both emotional and practical support. The agency's response to the sued worker's plight will also have an important effect on staff morale, as other employees watch to see whether the agency will stand by them in times of trouble.

Unless the agency's investigation determines that the worker acted in bad faith or deliberately beyond the scope of his or her official duties, counsel should be provided or paid for. Furthermore, in its statements and actions, the agency should be supportive of the worker both inside the agency and outside of it. This includes retaining the worker in a responsible position. (If the worker must be moved out of a line position pending the outcome of litigation, this should be done with sensitivity to the worker's feelings, and the worker should be given meaningful tasks in another part of the agency.)

If the circumstances of the case limit the degree to which the agency can publicly support the worker, it can still provide informal support by the way it treats the worker in personal dealings and by how it discusses the case in private conversations.

4. *Agencies should recognize that lawsuits are inherently stressful for all their workers, and that they must provide appropriate support to all agency workers.* The mood of the agency as a whole may go through a sequence of emotions similar to the grief reactions of an individual as described in the literature: denial, anger, depression, and, finally, acceptance.[8] Agency administrators should be sensitive to these reactions of staff and be responsive to them. "Stress literature consistently emphasizes that the first step in coping with a stressful situation is to develop an adequate understanding of it."[9]

Lack of information and rumors compound workers' fears. The agency's staff should be systematically informed about the lawsuit and the agency's response. For example, if the workers are to be provided with legal representation or if there is an agency insurance or indemnification program that protects them, this should be emphasized. Appropriate updates about

Chart 9-1
Massachusetts Case Investigation Unit's Policies and Procedures

The Case Investigation Unit, (a subdivision of the Office of Professional Services, Policy Unit) located at Central Office, conducts internal reviews of all DSS cases where a child in the custody of the Department or...known to the Department has died. The purpose of each investigation is to review the circumstances surrounding a child's death (or as related to the special incident report) as well as the Department's general provision of services to the child and the family.

Frequently a C.I.U. report highlights the need for the formulation of a new policy or for a change in current policy. The incorporation of the C.I.U. into the Policy Unit provides a more direct relationship between the results of the investigation and agency policies.

All deaths of children known to DSS need to be reported to the C.I.U., including deaths due to natural causes. In addition, the C.I.U. should be notified of the death of a child in a case closed within the last six months.

The C.I.U. also investigates other cases at the Commissioner's request. Such cases could involve injury to a child or allegations related to DSS handling of a particular case. In addition, Regional Directors can also request the Case Investigation Unit's intervention through the Deputy Commissioner.

In order for the C.I.U. to effectively conduct investigations, the following procedures have been developed:

1. The Area Director should immediately notify the Regional Director of the death of a child known to DSS. The Regional Director should insure that the case is reported by telephone to the C.I.U. Supervisor....

2. When notified of the incident, the C.I.U. will need to receive specific background information about the child and the case, including the child's name, date of birth, suspected cause of death, names of social work staff involved with family, and legal status of case. This information is collected on a special form...and is shared with the Commissioner, Deputy Commissioner and Assistant Commissioner for Professional Services.

3. Following this notification, the Case Record should be copied and immediately sent to the C.I.U. If the record is not up to date, the worker does not have to update it before it is sent to the C.I.U. The updated information should be forwarded as soon as possible. In addition, copies of the death certificate and autopsy report (if applicable) should be requested by the Area

Source: Massachusetts Department of Social Services, Boston, Document No. 84-006, undated.

Chart 9-1 (continued)

Director and sent to the C.I.U. (The Divisional Counsel may be effective in obtaining these documents.)

When the Commissioner requests the C.I.U. to investigate a case in which a child has been seriously injured or in situations where abuse/neglect is alleged as a cause of the child's death, an individual should be designated in either the Regional or Area Office to keep the C.I.U. abreast of new developments. If the child is injured, this designated staff person should maintain daily contact with the hospital, to ascertain the medical condition of the child....

The Regional or Area Director should forward all press calls to...the Director of the Communications Office at Central Office....

The C.I.U.'s investigation procedures involve four stages:

1. When a case is referred, the C.I.U. begins its investigation within two working days. An investigation usually entails reviewing the entire Case Record and coming out to the Area Office to interview social work staff. A decision will be made soon after the referral as to the type of report that will be done. For example, if a child dies as a result of a car accident where the circumstances and the information from the police report are straight-forward, the C.I.U. may do an abbreviated report.

If, however, a child does not die of natural causes there will be two reports. First, a preliminary report, which is a chronology of significant events in the case, will be done within two weeks of the referral. A more in-depth report will follow the preliminary one and will be completed a month after the referral.

2. The C.I.U. writes narrative reports based on the accounting of the facts in the case and information obtained from interviews with area staff. The report is reviewed by the Assistant Commissioner for Professional Services, the Deputy Commissioner and the Commissioner. The role of the C.I.U. is to gather and present facts. Only the Assistant Commissioner, Deputy Commissioner and the Commissioner draw conclusions from the report.

3. The report is forwarded to the Regional and Area Director within thirty days of receipt of the case. The Assistant Commissioner for Professional Services will make recommendations and/or comments which will accompany the report. These recommendations and/or comments will cover a range of issues including commendable casework practices demonstrated in the case, compliance with existing regulations and practice procedures, the need for new or revised policies or procedures, operational and administrative issues, etc.

4. Each report will be followed by an exit interview, within three weeks of the office's receipt of the report, between the C.I.U. investigator and area staff involved with the case. This will provide an opportunity for the

Chart 9-1 (continued)

area staff to give the C.I.U. investigator feedback on the process and to discuss the contents of the report.

There are some instances when the C.I.U. investigates a case jointly with an outside agency. For example, if a child dies in a Residential Care Facility the C.I.U. may interview program staff jointly with the Office for Children. If a case is contracted out, the C.I.U. investigates jointly with administrative staff from the private agency.

Area staff input into the Case Investigation process is essential. Supervisors should participate in the interviews with C.I.U. staff. In addition, DSS employees are entitled to the following rights during the investigation process:

1. Employees, if they so request, are entitled to union representation during the investigatory process.

2. Employees are shown the completed report and, if they so desire, they can respond in writing to the report's contents. This response will become part of the report.

There may be times when the C.I.U.'s report may be requested by the family involved or other concerned parties. A request for the C.I.U. report will not be granted automatically. The request will be considered carefully by the Deputy Commissioner and a decision will be made as to whether the report will be shared and to what extent a party identified in the report will be notified if the C.I.U. report is to be given to an outside party.

---

the progress of the case and the agency's response should also be made. Any resulting changes in agency policies or procedures due to the case should be fully explained to staff.

These should not be only didactic sessions. Agency administrators should encourage staff to ask questions and to express their feelings about the case and about legal vulnerability in general. Many agencies find it most effective to hold open, no-holds-barred meetings in which agency administrators and lawyers are available for questioning. Other agencies organize peer support sessions. The Massachusetts Case Investigation Unit, for example, does more than just investigate. It also provides supportive information and counseling for the workers involved in the case and for all the other workers in the same office.

5. *Agencies should seek public and professional support through careful public relations work.* The agency's future is dependent on public and

professional respect. In the face of negative publicity, it may be useful for the agency to disseminate its version of the events. Subject to the advice of legal counsel, the agency may decide to release the results of its own investigation together with a description of the history and functions of the agency. In doing so, it should try to educate the public about the underlying problems of the child welfare system, what child welfare agencies can reasonably be expected to do, and what they should not be expected to do. Such efforts might also include obtaining the public support of other local social service agencies, professional organizations, and schools of social work.

A well-thought-out and supportive agency response will pay large dividends. One worker summarized her experience: "Personally, I had a few bad moments and feelings of stress, but was well protected by my agency and received support from our attorney and my district director who went to court with me."[10] Such a result benefits the entire agency as well as the individual worker.

Personal Stress

Social workers who are the subjects of criminal or civil suits often perceive legal action as personal attacks. This can often lead to these workers feeling inadequate and helpless.

Criminal prosecutions are, of course, the most anxiety-provoking lawsuits. One indicted social worker said she wished she could "disappear from the face of the earth." Another worker, accused of sexually abusing a young client (based on what turned out to be insubstantial evidence), described it as the most "encompassing disaster I've ever had to face." She described herself as feeling "isolated, alienated, outraged." An indicted program director has written:

> The effects on us, the indicted, were extremely personal and pervaded our whole lives. Fear of the unknown, of incarceration took its toll, creating extreme tension in our lives. . . .The effects seem to be lasting to this day. Whenever I leave town there is a part of me that is afraid something might go wrong in my absence and that I will go back to face another charge.[11]

Civil lawsuits can be almost as stressful. As one social worker commented, "I became the client, the needy one." She could see that her preoccupation with protecting herself was a role reversal for her. Another worker described how she was "completely drained and felt emotionally—like a piece of elastic that's been stretched a bit too taut for a bit too long and loses its snap."[12]

Even social workers involved in relatively minor suits can find themselves reacting strongly. The director of a hospital social work department said she felt professionally attacked when she was sued by a student whom she had failed, despite the unanimous support of her colleagues and despite her objective knowledge that the suit was insubstantial. She was surprised to find herself preoccupied with the suit and uncharacteristically sensitive to criticism.

Some Common Problems
Depression was the most common reaction reported by social workers who had been sued. In interviews, they repeatedly spoke of sadness, tearfulness, labile moods, fatigue, and inability to concentrate. New or exacerbated physical illnesses including rheumatoid arthritis, back problems, and multiple minor illnesses in normally healthy people were common reactions.

The emotional stresses of malpractice suits were documented by the results of a survey published in the *American Journal of Psychiatry*.[13] The survey was based on questionnaires completed by 143 physicians who had been sued for professional malpractice. Thirty-nine percent of the respondents reported a cluster of symptomatic reactions that would fit the diagnosis of major depressive disorder. Another 20 percent had a group of symptoms with anger as a major theme. Eight percent reported the onset of a physical illness, such as a coronary, during the suit, and another 7 percent reported the exacerbation of preexisting illnesses, such as angina, hypertension, and ulcers. Only 4 percent of the respondents reported no emotional or physical symptoms related to the litigation. For the vast majority of physicians, the lawsuits adversely affected their ability to practice for periods ranging from weeks to years, despite the fact that none of the suits resulted in a verdict against them.

Such strong emotional reactions are to be expected. The impact of a lawsuit permeates one's life. A claim of malpractice is perceived as an attack on one's integrity.

> Although intent is not important in a malpractice case, to most professionals a malpractice suit implies that they are being accused of something that was morally wrong, ethically improper, or professionally incompetent, and this frequently is the cause of the greatest part of the anxiety that results.[14]

Professional problems—and even job loss—are also common. Even if the social worker is not at fault, the agency may be unsupportive and seek a scapegoat for its more generalized shortcomings. Workers often find themselves transferred to less prestigious jobs or denied promotions. Friendships with colleagues may become strained, and collaboration uncomfortable or impossible. One man described his situation with dramatic understatement: "It was rather difficult working in the agency as an indicted felon. We were unsure as to who supported us and who trusted us."[15] The atmosphere may become so poisoned that workers feel they must leave the agency. Some workers are simply fired, regardless of fault. One worker who was fired described herself as feeling "alone and bereft."

Social workers who have been forced to leave an agency because of a lawsuit often have difficulty finding a new job. Their professional confidence is so shaken that it interferes with the aggressive pursuit of a new job and with the successful handling of an interview. Moreover, the circumstances of the job termination are, at best, embarrassing to explain to a prospective employer. Even if the suit was ultimately settled in the worker's favor, the worker suffers a subtle stigma, because an employer may wonder whether the worker did anything wrong that contributed to the suit. As time goes by, finding a job becomes progressively more difficult because the worker's résumé reveals an increasing gap since the last employment.

Social workers in private practice who are sued are able to continue practicing, of course, but they may suffer a loss of clients and new referrals. After all, how likely is it that other workers would make a referral to someone who had been sued for professional malpractice? Would they not be concerned that, if something went wrong with the treatment of the client, they, too, might be sued for malpractice (that is, for a negligently made referral)?

Loss of self-confidence is a less tangible but more insidious professional cost of being sued. Many workers report a disproportionate sensitivity to criticism that often interferes with collegial relationships. Furthermore, having been sued once, many workers adopt a defensive approach to their other clients. They find themselves modifying their clinical judgments for fear of angering another client.

The upheaval of a lawsuit is not confined to the workplace. Just as personal problems impinge on work productivity, a work crisis can interfere with relationships and activities outside the job.

Financial fears are also a fundamental concern. Not only is there the prospect of legal fees but also the possibility of a substantial judgment to pay. Between these costs and possible loss of work, there may be increased financial dependence on family members. One social worker described poignantly how her husband had reluctantly supported her change of career to social work, which involved not only the cost of a social work education but also a lower salary than in her former career. When a lawsuit led to long unemployment, she felt highly guilty about her reduced financial contribution to the family, and her husband's increased resentment about her new profession led to a period of marital stress. Another worker was deeply upset by her need to turn to her parents for financial help to pay legal costs.

The emotional strain on the sued social worker necessarily affects the family. Most social workers worried that their preoccupation with the litigation took away from the energy available for their families, especially for their children. One woman admitted, "Everything in my life took a backseat."

Many workers spoke of the need for added support from their spouses. One said, "My husband was a rock...he has really gone through a lot."[16] In situations in which the spouse is less understanding, as in the example noted earlier, marital problems may result, much like unemployment strains some marriages.

The magnitude of the emotional reaction to being sued reflects the degree to which self-esteem is bound up in work. A lawsuit is perceived as a challenge to professional competence and is a narcissistic blow. As social workers know from their clients' reactions, forced unemployment or unwanted job changes can cause serious stress. Even when a lawsuit does not lead to the loss of a job, the dynamics are similar. Studies of unemployment have elucidated the multidimensional meaning of work.

> Clinical observations of recently unemployed persons seeking help from social service agencies found grief reactions, anger, guilt, feelings of loss, and a sense of losing part of the self. These responses are not unlike feelings of bereavement. Several studies of people anticipating and experiencing unemployment have found that these people suffer loss of self-esteem, loss of personal identity, worry and uncertainty about the future, loss of a sense of purpose, and depression.[17]

Social workers are particularly vulnerable to the emotional stresses of a malpractice lawsuit because of their generally high degree of emotional investment in their work. The nature of the work demands such involvement. The emotional satisfaction of helping people is a major factor in most social workers' career choice; many could work in better paying and less demanding jobs. The intense relationships that workers frequently develop with their clients lead them to feel especially betrayed and upset if a client turns against them by suing. This feeling of betrayal was repeatedly mentioned by social workers who have been sued. The apparent unfairness of many of these suits and the sense that they were being scapegoated by the community and abandoned by their agencies compounded their feeling of being helpless victims.

The attitudes of social workers toward their own profession, the law, and the legal system probably fuel this feeling of helplessness. As one therapist has written:

> Whenever I talk about legal liability for psychotherapy, I am struck by the intense anxiety and anger that the topic evokes. These feelings seem to arise because, in general, we therapists feel uncomfortable about being scrutinized and held legally accountable for our practices. Many of us do not seem confident about what we are doing or how it looks to others. From my talks with therapists, a picture has emerged of our collective view of the law. It is seen as an unreasonable and capricious parent, inventing full-blown duties and then holding us accountable retroactively (most notably, in the *Tarasoff* case); as a frustrating discipline that functions far better as an adversary than an advisor, rarely able to provide guidelines for avoiding problems; as a nit-picking nuisance concerned with form and not substance, where the complex realities of human

interaction are whittled away in semantics; and, finally, as a parent who does not understand or appreciate the difficulty of the task we have undertaken and who holds us accountable to patently unfair standards.[18]

Certainly, there is much about social work and those who enter the profession that makes the foregoing observations seem valid. But, if truth be told, most people feel this way about the law. Everyone, after all, feels a twinge of discomfort and even fear when legal papers appear unexpectedly in the mail.

Finally, lack of preparation for the possibility of a lawsuit adds to the high emotional stress experienced by social workers. Few schools of social work or agencies do more than make a passing reference to the danger of criminal prosecutions and malpractice suits. Anger at this lack of preparation was a recurrent theme in discussions with social workers involved in litigation. One said, "People are not trained and then they are held accountable." An indication of the failure of schools and agencies to orient social workers to the possibility of being sued is manifested by the large number of workers who fail to protect themselves through the purchase of liability insurance, despite its low cost.

Perhaps, the relative infrequency of litigation and the relatively recent emergence of the problem are partial explanations of this failure to address liability issues. However, there is also an element of denial, of preferring not to think about this worrisome subject. Such avoidance may prevent some workers from feeling anxious, but it also leaves them unprepared for the emotional as well as the practical consequences of being sued, even for what seems to be the most routine case.

> The family was referred to us by the school guidance counselor because the 13-year old son came to school with bruises on his back and stated he was beaten once a month by his father. I called on the parents as the initial part of my investigation and met with hostility, anger and denial.
>
> Suggestions were made with respect to the need for family therapy which the parents rejected. However, they gave me permission to see the boy at school and at home.
>
> I called a few days later to make arrangements to visit the boy at home and was told that the family attorney had advised them not to allow such a visit.
>
> A week later, I was advised by our assistant attorney general that I was being sued by the family for $50,000 for causing a detrimental effect on the family harmony, consortium, tranquility, privacy and emotional stability.

Personal Coping Strategies
From interviews with workers who have gone through the ordeal of litigation, together with the professional literature on coping with stress, a number of

recommendations can be made to help social workers who are confronting a lawsuit.

1. *Social workers should take steps to protect themselves.* Individual workers should assume responsibility for informing themselves about their growing legal vulnerability, and they should protect themselves by purchasing liability insurance. Insurance not only provides financial protection in the event of a suit, but it also reduces anxieties about liability for the overwhelming majority of social workers who will not be sued. Some social workers mentioned that their insurance company was supportive during a suit and that it provided a good lawyer to handle the case and advise the worker.

2. *When faced with a likely or actual lawsuit, social workers should recognize that the situation is highly stressful and that they must adopt an appropriate coping strategy.* Legal proceedings are inherently anxiety provoking, even though many are dismissed and most of the remainder are resolved before trial. As one writer explained:

> The reaction to a malpractice suit generates the potential for tremendous psychological stress for the professional. Realizing that the strong emotion invoked can be incapacitating is an essential first step in the successful handling of these emotions by the individual.[19]

The perceived attack on professional status is a significant loss. The stages of reactions to being sued as described by social workers often parallel the stages of reaction to grief as noted earlier: (1) denial, (2) anger, (3) depression, and (4) acceptance. Identifying some or all of these stages in one's reactions may be helpful in realizing that they are to be expected—and that they will pass.

Research on stress and burnout emphasizes the importance of accepting as normal emotional responses to difficult situations. Symptoms of burnout include lowered self-esteem, fatigue, illness, decreased work performance, irritability with the family, and labile moods.[20] "It is common for workers who are suffering from stress and burnout to believe that their reactions are unique and to imagine themselves defective when they experience them."[21] Some of the social workers embroiled in lawsuits have exactly this reaction. They should be reassured by the knowledge that theirs is a common—and entirely normal—response.

After recognizing the inevitable emotional impact of a suit, it is important for the social worker to identify and verbalize the specific way in which he or she is being affected. One social worker advised: "Feel and express feelings just as you would encourage clients to do." As in crisis counseling, the social worker should explore feelings, assess how well he or she is coping, then use these insights to cope in a more productive way.[22] As another social worker put it: "Express your feelings and then act."

Several workers found that, by viewing the suit in a more objective way, they were able to reduce self-blame. They recommended getting feedback from others as a way to check that emotional reactions were not leading to a preoccupation with the wrong issues or provocative expressions of anger. Some workers were able to mobilize their anger to defend themselves better. "I made my anger work for me," one worker said.

3. *Being sued does not necessarily mean that wrongdoing occurred.* Many suits are based on weak or even bogus allegations or lack of valid legal basis to support liability. Furthermore, many cases are brought not on the basis of a worker's negligence or other malfeasance but, rather, to test the legality of current laws, regulations, or procedures.

4. *The ability to cope with the stress of litigation is enhanced by the support of others.* The importance of colleagues, family, and friends is emphasized repeatedly by workers who have been sued. One indicted worker enthusiastically described the widespread support she received from the mental health community and court personnel.[23] Both she and her supervisor received oral and written support in her defense. A group of social workers who sued their agency for wage discrimination found themselves, as the case dragged on for four years, becoming progressively more preoccupied with their case and the responses of their colleagues. They began to question their own handling of the case and whether they should have brought it in the first place. When they felt especially unsettled by how things were going, they would meet for lunch several times a week to give each other support. One member of the group told how the meetings made her feel "less crazy."

As yet another worker suggested: "Mobilize your support. Allow yourself to be nurtured." This worker said that she "learned to enjoy" friends and colleagues bringing her food and flowers. They also organized a legal defense fund. These personal recommendations are in accord with the professional literature on burnout, which correlates high levels of social support with decreased symptoms of stress.[24]

5. *Explore other means of emotional and professional support.* Some workers have found psychotherapy to be a useful source of support during a lawsuit. The decision to begin psychotherapy, of course, is a highly individual one. As a general rule, though, any dramatic change in functioning, such as debilitating depression or serious marital problems, may suggest the need for a consultation. Workers with more mild symptoms may also find supportive psychotherapy worthwhile as a means to ventilate and clarify feelings and, thus, to gain more energy with which to deal with the suit.

The wider professional community is another important source of support. Grants from the NASW Legal Defense Service (LDS) mentioned earlier in this volume provide important professional support, as well as limited financial aid.[25] Various workers spoke glowingly of the LDS grants they had received: "The support was far beyond the money"; "others were standing up for my professional decisions"; "the grant meant a great deal, because of the feeling of being backed."

Local NASW chapters should also be approached for public support, as should other local professional organizations, social service agencies, and schools of social work.[26] Such outside organizations, agencies, and institutions can often band together to provide substantial public support to keep the beleaguered worker from succumbing to a sense of overwhelming helplessness.

6. *Obtain good legal counsel.* Good legal counsel is also an important source of support. Understanding the legal system and the likely progression of a lawsuit can lead to an increased sense of control. A lawyer's effective handling of a case includes helping the worker understand what is happening and what to expect next. A number of workers complained that the trauma of the suit was compounded by mediocre counsel. A lawyer should be selected carefully, and, if he or she proves to be unsatisfactory, a change may be worth the inconvenience and added expense.

7. *Continue working.* Continuing employment is strongly recommended for emotional as well as financial reasons. Staying at home during a suit increases one's sense of isolation and may lead to greater depression. If a worker is forced to leave employment, another job should be searched for immediately. A careful explanation of what happened should be developed, and professional credibility bolstered with strong references.

8. *Keep busy.* The literature on both stress and burnout emphasizes the importance of developing other interests and activities to divert one's thoughts and to gain a sense of positive accomplishment.[27] Breaking out of the lethargy and immobilizing effects of a lawsuit may be difficult, but the potential results make the effort well worthwhile. Family activities, artistic interests, gardening, reading, in fact, anything that is absorbing and relaxing can be helpful in reducing an unhealthy preoccupation with the suit and in returning to a normal mood and way of functioning. One worker who had at first reacted to a suit with depression felt better when she began to write a novel that drew on her experiences. Others directed their energies toward helping their lawyers collect materials and information for the suit. Some worked to change state child welfare regulations and laws whose requirements exposed social workers to unfair risks of legal liability.

Many workers discovered the revitalizing potential of exercise. Just as stress may trigger physical illness, fitness can reduce stress. For good reason, the benefits of exercise such as jogging, swimming, and aerobics are touted by the popular media. In two cases, by the way, social workers became marathon runners as a means of relieving the tensions they faced.

The emotional stresses of a criminal or civil proceeding can, at the time, seem insurmountable. But handled properly, as with other crises, they need not do permanent harm. An indicted social worker, whose case was ultimately dismissed, had this to say about her experience: "I think I am a much stronger person. I was brought up as a very sheltered girl. I learned a lot about the reality of life, about how much I can tolerate."[28]

Notes

1. See p. 158.
2. See, for example, E. Murphy-Hackett and N. Ross, "How One Agency Is Fighting Burnout," *Public Welfare,* 42 (Spring 1984), p. 23; N. Falconer and K. Swift, *Preparing for Practice* (Toronto, Ont., Canada: Children's Aid Society, 1983); M. Bramhall and S. Ezell, "How Burned Out Are You?" *Public Welfare,* 39 (Winter 1981), p. 23; Bramhall and Ezell, "How Agencies Can Prevent Burnout," *Public Welfare,* 39 (Summer 1981), p. 33; C. Maslach, "Job Burnout: How People Cope," *Public Welfare,* 36 (Spring 1978), p. 56.
3. See pp. 133–138.
4. C. Geminski, M. Casper, and E. Hutchinson, "Worker Liability: Who's Really Liable?" in C. Washburne, ed., *Looking Back, Looking Ahead: Selections from the Fifth National Conference on Child Abuse and Neglect* (Milwaukee: School of Social Work, University of Wisconsin, 1982), p. 122.
5. This case is discussed on p. 66.
6. Confidential material on file with the author.
7. Gembinski, Casper, and Hutchinson, "Worker Liability," p. 123.
8. See, generally, E. Kubler-Ross, *On Death and Dying* (New York: Macmillan Co., 1969).
9. C. Shannon and D. Saleeby, "Training Child Welfare Workers to Cope with Burnout," *Child Welfare,* 59 (September–October 1980), pp. 463, 468.
10. Unless otherwise indicated, any quoted statements by social workers were made to S. H. Besharov during confidential interviews.
11. Gembinski, Casper, and Hutchinson, "Worker Liability," pp. 116, 118–119.
12. Quoted in W. Holder, "Malpractice in Child Protective Services: An Overview of the Problem," in Holder and K. Hayes, eds., *Malpractice and Liability in Child Protective Services* (Longmont, Colo.: Bookmakers Guild, 1984), pp. 5–6.
13. S. Charles, J. Wilbert, and E. Kennedy, "Physicians' Self-Reports of Reactions to Malpractice Litigation," *American Journal of Psychiatry,* 141 (April 1984), p. 563.
14. W. Goodwin, "The Emotional Reaction of Dentists to Malpractice Suits," *Dental Clinics of North America,* 26 (April 1982), p. 405.
15. Gembinski, Capser, and Hutchinson, "Worker Liability," p. 117.
16. W. Holder, "A Personal View of Caseworker Liability," in Holder and Hayes, eds., *Malpractice and Liability,* pp. 95, 100.
17. T. Keefe, "The Stresses of Unemployment," *Social Work,* 29 (May–June 1984), p. 265.
18. B. Schultz, *Legal Liability in Psychotherapy: A Practitioner's Guide to Risk Management* (San Francisco: Jossey-Bass, 1982), pp. ix–x.
19. Goodwin, "The Emotional Reaction of Dentists to Malpractice Suits," p. 409.
20. See, for example, Falconer and Swift, *Preparing for Practice,* pp. 197–198; M.

Lauderdale, *Burnout* (Austin, Tex.: Learning Concepts, 1982), pp. 46–49; Bramhall and Ezell, "How Burned Out Are You?" pp. 23, 25–26.

21 Falconer and Swift, *Preparing for Practice,* p. 53.

22. L. Smith, "A Review of Crisis Intervention Theory," *Social Casework,* 59 (July 1978), pp. 396, 403.

23. Holder, "A Personal View of Caseworker Liability," p. 99.

24. See, for example, M. L. Davis-Sacks, S. Jayaratne, and W. A. Chess, "A Comparison of the Effects of Social Support on the Incidence of Burnout," *Social Work,* 30 (May–June 1985), p. 240.

25. See pp. 210–211.

26. See, for example, "Workers' Arrests Spur NYC Chapter Action," *NASW News,* 28 (February 1983), p. 8.

27. See, for example, Murphy-Hackett and Ross, "How One Agency Is Fighting Burnout"; M. Bramhall and S. Ezell, "Working Your Way Out of Burnout," *Public Welfare,* 39 (Spring 1981), p. 32; Maslach, "Job Burnout."

28. Holder, "A Personal View of Caseworker Liability," p. 101.

10

Afterword

Growing criminal and civil liability poses a serious threat to social work services for children and families. If present trends continue, large numbers of innocent workers will experience financial and career disaster. Defensive social work, now only a minor problem, could grow to immobilize responsible decision making.

All citizens—including lawyers—should be disturbed by these possibilities. This writer hopes that many lawyers will join him in supporting the general reduction of social worker liability recommended in this book. Lawyers, however, like social workers, have a professional obligation to their clients. As long as the law, however unfairly, provides a cause of action against social workers, lawyers must pursue such claims. Hence, many more suits— and judgments—can be expected.

Social workers should be deeply concerned about their new legal vulnerability, but they need not be paranoid. Although it is true that almost any case could result in a lawsuit, most will not. In addition, by maintaining professional standards of practice and obtaining financial protection through insurance or indemnification programs, social workers can substantially reduce their legal vulnerability.

More important, social workers should not feel powerless about the growth of civil lawsuits and criminal prosecutions against them. They should not meekly accept excessive—and unfair—liability; it is not an intrinsic part of our society. If the legal system is threatening the proper practice of social work, the law should be changed—not social work. As this book has described, the present level of liability is a relatively recent development, in large part the unintended consequence of changes in other areas of the law. Furthermore, as the "good faith" immunity legislation already passed in nine states demonstrates, it is a development that can be reversed by effective advocacy from the profession and its allies.

Chart 10-1
Needed Legal Reforms

- Statutes, agency procedures, and professional standards should be made more realistic about the capabilities of child welfare services;

- "Good faith" immunity should be granted to child welfare workers;

- Liability for failing to report suspected child maltreatment should be limited to "knowing" and "willful" violations of the law; and

- For publicly employed social workers, insurance, indemnification, and legal representation should be authorized or required.

To obtain the legal protections described in this book and summarized in Chart 10-1, social workers will have to change the societal attitudes that have fostered the tendency to blame individual workers unfairly for conditions beyond their control. To do this, they will have to be honest with themselves and the public about what the profession can do for children and parents—and what it cannot do. This is a difficult and unpleasant task for a profession eager to do as much as possible to help its clients, but it is a task necessary for the long-term good of the profession and its clients.

Appendix A
Materials on the Liability of Mental Health Professionals*

Alexander, C. "Professional Liability Insurance: Jeopardy and Ethics." Paper presented at the Professional Symposium, National Association of Social Workers, Washington, D.C., 21 November 1983.

Annotation. "Governmental Tort Liability for Injuries Caused by Negligently Released Individual." *American Law Reports 4th,* 6 (1981), p. 1155.

――――. "Liability of Governmental Officer or Entity for Failure to Warn or Notify of Release of Potentially Dangerous Individual from Custody." *American Law Reports 4th,* 12 (1982), p. 722.

――――. "Liability of One Releasing Institutionalized Mental Patient for Harm He Causes." *American Law Reports 3rd,* 38 (1971), p. 699.

Antler, S. *Policy Statement on Social Worker Liability. Child Welfare at the Crossroads: Professional Liability.* Boston: National Association of Social Workers, 1985.

――――. *Social Worker Liability: Issues All Social Workers Should Think About.* Boston: National Association of Social Workers, 1985.

Barton, W., and Sanborn, C., eds. *Law and the Mental Health Professions: Friction at the Interface.* New York: International Universities Press, 1978.

Benesohn, H., and Resnik, H. "Guidelines for 'Suicide Proofing' a Psychiatric Unit." *American Journal of Psychotherapy,* 27 (1973), p. 204.

Beresford, H. "Professional Liability of Psychiatrists." *Defense Law Journal,* 21 (1972), p. 123.

Bernstein, B. E. "Malpractice: Future Shock of the 1980s." *Social Casework: The Journal of Contemporary Social Work,* 62 (March 1981), p. 175.

――――. "Malpractice: An Ogre on the Horizon." *Social Work,* 23 (March 1978), p. 106.

――――, and McCutchan, B. "The Grand Jury vs. the Social Worker: Friends or Enemies?" *Social Work,* 28 (May–June 1983), p. 224.

Cassidy, P. "The Liability of Psychiatrists for Malpractice." *University of Pittsburgh Law Review,* 36 (1974), p. 108.

Cohen, R. *Malpractice: A Guide for Mental Health Professionals.* New York: Free Press, 1979.

――――. "*Tarasoff v. Regents of the University of California.* The Duty to Warn: Common Law and Statutory Problems for California Psychotherapists." *California Western Law Review,* 14 (1978), p. 153.

Daley, T. "Negligence and the Social Worker." *Ontario Association of Professional Social Workers Newsmagazine,* December 1982, p. 7.

Dawidoff, D. *The Malpractice of Psychiatrists: Malpractice in Psychoanalysis, Psychotherapy, and Psychiatry.* Springfield, Ill.: Charles C Thomas, Publisher, 1973.

――――. "The Malpractice of Psychiatrists." *Duke Law Journal, 1966* (1966), p. 696.

Eger, C. "Psychotherapists' Liability for Extrajudicial Breaches of Confidentiality." *Arizona Law Review,* 18 (1976), p. 1061.

---

*A majority of the materials listed here were not written specifically for social workers. Instead, most are directed to psychiatrists or "psychotherapists." However, except for certain issues concerning involuntary commitments, the prescription and administration of drugs, and particular diagnostic and therapeutic skills, the potential liabilities are analogous.

Feldman, R., and Ward, T. "Psychotherapeutic Injury: Reshaping the Implied Contract as an Alternative to Malpractice." *North Carolina Law Review,* 58 (1979), p. 63.

Fink, V. "Medical Malpractice: The Liability of Psychiatrists." *Notre Dame Lawyer,* 48 (1973), p. 693.

Fleming, J., and Maximov, B. "The Patient or His Victim: The Therapist's Dilemma." *California Law Review,* 62 (1974), p. 1025.

Furrow, B. "Defective Mental Treatment: A Proposal for the Application of Strict Liability to Psychiatric Services." *Boston University Law Review,* 58 (1978), p. 391.

———. *Malpractice in Psychotherapy.* Lexington, Mass.: Lexington Books, 1980.

Garcetti, G., and Suarez, J. "The Liability of Psychiatric Hospitals for the Acts of Their Patients." *American Journal of Psychiatry,* 124 (1968), p. 961.

Glenn, R. "Standard of Care in Administering Non-Traditional Psychotherapy." *University of California, Davis, Law Review,* 7 (1974), p. 56.

Green, R. K., and Cox, G. "Social Work and Malpractice: A Converging Course." *Social Work,* 23 (March 1978), p. 100.

Griffith, E., and Griffith, E. "Duty to Third Parties, Dangerousness, and the Right to Refuse Treatment: Problematic Concepts for Psychiatrist and Lawyer." *California Western Law Review,* 14 (1978), p. 241.

Grossman, M. "Right to Privacy vs. Right to Know." In *Law and the Mental Health Professions: Friction at the Interface,* edited by W. Barton and C. Sanborn. New York: International Universities Press, 1978. p. 137.

Gutheil, T., and Appelbaum, P. *The Clinical Handbook of Psychiatry and Law.* New York: McGraw-Hill Book Co., 1982.

Halleck, S. *Law in the Practice of Psychiatry: A Handbook for Clinicians.* New York: Plenum Publishers, 1980.

Harris, M. "Tort Liability of the Psychotherapist." *University of San Francisco Law Review,* 8 (1973), p. 405.

Hofling, C., ed. *Law and Ethics in the Practice of Psychiatry.* New York: Brunner/Mazel, 1981.

Howell, J. "Civil Liability for Suicide: An Analysis of the Causation Issue." *Arizona State Law Journal,* 1978 (1978), p. 573.

Kaplan, N. "*Tarasoff v. Regents of the University of California:* Psychotherapists, Policemen, and the Duty to Warn—An Unreasonable Extension of the Common Law." *Golden Gate University Law Review,* 6 (1975), p. 229.

Keeton, W. P., and Prosser, W. L. *Prosser and Keeton on Torts.* 5th ed. St. Paul, Minn.: West Publishing Co., 1984.

Kennedy, C. "Injuries Precipitated by Psychotherapy: Liability Without Fault as a Basis for Recovery." *South Dakota Law Review,* 20 (1975), p. 401.

Klein, J.; Macbeth, J.; and Onek, J. *Legal Issues in the Private Practice of Psychiatry.* Washington, D.C.: American Psychiatric Association, 1984.

Knapp, S. "A Primer on Malpractice for Psychologists." *Professional Psychology,* 11 (1980), p. 606.

Krauskopf, J., and Krauskopf, C. "Torts and Psychologists," *Journal of Counseling Psychology,* 12 (1965), p. 227.

Lathum, J. "Torts—Duty to Act for Protection of Another—Liability of Psychotherapist for Failure to Warn of Homicide Threatened by Patient." *Vanderbilt Law Review,* 28 (1975), p. 631.

Lebersohn, Z. "Defensive Psychiatry or How to Treat the Mentally Ill Without Being a Lawyer." In *Law and the Mental Health Professions: Friction at the Inter-*

face, edited by W. Barton and C. Sanborn. New York: International Universities Press, 1978.

Leroy, D. "The Potential Criminal Liability of Human Sex Clinics and Their Patients." *St. Louis University Law Journal,* 16 (1972), p. 586.

Levine, R. "Social Worker Malpractice." *Social Casework,* 57 (July 1976), p. 466.

Litman, R. "Medical-Legal Aspects of Suicide." *Washburn Law Journal,* 6 (1967), p. 395.

Lowe, R. "*Tarasoff v. Regents of the University of California*—Risk Allocation in Mental Health Care: Whether to Treat the Patient or His Victim." *Utah Law Review,* 1975 (1975), p. 553.

Martin, R. *Legal Challenges to Behavior Modification: Trends in Schools, Correction and Mental Health.* Champaign, Ill.: Research Press, 1975.

Mason, P., and Stitham, M. "The Expensive Dalliance: Assessing the Cost of Patient-Therapist Sex." *Bulletin of the American Academy of Law and Psychiatry,* 5 (1977), p. 450.

Mirakian, S. "Tort Law: California's Expansion of the Duty to Warn." *Washburn Law Journal,* 15 (1976), p. 496.

Morrison, J.; Frederick, M.; and Rosenthal, H. "Contracting Confidentiality in Group Psychotherapy." *Forensic Psychology,* 7 (1975), p. 4.

Morse, H. "The Tort Liability of the Psychiatrist." *Buffalo Law Review,* 16 (1967), p. 649.

Note. "Liability of Mental Hospitals for Acts of Those Patients Under the Open Door Policy." *Virginia Law Review,* 57 (1971), p. 156.

———. "Psychotherapists' Liability for the Release of Mentally Ill Offenders: A Proposed Expansion of the Theory of Strict Liability." *University of Pennsylvania Law Review,* 126 (1977), p. 204.

Olander, A. "Discovery of Psychotherapist–Patient Communications After *Tarasoff.*" *San Diego Law Review,* 15 (1978), p. 265.

Olsen, T. "Imposing a Duty to Warn on Psychiatrists—A Judicial Threat to the Psychiatric Profession." *University of Colorado Law Review,* 48 (1977), p. 283.

Perr, I. "Legal Aspects of Sexual Therapies." *Journal of Legal Medicine,* 1 (1975), p. 33.

———. "Suicide Responsibilities of Hospital and Psychiatrist." *Cleveland-Marshall Law Review,* 9 (1960), p. 427.

Pollack, S. "Psychiatric-Legal Problems of Office Practice." *Current Psychiatric Therapies* (1977), p. 31.

Riskin, L. "Sexual Relations Between Psychotherapists and Their Patients: Toward Research or Restraint." *California Law Review,* 67 (1979), p. 1000.

Rothblatt, H., and Leroy, D. "Avoiding Psychiatric Malpractice." *California Western Law Review,* 9 (1973), p. 260.

Sadoff, R. *Forensic Psychiatry: A Practical Guide for Lawyers and Psychiatrists.* Springfield, Ill.: Charles C Thomas, Publisher, 1975.

———. *Legal Issues in the Care of Psychiatric Patients.* New York: Springer-Verlag, 1982.

Sauer, J. "Psychiatric Malpractice—A Survey." *Washburn Law Journal,* 11 (1972), p. 461.

Saxe, D. "Psychotherapeutic Treatment and Malpractice." *Kentucky Law Journal,* 58 (1969–70), p. 467.

Schroeder, L. *The Legal Environment of Social Work.* Englewood Cliffs, N.J.: Prentice-Hall, 1982.

The Vulnerable Social Worker

Schultz, B. *Legal Liability in Psychotherapy: A Practitioner's Guide to Risk Management.* San Francisco: Jossey-Bass, 1982.

Schwartz, V. "Civil Liability for Causing Suicide: A Synthesis of Law and Psychiatry." *Vanderbilt Law Review,* 24 (1971), p. 217.

Schwitzgebel, R. L., and Schwitzgebel, R. K. *Law and Psychological Practice.* New York: John Wiley & Sons, 1980.

Seligman, B. "Untangling *Tarasoff: Tarasoff v. Regents of the University of California." Hastings Law Journal,* 29 (1977–78), p. 179.

Shaffer, T. "Under Influence, Confidential Relationship and the Psychology of Transference." *Notre Dame Lawyer,* 45 (1970), p. 197.

Sharwell, G. R. "Avoiding Legal Liability in the Practice of School Social Work." *Social Work in Education,* 5 (October 1982), p. 17.

―――. "Learn 'Em Good: The Threat of Malpractice." *Journal of Social Welfare,* 6 (Fall–Winter 1979–80), p. 39.

Shea, T. "Legal Standards of Care for Psychiatrists and Psychologists." *Western State University Law Review,* 6 (1978), p. 71.

Simon, R. *Psychiatric Interventions and Malpractice: A Primer for Liability Prevention.* Springfield, Ill.: Charles C Thomas, Publisher, 1982.

Slawson, P. "Psychiatric Malpractice: The California Experience." *American Journal of Psychiatry,* 136 (1979), p. 650.

―――; Flinn, D.; and Schwartz, D. "Legal Responsibility for Suicide." *Psychiatric Quarterly,* 48 (1974), p. 50.

Sloan, J., and Klein, S. "Psychotherapeutic Disclosures: A Conflict Between Right and Duty." *Toledo Law Review,* 9 (1977), p. 57.

Slovenko, R. "Legal Issues in Psychotherapy Supervision." In *Psychotherapy Supervision: Theory, Research, Practice,* edited by A. Hess. New York: John Wiley & Sons, 1980.

―――. "On the Legal Aspects of Tardive Dyskinesia." *Journal of Law and Psychology,* 7 (1979), p. 295.

―――. *Psychiatry and Law.* Boston: Little, Brown & Co., 1973.

―――. "Psychotherapy and Confidentiality." *Cleveland State Law Review,* 24 (1975), p. 375.

Stone, A. *Law, Psychiatry, and Morality: Essays and Analysis.* Washington, D.C.: American Psychiatric Press, 1984.

―――. "The Legal Implications of Sexual Activity Between Psychiatrist and Patient." *American Journal of Psychiatry,* 133 (1976), p. 1138.

―――. *Mental Health and Law: A System in Transition.* Washington, D.C.: U.S. Department of Health, Education and Welfare, 1976).

―――. "Suicide Precipitated by Psychotherapy: A Clinical Contribution." *American Journal of Psychotherapy,* 25 (1971), p. 18.

―――. "The *Tarasoff* Decisions: Suing Psychotherapists to Safeguard Society." *Harvard Law Review,* 90 (1976), p. 358.

Tancredi, L.; Lieb, J.; and Slaby, A. *Legal Issues in Psychiatric Care.* New York: Harper & Row, 1975.

Tarshis, C. "Liability for Psychotherapy." *University of Toronto Faculty Law Review,* 30 (1972), p. 85.

Trent, C. "Psychiatric Malpractice Insurance and Its Problems: An Overview." In *Law and the Mental Health Professions: Friction at the Interface,* edited by W. Barton and C. Sanborn. New York: International Universities Press, 1978.

―――, and Muhl, W. "Professional Liability Insurance and the American Psychiatrist," *American Journal of Psychiatry,* 132 (1975), p. 1312.

Tryon, W. "Behavior Modification Therapy and the Law." *Professional Psychology,* 6 (1976), p. 468.

Twardy, S. "The Issue of Malpractice in Psychiatry." *Medical Trial Techniques Quarterly, 1979* (1979), p. 161.

Valentine, G. "*Tarasoff v. Regents of University of California:* The Psychotherapist's Peril." *University of Pittsburgh Law Review,* 37 (1975), p. 155.

Van Hoose, W., and Kottler, J. *Ethical and Legal Issues in Counseling and Psychotherapy.* San Francisco: Jossey-Bass, 1977.

Waltzer, H. "Malpractice Liability in a Patient's Suicide." *American Journal of Psychotherapy,* 34 (1980), p. 89.

Wexler, D. "Patients, Therapists, and Third Parties: The Victimological Virtues of *Tarasoff.*" *International Journal of Law and Psychiatry,* 2 (1979), p. 1.

White, A., and Gross, R. "Professional Liability Insurance and the Psychologist." *Professional Psychology,* 8 (1975), p. 267.

Whiting, L., and Daniels, M. "Legal Vulnerability and Liability: A Guide for Social Workers." Silver Spring, Md.: National Association of Social Workers, 1982.

Wise, T. "Where the Public Peril Begins: A Survey of Psychotherapists to Determine the Effects of *Tarasoff.*" *Stanford Law Review,* 31 (1978), p. 165.

Appendix B
Materials on Liability in Child Welfare

Annotation. "Governmental Tort Liability for Social Service Agency's Negligence in Placement, or Supervision After Placement, of Children." *American Law Reports 3d,* 90 (1979), p. 1214.

Besharov, D. "Child Welfare Malpractice: Suing Agencies and Caseworkers for Harmful Practices." *Trial,* 20, No. 3 (Association of Trial Lawyers of America, 1984), p. 56.

———. *Criminal and Civil Liability in Child Welfare Work: The Growing Trend.* Chicago: American Bar Association, 1983.

———. "Liability in Child Welfare." *Public Welfare,* 42 (Spring 1984), p. 28.

———. "Malpractice in Child Placement: Civil Liability for Inadequate Foster Care Services." *Child Welfare,* 63 (May–June 1984), p. 175.

———. "Protecting Abused and Neglected Children: Can Law Help Social Work?" *Family Law Reporter,* Monograph No. 5, 23 August 1983; reprinted in *Child Abuse and Neglect,* 7 (1983), p. 421.

Bross, D. "Professional and Agency Liability for Child Protective Negligence." In *Legal and Ethical Aspects of Health Care for Children,* edited by A. E. Doudera and L. S. Rothberg. Ann Arbor, Mich.: Caupha Press, 1983.

Brown, R., and Truitt, R. "Civil Liability for Child Abuse Cases." *Chicago-Kent Law Review,* 54 (1978), p. 753.

"Can Public Agencies Do No Wrong?—Liability of Child-Serving Agencies." *Children's Legal Rights Journal,* 3 (November–December 1981); reprinted in *Child Welfare,* 61 (November–December 1982), p. 585.

Comment. "A Damages Remedy for Abuse by Child Protective Workers." *Yale Law Review,* 90 (1981), p. 681.

Corder, B.; Whiteside, R.; Silverstein, E.; and Rieder, M. "Legal Issues Affecting Residential Child Care Workers." *Child Welfare,* 63 (May–June 1984), p. 217.

Davidson, M. "Civil Rights and Child Welfare." Paper presented at the Professional Symposium, National Association of Social Workers, Washington, D.C., 20 November 1983.

DeFrancis, V. "Guest Editorial." *National Child Protective Services Newsletter* (American Humane Association), 2, No. 8 (Winter 1979).

Donnella, S. "Safe Foster Care: A Constitutional Mandate." *Family Law Quarterly,* 19 (Spring 1985), p. 81.

Downey, J. "Accountability for Failure to Protect Children." In *Legal Representation of the Maltreated Child,* edited by D. Bross. Denver, Colo.: National Association of Counsel for Children, 1979.

Gembinski, C.; Casper, M.; and Hutchinson, E. "Worker Liability: Who's Really Liable?" In *Looking Back, Looking Ahead: Selections from the Fifth National Conference on Child Abuse and Neglect,* edited by C. Washburne. Madison: University of Wisconsin, School of Social Work, 1982, p. 116.

Greenland, C. "Reflections on the Popen Inquiry Report." *The Social Worker,* 50 (Winter 1982), p. 155.

Griffin, W., and Kalinowski, J. "An Approach to Liability Concerns: Standard for Practice." *Family Life Developments* (College of Human Ecology, Cornell University) (April–May 1981), p. 1.

Holder, W., and Hayes, K., eds. *Malpractice and Liability in Child Protective Services.* Longmont, Colo.: Bookmakers Guild, 1984.

Horowitz, R., and Davidson, H. "Improving the Legal Response of Child Protective Agencies," *Vermont Law Review,* 6 (1981), p. 381.

Hutchinson, E., and Casper, M. "CPS Indictments in Kentucky and Their Aftermath." *National Child Protective Services Newsletter* (American Humane Association), 4, No. 6, (1981).

Kieffer, M. "Child Abuse and Foster Homes: A Rationale for Pursuing Causes of Actions Against the Placement Agency." *Saint Louis University Law Journal,* 28 (1984), p. 975.

Leahy, M., and Barnes, M. "Private Social Welfare Agencies: Legal Liabilities Facing Employees." *Public Welfare,* 35 (Fall 1977), p. 42.

Levine, R. "Social Worker Malpractice: A New Approach Toward Accountability in the Juvenile Justice System." *Journal of Juvenile Law,* 1 (1977), p. 101.

"Malpractice: Growing Liability for CPS Workers." *Virginia Child Protection Newsletter* (James Madison University) (Spring 1983), p. 10.

Rose, C. *Some Emerging Issues in Legal Liability of Children's Agencies.* New York: Child Welfare League of America, 1978.

Schultz, L. *Malpractice and Liability in West Virginia's Child Protective Services: A Social Policy Analysis.* Morgantown: West Virginia University, School of Social Work, 1981.

Spearly, J. "Caseworker Indictments—A Closer Look." *National Child Protective Services Newsletter* (American Humane Association), 3, No. 4 (Winter, 1981), p. 6.

Appendix C
Materials on Liability for Failure to Report Suspected Child Maltreatment

Aaron, J. "Civil Liability for Teacher's Negligent Failure to Report Suspected Child Abuse." *Wayne Law Review,* 28 (1981), p. 183.

Annotation. "Failure to Report Suspected Case of Child Abuse." *American Jurisprudence: Proof of Facts 2d,* 6 (1975), p. 345.

Brown, R., and Truitt, R. "Civil Liability in Child Abuse Cases." *Chicago-Kent Law Review,* 54 (1978), p. 753.

Clymer, J. "The Battered Child—A Doctor's Civil Liability for Failure to Diagnose and Report." *Washburn Law Journal,* 16 (1977), p. 543.

Collier, S. "Reporting Child Abuse: When Moral Obligations Fail." *Pacific Law Reporter,* 15 (1983), p. 189.

Curran, W. "Failure to Diagnose Battered-Child Syndrome." *New England Journal of Medicine,* 296, No. 14 (7 April 1977), p. 795.

Endicott, O. "Civil Liability for Failure to Report Child Abuse." *Child Abuse and Neglect,* 3, No. 2 (1979), p. 633.

Hannig, J. "Physicians and Surgeons—Infants—Physician's Liability for Noncompliance with Child Abuse Reporting Statute." *North Dakota Law Review,* 52 (1976), p. 736.

Isaacson, L. "Child Abuse Reporting Statutes: The Case for Holding Physicians Civilly Liable for Failing to Report." *San Diego Law Review,* 12 (1975), p. 743.

Kohlman, R. "Malpractice Liability for Failing to Report Child Abuse." *California State Bar Journal,* 49 (1974), p. 118.

Lehto, N. "Civil Liability for Failing to Report Child Abuse," *Detroit College of Law Review,* 1 (1977), p. 135.

McDonald, R. "Civil Actions Against Physicians for Failure to Report Cases of Suspected Child Abuse." *Oklahoma Law Review,* 30 (1970), p. 482.

Maidment, S. "Some Legal Problems Arising Out of the Report of Child Abuse." *Current Legal Problems,* 31 (1978), p. 149.

Mazura, A. "Negligence—Malpractice—Physician's Liability for Failure to Diagnose and Report Child Abuse." *Wayne Law Review,* 23 (1977), p. 1187.

Miles, L. "The Guardian Ad Litem and Civil Liability on California Child Maltreatment Cases." *University of California, Davis, Law Review,* 12 (1979), p. 701.

Roberts, M. "Civil Liability of Physician for Failure to Diagnose or Report Battered Child Syndrome." *American Law Reports 3d,* 97 (1980), p. 338.

Appendix D
Standards Relating to Child Welfare Programs

American Humane Association. *Child Protective Services Standards.* Denver, Colo.: American Humane Association, 1977.

American Public Welfare Association. *A Guide for Improved Service Delivery: Analysis of the Tasks, Knowledge and Skill Requisites and Performance Criteria of the Child Protective Functions.* Washington, D.C.: American Public Welfare Association, 1981.

————. *Standards for Foster Family Services System.* Washington, D.C.: American Public Welfare Association, 1979.

Child Welfare League of America. *Standards for Child Protective Service.* New York: Child Welfare League of America, 1973.

National Association of Social Workers. *NASW Standards for Social Work Practice in Child Protection.* Silver Spring, Md.: National Association of Social Workers, 1981.

U.S. Children's Bureau. *Model State Adoption Act and Model State Adoption Procedures* (Draft 1980). Reported in *Federal Register,* 45 (1980), p. 10622.

U.S. National Center on Child Abuse and Neglect. *Child Protection: A Guide for State Legislation.* Washington, D.C.: U.S. Department of Health and Human Services, 1983.

————. *Federal Standards for Child Abuse and Neglect Prevention and Treatment Programs and Projects.* Washington, D.C.: U.S. Department of Health and Human Services, 1981.

Appendix E
Standards for Mental Health Professionals

American Association for Marriage and Family Therapy. *Code of Professional Ethics.* Upland, Calif., 1982.

American Psychiatric Association. *Principles of Medical Ethics, with Annotations Especially Applicable to Psychiatry.* Washington, D.C., 1984.

————, Task Force on Electroconvulsive Therapy. *Recommendations Regarding the Use of Electroconvulsive Therapy.* Washington, D.C., 1978.

American Psychological Association. *Ethical Principles of Psychologists.* Washington, D.C., 1981.

————. *Specialty Guidelines for the Delivery of Services by Clinical Psychologists.* Washington, D.C., 1981.

National Association of Social Workers. *Code of Ethics.* Silver Spring, Md., 1980.

————. *Standards for the Practice of Clinical Social Work.* Silver Spring, Md., 1984.

————. *Standards for Social Work Practice in Child Protection.* Silver Spring, Md., 1981.

————. *Standards for Social Work Services in Long-Term Care Facilities.* Silver Spring, Md., 1981.

————. *Standards for Social Work Services in Schools.* Silver Spring, Md., 1978.

Note for Appendices F, G, and H

Caveat: The charts in Appendices F, G, and H identify state laws relating to insurance, indemnification, and legal representation for *publicly* employed social workers. They present a reasonably accurate general view of state laws, but, given the limited resources that were available for their preparation, inaccuracies in individual state law provisions are possible. In addition, no attempt was made to analyze court decisions interpreting these laws and no attempt was made to identify and list local laws or particular agency policies on the same subject. In addition, this is a rapidly changing area of the law, and specific state descriptions could quickly become out of date. Moreover, many of the laws listed here are permissive in nature, that is, they authorize but do not require the provision of insurance, indemnification, or representation. Therefore, the charts should be used for initial reference only. Definitive information on these subjects should be sought from the relevant agency or an attorney.

> *Code:* A = all agents
> E = all employees
> N/A = not applicable
> N/M = not mentioned
> O = all officers

State	Unit of Government	Mand. or Disc.	Insurable Coverage	Amount of Insurance	Who Is Covered	Effect of Insurance on Defense of Government Immunity	Other
AL	State—Ala. Code §36-1-6 (Michie Supp. 1983)	Disc.	"Liability arising out of . . . operation of a motor vehicle"	N/M	E	N/M	
	Ala. Code §36-1-6.1 (Michie Supp. 1984)	Mand.	Negligent or wrongful acts or omissions	Amount needed to provide basic coverage	E, A	N/M	
AK	None						
AZ	State—Ariz. Rev. Stat. Ann. §41-621 (1984)	Mand.	"For acts or omissions of any nature while acting in authorized proprietary and governmental capacities and in the scope of employment"	The extent deemed "to be necessary"	O, E, A	No effect	
	Cities and Towns—§9-497 (1977)	Disc.	Insurance for acts done while engaged in proprietary or governmental capacity	N/M	O, E, A	N/M	
	Counties—§11-261 (1977)	Disc.	Same as for cities and towns	N/M	O, E, A	N/M	
AR	None						
CA	Local public entity—Cal. Govt. Code §990 (1980)	Disc.	For any liability within scope of employment	N/M	E	No effect—§991.2	
CO	State—§24-10-116; §24-14-102 (1982)	Mand.	"For any liability for which he may be liable" if within scope of employment	Up to amount of indemnification	E	Public entity deemed to have waived	
	Public entity other than the state—Colo. Rev. Stat. §24-10-115 (1982)	Disc.	Same	Any amount	E	N/M	
CT	Local (town, city, borough)—Conn. Gen. Stat. Ann. §7-465 (Supp. 1984)	Disc.	Within scope of employment	N/M	E	Government immunity no defense	
DE	State and Political Subdivisions—Del. Code Ann. tit. 10, §4005 (Michie Supp. 1984)	Disc.	N/M	Only to extent of indemnification statute	O, E	N/M	
FL	State and Subdivisions—Fla. Stat. Ann. §768.28(13); §111.072 (West Supp. 1984)	Disc.	For any possible action for which they may be civilly liable	"For whatever coverage they may choose"	N/M	Immunity waived for claims brought pursuant to §768.28	

Appendix F (continued)
State Laws Relating to Liability Insurance for Public Employees and Officers

State	Unit of Government	Mand. or Disc.	Insurable Coverage	Amount of Insurance	Who Is Covered	Effect of Insurance on Defense of Government Immunity	Other
GA	State—Ga. Code Ann. §45-9-1(1982) (agency defined §45-9-1[b])	Disc.	Any civil liability	"The amount of such insurance shall be in the discretion of such agency"	O (as defined in §45-9-1[b]), E	N/M	May include any legal costs; existence of insurance or indemnification not to be suggested or disclosed
	§45-9-2	Disc.	Any personal liability	Decided by commissioner of administration	Members of organized militia	N/M	Only if act occurs while in the performance of duties and while on active duty
	§45-9-3	Disc.	Any personal liability	Decided by commissioner of administration	Law enforcement personnel in programs administered by Organized Crime Prevention Council	N/M	
	Municipality, county, public body— §45-9-20 (1982)	Disc.	Any personal liability arising out of the performance of their duties	Left to discretion of governing body	Supervisors, administrators, E, O	N/M	The existence of the insurance not be brought into evidence
HI	None						
ID	State—Idaho Code §6-919 (1979)	Mand.	Tort claims and civil lawsuits	Minimum: $500,000 for all claims	E	Remains in effect §6-903(f)	If insurance exceeds limits of indemnification, the controlling limit shall be the amount of insurance §6-926; no punitive damages §6-918
	Political Subdivisions—§6-923 (1979)	Disc.		Same	E		
IL	Local Public Entity—Ill. Ann. Stat. Ch. 85, §9-103 (Smith-Hurd Supp. 1984)	Disc.	Acts that could cause tort liability	N/M	E	N/M	The insurance company issuing the policy must waive any right to deny liability by reasons of immunities given to the insured public entity
IN	State and Political Subdivisions— Ind. Code §34-4-16.5-18(a) (Supp. 1983)	Disc.	Acts that could result in the E's tort liability	N/M—However, insurers may not settle for an amount that exceeds insurance coverage without approval of the governor (for state E) or mayor (for city E)	E	Not to be construed as waiver §34-4-16.5-5	

Appendix F (continued)
State Laws Relating to Liability Insurance for Public Employees and Officers

State	Unit of Government	Mand. or Disc.	Insurable Coverage	Amount of Insurance	Who Is Covered	Effect of Insurance on Defense of Government Immunity	Other
IA	State and Political Subdivisions—Iowa Code Ann. §517A.1 (West Supp. 1983)	Disc.	Any individual, corporate, or quasi corporate liability that said...officers or E may incur	N/M	O, E	Immunity waived and policy provisions on defense and settlement apply	The form and liability limits of the insurance policy purchased by the state require A.G. approval
	Municipality—§613A.7 (West Supp. 1983)	Disc.	Any liability that can be incurred under §613A.2, A.4, or A.8	N/M	O, E, A	Constitutes a waiver of the defenses of government immunity listed in §613A.4 to extent stated in policy	Any reference to the existence of the insurance or lack of same shall be grounds for mistrial
KS	Government Entity—Kan. Stat. Ann. §75-6111 (Supp. 1983)	Disc.	For tort claims, including civil rights actions, but must be within the scope of employment	May be in excess of limits imposed by indemnification statute	E	Insurers may avail themselves of any defense that would be available to a government entity defending itself in an action within the scope of the act; enumeration of exceptions to liability not to be construed as waiver of immunity as to any other acts of discretionary nature §75-6104	
KY	None						
LA	None						
ME	State and Political Subdivisions—Me. Rev. Stat. Ann. tit. 14, §8116 (West Supp. 1983)	Disc.[1] Mand.[2]	Any claim against state or its employees including personal liability	May be in excess of limits imposed by indemnification statute	E	Insurance may be procured in areas where the government entity is immune, and if procured, this is a waiver up to the level of insurance §8116 (West Supp. 1983)	
MD	State—Md. Ann. Code art. 95, §27 (Michie Supp. 1984)	Mand.	Settlement or judgment if certified by Board of Public Works	N/M	O, E	Waived to extent of insurance coverage	

[1] Disc.—for acts occurring out of or in the scope of employment.
[2] Mand.—$10,000 coverage for employer's liability under §8103(3).

State Laws Relating to Liability Insurance for Public Employees and Officers

State	Unit of Government	Mand. or Disc.	Insurable Coverage	Amount of Insurance	Who Is Covered	Effect of Insurance on Defense of Government Immunity	Other
MA	State and Local Public Employer—Mass. Ann. Laws Ch. 258, §8 (West Supp. 1983-84)	Disc.	N/M	"May procure insurance for payment of damages"	N/M	N/M	
MI	State and Political Subdivisions—Mich. Comp. Laws Ann. §691.1409 (1966)	Disc.	Personal injury and property damage	N/M	Some or all of the agents, O, E	Not a waiver of any defense available	
MN	State—Minn. Stat. Ann. §3.736 (8) (1977)	Disc.	Tort action	N/M	E	"Constitutes a waiver of the defense of government immunity to the extent" of the policy	
	Municipality—§466.06 (1977)	Disc.	Tort action	N/M—policy may exceed limits of liability in §466.04	O, E, A	Same	
MS	Municipality—Miss. Code Ann. §21-15-6 (Harrison Supp. 1984)	Disc.	N/M	N/M	O, E	Does not constitute a waiver. Recovered to the extent of the insurance policy	Existence of insurance cannot be made evidence in a trial
MO	State and Political Subdivisions—Mo. Ann. Stat. §537-610, §105-721 (Vernon Supp. 1985)	Disc.	Tort claim	Maximum: $100,000/person; $800,000/occurrence. No recovery for punitive damages	Actions against the state or political subdivision	Constitutes a waiver of immunity only to the extent of the insurance policy	
MT	State—Mont. Code Ann. §2-9-201 (1983)	Mand.	N/M	N/M	State and instrumentalities	N/M	
	Political Subdivisions—§2-9-211	Disc.	N/M	N/M	N/M	N/M	
NE	State—Neb. Rev. Stat. §81-8, §239.02 (1981)	Mand.	Compensable civil liability and fidelity claims	N/M	O, E, A	Creation of insurance fund shall not be interpreted as expanding liability	
	Political Subdivisions—§23-2413 (1983)	Disc.	Claims under act	N/M	O, E, A	Waiver as to excepted claims up to amount of insurance	
NV	State and Local Government—Nev. Rev. Stat. §41.038 (1981)	Disc.	Tort liability or any liability not given immunity	N/M	O, E, and peace officers used by school districts	N/M	
NH	State—N.H. Rev. Stat. Ann. §99D:3 (Supp. 1983)	Mand.	All damages, losses, expenses except employee injury	N/M	N/M	N/M	State to self-insure
	Local—§31-107	Disc.	All claims for which O indemnified	N/M	O	N/M	

State	Unit of Government	Mand. or Disc.	Insurable Coverage	Amount of Insurance	Who Is Covered	Effect of Insurance on Defense of Government Immunity	Other
NJ	None						
NM	State—N.M. Stat. Ann. §41-4-20(2) (1982)	Mand.	Every risk or liability for which immunity has been waived	N/M	E	N/M	
	Local Public Bodies—§41-4-20(1) (1982)	Mand.	Every risk or liability for which immunity has been waived	N/M	E	N/M	
NY	City, County, Town, Village, School and Fire District—N.Y. Gen. Mun. Law §52 (McKinney Supp. 1984–85)	Disc.	For actions done in good faith purporting to perform these duties	N/M	O, E	N/M	
	Local Public Entity—N.Y. Pub. Off. Law §18(8) (1984–85)	Disc.	Against liability for any indemnification provided by the locality	N/M	E	Immunity not impaired, altered, limited, modified, abrogated or restricted	May also act as self-insurer
NC	State—N.C. Gen. Stat. §143B-424.1 (Michie Supp. 1983)	Disc.	Professional liability of state officials	Amount in excess of protection provided under statute	O, E	Not deemed waived	
	City, County Authority—N.C. Gen. Stat. §160A-167(b) (Michie Supp. 1983)	Disc.	Civil liability resulting from actions within the scope of employment	N/M	O, E (and former O, E)	Purchase of insurance shall not be deemed an assumption of liability beyond the scope of the policy	
ND	State—N.D. Cent. Code §32-12.1-15 (Supp. 1983)	Disc.	Against civil liability provided by this chapter	N/M	E	Government waives its immunity only for the types of insurance coverage provided and to extent of policy limit	The insurance policy cannot cover punitive damages
	Political Subdivision—§32-12.1-05 (Supp. 1983)	Disc.	Against civil liability provided by this chapter and additional coverage as government body determines appropriate	N/M	E	N/M	The policy may not be procured for more than 5 years' duration; does not cover punitive damages
OH	State—Ohio Rev. Code Ann. §9.87(c) (Page Supp. 1984)	Disc.	Civil actions arising from acts within the scope of employment	Coverage in excess of $1,000,000 per occurrence	E, O	N/M	
	County—Ohio Rev. Code Ann. §307.441 (Page Supp. 1984)	Disc.	For liability within the performance of official duties	N/M	E, O	No effect	

Appendix F (continued)
State Laws Relating to Liability Insurance for Public Employees and Officers

State	Unit of Government	Mand. or Disc.	Insurable Coverage	Amount of Insurance	Who Is Covered	Effect of Insurance on Defense of Government Immunity	Other
OK	State—Okla. Stat. Ann. tit. 57, §553 (West Supp. 1984–85)	Disc.	Acts performed while discharging his duties	$100,000 for each E insured	E of Department of Corrections	No effect	
	Municipalities—tit. 56, §168, School districts—tit. 51, §168, Counties— tit. 51, §169 (West Supp. 1984–85)	Disc.	Acts within scope of employment	N/M	E	N/M	
OR	Local Public Body—Or. Rev. Stat. §30.282 (1983)	Disc.	"Against liability"	N/M	O, E, A	N/M	Local public body may establish self-insurance fund or contract with state and make payment into State Liability Fund
PA	Local Agency—Pa. Stat. Ann. tit. 42, §8564 (1982)	Disc.	"For any liability within scope of employment and in performance of their duty"	N/M	E	N/M	Localities may join together to develop group risk management program or to purchase insurance; may self-insure
RI	None						
SC	State—S.C. Code §1-11-140 (Supp. 1983)	Disc.	To protect against tort liabilities while within the course of employment	N/M	E	N/M	
	Political Subdivisions—S.C. Code §1-11-140 (Supp. 1983)	Disc.	Same	N/M	E	N/M	
SD	State—S.D. Codified Laws Ann. §21-32-15 (Supp. 1984)	Disc.	N/M	"To the extent…deemed expedient"	O, E, A	Waiver to extent of coverage	
	Municipality—§9-12-7 (1981)	Disc.	Acts committed in the performance of official duty	N/M	O, E	N/M	
TN	State and Local Governmental Entities— Tenn. Code Ann. §29-20-406 (1980)	Disc.	Injury or damage resulting from negligent acts	Minimum: $40,000/person; Minimum: $80,000/accident of others; $20,000/ property; automobile cases have a $100,000/person; $300,000/accident minimum	E	N/M	If government entity not insured, limit of liability is $20,000/person; $40,000/ accident; $10,000/property
TX	State and all other units of government—Tex. Rev. Civ. Stat. Ann. art. 6252 §19 (1970)	Disc.	Against civil claims arising under this act	N/M	O, E, A	N/M	Provision for insurance not admissible at trial

The Vulnerable Social Worker

State	Unit of Government	Mand. or Disc.	Insurable Coverage	Amount of Insurance	Who Is Covered	Effect of Insurance on Defense of Government Immunity	Other
UT	State and Political Subdivisions—Utah Code Ann. §63-30-33 (Supp. 1983)	Disc.	For injury or damage resulting from act occurring during performance of an E's duties, within the scope of employment or under color of authority	May be in excess of limits imposed by indemnification statute	E	N/M	
VT	State—Vt. Stat. Ann. tit. 29, §1401 (1970), §1406 (Supp. 1984)	Mand.	For actions committed while performing official duties (civil)	N/M	E	Waiver in extent of policy coverage—§1405	
	Municipal Corporation—tit. 24, §1092 (Supp. 1984)	Disc.	"To secure benefits . . . for the employees"	N/M	E	N/M	
VA	State—Va. Code §2.1-526.8 (1984)	Mand.	Acts/omissions of any nature while acting in governmental or proprietary capacity	N/M	O, E, A	Not express or implied waiver	Insurance plan to be established and may include purchased or self-insurance
	State—Va. Code §15.1-506.2 (1981)	Disc.	Conduct in the discharge of duties (civil)	N/M	O and E of local departments and boards of welfare and social service	N/M	Va. Code §46.1-39(b)(1980) provides that a liability insurance policy of a police officer appointed by Commissioner of Motor Vehicles be paid out of funds appropriated to enforce motor vehicle laws
	County and any political subdivisions—§15.1-506.1 (1981)	Disc.	Conduct in the discharge of duties	N/M	O, E, volunteers	N/M	
WA	County, City, Town, School District, etc—Wash. Rev. Code Ann. §§36.16.136, 138 (Supp. 1983)	Disc.	Any action arising out of performance of duties	"With such limits as [deemed] reasonable"	O, E, A, commissioners, council and governing board members, directors	N/M	
WV	Municipality—W.Va. Code §842.7 (1976)	Disc.	Bodily or personal injury or property damage or damage while in the performance of their official duty	N/M	O, E, A	N/M	
WI	State and Municipality—Wis. Stat. Ann. §66.18 (West Supp. 1984-85)	Disc.	N/M	N/M	O, E, A	N/M	
WY	State and local Governmental Entity—Wyo. Stat. §1-39-118 (Supp. 1983)	Disc.	Any acts or risks	May be in excess of $500,000 limit on government liability	N/M	N/M	

Appendix G
State Laws Relating to Indemnification for Public Employees and Officers

State	Unit of Government Authorizing Indemnification	Mandatory or Dis-cretionary	Criminal Penalties Covered?	Discretionary Indemnification: Who Makes Decision	Limits on Indemnification	Who Is Covered
AL	None					
AK	None					
AZ	None					
AR	State—Ark. Stat. Ann. §§12-3401-3402 (1979 replacement volume)	Mandatory	N/M	N/A	No recovery for punitive damages	O (defined in §12-3406), E
	Local—§12-3407 (Michie Supp. 1983)	Mandatory	N/M	N/A	No recovery for punitive damages	E of city, town, county
CA	Public Entity—Cal. Govt. Code §§825, 825.4 (1980)	Mandatory	N/M	N/A	No recovery for punitive or exemplary damages	E and former E (state and local)
CO	Public Entity—Colo. Rev. Stat. §24-10-110 (1)(b)(1) (1982)	Mandatory	N/M	N/A	No recovery for punitive damages (§24-10-115[b][1]). Limit of $150,000/person injured; $400,000/incident	E (state and local)
CT	State—§4-16a (West Supp. 1984)	Mandatory	N/M	N/A	N/M	All department heads
	State—§4-165 (West Supp. 1984)	Mandatory	N/M	N/A	N/M	O, E
	Towns, Cities, Boroughs—Conn. Gen. Stat. Ann. §7-465 (West Supp. 1984)	Mandatory	N/M	N/A	No indemnification for libel or slander suits or suits brought by fellow E	E, except for fireman covered under §7-308
	Municipality—§7-308 (West Supp. 1984)	Mandatory	N/M	N/A	No indemnification for suit brought by fellow fireman	E
	Board of Education—§10-235 (1984)	Mandatory	N/M	N/A	N/M	E
DE	State—Del. Code Ann. tit. 10 §4002 (Michie Supp. 1984)	Mandatory	N/M	E's agency head must secure the approval of Governor and A. G. if settlement; automatic if judgment for E or determination that no claim existed or good faith act of discretion (§4001)	Maximum against E of political subdivision is $300,000/occurrence or amount of insurance coverage if higher	O, E (county and municipal E defined in §4010) (state and local)
	Political Subdivisions—Del. Code Ann. tit. 10, §4003 (Michie Supp. 1984)	Discretionary	N/M	To determine its own procedure for settlement	N/A	N/A
FL	State, County, Municipality or Political Subdivisions—Fla. Stat. Ann. §111.071, §768.28 (1984)	Discretionary	N/M	N/M	$100,000/person; $200,000/incident. Legislature may increase this amount. In §1983 actions, no limit unless act was intentional (§768.38[5] [1983])	O, E, A (state and local)
GA	State—Ga. Code Ann. §45-9-60 (1982)	Discretionary	N/M	The A. G. (§45-9-60 [1982])	N/M	O, official
	Municipality, County—§45-9-22 (1982)	Discretionary	Yes	The local entity (§45-9-21 [1982])	"May pay part or all of any claim or judgment"	O, E (as defined by governing body, under §45-9-21
HI	None					
ID	Governmental Entity—Idaho Code §6-903 (1985)	Mandatory	N/M	N/A	No recovery of punitive damages (§6-918). Only for a pro rata share of the damages which is attributable to the conduct of E $500,000 per occurrence regardless of number of claimants	E (state and local)

252

Notice Requirement	Indemnification Limited to Acts or Omissions	No Indemnification for Behavior That Is...	Reimbursement to or from Employee?	Effect of Insurance	Other
Notify A. G. promptly (§12-3404)	Within scope of employment and in the performance of his official duties	Malicious or lacks good faith	N/M	Indemnification reduced to amount in excess of coverage	
N/M	Same	Same	N/M	N/M	
10 days prior to trial	Within scope of employment	Malicious, or fraudulent, or when E fails to conduct or cooperate in a defense(§825.2)	Reimbursement to public entity permitted under limited circumstances, such as when action was malicious, fraudulent, corrupt, or E failed to cooperate with defense (§825.6)	N/M	
Within a reasonable time of the incident	Within scope of employment or duty	Willful or wanton	Reimbursement to public entity for reasonable attorney fees if act not within scope of employment or willful or wanton conduct (§24-10-110 [3][a][1])	Damages limited to amount of insurance coverage	
N/M	Within scope of employment or duty	Wanton, reckless, or malicious	N/M	N/M	
N/M	Same	Same	N/M	N/M	
N/M	Same	Willful or wanton	N/M	N/M	
N/M	Same	Willful, reckless, or malicious	N/M	N/M	
N/M	Same	Same	N/M	N/M	
N/M	Within scope of employment or duty	Not in good faith or not in the belief that the public interest would be best served; gross or wanton negligence	N/M	No indemnification beyond insurance (§4005)	If case does not reach court or administrative tribunal or court does not decide no cause of action exists, render judgment for E, or find good faith act within discretion, employee may request head of his or her unit (i.e., department or agency) to grant his or her request for indemnification. Head of unit must secure approval of Governor and A.G. before indemnifying employee (§4004)
N/A	N/A	N/A	N/A	N/A	
N/M	Within scope of employment or duty	An intentional violation of civil rights; bad faith, malicious purpose, or manner exhibiting wanton and willful disregard of human rights, safety, or property	N/M	N/M	Indemnification is not intended to be a waiver of any defense or immunity available in such lawsuits. (§111.071[4] [1982])
N/M	Within scope of employment or duty	A breach of duty imposed by law	N/M	N/M	A. G. decides whether O's omission or commission constituted a breach of duty imposed by law. If A. G. is the one seeking indemnification, the governor decides whether the A. G.'s acts constituted a breach of duty imposed by law.
N/M	Same	A theft, embezzlement, or like crime	N/M	N/M	
N/M	Within scope of employment or duty	Malicious or with criminal intent	Yes—but a rebuttable presumption in favor of E that he was acting within scope of employment and without malice or criminal intent	Indemnification reduced to the amount in excess of coverage	Neither the fact of indemnification nor the government's willingness to pay legal fees may be introduced into evidence.

Appendices

State	Unit of Government Authorizing Indemnification	Mandatory or Dis- cretionary	Criminal Penalties Covered?	Discretionary Indemnification: Who Makes Decision	Limits on Indemnification	Who Is Covered
IL	State—Ill. Ann. Stat. ch. 127, §1302(2)(d) (Smith-Hurd Supp. 1984)	Mandatory	N/M	N/A	N/M	E
	State—Ch 111-1/2 §217.1 I (Smith-Hurd Supp. 1983)	Mandatory	N/M	N/A	N/M	Individuals on advisory boards of Department of Nuclear Safety
	Municipality (over 500,000 pop.) —Ch. 24, §1-4-5 (Smith-Hurd Supp. 1984)	Mandatory	N/M	N/A	N/M	Policeman (defined in §1-4-5; §1-4-6)
	Municipality (less than 500,000 pop.)—(Smith-Hurd Supp. 1984)	Mandatory	N/M	N/A	Maximum: $100,000	Same as above
	Local Public Entity—ch. 85, §9-102 (Smith-Hurd Supp. 1984)	Mandatory	N/M	N/A	N/M	E
IN	Governmental Entity—Ind. Code §34-4-16.5-5 and 16.7-1 (1982 Supp.)	Mandatory	N/M	The governor or the governing body of the level of government (§34-4-16.5-5[b] 1982)	No recovery for punitive damages (§34-4-16.5-4); $300,000/injury or death of 1 person; $5,000,000/ occurrence	E (state and local)
IA	State—Iowa Code Ann. §§25A.21, 22 (1978)	Mandatory	No	N/A	No recovery of punitive damages	E
	Governing Body—§613A.8 (West Supp. 1983)	Mandatory	N/M	N/A	Same	O, E (local)
KS	Governmental Entity—Kan. Stat. Ann. §75-6109 (Supp. 1983)	Mandatory	N/M	N/A	No recovery for punitive or exemplary damages. Maximum: $500,000/occurrence (§75-6105)	E (state and local)
KY	None					
LA	State—La. Rev. Stat. Ann. §13-5108.1(A) (West Supp. 1985)	Mandatory	N/M	N/A	Legislature will appropriate a sum to reimburse O or E (§13-5108.1[E])	O, E
	State—§13-5108.2(B) (West Supp. 1985)	Mandatory	N/M	N/A	Same (§13.5108.2[F])	O, E, including an E of a harbor, terminal district, or deep-water port
ME	Governmental Entity—Me. Rev. Stat. Ann. tit. 14, §8112 (1980)	Mandatory —when the governmental entity *would* be liable for the act done (§8112.2) Discretionary —when the governmental entity would not be liable for the act done (§8112.2)	N/M	Governmental entity (§8112 [1980])	No recovery for punitive or exemplary damages (§8105); $300,000/ occurrence; legislature may give special authorization for an increased limit	E (state and local)
MD	State—Md. Ann. Code art. 78A, §12-310 (Michie Supp. 1984)	Mandatory (civil) Discretionary (criminal)	Yes	A. G.	Civil—Court costs, attorney fees, and other reasonable expenses Criminal—attorney fees	O, E
MA	State—Mass. Ann. Laws Ch. 258, §2 (West Supp. 1985)	Mandatory	N/M	N/A	No recovery for punitive damages or interest prior to judgment. Maximum: $100,000	E
	State—Ch. 258, §9 (West Supp. 1984-85)	Discretionary	Civil	Public employer (immediate agency head). (§9 [West Supp. 1983])	Maximum: $1,000,000	E
	State—Ch. 258, §9A (West Supp. 1984-85)	Mandatory	N/M	N/A	$1,000,000	Members of state police and metropolitan district police
	Local—Ch. 258, §13 (West Supp. 1984-85)	Mandatory for cities and towns accepting provision	N/M	N/A	$1,000,000	O
	City or Town—Ch. 258, §13 (West Supp. 1983)	Mandatory	N/M	N/A	$1,000,000	Municipal officers, elected or appointed

State Laws Relating to Indemnification for Public Employees and Officers

Notice Requirement	Indemnification Limited to Acts or Omissions	No Indemnification for Behavior That Is...	Reimbursement to or from Employee?	Effect of Insurance	Other
N/M	Within scope of employment	Intentional, willful, or wanton, not intended to serve or benefit interest of state	N/M	N/M	This provision does not deprive E of any defenses that are available. This provision applies regardless of whether E is sued in his individual capacity.
N/M	Within scope of their service	Willful or wanton	N/M	N/M	
N/M	Within scope of their duty (§1-4-5)	Willful misconduct	N/M	N/M	
Written notice 10 days after process is sent (§1-4-6)	Same (§1-4-6)	Same	N/M	N/M	
N/M	Within scope of employment	N/M	N/M	N/M	
N/M	Within scope of employment	N/M	N/M	N/M	Before payment, the governor, in the case of a state E, or the governing body, in the case of a political subdivision, must decide that the payment is in the best interests of the governmental entity.
Original notice to be served on E and A. G.	Within scope of employment	Involving malfeasance or willful or wanton	N/M	Policy provisions on defense and settlement will apply	
N/M	Within scope of employment or duty	Willful and wanton	Yes—to municipality if court finds E's conduct willful or wanton	Municipality may purchase insurance to protect O, E, against personal liability for punitive damages	
N/M	Within scope of employment	Fraudulent or malicious	Yes—if E does not cooperate in good faith in the defense of the claim or if court finds actual fraud or malice (§75-6109)	Government not liable for judgments or settlements paid through policy of insurance	
Notice to A. G. within 5 days of service on O or E prerequisite to indemnification (§13-5108.1[R])	Within scope of employment or duty	Intentionally wrongful or grossly negligent	Reimbursement of attorney fees for private counsel if court finds O or E acting within discharge of duties and scope of employment and no intentional wrongful act or gross negligence	Rights and obligations of insurer not impaired, limited, or modified (§13-5108.1[F])	Court must first decide that employee met all the requirements of the statute before any payment can be made (§13-5108.1 [D])
Same as above (§13-5108.2[C])	Same	Same	Same (§13-5108.2[C][3])	Same (§13-5108.2[H])	
30 days after receiving a claim or 15 days after summons	Within scope of employment or duty	N/M	Yes—(§8122.[3]) if court later determines act occurred within the scope of employment, governmental entity must also pay attorney fees and court costs	Governmental entity may purchase insurance for amounts higher than ordinary indemnification limits	
N/M	Within scope of employment or duty	Malicious or gross negligence	$100,000 per individual claim; $500,000 per occurrence (§12-104)	N/M	In cases of doubt, Board of Public Works decides if O or E is a *state* O or E. Decision cannot be appealed.
N/M	Within scope of employment or office	N/M	N/M	N/M	E shall provided reasonable cooperation to the public employer.
N/M	Within scope of employment or duty	Grossly negligent, willful, or malicious	N/M	N/M	Indemnification allowed for intentional torts and civil rights violations.
N/M	Within scope of official duty	Willful, wanton, or malicious	N/M	N/M	
N/M	Within scope of employment or duty	Intentional violation of civil rights	N/M	N/M	Voters in each city and town to decide whether provision will apply
N/M	Same	Same	N/M	N/M	

Appendices

State	Unit of Government Authorizing Indemnification	Mandatory or Discretionary	Criminal Penalties Covered?	Discretionary Indemnification: Who Makes Decision	Limits on Indemnification	Who Is Covered
MI	Government Agency—Mich. Comp. Laws Ann. §691.1408 (West Supp. 1984–85)	Discretionary	N/M	Government agency	N/M	O, E (state and local)
MN	State—Minn. Stat. Ann. §3.736(9) (West Supp. 1985)	Mandatory	N/M	N/A	No recovery for punitive damages (§3.786[3]); $200,000 per claim; $600,000/occurrence (§3.736[4])	E
	Municipality or any instrumentality thereof—§466.07 (West Supp. 1985)	Mandatory	N/M	N/A	Same	O, E
	Local—§461.45 (1977)	Discretionary	N/M	Governing body of government subdivisions (§471.45 [1977])	N/M	Sheriff, deputy sheriff, police, and peace officers
MS	Municipality—Miss. Code Ann. §25-1-47(2) (1972)	Discretionary	Yes	Governing body of the municipality (§25-1-47 [1983])	N/M	O, E, A
MO	State—Mo. Ann. Stat. §105.711 (Vernon Supp. 1985)	Mandatory	N/M	N/A	In tort actions, limit of $800,000/ occurrence; $100,000/claim	O, E
MT	Governmental Entity—Mont. Code Ann. §2-9-305 (1983)	Mandatory	No	N/A	N/M	E (state and local)
NE	State—Neb. Rev. Stat. §81-8.239-05 (Supp. 1981)	Mandatory	No	N/A	Not to exceed whatever could have been collected from O, E, A	O, E, A, or former O, E, A
	Political Subdivisions—§23-2419 (1983)	Discretionary	N/M	N/M	N/M	E
NV	State and Political Subdivisions— Nev. Rev. Stat. §41.0349 (1981)	Mandatory	N/M	N/A	$50,000/claimant in tort actions (§41.035)	O, E, and former O, E (state and local)
NH	State—N.H. Rev. Stat. Ann. §99-D:2 (Supp. 1983)	Mandatory	N/M	N/A	N/M	O, E, official, trustee
	City, County, Town, Village, District, Precinct, or any Municipal Corporation —§31:105 & 106 (Supp. 1983)	Discretionary	N/M	By vote of governing body (§31:105 [1983])	N/M	Any person employed by the unit of local government
NJ	State—N.J. Stat. Ann. §59:10-1 (1982)	Mandatory	No	N/A	No recovery for punitive or exemplary damages	E or former E
	Local Public Entity—§59:10-4 (1982)	Discretionary	N/M	The local public entity (§59:10-4 [1982])	Same	E
NM	Governmental Entity—N.M. Stat. Ann. §41-4-4 (1983)	Mandatory	N/M	N/A	Will pay punitive damages under substantive law of another State (§41-4-4C). $100,000/property; $300,000/personal injury; $500,000/ occurrence. No punitive damages (§41-4-19)	E (state and local)
NY	State—N.Y. Pub. Off. Law §17-3 (McKinney Supp. 1984–85)	Mandatory	Yes (§19), for legal fees if within scope of employment and acquittal or dismissal of charges	N/A	No recovery for punitive or exemplary damages	E
	Local Public Entities—§18 (McKinney Supp. 1984–85)	Discretionary (the law allows localities to adopt a mandatory program)	N/M	N/A	N/M	E
NC	State—N.C. Gen. Stat. §143-300.6 (Michie 1983)	Mandatory	Yes	N/A	N/M	E
	City, County—§160A-167(b) (Michie 1983)	Discretionary	N/M	Governing body (§160A-167[b] [Michie Supp. 1983])	N/M	O, E (and former O, E), member of volunteer fire squad or rescue squad and county alcoholic beverage control board
	Public School Employees— §143-300.14 (Michie 1983)	Mandatory	Civil	N/A	N/M	E

Notice Requirement	Indemnification Limited to Acts or Omissions	No Indemnification for Behavior That Is...	Reimbursement to or from Employee?	Effect of Insurance	Other
N/M	Within scope of authority and within employment	N/M	N/M	N/M	
N/M	Within scope of employment or duty	Willful or wanton, or involves neglect of duty, or malfeasance	N/M	N/M	
N/M	Same	Willful or wanton neglect of duty or malfeasance	N/M	N/M	
N/M	Same	Not in good faith	N/M	N/M	
N/M	"While acting as such" (O, E, A, etc.)	N/M	N/M	N/M	
N/M	Within official duties on behalf of state	N/M	N/M	No payment from state fund on policy of insurance procured by state until benefits provided by any other policy of insurance exhausted	
Yes, must be written	Within scope of employment	Oppressive, fraudulent, malicious, or involves a criminal offense. Also, no indemnification for settling without the consent of the governmental entity	N/M	N/M	Recovery against governmental entity bars suit against employee in any capacity
N/M	Within scope of employment	Willful, wanton, or malicious	N/M	N/M	This section does not extend the personal liability of state, agencies, officials, or employees (§81-8.239.02)
N/M	N/M	N/M	Political Subdivision may bring actions against E to recover settlement or award	N/M	
Must be a "timely request"	Within scope of public duty	Wanton, malicious, or involves a lack of cooperation	N/M	N/M	
Yes, within 7 days of service	Within scope of employment	Wanton or reckless	N/M	N/M	
N/M	Same	Malicious	N/M	N/M	
To A. G. within 10 days after receiving summons or complaint	Within scope of employment	Actual fraud, actual malice, or willful misconduct	N/M	N/M	
Same	Same	Same	N/M	N/M	
N/M	Within scope of official duty	Fraudulent or malicious	Yes, if E acted fraudulently or with actual intentional malice	N/M	
Within 5 days after summons	Within scope of employment or duty	Intentional wrongdoing or recklessness	N/M	Statute does not impair, alter, limit, or modify rights of insurer under policy	E may be indemnified for a violation of a prior order, judgment, consent decree, or stipulation of settlement. (E must have acted within scope of employment and without willfulness.) (§173[c], §18-4[c])
Written request within 10 days after summons	Within scope of official duties	Same	N/M	Same	
N/M	Within course of employment	N/M	N/M	Coverage in excess of commercial liability insurance policy up to limits established by statute	
Notice must be sent before judgment is rendered (§160A.174[c])	Same	Fraudulent, corrupt, or malicious	N/M	N/M	
N/M	Within course of duties	N/M	Yes (§143-300.17)	Coverage in excess of any commercial insurance liability coverage E may have	

State	Unit of Government Authorizing Indemnification	Mandatory or Discretionary	Criminal Penalties Covered?	Discretionary Indemnification: Who Makes Decision	Limits on Indemnification	Who Is Covered
ND	Local Political Subdivisions—N.D. Cent. Code §32-12.1-04 (Supp. 1983)	Mandatory	N/M	N/A	Political subdivision may be held liable for punitive damages if behavior is willful and wanton, which may exceed ordinary limits of: $250,000/person; $500,000/occurrence (§32-12.1-03 [1983])	E
OH	State—Ohio Rev. Code Ann. §9.87 (1984)	Mandatory	N/M	N/A	No recovery for punitive; $1 million/occurrence	O, E
OK	State and Political Subdivisions—Okla. Stat. Ann. tit. 51, §153 (West Supp. 1984-85)	Mandatory	No	N/A	$25,000 per claimant for loss of property arising out of single occurrence; $100,000 for any other loss arising out of single occurrence; maximum: $1,000,000/occurrence; no punitive damages	E
OR	Public Body—Or. Rev. Stat. §30.285 (1983)	Mandatory	N/M	N/A	No recovery for punitive damages; $50,000/claimant for property damage; $100,000/claimant for other claims; $300,000/occurrence	O, E, A (state and local)
PA	Local Agency—Pa. Stat. Ann. tit. 42, §8548 (1982)	Mandatory	N/M	N/A	$500,000/occurrence (§8553 [1982])	E
RI	State—R.I. Gen. Laws §9-31-12 (Supp. 1984)	Discretionary	N/M	"State reserves the right" (§9-31-12)	$50,000 (§9-31-12)	E
SC	None					
SD	State and Governing Board and Political Subdivisions—S.D. Codified Laws Ann. §3-19-1 (1980)	Discretionary	N/M	Governing Board of political subdivision or A. G. (§3-19-3)	$10,000 (§3-19-3)	E (state and local)
TN	State—Tenn. Code Ann. §8-42-103, 104 (Supp. 1984)	Mandatory	Yes	N/A	N/M	E
	Local Education Agency—Tenn. Code Ann. §49-6-4211(a) (1983)	Mandatory	N/M	N/A	N/M	Principals, teachers
TX	State—Tex. Rev. Civ. Stat. Ann. art. §6252-26, §1 (Supp. 1985)	Mandatory	N/M	N/A	$100,000/person; $300,000/occurrence; $10,000/property damage	O, E, and former O, E, physicians contracted with state government, or their estates
	Political Subdivisions—Tex. Rev. Civ. Stat. Ann. art. §6252-19b(2) (Supp. 1985)	Discretionary	N/M	N/M	Same	E
UT	Governmental Entity—Utah Code Ann. §63-30-36(2-3), §63-30a-2 (Supp. 1983)	Mandatory	N/M	Yes	$250,000/person; $500,000/occurrence; $100,000/property damage (§63-30-34)	E (state and local)
VT	State—Vt. Stat. Ann. tit. 12, §5601 (1973)	Mandatory	N/M	N/A	$75,000/person or $300,000/occurrence	E
	State—Vt. Stat. Ann. tit. 3, §1103(a) (Supp. 1984)	Discretionary	Yes (§1104)	A judgment would be an emergency, and, as such, would be up to the discretion of the Emergency Board. Compromise or settlement is up to the discretion of the A. G. (§1103[a] [Supp. 1983])	$100,000	E

State Laws Relating to Indemnification for Public Employees and Officers

Notice Requirement	Indemnification Limited to Acts or Omissions	No Indemnification for Behavior That Is...	Reimbursement to or from Employee?	Effect of Insurance	Other
N/M	Within scope of employment or office	N/M	Yes, if court determines E acted outside scope of employment. E jointly and severally liable for punitive damages.	N/M	All actions against E are to be brought against political subdivision.
N/M	Within scope of employment or duty	In bad faith, wanton, reckless, or malicious	N/M	No indemnification	No indemnification for any unreasonable settlement
N/M	Within scope of employment	N/M	Yes, if E's conduct outside scope of employment or E fails to cooperate in good faith	Terms of policy govern investigation, settlement, payment, and defense of claims	
N/M	Within scope of duty	Involving malfeasance in office or willful or wanton neglect of duty	If not represented by A. G. and E can establish act not willful or wanton neglect of duty and arose in performance of duty	N/M	
Timely written notice	Within scope of duty or office	Fraudulent, malicious, or willful misconduct (§8550)	No E liable to local agency for any surcharge, contribution, indemnity or reimbursement if act reasonably believed to be within scope of office or duties	Holder of judgment may use methods of collecting provided by policy to extent of limits of coverage	E must fully cooperate with local agency
N/M	N/M	N/M	N/M	N/M	
N/M	Within scope of employment	N/M	N/M	N/M	Indemnification for one or more of the following: court costs, reasonable attorney fees, judgment based on claim, compromise, or settlement of claim.
Written notice within 10 days	Within course of assigned duties	N/M	Civil—state not to cover for attorney fees, court costs, and incidental expenses if punitive damages awarded; many cover all costs if compensatory damages given. Criminal—state to cover no costs if E convicted		
N/M	Within scope of duties	Willful, wanton, or malicious wrongdoing	N/M	N/M	
Within 10 days of service	Within scope of employment, office, or contractual performance	Willful or wrongful, gross negligence in bad faith when depriving someone of their constitutional rights and privileges and immunities	N/M	N/M	
N/M	Within scope of employment	Willful, wanton act constituting gross negligence	N/M	Same	
Written request within 10 days after service or as long as not prejudicial to government's case	Within scope of employment	Fraudulent or malicious	Yes, if E can later establish eligibility	E	Governmental entity may agree to pay only after the court determines that E's act or omission occurred within the scope of employment (§65-30-36[3]). Governmental entity to pay attorney fees and court costs if indictment or information quashed or dismissed or results in acquittal unless quashed or dismissed on motion of .D. A.
N/M	Within scope of employment	N/M	N/M	Does not permit insurance carrier to bring action to recover payments made as a result of private contract between carrier and state E	A. G. may settle up to amount of $500
N/M	N/M	N/M	N/M	N/M	

Appendices

State	Unit of Government Authorizing Indemnification	Mandatory or Discretionary	Criminal Penalties Covered?	Discretionary Indemnification: Who Makes Decision	Limits on Indemnification	Who Is Covered
VA	None					
WA	State—Wash. Rev. Code Ann. §4.92.070 (West Supp. 1985)	Mandatory	N/M	N/A	N/M	O, E
	County—Wash. Rev. Code Ann. §36.16.134 (Supp. 1985)	Discretionary	N/M	Legislative authority of county (§36.16.134 [Supp. 1983])	N/M	O, E, A
WV	Municipality—W. Va. Code §8-12-7(b) (1976)	Discretionary	Yes ("any and all liability")	The municipal authority (§8-12-7 [1976])	N/M	O, E, A
WI	State and Political Subdivisions— Wis. Stat. Ann. §895.46 (1983)	Mandatory	N/M	N/A	N/M	O, E, A
	Local Governments—§895.35 (1983)	Discretionary	Yes	Governing body (§895.35)	N/M	O
WY	Governmental Entity—Wyo. Stat. §1-39-104 (Supp. 1983)	Mandatory	N/M	N/A	$500,000/occurrence	E (state and local)

Notice Requirement	Indemnification Limited to Acts or Omissions	No Indemnification for Behavior That Is...	Reimbursement to or from Employee?	Effect of Insurance	Other
N/M	Within scope of official duty or purported to be in good faith	N/M	N/M	N/M	State to cover expenses of defense
N/M	Same	N/M	N/M	N/M	Requires approval of the county legislative authority. May cover cost of defense and any money judgment against O, E.
N/M	Within scope of official duties	N/M	N/M	N/M	
As soon as reasonably possible	Within scope of official capacity or while carrying out duties as official or employee	N/M	N/M	Indemnification reduced to the amount in excess of coverage	No reimbursement for attorney fees and expenses if O, E refuses legal counsel offered
N/M	Within scope of official duties	N/M	N/M	N/M	No reimbursement unless action discontinued, dismissed, or determined favorably to O, or if determined adversely and based on constitutionality of statute not previously construed
N/M	Within scope of employment or duty	N/M	N/M	N/M	

Appendix H
State Laws Relating to Legal Representation for Public Employees and Officers

State	Unit of Government Authorizing Indemnification	Mandatory or Discretionary	Type of Proceedings	Who is Represented	Notice Requirement	Cooperation Requirement	Representation Limited to Acts or Omissions
AL	State—Ala. Const. Amend. 111 sec. 137 (1905)	Legislature's discretion	"Any and all suits"	O, E of state, political subdivision, and school boards	N/M	N/M	N/M
AK	None						
AZ	State—Ariz. Rev. Stat. Ann. §41-192.02a (West Supp. 1984)	Discretionary	Civil	O, E	N/M	N/M	N/M
	State—§41-621J (West Supp. 1984) (if state provides self-insurance)	Mandatory	Civil	O, E, A	N/M	"shall cooperate fully with A.G."	N/M
	State—§41-193A (West Supp. 1984)	Mandatory	Civil and criminal	O	N/M	N/M	Within official capacity
AR	State—Ark. Stat. Ann. §§12-701, 12-709 (1979)	Mandatory	Civil and criminal	O	N/M	N/M	N/M
	Local—§12-3407 (Michie Supp. 1983)	Mandatory	Civil	A. G. defends employees of cities, towns, and counties, when they assist the state and its employees	N/M	N/M	Within the scope of employment and in performance of official duties
CA	Public Entity—(defined in §811.2) Cal. Government Code §995 (1980)	Mandatory/Discretionary	Civil—Mandatory Criminal—Discretionary (§995.8) Adm. proceedings—Discretionary (§995.6)	E and former E (defined in §810.2) (state and local)	Written notice must be given 10 days before trial	Yes	Within scope of employment
CO	Public Entity—(defined in §24-10-103[5]) Col. Rev. Stat. §24-10-110(1) (1982)	Discretionary	Civil	E (defined in §24-10-103[4]) (state and local)	Within reasonable time of the incident	N/M	Within scope of employment and performance of duties
	State—§24-31-101(4) (1982)	Mandatory	Civil and administrative	E	N/M	N/M	Within official duty
CT	State—Conn. Gen. Stat. Ann. §3-125 (West Supp. 1984)	Mandatory	"All suits and other civil proceedings, except upon criminal recognizance and bail bonds"	All heads of departments and state boards, state commissioners, agents, inspectors, chemists, directors, harbor masters, librarians	N/M	N/M	N/M
DE	State-Del. Code Ann. tit. 10, §3925 (Michie Supp. 1984)	Mandatory	Civil and criminal	O, E	N/M	N/M	Within scope of employment or function
FL	State, county, municipality—Fla. Stat. Ann. §111-07 (West. Supp. 1984)	Discretionary	Civil, including §1983 actions	O, E, A (state and local)	N/M	N/M	Within scope of employment or function
GA	State—§45-15-70	Discretionary	Any action	O, state board or bureau member	N/M	N/M	Within administration of duties
	Municipality, county, public bodies—Ga. Code Ann. §45-9-21 (1982)	Discretionary	Civil, criminal and quasi-criminal	O, E (local)	N/M	N/M	Within scope of duties or in any way connected therewith
HI	State—Haw. Rev. Stat. §662-16 (1976)	Discretionary	Civil	E	Promptly after service	N/M	Within scope of employment
ID	Governmental Entity—Idaho Code §6-903 (Michie Supp. 1984)	Mandatory	Civil	E (defined in §6-902.4) (1984) (state and local)	N/M	N/M	Within scope of employment or duties

No Representation for Behavior That Is...	Eligibility Determined by	Who Defends	Does Counsel Have Authority to Settle?	Reimbursement If the Court's View of the Employee's Actions Differs from Prior Decision Concerning Representation	Effect of Insurance	Other
N/M	N/M	A. G.	N/M	N/M	N/M	
N/M	A. G.	A. G.	N/M	N/M	N/M	
N/M	N/M	A. G.	Up to $25,000 with approval of A. G. and Director of Administration. Over $25,000 requires additional approval of Legislative Budget Committee.	N/M	N/M	
N/M	N/M	N/M	N/M	N/M	N/M	
N/M	N/M	A. G. or Special Counsel	N/M	N/M	N/M	
Lacking good faith, or malicious	N/M	A. G.	Yes	N/M	N/M	
Lacking good faith, fraudulent, corrupt, or malicious	N/M	Public entity's own attorney or outside counsel	Yes	Yes (§996.4)	N/M	Public entity's counsel may refuse to defend if conflict of interest arises (§995.2[c])
Willful or wanton	N/M	Public entity's own counsel or outside counsel if government chooses	Yes	Yes (§24-10-110[3][a][I])	N/M	
Action or proceeding brought by state	N/M	A. G.	N/M	N/M	N/M	
Willful or wanton	N/M	A. G.	N/M	N/M	N/M	
N/M	The judge	In civil action, judge appoints attorney from Department of Justice or other licensed attorney. In criminal prosecution, from Office of the Public Defender or Department of Justice	N/M	N/M	N/M	
Malicious, in bad faith or in willful or wanton disregard of human rights, safety, or property. (This limitation applies only to tort cases)	N/M	For state E, an attorney may be provided from Department of Legal Affairs	N/M	Yes (§111-07) "Then said agency, county, municipal or political subdivision shall reimburse any such defendant who prevails in the action"	N/M	
N/M	N/M	N/M	N/M	N/M	N/M	
Theft, embezzlement, or similar crimes	If A.G. decides against representation, the Governor may direct the A.G. to provide counsel. If A.G. still refuses to provide counsel, Governor may appoint counsel (§45-15-70)	Regular counsel is provided by A.G., unless appointment by governor	N/M	N/M	N/M	
N/M	A.G.	A.G.	Yes	N/M	N/M	
Malicious or has criminal intent	N/M	N/M	No, only the governing body of each political subdivision may compromise and settle (§6-912)	Yes	It must pay because the government duty is secondary to the obligation of the insurer	There is a rebuttable presumption that the E acted within the scope of employment and without malice or criminal intent

Appendices

Appendix H
State Laws Relating to Legal Representation for Public Employees and Officers

State	Unit of Government Authorizing Indemnification	Mandatory or Discretionary	Type of Proceedings	Who is Represented	Notice Requirement	Cooperation Requirement	Representation Limited to Acts or Omissions
IL	State—Ill. Ann. Stat. Ch. 127, §1302 (Smith-Hurd Supp. 1984–85)	Mandatory	Civil, including §1983 actions	E, O	Timely and appropriate; physicians of Department of Corrections or Mental Health or Developmental Disabilities must give notice within 15 days after notice of claim	Yes—"an agreement by the state employee to cooperate with the Attorney General"	Within scope of employment
	Local—Ch. 85, §2-302 (1966)	Discretionary	Civil	E	Service to secretary or clerk of local entity	N/M	Within scope of employment
IN	State—Ind. Code §34-4-16.5-24 (Supp. 1982)	Mandatory	Contract actions	E	N/M	N/M	Contracts entered into for E's agency
	§4-6-2-1.5 (1982)	Mandatory	Civil and criminal	O	N/M	N/M	N/M
IA	State—Iowa Code Ann. §13.2 (1978)	Mandatory	Civil and criminal	O	N/M	N/M	In his official capacity
	State—§25A.21 (1978)	Mandatory	Civil, including §1983 actions (§25A.22)	E	N/M	N/M	In the scope of employment
	Governing Body—§613A-8 (West Supp. 1983)	Mandatory	Civil, including §1983 actions	O, E (local)	N/M	Right of indemnification for failure of E to cooperate	Within scope of employment
KS	Governmental Entity—Kan. Stat. Ann. §75.6108 (Supp. 1983)	Mandatory	Civil	(E (defined in §75-6102)	In writing to A. G. or government body within 15 days after service	Government may recover judgment, costs, and fees if E fails to cooperate in good faith	Within scope of employment and in official or individual capacity
KY	State—Ky. Rev. Stat. §§12.211, 212, 213 (1980)	Discretionary	Civil	E	N/M	N/M	Within scope of employment and in official or individual capacity or both
LA	State—La. Rev. Stat. §13-5108.1, §13-5108.2 (1985)	Mandatory	Civil	O, E, including an E of deep-water port, harbor, terminal district, deep-water port commission	Within 5 days after receiving a complaint, E shall send a copy to A. G. or attorney authorized to represent department, office, etc.	Yes—"E shall cooperate fully"	Within scope of employment and discharge of duties
ME	Governmental Entity—Me. Rev. Stat. Ann. tit. 14, §8112 (1980)	Discretionary (when the governmental entity would not be liable for the act done (§8112{1}) Mandatory (when the governmental entity would be liable for the act done) (§8112{2})	Civil	E (state and local)	30 days after receiving a claim or 15 days after summons	N/M	Within scope of employment

No Representation for Behavior That Is...	Eligibility Determined by	Who Defends	Does Counsel Have Authority to Settle?	Reimbursement If the Court's View of the Employee's Actions Differs from Prior Decision Concerning Representation	Effect of Insurance	Other
Intentional, willful, or wanton misconduct	A.G.	A.G.	Yes	Yes	N/M	
Willful or wanton negligence or bad faith	N/M	N/M	Compromise or settlement by governing body or person with authority to make policy decisions	N/M	N/M	
N/M	N/M	A.G., or A.G. may employ other counsel	N/M	N/M	N/M	
N/M	N/M	N/M	N/M	N/M	N/M	
N/M	N/M	A.G.	N/M	N/M	N/M	
Malfeasance or willful or wanton	N/M	N/M	Yes (§25A.9)	N/M	N/M	
Willful or wanton conduct	N/M	Governing body	No, only the governing body may compromise or settle (§613A.9)	If conduct found willful or wanton in action brought by municipality	N/M	
Fradulent, malicious or lacks good faith	N/M	Governmental entity's own attorney or other counsel may be employed	Yes—A.G. with the approval of the State finance council; governing body may do the same (§75-6106)	Yes (§75-6106[d])—if E found to have acted within the scope of employment and without fraud or malice	If the policy states that the insurer provides the defense, the government need not do so	If a conflict of interest would take place if the governmental entity defended the E, then the government may refuse to provide the defense The authority to settle is subject to the terms of an insurance contract (§75-6106)
Fraudulent, corrupt, or malicious	A.G., or A.G. may delegate authority to the chief administrative authority of any agency, board, institution, or commission, whose E is to be defended	A.G. or other counsel employed for this purpose or counsel assigned to the E's unit of government (§12.213)	N/M	N/M	The government need not provide representation if the policy does so (§12.213)	If a conflict of interest would exist if the governmental entity defended the E, then the government may refuse to provide the defense No representation if the A.G. decides that a defense of the action would not be in the state's best interest
Intentional wrongful act or gross negligence	A.G. or attorney representing the E's unit (e.g., Harbor's attorney)	A.G. or attorney representing E's unit	Yes. Upon advice and with concurrence of A.G., D.A., or proper official	Reimbursement for attorney's fees when private counsel obtained and court finds E acting in discharge of duties and within scope of employment and not intentional wrongful act or gross negligence (§13-5108.2[c][3])	The insurance provides the defense. Obligations of insurer not impaired, limited, or modified	
N/M	The governmental entity	N/M	N/M	Yes (§8112.3)—if Court determines act occurred within the scope of employment Governmental entity may discontinue the defense if it determines that the act occurred outside the scope of employment	The rights and obligations of the insurer (including representation) are in no way modified or limited (§8112[6])	If a conflict of interest exists between the governmental entity and the E, the governmental entity shall pay the E for reasonable attorney fees and court costs (§8112.2) If the governmental entity determines that the E's acts were outside his scope of employment and continues to defend him, the defense cannot be terminated thereafter

Appendices

Appendix H
State Laws Relating to Legal Representation for Public Employees and Officers

State	Unit of Government Authorizing Indemnification	Mandatory or Discretionary	Type of Proceedings	Who is Represented	Notice Requirement	Cooperation Requirement	Representation Limited to Acts or Omissions
MD	State—Md. Ann. Code art. 32A, §12-305 (1984)	Mandatory	Civil or special proceeding	O, E	There must be a written request to A.G.	A.G. to require O or E to enter agreement for reimbursement of state and no liability for judgment	Within scope of employment
	State—Md. Ann. Code art. 32A, §12-313 (1984)	Prohibited	Criminal	O, E	Written application to Board of Public Works for reimbursement	N/M	
MA	State—Mass. Ann. Laws ch. 12, §3E (West Supp. 1984–85)	Mandatory	Any action involving intentional or unintentional tort, violation of civil rights, or other wrongful act or omission (Civil)	O, E (of executive office of Deparments of Human Services and Education only)	There must be a written request to A.G.	N/M	Within scope of official duties of employment
	State—Ch. 258, §9A (West Supp. 1984–85)	Mandatory	Claim for alleged intentional tort or for alleged violation of civil rights (Civil)	Members of state and metropolitan police	The affected police officer must make a request to the Commonwealth	N/M	Within official scope of duties
	State—Ch. 258, §6 (West Supp. 1984–85)	Mandatory	Civil	Public employee	Service on public attorney after presenting a claim in writing to public employer	Reasonable cooperation	Within official scope of office or employment
MI	Government agency—Mich. Comp. Laws Ann. §691.1408 (West Supp. 1984–85)	Discretionary	Civil and criminal	O, E (state and local)	N/M	N/M	Within scope of authority and employment or if reasonable belief that acting within scope of employment
	County—§49.73 (West Supp. 1984–85)	Mandatory	Civil	Elected county officers	N/M	N/M	Official act or duty of the office
MN	State—Minn. Stat. Ann. §3.736 (West Supp. 1985)	Mandatory	Any tort claim or demand or any claim arising from issuance or sale of any securities by the state	E	N/M	Representation if E provides "complete disclosure and co-operation"	Within scope of employment
	State—Minn. Stat. Ann. §806 (1977)	Mandatory	N/M	O, boards, commissions	N/M	N/M	Within official duties
	Municipality and any instrumentality thereof—Minn. Stat. Ann. §471.44 (1977)	Mandatory	In all actions for alleged false arrest or alleged injury to persons, property, or character	Sheriff, deputy sheriffs, police, or police officers	N/M	N/M	Within scope of official duties
	§466.07(1a) (West. Supp. 1984–85)	Mandatory	Tort claim or demand	O, E (local)	N/M	N/M	Within scope of employment or official duties
MS	State—Miss. Code Ann. §7-5-39 (1972)	Mandatory	Any suit touching upon any official duty or trust (civil and criminal)	O	N/M	N/M	Within scope of official capacity
	State—§7-5-43 (1972)	Discretionary	Civil and criminal, and if called as witness by federal civil rights commission	O, E (state and local)	Written notice must be sent	N/M	Within discharge of official duties or growing out of official action/inaction
	Municipality—§25-1-47 (1972)	Discretionary	Civil and criminal	O, E, A (state and local)	N/M	N/M	While acting within the capacity of such O, E, A

The Vulnerable Social Worker

No Representation for Behavior That Is...	Eligibility Determined by	Who Defends	Does Counsel Have Authority to Settle?	Reimbursement If the Court's View of the Employee's Actions Differs from Prior Decision Concerning Representation	Effect of Insurance	Other
Malicious or involving gross negligence	A.G.	A.G. or by his assistant or by a special counsel or private attorney retained by A.G.	Yes	Yes, if court determines within scope of employment or duties, not malicious or grossly negligent, or sovereign immunity applies	the A.G. need not provide representation (§12B)	
N/A	A.G.	N/A	N/A	Yes, if not guilty or nolo contendere		
N/M	A.G.	A.G.	Yes	N/M	N/M	
Willful, wanton, malicious	N/M	N/M	N/M	N/M	N/M	
N/M	N/M	Public attorney	Executive officer of public employer with consent of public attorney	N/M	N/M	
N/M	N/M	"Furnish the services of an attorney"	No, only the government agency can settle	N/M	N/M	
N/M	N/M	"Shall employ an attorney" (if the prosecuting attorney or county or corporate counsel is unable to represent)	N/M	N/M	N/M	
Willful or wanton neglect of duty or involves malfeasance in office	E's appointing authority, whose determination may be overruled by the A.G.	N/M	N/M	N/M	N/M	A determination that the E did not act within the scope of his employment shall not be evidence provided to the jury
N/M	N/M	A.G. or special counsel	N/M	N/M	N/M	
Not in good faith	N/M	Required to furnish legal counsel	N/M	N/M	N/M	
Malfeasance or willful or wanton neglect of duty	N/M	N/M	N/M	N/M	N/M	
N/M	N/M	A.G.	N/M	N/M	N/M	
N/M	N/M	A.G. assistants or representatives	N/M	N/M	N/M	
N/M	Governing authorities	Provide legal counsel	N/M	N/M	N/M	

State	Unit of Government Authorizing Indemnification	Mandatory or Discretionary	Type of Proceedings	Who is Represented	Notice Requirement	Cooperation Requirement	Representation Limited to Acts or Omissions
MO	State—Mo. Ann. Stat. §105.716 (Vernon Supp. 1985)	Mandatory	N/M	O, E	N/M	Yes	Within official duties on behalf of state
	Political Subdivisions—§537.165 (Vernon Supp. 1985)	Mandatory	In any action for claims of injury to persons or property from operation of motor vehicle by fire department	Fire fighters	N/M	N/M	Arising out of operation of motor vehicle in the performance of their duties
MT	State, county, city, town government entity—Mont. Code Ann. §2-9-305 (1983)	Mandatory	Civil negligence actions and §1983 actions	E (state and local)	Written notice must be sent	"Failed to cooperate" is grounds for not providing defense	Within scope of employment or office
NE	State—Neb. Rev. Stat. §81-8, 239.06 (1981)	Mandatory	Civil	O, E, A	Written request must be sent	If E is not cooperative or has acted to prejudice the claim, A.G. may terminate the defense	In course of employment
	Political Subdivisions—§23-2403 (1983)	Discretionary	Civil	O, E, A	N/M	N/M	N/M
NV	State and Political Subdivisions—Nev. Rev. Stat. §41.0339 (1981)	Mandatory	Civil	O, E, and former O, E (state and local)	15 days after service, a written request must be sent	N/M	Relating to public duties
NH	State—N.H. Rev. Stat. Ann. §99-D:2 (Supp. 1983)	Mandatory	Civil and any claim seeking equitable relief	O, E, official, trustee	Seven days after summons or complaint	N/M	Within scope of official duty for the state
NJ	State—N.J. Stat. Ann. §59:10A-1 (1982)	Mandatory/Discretionary	Civil—mandatory Criminal—discretionary, "if representation is in the best interest of the State" (§59:10A-3)	E or former E	To A.G. within 10 days after receiving summons or complaint	"Shall cooperate" (§59:10A-4)	Within scope of employment (§59:10A-1)
NM	Governmental Entity—N.M. Stat. Ann. §41-4-4.B (1983)	Mandatory	Any tort and §1983 actions	E and former E (state and local)	N/M	N/M	Within scope of duty
NY	State—N.Y. Pub. Off. Law §17-2 (McKinney Supp. 1984–85)	Mandatory	Civil, including §1983 actions. Criminal—state reimbursement for legal fees only if dismissed or acquitted and within scope of employment (§19)	E	Within 5 days after summons, otherwise no defense or indemnification required	E must give "full cooperation" (§17-4)	Within scope of public employment or duties
	Local Public Entity—§18 (McKinney Supp. 1984–85)	Discretionary (the law allows localities to adopt a mandatory program)	Civil	E (local)	Within 10 days after summons, otherwise no defense or indemnification required	E must give "full cooperation" (§18-5)	Same as above
NC	State—N.C. Gen. Stat. §143-300.3 (Michie Supp. 1983)	Discretionary	Civil and criminal	E and former E	N/M	N/M	Within scope of employment
	State—§143-300.14 (Michie Supp. 1983)	Mandatory	Civil	Public school E (teachers, nurses, and supervisors)	Must be sent to A.G. 10 days after complaint	N/M	Acts or omissions causing personal injury
	Governing body of city or county—§160A-167(a) (Michie Supp. 1983)	Discretionary	Civil and criminal	O, E (and former O, E), member of volunteer fire squad or rescue squad and county alcoholic beverage control board (local)	N/M	N/M	Within scope and course of employment or duty

The Vulnerable Social Worker

No Representation for Behavior That Is...	Eligibility Determined by	Who Defends	Does Counsel Have Authority to Settle?	Reimbursement If the Court's View of the Employee's Actions Differs from Prior Decision Concerning Representation	Effect of Insurance	Other
N/M	N/M	A.G. or lead counsel of governmental entity	Yes	N/M	N/M	
N/M	N/M	N/M	N/M	N/M	N/M	Applies to political subdivisions with salaried, full-time fire department
Oppressive, fraudulent, malicious, or involves a criminal offense. Also, no representation if E settled case of the governmental entity	Government employer	N/M	The Department of Administration can compromise and settle subject to the terms of insurance, if any (§2-9-303); same for political subdivisions (§2-9-304)	N/M	Ability to compromise or settle is subject to the terms of the insurance contract	If there is a dispute between E and governmental entity on whether the E is eligible for government-paid defense, the governmental entity must pay for E's defense until Court decides in the government's favor
Willful or wanton neglect of duty or involves malfeasance	A.G.	A.G.	Yes (§81-8-218)	Yes—if Court decision goes against E, the E must reimburse the state, and if court goes against government, it must pay "reasonable costs"	Provisions of policy will apply	
N/M	Governing body	N/M	Yes	N/M	Same	
Performed or omitted without good faith (§41.0339[2]) and other conditions, such as wanton or malicious behavior, as listed in §41.0346	Official attorney (defined in §41.0338)	Official attorney	The State Board of Examiners and the governing body of a political subdivision may settle up to $50,000 (§41.037)	N/M	Official attorney may tender defense to insurer	The court or jury is required to return a special verdict stating that the O or E was acting within scope of public duty or that their acts or omissions were wanton or malicious (§41.0348)
Wanton or reckless	A.G.	A.G. or outside counsel if action is against A.G.	Yes	N/M	N/M	
Fraudulent, willful misconduct, or malicious	A.G. (§59:10A-2)	A.G.	N/M	Yes—however, E must prove he acted within scope of employment and the state must fail to show he acted with fraud and willful misconduct	N/M	A.G. is removed if a conflict of interest arises (§59:10A-2)
N/M	N/M	N/M	N/M	Government recovers if E acted with fraud or malice (§41-4-4E)	The insurance provides the defense (§41-4-4)	
No representation if action brought by governmental entity (§17-2[a])	A.G.	A.G.	Yes—requires A.G. approval (§17-3[b])	N/M	Statute does not impair, alter, modify, or limit obligations of insurer under terms of policy	When A.G. or locality's chief legal office determines a conflict of interest exists and to represent E "would be inappropriate," the state or locality pays for private counsel (§17-2[b] and §318-3[b])
Intentional wrongdoing or recklessness or when action brought by public entity	The "public entity"	Chief legal officer or other designated counsel	N/M	N/M	Same	
Fraudulent, corrupt, or malicious	A.G. or agency head authorized by A.G.	A.G., or other counsel, insurer's counsel, agency's counsel, or counsel employed by agency	Yes—§143-300-6(b)	N/M	N/M	A.G. need not provide defense when a conflict of interest exists, or it is not in the state's best interests (§140.300.4[a][3-4])
Same	A.G.	A.G.	Yes	Yes, E may be required to repay state if judgment for P	N/M	Same
N/M	N/M	Locality's counsel, other counsel or insurer's counsel	N/M	N/M	N/M	

Appendices

State Laws Relating to Legal Representation for Public Employees and Officers

State	Unit of Government Authorizing Indemnification	Mandatory or Discretionary	Type of Proceedings	Who is Represented	Notice Requirement	Cooperation Requirement	Representation Limited to Acts or Omissions
ND	State—N.D. Cent. Code §32.12.1-15 (Supp. 1983)	Mandatory	All actions or procedures for alleged negligence	E	N/M	N/M	Within scope of employment
	Political Subdivisions—§32-12.1-04 (Supp. 1983)	Mandatory	Same	E	N/M	N/M	Same
	State and Political Subdivisions—§44-08-11 (Supp. 1983)	Mandatory	Civil	Law enforcement officer (state and local)	N/M	N/M	Within scope of official duties
OH	State—Ohio Rev. Code Ann. §109.361 (1984)	Mandatory	Civil	O, E	Written notice must be sent	Yes	Within scope of employment
OK	State—Okla. Stat. Ann. tit. 74, §20F (West Supp. 1983)	Mandatory	Civil or special proceeding	O, E	15 days after service	Yes	Within scope of employment
	State and Political Subdivisions—tit. 51, §161, 162 (West Supp. 1984–85)	Mandatory	Civil, violation of constitutional rights	E	N/M	Cooperation in good faith	Within scope of employment
	County—Okla. Stat. Ann. tit. 19, §215.25, 26 (West Supp. 1983)	Mandatory	Civil or special proceeding	E (county)	15 days after service	N/M	In course of employment
	Municipality—Okla. Stat. Ann. tit. 11, §23-101, 102 (West Supp. 1984–85)	Mandatory	Civil or special proceeding	O, E, A (local)	10 days after service	N/M	In course of employment
OR	State and Local Public Body—Or. Rev. Stat. §§30.285, 287 (1983)	Mandatory	Civil, §1983 actions (§30.265[1])	O, E, A	Written notice must be sent	Shall cooperate fully	Within scope of employment and duty
PA	Commonwealth—Pa. Stat. Ann. tit. 42, §8525 (1982)	Mandatory	Civil	E	Prior notice to A.G. required	N/M	Within scope of office or duties
	Local Agency—tit. 42, §8547 (1982)	Mandatory if alleged to be within scope of employment; discretionary if not so alleged	Civil	E (local)	Written request required	Yes (§8547[c])	Within scope of office or duties
RI	State and Political Subdivisions—R.I. Gen. Laws §9-31-8 (Supp. 1984)	Mandatory	Any action brought on account of an act or omission within scope of employment (civil)	E and former E	Within 10 days after receiving summons	Yes	Within scope of employment
SC	State and Political Subdivisions—S.C. Code §§1-7-50, 60 (1977)	Mandatory	Civil, criminal, and special proceeding	O, E (state and local)	A written notice must be sent to A.G.	Yes	Within scope of employment
SD	None						
TN	State—Tenn. Code Ann. §8-6-109(b)(1) (Supp. 1984)	Mandatory	Civil and administrative proceedings	O	N/M	N/M	N/M
	State—§8-42-103, 104 (Supp. 1984)	Discretionary	Civil and criminal	E	Written notice within 10 days	N/M	Within course of assigned duties
	Local Education Agency—§49-6-4211 (1983)	Mandatory	Civil	Principals and teachers	N/M	Yes	N/M
TX	State—Tex. Rev. Civ. Stat. Ann. art. 6252-26, §3(a) (West Supp. 1985)	Mandatory	Civil	O, E (and former O, E) physicians contracting with state government, or their estates	Process must be sent to A.G. not later than 10 days after service	N/M	Within scope of office, contractual performance, or employment
	Political Subdivisions—art. 6252-19b (West Supp. 1985)	Discretionary	Civil	E	N/M	N/M	Within scope of employment

The Vulnerable Social Worker

State Laws Relating to Legal Representation for Public Employees and Officers

No Representation for Behavior That Is...	Eligibility Determined by	Who Defends	Does Counsel Have Authority to Settle?	Reimbursement If the Court's View of the Employee's Actions Differs from Prior Decision Concerning Representation	Effect of Insurance	Other
N/M	N/M	A.G.—unless conflict of interest arises	N/M	N/M	The insurer provides the defense	
N/M	N/M	N/M	N/M	N/M	N/M	
Not in good faith	N/M	State or Political Subdivision must furnish legal counsel	N/M	N/M	N/M	
Malicious, in bad faith, or reckless	A.G.	A.G., Assistant A.G., special counsel appointed by A.G.	N/M	O or E may recover reasonable expenses where representation denied and Court finds it should have been granted	The insurer provides the defense	
Fraudulent, corrupt (§162)	A.G.	A.G. or staff	N/M	Yes—E pays if Court determines acts were outside of official authority	N/M	
Same	N/M	A.G. or authorized attorney	Yes	Yes	Terms of policy apply	
Not in good faith or failure to perform statutorily required duty	District Attorney	District Attorney	N/M	Yes—E pays if Court determines acts were outside of official authority	N/M	
Same	Government body	Municipal attorney or other legal counsel	N/M	Same	N/M	
Malfeasance in office or willful or wanton neglect of duty	A.G.	A.G.	N/M	Yes—Commonwealth or local agency will reimburse E for amount that court determines; E to pay costs if court determines not within performance of duties	N/M	
N/M	A.G.	A.G.	N/M	Yes—Commonwealth or local agency will reimburse E for amount that court determines		
Crime, actual fraud, malice, or willful misconduct	Local agency	N/M	N/M	Yes—if local agency refuses request to defend and court determines act was within scope of employment (or E reasonably believed it to be) and did not constitute crime, fraud, malice, or willful misconduct	N/M	
Fraudulent, willful misconduct, or actual malicious behavior (§9-31-9)	A.G.	A.G.	Yes, but approval of court required	N/M	N/M	If a conflict of interest exists or A.G. determines that it is in state's best interests not to represent E, then state pays reasonable counsel fee (§9-31-11)
Malicious or involves bad faith	A.G.	A.G. or staff	N/M	N/M	The insurer provides the defense (§1-7-60)	The information gathered in A.G.'s investigation cannot be used as evidence in court (§1-7-70)
N/M	N/M	N/M	N/M	N/M	N/M	
N/M	Civil—Defense Counsel Commission; Criminal—Board of Claims	Hired counsel	N/M	Civil—Yes, if punitive damages awarded; Criminal—yes, if convicted	N/M	
Willful, wanton, or malicious wrongdoing	Board of Education or agency	N/M	N/M	N/M	N/M	
N/M	N/M	A.G.	Yes	N/M	Can relinquish representation under terms of policy	
N/M	N/M	County attorney/attorney of political subdivision	Yes	N/M	Same	

State	Unit of Government Authorizing Indemnification	Mandatory or Discretionary	Type of Proceedings	Who is Represented	Notice Requirement	Cooperation Requirement	Representation Limited to Acts or Omissions
UT	Governmental Entity—Utah Code Ann. §§63-30-36 and 37 (Supp. 1983)	Discretionary	Civil	E (state and local)	Written request within 10 days after service or as long as not prejudicial to government's case	Yes	N/M
	§63-30a-3 (Supp. 1983)	Discretionary	Criminal	E	N/M	N/M	N/M
VT	State—Vt. Stat. Ann. tit. 3, §§1101, 1102 (Supp. 1984)	Mandatory	Civil and criminal (§1104)	E	Yes	Yes	Within scope of official duties
VA	State—Va. Stat. §2.1-121 (Michie Supp. 1984)	Discretionary	Civil actions	O, E, A (of designated agencies listed in §2.1-121 only)	N/M	N/M	Within scope of official duties
	State—§46.1-40 (1980)	Discretionary	Criminal	Police officers in Motor Vehicle Department	N/M	N/M	Discharge of official duties
	Local—§15.1-506.2 (1981)	Mandatory	"Whatever legal services are required" (civil)	O, E (of local departments and boards of welfare or social services only)	N/M	N/M	Within scope of official duties
WA	State—Wash. Rev. Code Ann. §4.92.060 (Supp. 1985)	Mandatory	Action or proceeding for damages	E, O	O or E may request A.G. to represent them	Yes	Within scope of official duties (or purported in good faith to be within official duties)
	County—§36.16.134 (Supp. 1985)	Discretionary	Action or proceeding for damages	E, O (local)	N/M	N/M	Same
WV	State—W. Va. Code §5-3-2 (1979)	Mandatory	Civil and criminal if state not "interested" in case against officer	O	N/M	N/M	Within scope of official capacity
WI	State and Political Subdivisions—Wis. Stat. Ann. §895.46(1)(a) (1983)	Discretionary	Civil and special proceeding	O, E, A (state and local)	Yes—as soon as reasonably possible	Yes	Within scope of employment
WY	State—Wyo. Stat. §9-1-606 (1982)	Mandatory	Civil not involving tort action covered by §1-39-104	O (state)	N/M	N/M	Within scope of duty
	Governmental Entity—Wyo. Stat. §1-39-104 (Supp. 1983)	Mandatory	Civil	E (state and local)	N/M	N/M	Within scope of duty

No Representation for Behavior That Is...	Eligibility Determined by	Who Defends	Does Counsel Have Authority to Settle?	Reimbursement If the Court's View of the Employee's Actions Differs from Prior Decision Concerning Representation	Effect of Insurance	Other
N/M	N/M	N/M	Yes	Yes—to E, if he proves his actions were done in good faith and within the scope of his employment and the government fails to establish fraud or malice	N/M	
N/M	N/M	N/M	N/M	N/M	N/M	E may request defense of criminal charge or indictment
N/M	A.G.	A.G. or assistant A.G. If A.G. cannot represent, state will reimburse E for legal counsel	Yes (§1203)—but not for more than $100,000, without E's approval	N/M	Insurer provides defense	E may appeal A.G.'s denial of representation to state labor relations board (§1102[c])
N/M	A.G.	A.G. or special counsel	Yes (§2.1-127)	N/M	N/M	
N/M	N/M	Commonwealth attorney or city attorney or county attorney, as appropriate	N/M	N/M	N/M	
N/M	Commissioner	Special counsel	N/M	N/M	N/M	
N/M	N/M	A.G. (§4.92.070)	Yes, with approval of court (§4.92.150)	N/M	N/M	
N/M	N/M	N/M	N/M	N/M	N/M	
N/M	N/M	N/M	N/M	N/M	N/M	
N/M	N/M	N/M	N/M	Yes—to E reasonable attorney fees unless state court determines E did not act within scope of employment	N/M	A.G. may appear on behalf of state without waiving immunity if employing agency or A.G. denies that O or E was acting within scope of employment
N/M	N/M	A.G. or by contracting at state expense	N/M	O must reimburse the state if shown to have acted outside the scope of employment	N/M	
N/M	Governmental entity	N/M	Yes—up to $10,000	N/M	N/M	

Appendices

About the Authors

Douglas J. Besharov practices law in Washington, D.C., and New York. He also directs a social policy project for the American Enterprise Institute for Public Policy Research in Washington, D.C.

Mr. Besharov was the first Director of the U.S. National Center on Child Abuse and Neglect, from 1975 to 1979. Before that, he was Executive Director of the New York State Assembly Select Committee on Child Abuse.

Currently on the Adjunct Law Faculties of Georgetown and American Universities, Mr. Besharov has taught family law, torts, and criminal law at New York University, University of Maryland, College of William and Mary, and Osgoode Hall Law School in Toronto, Canada.

Mr. Besharov is the author of more than 50 articles and eight books, including *Reporting Child Abuse and Neglect: A Guide for Professionals* and *Juvenile Justice Advocacy.* Each year, he writes the Practice Commentaries for *McKinney's New York Family Court Act*.

Susan H. Besharov, author of Chapter 9 on reducing agency and personal stress, is a psychiatric social worker in the Department of Psychiatry, Children's Hospital National Medical Center, Washington, D.C. Ms. Besharov has many years of experience working with children and families in mental health and school settings and in private practice. She has a long-standing interest in parents' groups and has been a sponsor of a Parents' Anonymous group.

Appendices   **275**